READINGS IN PSYCHOLOGY

READINGS
IN
PSYCHOLOGY

EDITED BY

JOHN COHEN

Professor of Psychology
University of Manchester

London

GEORGE ALLEN & UNWIN LTD

RUSKIN HOUSE MUSEUM STREET

PRINTED IN GREAT BRITAIN
in 11 on 12 pt. Fournier type
BY UNWIN BROTHERS LIMITED
WOKING AND LONDON

PREFACE

This book is designed to introduce the student and the general reader to selected topics in contemporary psychology. Inevitably a composite volume suffers from certain limitations, in particular the lack of a single pervasive theoretical viewpoint, though this perhaps carries its peculiar advantages. Furthermore, the choice of topics is unavoidably biased. This, however, could hardly be otherwise, for an editor's task is to select, and no selection could please everyone.

What actually guided the choice of the chapters was the fact that they seemed to combine unusual interest with high quality. And their diversity in outlook did not deprive them of some basic unity. I hope the volume will prove of interest not only to professional students of psychology but also to students of medicine, psychiatry, the humanities, and the sciences.

No attempt has been made to range over the entire field of psychology. Nor are the themes of the chapters necessarily the most 'important' ones. What is 'important' is, in any event, a matter of opinion. Some readers may look for chapters on insanity or crime, on social psychology or personality, or on a hundred and one other subjects that might have been discussed. Their exclusion is no slur on their significance or on the legitimacy of their study but is imposed by limitations of space. These other topics could more suitably be discussed in separate volumes.

The sequence of chapters is intended to be methodical though this may not be obvious. Beginning with a 'point of view' by the editor which is not necessarily shared by any of the other contributors, Chapters 2 and 3 are historical; Chapters 4, 5 and 6 deal with theoretical issues; Chapters 7 and 8 with body-mind relationships; Chapters 9 and 10 with perception; Chapters 11 and 12 with thought processes; Chapters 13, 14 and 15 with problems of communication; Chapters 16 and 17 with memory and intelligence; and Chapter 18 with problems of emotional behaviour. Chapters 19 to 23 are concerned with rather more specific themes; stress, integration, research in psychoanalysis, applications of psychology in industry, and studies of animal behaviour.

I wish to record my warm thanks to all who have contributed to this volume, not only for providing the chapters and adapting them to the form required but also for answering patiently the many queries that necessarily arose.

I am also much indebted to Mr Peter Cooper for a number of valuable suggestions and particularly for constructive criticisms of the drafts of my two chapters, and for help in editing the material for Professor Zangwill's chapter. Miss Gillian Lighton deserves special praise for her meticulous checking of texts, sources, proofs, for revising and standardizing the references, and for compiling the Index. Finally, it is a pleasure to thank Miss Nora Williamson, Mrs Thelma Pearce, Mrs. Laura Miles and Miss Beulah Morris for their splendid secretarial assistance.

CONTENTS

A*

Contributors

B. V. BOWDEN

M.A., Ph.D., M.I.E.E., Principal of the Manchester College of Science and Technology

DONALD E. BROADBENT

M.A., Ph.D., Director, Medical Research Council, Unit of Applied Psychology, Cambridge

SIR CYRIL BURT

M.A., D.Sc., Hon.LL.D. (Aberdeen), Hon.D.Litt. (Reading), Emeritus Professor of Psychology, University of London

JOHN COHEN

M.A., Ph.D., F.B.Ps.S., Professor of Psychology, University of Manchester

JAMES DREVER

M.A., Professor of Psychology, University of Edinburgh

PAUL FRAISSE

Docteur ès Lettres, Docteur de l'Institut Supérieur de Philosophie de Louvain, Professor of Experimental Psychology and Director of Psychological Laboratories, Sorbonne

EDWARD GLOVER

M.D., LL.D., Chairman of the Scientific Committee, Institute for the Study and Treatment of Delinquency

L. S. HEARNSHAW

M.A., Professor of Psychology, University of Liverpool

GEORGE HUMPHREY

M.A., Ph.D., F.R.S.C., formerly Professor of Psychology, University of Oxford

IAN A. HUNTER

M.A., Ph.D., Professor of Psychology, University of Keele

BÄRBEL INHELDER

D.Phil., Professor of Child Psychology, Institut des Sciences de L'Éducation, University of Geneva

C. DAVID LEGGE

B.Sc., Assistant Lecturer, University College, University of London

C. A. MACE

M.A., D.Litt., F.B.Ps.S., Professor of Psychology, Birkbeck College, University of London, 1944–61

DONALD M. MACKAY

M.A., D.Phil., Professor of Communication, University of Keele

G. PATRICK MEREDITH

M.Sc., M.Ed., Ph.D., F.B.Ps.S., Professor of Psychology, University of Leeds

R. C. OLDFIELD

M.A., Professor of Psychology, University of Oxford

ALEC RODGER

M.A., F.B.Ps.S., Professor of Occupational Psychology, Birkbeck College, University of London

HANNAH STEINBERG

M.A., Ph.D., Reader in Psychopharmacology, University College, University of London

ARTHUR SUMMERFIELD

B.Sc.(Tech.), B.Sc., F.B.Ps.S., Professor of Psychology, Birkbeck College, University of London

W. H. THORPE

M.A., Sc.D., F.R.S., Reader in Animal Behaviour, Jesus College, Cambridge

MAGDALEN D. VERNON

M.A., Sc.D., Professor of Psychology, University of Reading

PHILIP E. VERNON

M.A., Ph.D., D.Sc., Professor of Educational Psychology, Institute of Education, University of London

OLIVER ZANGWILL

M.A., Professor of Experimental Psychology, University of Cambridge

ACKNOWLEDGMENTS

To the Editors of *Advancement of Science, Nature, The British Journal of Psychology* (General Section) and the Cambridge University Press, *The Bulletin of the British Psychological Society, The Hibbert Journal,* to Messrs Gollancz, Messrs Simon and Schuster, Messrs Methuen and Messrs Wiley (for permission to reprint a revision of Chapter X, pp. 308-15 of *Thinking,* by Professor George Humphrey, 1951), to NATO and the Pergamon Press, to Sir Isaac Pitman & Sons Ltd, and to UNESCO, for permission to reprint, in Professor MacKay's chapter, parts of an article entitled 'Information Theory and Human Information Systems' first published in *Impact of Science on Society* (1957).

CHAPTER I

A PERSPECTIVE FOR PSYCHOLOGY*

BY JOHN COHEN

I

In the contemporary study of cognition—perceiving, learning, thinking, and remembering—the central question is: *How do we represent within us the world outside?* How, in other words, do we first encode 'signals' from the outside world, and then store and decode them? This huge and unmanageable question may be resolved into relatively simpler ones: (i) how does one event come to signify for us some other event or range of events? How, for instance, does an unexpected knock at the door come to mean the arrival of an eagerly awaited guest or of an even more eagerly unwanted bore? (ii) How does our cumulative experience constitute a living 'filing system'? What shapes the material of memory between reception and recall? (iii) How, again, does our interpretation of events acquire a private probability of its own? How does one politician come to hold with supreme assurance that the possession of thermonuclear weapons acts as a deterrent to war while another is convinced that war is made more likely by the possession of such weapons? (iv) And what exactly do we mean when we say that one thing *signifies* another?—that, for example, in the USA an egg-shaped head *stands for* massive erudition?

We can include emotional with cognitive representation. We can inquire into the manner in which a man becomes enamoured of his neighbour's wife and bedazzled by her charms as well as into the way he learns to embezzle the bank in which he is employed. These situa-

---

* An adaptation of 'Cyclopean Psychology', *The Hibbert Journal*, 1961, *59*, 236, and 'The Metaphorical Consciousness' (address to the Glasgow meeting of the British Association for the Advancement of Science), *The New Scientist*, 1958, *950*, 996.

tions illustrate the fundamental problem: How do we represent within us the world outside?

But this question, majestic though it is, cannot survive in lonely isolation. It needs the solace of another, namely: *How do we represent outside us the world we create within?* How, in other words, do we encode, store, and decode the 'signals' that are generated in the inner realm of private experience?[1] This, too, may be reduced to simpler questions: how do we find words, melodies, patterns of colour, masses and shapes of stone or bronze to convey that which cannot be put in any other medium? What imperative impulse insists on our doing these things? How can the poet tell that he has chosen the correct words in the correct order? And what causes us to be moved by his striking metaphors? For the elucidation of these questions we need an Information Theory, so to speak, in reverse.

Clearly, the word 'world' in our two basic questions is employed in different senses. When we speak of the world *outside*, we think of motor-cars, mistresses, and missiles. When we speak of the world *within*, we do not think of palpable things, people or events. We think rather of thoughts, feelings and emotions, part of which we can express with ease, part with difficulty, and part perhaps not at all. We think of those beliefs and feelings, hopes and regrets, longings and loathings which are so tenuously and obscurely related to external events that they seem to us to be generated within. We think of secret memories and intentions, of faint emotional reverberations. We think of the birth of myth, of the making of poetry, art and music, and of visionary experience. These cannot properly be described as transactions between us and the external world, for they are engendered in relative independence of our environments.

It goes without saying that we cannot draw a hard and fast line between the two questions. Mental life does not consist of two distinct kinds of process, one which sorts and recodes 'information' streaming into us from without and the other which weaves a fanciful inner web for display in the market-place. Such a division would be both arbitrary and artificial, for several reasons.

In the first place, we do not passively represent within us what goes on outside. When, for instance, I gaze at the moonlit sky, no copy of moon or stars is imprinted on my mind. Certainly a pain in my finger does not represent the pin that pricked me; and things seem to us to retain their size, shape and colour in spite of the fact that they are 'actually' different.

Secondly, our perceptions of the external world are *interdependent*, unlike the physical stimuli by which they are prompted which are mutually *independent*. Thirdly, our state of mind itself determines the reception of signals from outside. We respond to what we believe things or people are like, not to what they are *really* like, whatever that may be. We see what we expect or hope or fear or believe or know to be there. We are apt to treat things and people as a canvas on which to depict our loves and hates, our convictions and preconceptions. The blankest look is full of meaning, a sign that the situation has been taken in, for interpretation enters in the simplest act of perception. And, conversely, our states of mind are themselves ultimately linked with situations outside us. The inner web is woven from materials and patterns provided by external events. In some dim and esoteric way the fabulous visions of a Swedenborg, a Factor Analyst, or even a Learning Theorist undeniably constitute an attempt to interpret his world.

All the same, when every allowance has been made for the kinship between the two questions, they obstinately retain their separate identity. For there are elements of experience which cannot be understood in terms of the 'physical dimensions of consciousness'.[2]

II

Even those forms of experience which *are* intelligible in these terms may be governed by inner rules. A mass of evidence from psychophysics could be adduced to support this statement, but let me take an illustration from a recent experiment on the determination of the subjective value of a 'bit' of information. Suppose you present someone with a page on which there are a number of circles and you tell him to guess which circle you (the experimenter) are thinking of. Before making his guess he is allowed to ask you questions, but only questions which can be answered by 'Yes' or 'No'; and he must tell you how many questions (i.e. the minimum number) he would have to ask in order to guess correctly. Under such conditions, if what goes on in his 'mind' accurately represented the objective 'information' on the page, the number of questions he would believe necessary should correspond to the number of 'bits' of information on the page. In point of fact, the number of questions which he actually believes it is necessary to ask is usually in excess of this. Young children believe the number is *greatly* in excess, and at all ages the number increases logarithmically as the number of circles or 'bits' of information increases.[3]

A second example from a study of evidence will illustrate the same point. It appears that for the majority of people, the *total* weight of evidence counts more than the *balance* of evidence. For instance, most people seem to think that, in a typical situation, 10 witnesses *against* a defendant and 10 *for* him are more incriminating than 5 *against* and 5 *for*. Similarly, 5 *against* and 5 *for* are considered more incriminating than 2 *against* and 2 *for*. Still more significant is the fact that many people consider 5 against 3 as more incriminating than 2 against 1, although the balance against the defendant is greater in the second case than in the first.[4] Thus even in the domain of the first question we are guided by principles which are psychologically *sui generis*.

Our two questions seem to demarcate realms of experience which, though related and overlapping, remain disparate. If we identify their distinctive features we shall find that the first question is a competent guide only for the Constable landscapes of the mind and it would be of little use in the Hieronymus Bosche zone or the Proust territory of the second question.

As a heuristic device our difficulty in relation to the distinctive features, might be resolved in this way. We may be said to concern ourselves with the first question when we take things at their face value, but when we take them figuratively we occupy ourselves with the second question. Mental activities of a logico-scientific character are primarily directed to the face value of things or words, to their literal or factual sense. But we can also take things and words in a non-literal or symbolic sense, which is not, however, to be labelled as inferior. For man is not only capable of inquiring in a matter-of-fact way into the objective world existing independently of him as an observer. He does not wholly or even primarily take things at their face value. He takes them symbolically as well.

The non-literal efforts of man are encountered in myth and poetry, in drama and music. They do not represent a lowly stage of mental evolution from which we climb to higher levels, from the theological through the metaphysical, to the scientific, as Comte would have us believe. They allow a symbolic representation in a different mode from the logico-scientific, and they result from a transfiguration which colours the way the observer perceives no less than the way he thinks, leading him beyond outer appearances and beyond literal meanings. Things and words are then invested with a significance which is not less real because it does not refer to anything physically existing independently of the observer.

Figurative or symbolic 'knowledge' does not tell us of some ethereal reality which delights in a Platonic existence, or of some poetic or mystical reality that exists in the sense that tables or electrons exist. The 'reality' it intimates is sufficiently accredited by the personal significance it has for us.

The novelist and the artist stake more ambitious claims, for the creatures they invent are more real to them than their neighbours. Dickens wept bitterly when Little Nell died, and when Jules Sandeau spoke to Balzac about his sister's illness, Balzac listened absent-mindedly for a while and then impatiently interrupted his visitor: 'All that, my friend, is very well, but let us return to reality; let us talk of Eugenie Grandet!'[5] 'Reality', declared Picasso, 'is more than the thing itself. I always look for its super-reality. Reality lies in how you see things. A green parrot is also a green salad *and* a green parrot. He who makes it only a parrot diminishes its reality. A painter who copies a tree blinds himself to the real tree. I see things otherwise. A palm tree can become a horse.' When a lady contemplating a picture in Matisse's studio said to him, 'Surely the arm of this woman is much too long', the artist replied, 'Madame, you are mistaken. This is not a woman. This is a picture.'[6]

Such varieties of experience and reality have nothing to do with the accumulation of knowledge which comes from stuffing our heads with facts. The line 'The mortal moon hath her eclipse endured' was never intended to communicate a proposition, and there are other non-propositional experiences which, in the words of Satchinananda Murti, 'turn a man upside down and churn his very being'.

Theories of symbolism in general and of the metaphor in particular should therefore not rely exclusively on 'reality-testing' as the single path to true knowledge.[7] For this leads to the conclusion that symbolization occurs only when the mind is unequal to grasping a set of ideas, the incapacity being due to fatigue or illness, and to have arisen when the mental capacity of the race was not yet able 'to grasp an idea which some day in the future it will'. A symbol or metaphor becomes then no more than a sign of failure of apprehension. If this were so, it would make nonsense of the fact that it is largely by their sublime use of metaphor that we judge the excellence of Homer and Shakespeare. Was Homer tired when he wrote the *Odyssey* or Shakespeare ill when he wrote *Lear?*

III

In the half a century they have devoted to the testing of intelligence, psychologists have largely been barking up the wrong tree, an arboreal skill evidently transmitted to them by their philosophical forebears.

'Most of the errors of philosophers', wrote Shelley, 150 years ago, 'have arisen from considering the human being in a point of view too detailed and circumscribed. He is not (only) a moral and intellectual— but also, and pre-eminently, an imaginative being.'[8]

A comprehensive view of mind or brain cannot ignore activities which appear to be beyond the reach of the logical or scientific intelligence. Nor can it be limited to what seems to be the 'evidence' of the senses or to the incomplete world picture of natural science. A comprehensive view, if it has pretensions to scientific status, must embrace the full range of mental operations, not only those which are thought to be relevant to establishing verifiable knowledge. Outside natural science, men have always acknowledged different varieties of experience, if not different kinds of knowledge and even different orders of reality—poetic, musical, religious, mystical. These other orders are subjectively as real in their way as the solid earth beneath our feet. We act upon them, and they govern our lives.[9]

Of such symbolic orders of experience neurology as such can know nothing. Even Lashley,[10] the fervent advocate of psychoneural reductionism, recognized this when he declared that 'psychology is today a more fundamental science than neuro-physiology', because, he went on to say, the latter offers few principles from which we predict the normal organization of behaviour, whereas the laws of nervous action in behaviour *must* conform to demonstrable psychological facts.[11]

For this reason alone it is hard to justify the demand for translatability as a criterion in psychological science.[12] It is necessary, some theorists tell us, that the student of psychology should talk in terms which are translatable into neurology. If we ask 'Why?', we should no doubt be informed that it is more productive to do so. But whether this is so or not is surely a matter of *meta*-scientific opinion, for there is no other criterion of scientific productivity. Mental 'models' or analogies, as they should perhaps be called, may be as adequate as neural 'models' in leading to experiment, prediction, and understanding, although the two types of model need not be mutually exclusive. In the end, it may be a matter of taste whether the theorist prefers a psychological or neural 'model' and whether he feels one or the other to be intellectually more satisfying.

IV

The dazzling ascent of modern science need not deter us from seeking the obscure paths whereby the pinnacle of achievement has been reached. Far from being *pre*-logical or *pre*-scientific, what we may call 'non-literal' mental activities are perhaps a necessary feature in scientific inventiveness itself. We need not suppose that there is such a thing as a 'scientific intelligence' which operates independently of what is popularly called the 'imagination'. Nor is scientific thinking a conscious exercise which can be wholly recaptured by introspection. Those who have attempted to catch themselves unawares whilst in the act of discovery have felt like the small boy who stood in front of a mirror with his eyes closed to see what he looked like when asleep. Thinking in science is not a series of step-by-step operations that we can follow from the beginning to the end, and it never keeps to the ways prescribed by logic. The scientific intelligence is not, in fact, a sharply defined cognitive process. It has a penumbra of tacit and possibly unspecifiable elements which are indispensable if it is to function at all.

The importance of such elements may be illustrated from the biographies of eminent scientists. Charles Babbage's celebrated Analytical Engine was the principal precursor of modern computing machines. How did Babbage arrive at his novel idea? This is what he wrote:

The earliest idea that I can trace in my own mind of calculating arithmetical Tables by machinery arose in this manner: One evening I was sitting in the rooms of the Analytical Society at Cambridge, my head leaning forward on the table in a kind of dreamy mood, with a table of logarithms lying open before me. Another member, coming into the room and seeing me half asleep, called out, 'Well, Babbage, what are you dreaming about?' to which I replied, 'I am thinking that all these Tables (pointing to the logarithms) might be calculated by machinery.'[13]

A 'dreamy' mood is very unlike the intense concentration and concern with representation of the external world which might be expected to favour scientific inventiveness. Yet a 'dreamy mood' may generate the imagery which liberates the mind from the perceptual field and endows it with a mobility otherwise perhaps unattainable.

Consider Clerk Maxwell, the greatest theoretical physicist of the nineteenth century, in whose scientific imagination, as in Kepler's, there appear to have been vital 'religious' elements. It may be that we owe to them the derivation of the general equations of the electro-magnetic field, for it was evidently because of them that the equations 'were more real to him [Clerk Maxwell] than the material phenomena he could know in the laboratory'.[14] Faraday provides perhaps an even more telling example, for his special gift lay in inexhaustibly reflecting on analogies between the known and the unknown.

The imaginative detecting of analogies, the seeking and dwelling on resemblances between different ideas or images may be a fundamental feature of thought itself. It has been described as the art of 'dancing' around an idea, of lingering on a point, of decorating and transforming it until it produces a sense of novelty in the mind. Scientific inventiveness may itself depend on the assimilation of new analogies; and in so far as language enters into this it is a sort of verbal 'museum' where we encounter 'the relics of the extravagant fancies and analogies of dead and forgotten poets'.[15] In physics, the task of analogy is to render the unfamiliar familiar. In psychology, it may be the other way round, for the data of psychology are often too familiar.

V

We may further distinguish the systems of representation relating to our first and second questions with respect to the part which 'evidence' plays in them, and by 'evidence' I mean sensory signals for action. The first system may be defined as tied to action, which is to be taken only when the signal warrants it, for instance, telephoning the doctor when sufficient spots on baby's tummy warrant it, or calling the fire-brigade when, in the fireman's opinion, there is enough smoke to justify the call, 'enough' being measured by the relative frequency with which such an amount of smoke has led to a fire in the past. If a man calls the fire-brigade when there is too little smoke, or if he waits before doing so until his house is crumbling in flames, he is acting on 'evidence' which deviates from the optimum. On the other hand, we can regard the second system of representation as having no direct relevance for action. 'Evidence', then, is here of no consequence.

So far we have only offered definitions. Let us now take the bull by the horns and make the assumption that the first and second systems relate to the two types of activity that we very vaguely contrast as 'intelligent' and 'imaginative' respectively. It is not at all necessary for my main argument that I should make this assumption. I could just as well employ the symbols 'X' and 'Y' instead of 'intelligent' and 'imaginative'. My reason for not doing so is to try and kill two birds with one stone, that is to say, to clarify this ancient antithesis between 'intelligent' and 'imaginative' while distinguishing the two types of representation in terms of 'evidence'.

This antithesis will become clearer in the light of the kinship between animal and man, so far as the role of evidence is concerned. In many animals the same behaviour patterns may occur either as a result of a strong stimulus applied when the need is weak, or by a weak stimulus applied when the need is strong; the longer a need remains unsatisfied, and hence becomes more powerful, the lower the threshold of the stimulus can afford to be. In the limit, when the threshold reaches zero the reaction takes place *in vacuo*—the so-called *Leerlaufreaktion*; the organism, we may say, explodes. This relationship between need and stimulus might be described as the Law of Substitutes, which means that as the need grows in intensity, the readier the animal is to accept second, third or fourth best.

The animal's interpretation of its environment accordingly depends[16] on two inversely related factors, namely, (i) resemblance, and (ii) the biological relevance of the stimulus. This also appears to be true of man. The starving man will eat cat's meat, a drowning man will clutch at a straw, the parched desert traveller pursues a mirage.

Now we come to the point. Let us assume that there are experiences which must be realistically attuned to the external world if we are to survive and other experiences which may vary without affecting the chances of survival. The first category we may regard as appropriate for 'intelligent' activity and inappropriate for 'imaginative' activity, and conversely for the second category of experiences. The 'vacuum-reaction' is 'unintelligent' if elicited in a situation which calls for internal control over the delay which supervenes between desire and fulfilment; but may be highly imaginative in a situation which calls for no action in the external world. E. H. Gombrich has remarked that an artist can afford to omit a vital feature suggested by the context; the more vital the feature, the more intense is the 'completing' process instigated in the viewer. Hence the life-like expression in the masterpieces of Leonardo and Rembrandt were achieved by leaving the eyes of their most moving portraits in the shade, thus compelling the viewer to share in the act of creation. This phenomenon is familiar in the sphere of erotic behaviour. That is why film-makers are fond of such titles as 'The Naked Earth', 'The Naked Edge', or 'The Naked Truth', for anything naked is bound to stir the craving of a sex-starved public.

The view we are led to is this. Following a suggestion of Prof. D. M. MacKay, we can say that an action may be described as 'intelligent' if it occurs at the correct threshold of evidence. If the threshold is too high, measured by what the situation has demanded in the past, action will take place too rarely; if it is too low, action will take place too frequently, whilst an optimal threshold of evidence may be located between these extremes.[17] Thus there are two contrasting types of 'unintelligent' behaviour. To this we can add that an activity may be described as 'imaginative' to the degree that it does not lean on evidence from without provided the situation does not require a realistic appraisal of signals in the interests of survival. The appreciative viewer of Rembrandt's portraits is behaving 'imaginatively', but the unsatisfied man who goes to the cinema merely because he is attracted by the ambiguity of the title 'Fire Down Below' is behaving 'unintelligently'. This formulation may be taken as provisional but I hope it will serve to indicate what I am trying to convey.

VI

The diverse orders of experience to which I have earlier referred vary in process as well as in content. In order to investigate them we need more than introspective analysis. This remark may be justified by distinguishing between experience and consciousness in terms of a multi-filter model.

Experience may be regarded as channelled into consciousness through an intricate sequence and variety of filters. Let us call the two principal ones F_1 and F_2. F_1 is an economy filter under our direct control, and it allows into awareness only those elements to which we are set or 'tuned in'. Only part of what we see is actually *looked at* by us, just as only part of what we hear is actually *listened to*, and so with the other avenues of sense; but with an effort we can shift our attention as we please. F_2, the second filter, is not under our direct control. It prevents the entry into awareness of any items of experience which might provoke that highly distressing state of mind we call anxiety. It is selective both positively and negatively; that which it shuts out from awareness is deliberately excluded. The method of introspection can circumvent F_1, but it can make little of those processes (operation, contents) of consciousness which cannot pass through F_2. The more subtle method of phenomenological analysis can, however, elude F_2 as well, and hence penetrate into otherwise inaccessible realms of experience. Its subtlety resides, I should explain, not in any special technique of exploration but in the type of question it prompts and in the depth of its probe.

Analysis of experience is a much more ambitious undertaking than the introspective report we ask of our experimental subjects. When I introspect, I treat myself or the content of my consciousness as an object. If it were practicable, I would invite the experimenter to enter my mind and see for himself what is going on there. He could then describe my after-image for himself, and his description would not differ materially from my own. That is to say, in introspection, I act as internal deputy of the outside observer. In phenomenological analysis, by contrast, I cannot say to the experimenter 'Look and see for yourself', for my aim is not so much to provide a description such as, he, as an external observer, might give if he were 'inside me', but to describe what is happening to *me* from a subjective point of view. It is *my* personal experience that I am describing, and he would feel differently in my situation. In phenomenological analysis, I am not trying to be a detached spectator describing my bodily changes when I am afraid, hungry, jealous, or in agony. I am not acting as an agent for an observer to whom my experiences are inaccessible. I am conveying to him what is undergone by me as an experiencing subject, with a distinctive life-history, and I am doing what would be altogether impossible for anyone else to do without, in fact, becoming me.

Phenomenological analysis can bring to awareness our implicit or tacit knowledge of events and relationships. By this I do not mean that it is a cunning way of describing how some skilled performance is executed. I mean rather that it explores unverbalized experiences of emotional engagement and social involvement. These play a much bigger part in our lives than is commonly supposed. We are not by any means aware of and therefore cannot articulate all that we organically 'know' with our bodies, that is, all that which is excluded by F_2. The preoccupation of psychologists with verbal behaviour, and with repressed unconscious phenomena, has led to the neglect of the 'reverberation' of experience, of that which we assuredly 'know', but which we can only make explicit with great effort.

Let us not forget, too, that non-propositional silence may be more eloquent than the wisest speech. 'If I were to render my silence in music', said Canabis, 'I should need three military orchestras.' When the dinner partner of a famous actress had sat in perfect silence for half an hour, she turned to him and said: 'Let's talk about something else now!'

Naturally, when experience does not 'reverberate', no problem arises of phenomenological analysis. When, for example, a lover on the celluloid film screen declares to a young woman: 'I love you', we are not greatly impressed. We may even feel revolted, for we realize the sham character of this quasi-amorous declaration. It is not operational, for it leads nowhere. Nothing is intended, implied or received. But in real life the situation is different. The young man who first utters these fateful words is well aware that he is crossing his Rubicon. And the young woman who hears them for the first time at once conjures up in her mind an album of images of domestic bliss, a fertile bed, a labour-saving kitchen, and a husband to boot. Fortunately the echoes of these words resounding in the boudoir and vaults of her mind need not be lost forever. She can, if she wishes, recapture them, for the lasting edification of the phenomenological psychologist.

VII

Finally, here is a word of reassurance. Some theorists have charged psychologists with agoraphobia, namely, a tendency to imprison their subject within the organism and to deal exclusively with the world within. The neglected environment, they say, should be granted equal marital status with the organism. But the boot is surely on the other foot! Self-imprisonment there has scarcely been at all. On the contrary, many psychologists have drifted away if not exiled themselves from their native terrain, and are ready to explore anything so long as it has nothing to do with the inner history and geography, and the flora and fauna of their own minds.

For this reason perhaps, in so far as a coherent conception of the human mind emerges from contemporary academic psychology, it seems incomplete. For it suggests that the mind is an intellectual instrument for acquiring certain kinds of 'objective' knowledge, our feelings, emotions and 'drives' being thought of as motivating or disrupting elements. This notion comprises only those features which supposedly govern logical, mathematical or scientific thinking, which alone are believed to be truly characteristic of civilized man. Other features which do not provide 'objectively' correct knowledge of our environment are stigmatized as inferior or illusory. If not ignored entirely, they are treated as merely subjective, or as pre-logical or pre-scientific thinking, and they are denied validity. Thus all experience is judged by a criterion which is appropriate only to limited aspects of it.

The task of the psychologist, I would suggest, is to illumine the world of meaningful experience by resolving the subjective-objective antithesis. Such an achievement requires the two-edged sword constituted by our two basic questions. The psychological would thus be rendered 'objective' and the so-called 'objective' would be recognized as, in the last resort, psychological.

NOTES AND REFERENCES

1. It is conceivable that a neurophysiological correlate of this internal activity will one day be demonstrated. For there is evidence of considerable endogenous discharge of neurons in the central nervous system, although little seems to be known about the manner in which the brain selects discharges evoked by messages in its own environment from those that constitute its background activity. (See BRAZIER, M. A. B., 1963, 'How can models from Information Theory be used in Neurophysiology?' in FIELDS, W. S. and ABBOTT, W. (ed.), *Information Storage and Neural Control*, Springfield, Ill.: Thomas.)

2. BORING, E. G., 1933, *The Physical Dimensions of Consciousness*, New York: Appleton-Century.

3. COHEN, JOHN, and COOPER, PETER, 1962, 'Subjective Value of a "Bit" of Information', *Nature, 196*, 360.

4. COHEN, JOHN, COOPER, PETER, and THORNE, PAUL, 1962, 'Les degrés d'évidence', *J. de Psychol., 3*, 225.

5. HARDING, R. H. M., 1948, *Anatomy of Inspiration*, Cambridge: Heffer.

6. Quoted by GOMBRICH, E. H., 1960, *Art and Illusion*, p. 115, London: Phaedon Press.

7. It was on the basis of Freud's conception of scientific intelligence as a 'secondary' process that Ernest Jones elaborated his reductionist theory of symbolism, according to which 'symbolic modes of thought are the more primitive, both ontogenetically and phylogenetically, and represent a reversion to some simpler and earlier stage of mental development'. (G. JONES, 1923, 'Symbolism', in *Papers on Psycho-Analysis*, London: Baillière, Tindall and Cox.) It is true that there are certain primitive myths which, taken literally, and considered as serious attempts to explain the origin of the universe, are superseded by science. But many of such myths have a beauty and grandeur which survive their obsolete pre-science.

8. SHELLEY, P. B., 1886, 'Speculations in Metaphysics' (A Fragment), IV, in *Essays and Letters*, London: Scott. 'The imagination', wrote Kierkegaard, 'is what providence uses in order to get men into reality, into existence, to get them far enough out, or in, or down in existence. And when imagination has helped them as far out as they are meant to go—that is where reality properly speaking begins.' (KIERKEGAARD, S. A., 1958, *The Journals*, 1834–54, p. 243 (ed. and trans. by Dru, A.), London: Fontana Books.)

9. COHEN, JOHN, 1958, 'The Metaphorical Consciousness' (address to the 1958 meeting of the British Association), *New Scientist, 950*, 996.

10. LASHLEY, K. S., 1960, *The Neuropsychology of Lashley*, New York: McGraw-Hill, quoted by Lord Russell Brain, 1961, 'Body, Brain, Mind and Soul' in HUXLEY, SIR JULIAN (ed.), *The Humanist Frame*, London: Allen and Unwin. See particularly, WELLEK, A., 1963, 'Die Wissenschaftsproblematik der Psychologie als einer anthropologischen Disziplin', *Psychologische Rundschau, 14* (2), 75.

11. For this reason alone we cannot accept the assertions of McCulloch and Pitts that 'the formal and the final aspects of that activity which we are wont to call mental are rigorously deducible from present neurophysiology', and that 'diseased mentality can be understood without loss of scope or rigour, in the scientific terms of neurophysiology'. (MCCULLOCH, W. G., and PITTS, W. H., 1943, 'A Logical Calculus of the Ideas Immanent in Nervous Activity', *Bull. Maths. Biophys.*, 5, 115.) I should add that the attempt to reduce psychology to neurophysiology is not analogous to the explanatory reduction of, say, chemistry to physics. The two-sidedness of psychological phenomena, the fact that they can be looked at from the 'inside' as well as from the 'outside' puts them logically in a class apart.

12. HEBB, D. O., 1951, 'The Role of Neurological Ideas in Psychology', *J. Person.*, 20, 39.

13. BABBAGE, C., 1864, *Passages from the Life of a Philosopher*, p. 42, London: Longmans Green.

14. CROWTHER, J. G., 1935, *British Scientists of the Nineteenth Century*, pp. 311–12, London: Routledge and Kegan Paul.

15. HULME, T. E., 1955, *Further Speculations*, pp. 91–2, Minneapolis: University of Minnesota Press.

16. GOMBRICH, E. H., 1951, 'Meditations on a Hobby Horse or the Roots of Artistic Form', in WHYTE, L. L. (ed.), *Aspects of Form: A Symposium on Form in Nature and Art*, London: Lund Humphries.

17. MACKAY D. M., 1958, 'Operational Aspects of Intellect', in *Mechanization of Thought Processes*, N.P.L. Symposium, London: H.M.S.O., and other papers by the same author.

CHAPTER 2

EXPERIMENT IN PSYCHOLOGY—
A CENTENARY AND AN OUTLOOK*

BY R. C. OLDFIELD

I

Custom—for once reasonably apt—attributes the beginnings of experimental psychology to the publication in 1860 of Fechner's *Elements of Psychophysics*. A hundred years in the history of science is a long time. A century ago the *Origin of Species* had been in the bookshops less than a year. Sigmund Freud was a little boy of four, Charles Sherrington a year his junior. Even Pavlov, born in 1849, however precocious, could scarcely have taken the first steps towards the discovery of the conditioned reflex. As to those names which mark for us the period between the wars, Köhler, Lashley, Bartlett, Hull, to name but four, twenty years were to pass before even their parents were to think of them. Since 1860 there has been great, and positively accelerated, activity. Fechner himself inspired an immense quantity of work distinguished more by bulk than scientific outcome, yet it remains true that he was the originator of surprisingly much that remains central to experimental psychology as we know it today.

I would like to pick out from the story[1] which follows Fechner's *Elements* a few samples chosen for their bearing on the question of what part experiment has to play in psychology. Views about this have differed a good deal during the past century. Some have held that the very character of the subject precludes experiment having any place at all: others that nothing can claim the status of psychological research which does not conform to the basic pattern of the conditioned

* An address delivered to Section J (Psychology), on Friday, September 2, 1960, at the Cardiff meeting of the British Association for the Advancement of Science, published in *Advancement of Science*,1960, *17*, 364.

reflex experiment. We need not worry with extremes such as these. But lesser degrees of doctrinaire finality are still in evidence today. As a consequence not only the worthy research student, but his elders and betters, are sometimes condemned to routines which are dreary in execution and too often trifling in result. Most psychologists nowadays will agree that experiment has a contribution to make. Many would hold that contribution to be vital. I myself would go so far as to say that psychology can only make progress in the long run in so far as it is able and willing to submit its basic propositions to empirical test in an experimental framework. But this certainly does not mean that we all ought to plunge furiously into some experimental activity or other as the only alternative to a guilty feeling that we are not doing our job. On the contrary, it seems to me, we should try to be as selective and discriminating as possible in our use of experiment. There is at least one good reason for this. Experiments are time-consuming: we need more good ones and ought not to waste time on bad. It is not easy to say what the characteristics of a good experiment are in this connection. Certainly in a subject so wide in scope, which started from scratch no more than 100 years ago, it seems likely that there will be different sorts of 'good' experiments—and an even greater variety of 'bad'. In looking at them it will be useful to keep a number of questions in mind. First of all, to what extent and in what particular connections ought we to strive to be quantitative? Again, with regard to the relation of experiment to theory, what kinds of experiments generate useful theory, and conversely, what sort of theoretical formulation helps to build a coherent empirical structure capable of sound extension beyond any particular theory and giving rise to new connections of ideas? Finally, we shall do well to bear in mind the circumstance, humiliating but not uncommon in psychology, that having devised experiments respectably scientific and theories which interact with them, we find ourselves remote from the crude facts of everyday life which originally aroused our curiosity and which it is our aim to interpret and explain on a rational scientific basis. Scrutiny of the past will give no complete answers to questions of this kind. But it may at least tell us where some of the pitfalls lie. Let us go back 100 years and start with Fechner.

II

Fechner was a professor of physics by trade, by temperament a rather unbalanced, quixotic, romantic humanist. (Fortunately before these latter tendencies gained the upper hand he had absorbed the lessons offered by the experimental study of electricity.) In an increasingly materialist world he burned with zeal to enlarge the status of the human spirit. This, he concluded, could only be done by deciding what relationship there is between body and mind. A physicist trying to understand something material tends to measure it. Could not events in the mind also be measured, and the connection between the two established as a quantitative functional relation? Not directly, for, he writes, 'the measure only of the physical is directly accessible, so that the measure of the psychical must in the first instance be achieved through its dependence upon the former'. One fact emerges straight away from any systematic exploration of the sensations resulting from stimuli of different strengths. This fact is that two stimuli which are quantitatively distinguishable by physical measurement of their intensities are not always distinguishable by the sensations they provoke. They only become so when the physical differences reach a certain magnitude. This finding, adumbrated by Bouguer in the mid-eighteenth century and studied in some detail by E. H. Weber in the early nineteenth, provides Fechner with his starting point. If we suppose (and I cannot discover that Fechner ever questioned this assumption) that to *every* stimulus-intensity there corresponds one and only one sensory magnitude, then we should be justified perhaps in taking the sensation interval which corresponds to the difference of any two just discriminable stimuli as constant. We could then use it as a unit of sensation. And as a measure of its strength we could allot to every sensation a number corresponding to the number of steps of just perceptibly different physical intensities from the minimum intensity at which there is no sensation at all. With this idea in mind, Fechner embarked on a study of just discriminable stimulus intensities and especially of the way in which the discriminable difference varies with the absolute value of the intensity itself. It is not easy now to be sure that we fully grasp Fechner's meaning. Many people would certainly feel that there is something fishy about his argument. Certainly it started a far-reaching but largely futile controversy over the measurement of sensation which deflected the attention of most of his successors from more profitable enterprise. Ought we then to hold up Fechner as an example of how not to go about experimenting in psychology? I do not think so. Notice how, with an intuition which perhaps he owed to his training in the physics laboratory, Fechner moves from questionable convictions about body and mind, via a shaky argument, to an experiment with a definite outcome which can be expressed wholly in terms of physical measurements. The experiment and its result have a standing independent of their *rationale*, and offer scope for the classical device of seeking functional relationships among variables. The whole procedure might still, of course, have had merely trivial results. But this did not happen. Precisely these relationships among stimulus intensities are very much the subject of active enquiry and speculation at the present time.

Trying to refine and enlarge the work started by Weber, Fechner came across a difficulty which must have been particularly tiresome to a physicist. This is the inescapably variable response of the human organism to any given stimulus. If a human being tries to decide which of two weights is the heavier by poising them in his hands, the variability of his judgments on different occasions is far greater than any variation which crops up when weighing them on a balance. How discouraging and baffling such a situation might be to a pioneer without ready-made techniques, is not easy for us to appreciate. Like the first-year student trying to apply the Constant Method, Fechner might well have been excused for concluding that there is no scope for quantitative study in this field. His pertinacity in perfecting and applying his psychophysical methods in the face of such striking inconsistency in the observable facts stands out as a major achievement of nineteenth-century biology. As much more recent students of living organisms have realized, biology is full of cases where progress can only be made by using statistical reduction of the raw data. It is entertaining to recall that the particular mathematical device he used in connection with the Constant Method is the direct forerunner of what now goes under the name of Probit Analysis. This today is the method of choice for testing the efficacy of insecticides: the tendency of any individual insect to respond mortally to a given dose is as tiresomely unreliable as the human subject's to respond to an auditory stimulus by reporting a sound.

Fechner could never have made the progress he did had he not stuck, with unwitting boldness, to the idea that there *is* a quantity to be measured, and that the variability of experimental results is attributable to the operation of numerous small random contingencies, the effects of which we can with care diminish, though not wholly eliminate. So far as I can see, he did *not* contemplate the possibility, as we sometimes do today, that the quantity itself has no more than a statistical definition in the last resort and is ultimately indeterminate. The straightforward nineteenth century physicist's view of measurable quantities stood him in good stead. The theory of errors of observation could be invoked and it allowed Fechner to arrive at most probable estimates of psychophysical variables, together with some estimate of the uncertainty of the values. It is forbidding to speculate about what might have happened had psychophysics had to start its career against a background of modern quantum theory.

When Fechner gave us the psychophysical methods he showed how purely physical measurements could be used to attack psychological problems. But he did far more than this. The framework of experiment he introduced was so fundamental that it is applicable in psychology outside the range of phenomena he was primarily concerned with. He gave us the stimulus-response method itself, and upon this practically all that we nowadays regard as experimental psychology rests. This, too, joins psychology directly on to physiology. While Fechner was composing the 'Elements of Psychophysics' his great contemporary Claude Bernard was engaged, in his laboratory, in provoking a known change in the environment of his animal preparation, noting and measuring the change of behaviour, and drawing conclusions as to the mechanism underlying the function in which he was interested. But Bernard was fortunate in being able to control the conditions of his experiment closely enough to make it repeatable within the limits required by his arguments. In experiments upon the intact human organism, on the other hand, the use of the stimulus-response method is inseparable from recourse to the experimental and statistical framework provided by Fechner.

The immediate result, however, of Fechner's efforts was to generate a controversy as to the measurability of sensation which might well have led any outside observer to conclude that the fear rather than the hope of a solution was responsible for its continuance. There are those for whom this question, translated into suitable operational terms, is still a real issue. But for the most part the controversy itself lies buried in the dustbin of history, and is best remembered by the epitaph William James pronounced over it.[2]

Fechner did more than start an arid controversy. He directly inspired Wilhelm Wundt. Wundt had the background, commanded the means and disposed of the compulsive energy which can do duty for enthusiasm, to make Leipzig the capital of a new empire and to set it about with an armamentarium of brass instruments. The outcome resembled that of other empires. Some who found it a centre of attraction and a fount of ideas and methods later went their pioneering ways. Others became high priests and ambassadors. In due course the weapons, originally intended for attack upon problems, became fetish

B

objects endowed with magical powers of defending established notions. Research deteriorated into ritual. None the less, Wundt's most outstanding achievement was, perhaps, the introduction of 'instrumentation' into psychology. There comes a time in the development of every science when *one* condition of success in tackling a problem is to look at it from the point of view of the instrumental resources that would be required to solve it—to consider how far they already exist and, if not, whether and how they could be devised. It is, for example, useless to ask a question the reply to which would require the measurement of time to a millionth of a second if the best means we have of measuring time is accurate only to within a thousandth. We must either reformulate the original problem so as to pose another interesting question which the clocks we have can answer or else set about devising a more accurate method of measuring time. Either outcome is likely to start new lines of enquiry. In another way Wundt's establishment of the psychological laboratory, with its acknowledged instrumentation and the identifiable forms of its inmates' activities, proved less fortunate. Rather prematurely, experimental psychologists acquired a consciousness of professional unity. Outcrops of parochialism and defensiveness against influence from outside has sometimes been the result.

III

Perhaps it is not accidental that the next outstanding innovator was no product of the Wundtian stable. Hermann Ebbinghaus never got closer to Leipzig than the University of Halle, disposed of no brass instruments, and worked alone. His experimental attack upon memory[3] is truly distinguished and is in many ways a model of good experimental research in psychology. First, he picked out of what at that time was the most coherent and articulated set of ideas about the subject—namely those of the English empiricists—just what could be made the subject of precise experiment yet did not saddle him unduly with hidden presuppositions. Secondly he appreciated the need, even when trying to study the higher mental processes, to make experiment yield behavioural and quantitative data, and to use every means in his power to control the conditions. Thus, even at the risk of artificiality, he broke down the complex material with which he had to deal into small elements—the famous nonsense syllables. If not identical, these could *prima facie* be regarded as equivalent. By making these elements small, and using a lot of them, he was able to get a reasonably continuous scale in respect of quantity. This ruthless pruning and shaping of his problem, which led others to assert later that Ebbinghaus had studied only a small, and not the most interesting, part of what we mean by memory is none the less highly characteristic of experimental science. So cavalier a treatment of what we all know to be a rich and complex field of phenomena fully justifies itself when some simple form of relationship emerges in the results. Ebbinghaus's two most important findings, that oblivescence broadly speaking follows a course of exponential decay and that the structure of the material and not only its elements plays an important part in retention, suggestively point in opposite directions. The first conclusion might seem to bear out a view of memory which made retention dependent upon some sort of trace in the brain, some physico-chemical or physiological disequilibrium which resolved itself in course of time by a process of leakage or of tissue change. Had physiology been further advanced in Ebbinghaus's day than it was, or indeed than it is now, such a finding might have encouraged a variety of hypotheses suitable for experimental test at a physiological level. As things have turned out, Ebbinghaus's simple, provisional, experiment and conclusion have proved, after a long interval, a stimulus in other directions. They have provided a starting point on which the fresh impetus, first of Hullian conditioned reflex behaviour theory, and later of information theory could extend their hypotheses into the field of memory.

The implications of Ebbinghaus's second finding, that organization of material is a factor in retention, seem to have been rather neglected. A fresh attack upon this aspect of remembering developed from other preoccupations. What Ebbinghaus wrote in his *Grundzüge* makes it clear that he was by no means unaware of a reconstructive aspect of recall. But it was left to Bartlett to make this feature the object of original experimental attack. Bartlett's approach,[4] by comparison with that of Ebbinghaus, is not at all quantitative and not very systematic. But it is one which is quite indispensable at certain stages in the development of a science, notably when more limited and rigid methods have lost the initial impetus of their early success. Bartlett's methods of *Repeated Reproduction* and of *Serial Reproduction* allowed scope for the operation of complex and important factors in recall that were carefully, and from his point of view rightly, excluded by Ebbinghaus. Bartlett's investigations are related to those of the philologist tracing the evolution of the meanings and forms of words, of the archaeologist following the development of a decorative or symbolic *motif* or of the social anthropologist who tracks down the origins of myth, legend and folk-tale, rather than to the manipulations of the laboratory scientist. Successful use of methods such as these is limited to certain fields. It requires a firm grasp of their limitations and an unusual amount of implicit discipline. Little, if any, conventional experimental scaffolding is there to prevent the work from going astray. The possibility of physiological check is remote. Bartlett's methods do not lend themselves much to further refinement in the direction of systematic quantitative experimental design. They remain somewhat esoteric, their precise character less important than the conclusions of the man who devised and used them. His clear demonstration of the reconstructive, as opposed to the merely reproductive, character of memory processes effectively put a stop to the idea that memory could be directly interpreted in terms of a conglomeration of simple independent storage processes. Effort in the laboratory was thereby led into more fruitful channels, and clinical studies of memory and language disorders refreshed. Another important—if perilous—consequence of Bartlett's work was the importation into psychology of Head's concept of the *Schema*.[5] Perhaps the chief merit of this has been that it enables us to move with conceptual ease among a great variety of psychological phenomena, many of them very obscure, and reaching far beyond memory itself. In the fields of thinking, skill, language and perception, the navigational aids provided by older views prove inept, or would confine us to certain limited paths.

In this connection it ought to be said that the value of this new freedom of movement could prove illusory. There is a current tendency—and it is to be seen in institutes of clinical neurology as well as in psychological laboratories—to invoke the word 'schema' wherever there is difficulty in describing clearly some aspect of psychological or physiological organization. It is no disparagement of Bartlett's personal and unique achievement to say that the word 'schema' has an important role in contemporary psychology largely because it stands for something of which we are ignorant. There is everything to be said for replacing worn-out myths by fresh ones, but we ought not to forget that myths can sustain complacency as well as urge action. Some people, but I am not one of them, may think that psychology has no further need for workers like Bartlett. Certainly we cannot command or contrive their appearance on the scene. The taste, the flair and the peculiar variety of empirical logic demanded by such work seem to arise before the age of intellectual training.

IV

In two respects there is a similarity between the contributions of Bartlett and those of the Gestalt[6] school. The latter also arose out of dissatisfaction with earlier views, especially in their atomistic aspect, and a determination to demonstrate experimentally their inadequacy. In the same way, too, it gave to psychology—indeed to the world at large—more than one useful catchword device for the denotation of the ineffable. No one can impugn the brilliant experimental achievements of the Gestalt school nor deny the powerful impact its theoretical formulations had on the development of psychology in the first half of this century. None the less the impetus eventually petered out. Why was this? Basically, it seems to me, because of an inappropriate relation between theory and experiment. Wertheimer's early work on the perception of pattern rather over-endowed Gestalt theory with terms which could not be defined on a more fundamental or unitary basis. We are still very far from being able to give any coherent account of everything we mean by the words 'form', 'shape', and 'pattern'. Wertheimer, apart from being able to draw upon conceptions deriving from geometry, such as similarity, proximity and symmetry, had to invent expressions as best he could and some of his inventions have today a rather figurative, if not metaphysical, ring. The philosopher von Ehrenfels had bequeathed him the term *Gestaltqualität*. He added such other terms as 'common fate', 'good continuation', and '*Prägnanz*'. These curiosities, especially the word *Gestalt*, served their purpose so well in articulating Wertheimer's attack on the elementaristic hypothesis that most people were convinced of the facts so brilliantly emphasized by his demonstrations. That this controversy is nowadays a matter of history, and that we tend to wonder what the fuss was all about, testifies to the distinction of Wertheimer's work.

At that time some people were intrigued by the incursion of exciting ideas like Gestalt into experimental psychology. Others, acknowledging the brilliance and interest of the great train of experiments thereby set off, remained cautious as to the terminology. Sherrington, for instance, reportedly said of Gestalt psychology, when it had acquired the rounded aspect of a school, 'Ah, it's all laid up in Heaven.' The general idea certainly stirred fresh thought in a number of fields outside the experimental. Psychopathology, neuropsychology, social psychology and aesthetics all gained fresh mobility. In the experimental field although, especially among Köhler's research associates at Berlin, the impetus was well maintained, the theoretical framework did not encourage investigations which could transform the concepts and bring them into more direct relation with what can be physically measured. This is scarcely surprising, for they had originally been devised to allow escape from the trammels of an inadequate physiology. In a later phase, attention centred upon the concept of isomorphism. In 1921 Köhler had tried by an effort of virtuosity to bring the concept of Gestalt into direct relationship with the properties of appropriate physico-chemical systems. The austerity of his theory of *Physische Gestalten* did not altogether commend itself to his followers. They accepted the general idea of a *field*, and endowed this with convenient, if ill-defined properties. Only certain, not unsympathetic, sceptics took the idea that this field is in the brain seriously. Concrete, quantitative reference to its physico-chemical or physiological characteristics was more than discreet. Once again the theoretical formulation and the experiments which proceed from it, did not conduce to any explicit picture of the mechanisms at work.

The birth, decline and fall of the Gestalt idea are certainly not without their lessons for contemporary psychology. To invent fresh concepts in order to gain empirical mobility is tempting, and often immediately rewarding. But disappointment may follow unless these concepts can be refined quantitatively, or in some other explicitly logical sense. None the less, Gestalt psychology was a glorious revolution. Pregnant figures are no longer shameful, to be explained away— if at all—by unconscious inference!

V

But at the same time another and probably far more significant revolution was in progress. Behaviourism had something which Gestalt psychology did not—an origin in a physiological discovery. It also had John B. Watson,[7] a man who expressed views so outrageous that neither the cold steel of logic nor the white heat of passion found them entirely easy to dispose of. Psychology ought to be grateful to him, for the resulting controversies of the 1920's about Consciousness, Introspection, Instinct, and Purpose, together with the proper subject and methods of psychological science, were so profound that when the dust had settled a fresh start in simpler style and freer from past tradition was possible. Much that had been thought before could never be thought again, and stocks of ammunition for unprofitable controversy were a good deal depleted. Watson, however, was no mere professional *enfant terrible*. He was one of a group of workers, chiefly in the United States, who were laying the foundations of comparative and physiological psychology as we know it today. Watson's attempts, armed with Pavlovian bell and candle, to exorcise the ghost in the machine, were sustained by considerable publicity. Very much less in the public eye were the more patient efforts of Lloyd Morgan, E. L. Thorndike, Shepherd Ivory Franz, Karl Lashley, and of Watson himself, to set about investigating animal behaviour and its mechanisms on a solid scientific basis. This work as a whole comprised a number of different elements. Lloyd Morgan[8] contributed the Canon which allowed escape from the anecdotalism of earlier students like Romanes. He also initiated systematic controlled experiment. Thorndike's invention of the Puzzle-Box in 1898[9] was the beginning of a long series of pieces of special laboratory apparatus, such as the maze, the Lashley jumping stand and the operant conditioning box, which enable performance to be quantitatively assessed. Yerkes, foreseeing a need to move beyond the cats, dogs, hens, and rats commonly employed, undertook a major study of the general behaviour and mode of life of primates. When, within the last fifteen years, laboratory workers have increasingly turned their attention to these animals, the background knowledge gained by Yerkes has been invaluable. Another essential feature in the story dates back farther. In the first quarter of the nineteenth century Pierre Flourens[10] first practised the surgical removal of parts of the cerebral hemispheres as a means of determining their functions. Throughout the nineteenth century this technique became progressively more refined in the hands of Ferrier, Goltz, Munk, and other workers.[11] By the end of the nineteenth century an inconclusive phase had been reached because of the lack of any but qualitative observational methods for assessing the resultant disturbance of function. This was rectified in 1902 by S. I. Franz[12] at the Harvard Physiological Laboratory, who first took the vital step of combining the method of ablation with the quantitative techniques of behaviour measurement devised by Lloyd Morgan and Thorndike. Franz's findings, which had to do with the functions of the frontal lobes in the cat, could scarcely be regarded as conclusive by present-day standards. He gives no detailed post-mortem account of the extent of the lesions (although he promises one, including microscopical appearances, for later publication). But this paper is a landmark, for in every other respect it is the first representative of a method of discovering the mechanisms underlying behaviour which, gaining momentum over the next half-century, now promises to be as fruitful as any.

Franz made a second outstanding contribution when he encouraged Lashley to widen the scope of this attack so as to cover generally the role of the cerebral cortex in intelligent and learned behaviour. 'The whole theory of learning and of intelligence', wrote Lashley[13] some ten years later, 'is in confusion. We know at present nothing of the organic basis of these functions and little enough of either the variety of uniformities or their expression in behaviour.' This is, indeed, too favourable a view of the situation at the outset of his adventure. Seventy years of clinical observation on brain-injured and brain-diseased human subjects and a half-century of animal experiment had afforded a limited number of conclusions, chiefly regarding sensory and motor function. But over these crude landmarks there swirled a mist of sophisticated speculation and controversy. Originally directing his work, Lashley tells us, 'toward the tracing of conditioned reflex arcs through the cortex, as the spinal paths of simple reflexes seems to have been traced through the cord', he cut down his problem to essentials so bare that it might have seemed his findings could be of no general interest at all. But, at long last, a systematic experiment on the cerebral mechanisms of behaviour was carried out. Removal of various amounts of tissue from various parts of the brains of rats, careful post-mortem verification of the lesion, training of the animals in standardized tasks of varying complexity before or after operation were the features of an experiment which gave repeatable results. With these findings, any theory must come to terms, and as Lashley notes, the findings never fitted in to a conditioned reflex scheme. Perhaps because they found this comforting, some people did not hesitate to extend Lashley's tentative conclusions, as expressed in the principles of Mass Action and Equipotentiality, to higher level brains, not excluding man's. Others set about exploiting the basic methodology and extending its application to different species of animal and to a great variety of more special aspects of behaviour. These latter now include not only cognitive but appetitive and affective functions. If today we can say that the experimental approach we owe to Franz and Lashley is perhaps the most powerful at our disposal, this does not mean that it provides a royal road to the solution of every problem even of animal psychology. But from present indications it seems clear that there is still a lot of life in it.

VI

After the First World War direct observational study of instinct and appetite fell on evil days. McDougall,[14] stirred beyond mere scientific zeal by Watsonian behaviour and unable to accept the particular form of unity which Freudian theory offered, stretched too much the existing knowledge of instinctive behaviour in his efforts to attain a solid theoretical structure. This, together with the increasing scope and success of quantitative experiments on cognitive functions, deflected attention from the problem of what it is that makes animals tick. Pioneers had to be born afresh. Of these, there must have been a number in various countries who were curious and fascinated enough by animals in their natural habitat not only to observe them closely but to try varying systematically that we should now call the 'stimulus parameters'. (In practice, this consisted in such simple measures as substituting billiard balls and wooden cubes for the eggs of a nesting gull.) In this country we ought not to forget the names of Eliot Howard and F. B. Kirkman[15] in this connection. Amateur naturalists both, they pointed the way between them to two methodological principles which, in the hands of Lorenz, Tinbergen[16] and their colleagues, have introduced a fresh and powerful element into the study of behaviour. First, establish by quantitative observation the temporal sequence and topographical pattern of an animal's appetitive activities: second, ascertain by simple but systematic interference with the environment the stimuli which arouse and at every stage control the behavioural sequence. Simple and straightforward as these principles might appear, the adoption of the second must certainly have required notable freedom from anthropomorphic sentiment. It is difficult, watching a nesting goose, not to suppose that to the bird her eggs are eggs—not just coloured shapes. The decision to find out what range of objects will evoke the same behaviour as the egg is a considerable step forward. There are some branches of human psychology in which almost equally crude approaches might not be unprofitable. The work of the (self-styled) 'Ethologists' has provided a mass of concrete knowledge. Moreover this is in a form which we may expect can be greatly extended and refined by the use of physiological and pharmacological expedients. From the existing data some interesting fresh conceptions have emerged such as the idea of the innate releasing mechanism, of displacement activity and of the distinction between a consummatory act and the satisfaction of a need. These ideas, though incisive, are not rigid and seem capable of considerable modification before they give way to others more precise. At a more theoretical level, the ethologists have formulated interesting schemes for the mechanisms which they suppose to underlie the functions they observe. Not everybody, in particular those wedded to a more strictly be-

B*

haviouristic approach, approves of them. Here, as in the case of the 'black box' theories evolved by the Hullian school, there is a need for direct check by physiological observation. The ethologists, however, would be the first to agree that theories based on behavioural observation ought to lead toward, rather than away from, the possibility of physiological confirmation. This can less confidently be asserted of the followers of Hull, who seem rather inclined to keep their theories locked up in black boxes with a view to guaranteeing the independent status of psychology against the physiological enemy without. Even among them, however, there have been recent signs of a change of heart.

VII

There must be a great many people who, while they acknowledge the interest and suggestiveness of research upon animals, feel that experimental psychology is burking the issues and evading its responsibilities unless it tackles problems of human behaviour by experiments on human subjects. Personally, I am not wholly in agreement with this view. I believe we are only at the beginning of what we can learn about ourselves by studying animals. Nevertheless it is exciting when new ways of approach to understanding human functions open up in the laboratory and lend themselves to satisfactory experimental treatment. At the present day there are a number of such but time forbids mention of more than one. I choose some recent work on speech and language because it exemplifies the way in which practical requirements can evoke attack upon old problems from an entirely fresh angle, and how once such an attack develops on a narrow and minor front it may widen into something of a campaign. When, shortly after its invention by Graham Bell in 1876, the primitive telephone was demonstrated to Lord Rayleigh, he expressed his admiration but doubted whether it would ever be of any practical importance. For a number of years after that the efforts of engineers were devoted to perfecting the faithfulness of speech transmitted down a wire or through the ether. In the meantime Lord Rayleigh had been proved wrong and two new problems presented themselves and became acute in the flurry of war. The first was that of how to economize channel-space. Copper wires and radio wave-bands are not unlimited. The second arose because existing circumstances and technical resources could and did make several separate communication channels converge upon the same human being. The question of his capacity to sort out and act upon a number of messages arriving simultaneously or in quick succession became literally a vital one. Awareness of the first of these problems led engineers, pre-eminently Claude Shannon[17] of the Bell Telephone Laboratories, to ask what is basically involved in the transmission of information. He concluded that it consists in a decision by the listener, or receiver, as to which of a finite number of possible messages was sent by the speaker, or transmitter. In practice, if less than the whole of a verbal message arrives at the receiving end, we can often make a guess, based on our implicit knowledge of the probabilities of word-sequences, at what the missing words were. This means that for speech to be understood it is not necessary to burden the communication channel with the whole of it. To this extent, language is redundant and telephone lines and radio channels can be economized. In order to study the redundancy of language, Shannon devised means of constructing messages on a statistical basis in which the word-sequence is determined only by the transition probabilities between words, and not by any intention to say anything. Thus a sixth-order approximation to English is obtained by choosing each word only in the light of the preceding five. Shannon also found a way of estimating the redundancy of specimens of actual English utterance. Such measures provide a new quantitative dimension of language, and this has proved very useful in experiments that have been done on the second problem I mentioned above, that of the mechanism by which we sort out a number of messages arriving simultaneously in our ears and pay attention to one. A good deal of work has recently been devoted to this question by Broadbent, Cherry, Taylor and others.[18] It would seem clear that if we are able to give evidence of attending to one message either by repeating it aloud as it comes or giving its substance later, this must be because other, competing messages are rejected or filtered out. The question is, upon what clue do these filters operate? If we can find this out, we might eventually be able to localize them in the hierarchy of neural functions. A large number of experiments have established that at least part of the filtering is carried out in accordance with differing physical properties of the messages. Thus, if two messages come from spatially separate sources, or are of different pitches like a man's and a woman's voice, this helps to separate them. A filter working on this principle, without reference to any aspect of meaning, could evidently be situated relatively low down in the neural hierarchy. But it is clear that this is not the only filter in operation. If, in accordance with a procedure first used by Cherry, we get a subject to repeat a message that is coming into his right ear while a second one is being delivered to his left, he can do this, and can afterwards give no evidence that he was in any way aware of the content of the rejected message. Indeed, if the language in which the message is spoken is changed from English to, say, German, he simply fails to notice the fact. Certainly, part of the capacity to accept and respond to one message in competition with another has to do with the prob-ability structure of the message. Other things being equal, the more a message incorporates accustomed sequences and a continuing theme, the easier it is to be accurate in repeating it aloud. Miss Taylor had subjects repeat aloud 'shadow' messages which were in fact only statistical approximations to English of various orders. The competing message in the other ear was normal English. She was able to show that the number of errors made was a very simple function of the order of approximation. But differences at the physical level, and at the level of linguistic structure are certainly not the only factors which operate the filtering system. Everybody knows that at a cocktail party, when one's ears are beset by a most complicated pattern of sound waves, and one is filtering out everything except the voice of the person one is talking to, one's attention can still be caught by hearing the sound of one's own name. This phenomenon has been verified under care-fully controlled conditions by Moray and Miss Taylor. It certainly adds fascination to the whole problem, for we may well ask what kind of a system is this which filters out unwanted sounds in accordance with their mere physical characteristics or their mere statistical structure, yet somehow remains on guard at the level of meaning, ready to ring an alarm bell when there may be good reason for turning one's atten-tion elsewhere.

I have not referred to these experiments because of their intrinsic interest but because, as it seems to me, they represent a happy instance in which easily observable facts, lending themselves unexpectedly to quantification can be exploited so as to throw light on very different matters such as attention and meaning. A century ago these would have been thought incapable of any exact inquiry.

VIII

It will by now be clear that I have not tried to give any balanced outline of the past 100 years of experiment in psychology. But perhaps even the limited view we have gained may suggest some points about the practice of our craft. If, for brevity, I put these as injunctions, I hope I shall not be misunderstood. First: neither be deceived by the sophis-tication and respectability of a well-established controversy, nor attempt directly to settle it in the terms in which it is conducted. You will certainly fail, and the terms are probably unreal anyway. Instead, take some question connected with it, however crude and simple, which has not yet been answered and try to answer it. Other questions will follow. Second: try, whenever possible, to be quantitative. Words and ideas without numbers have an almost unlimited power of evading logic. Third: do not invent new descriptive terms and concepts more than is strictly necessary. They are apt to get out of control. Fourth: in pursuing experimental work, try to keep in as close touch with physiological and anatomical factors as possible, not with any immediate hope of explanation in these terms but because experience shows this to be an effective way of opening up fresh and often unsuspected phenomena for study. Fifth: do not neglect the opportunities offered by a systematic natural history approach, especially when strict experiment seems to come to a dead end.

So much for the centenary. What of the outlook? There is a good deal of talk today about the need for much more research in the human sciences. Many people urge that a great deal more money ought to be spent on these and some seem to assume that, if it were, commensurate results would follow. Psychology is one, perhaps the most basic, of the human sciences. Money is the root of nearly all evil, but so far as psychology is concerned I would think it is true to say that if all the research which could now profitably be done were in progress a great deal more money would have to be spent than is being spent at present. Many fresh fields are opening up in which, especially in collaboration with physiologists, zoologists, pharmacologists, geneticists and engineers, the experimental psychologist can work with every prospect of being led to basic issues. A vast development of psychology like that in the United States would not, perhaps, commend itself to our temperament. But it must be said that on any count which gives due weight not only to quantity but quality, this country is some way behind America in behavioural research. The prospects for experimental psychology here may nevertheless be good. To make the best of them, however, may require some re-orientation on the part of all of us who pursue the subject. The future will turn not on individual sallies of brilliance, nor on the worthy pursuit of the solid and impeccable. What will matter is the quality of the young people who are drawn into the subject. Once attracted, they must at first get their encouragement and the confirmation of their enthusiasm from what goes on in teaching and research laboratories. If not anybody's guess, at any rate it is a matter of opinion as to what will most contribute to a favourable atmosphere. May I be allowed to finish by giving my view—briefly but frankly?

First, I will affirm a belief, which I think many people share, that the growth of psychology will be within the framework of the biological sciences. This means striving to regard human behaviour *as* objectively as the biologist looks at the behaviour of animals. It cannot be too strongly asserted that this implies no lack of sympathy, respect or love. Nor does it mean that psychology is for ever constrained within any existing framework of biological ideas. It is far more likely that psychology will be instrumental in extending the range of fundamental biological conceptions. Secondly, so it seems to me, we have no need to wax protective about our subject—to expend effort on advertising the special and individual character of its approaches, methods, concepts, and theories. There is no point in emphasizing the 'psychologist's' view of human beings and their behaviour. For better or worse, experimental psychology is an established activity, whether it is carried out at a department which has Psychology, Zoology, Medicine, or Engineering on the door. Its future will lie in the hands of those who pursue it, not in the maintenance of frontiers. I say this because I sometimes feel that we who call ourselves psychologists stand in some danger of worshipping the Idols of the Parish.

But there are less distasteful thoughts. If the work of the past century has done nothing else it has recast some problems, and uncovered others, in forms susceptible to direct systematic attack. At the same time appropriate technical and instrumental resources have emerged. The usefulness and the limitations of work upon animals have become much more clearly appreciated. We no longer suppose that even careful controlled experiments on the abilities of rats to run mazes after removal of part of their brains is likely to make any particular contribution to the general problem of our own cerebral processes. But specific possibilities, such, for instance, that the maintenance of conscious vigilance is effected by some kind of closed circuit system, into which stimuli from the outside world are fed via two separate channels, can be looked into with a precision undreamed of twenty years ago.

Another unquestionably favourable feature is the increasing scale and freedom of collaboration between psychologists and those who work in a great variety of other fields. That this takes place is partly due to another factor which I personally would rank as the most important element of all. This is the growing number of young people coming into the subject whose ability would distinguish them in many other fields. Do these gain, during their time as undergraduates and postgraduates, the knowledge and experience of problems and methods which will stand them in best stead later, whether in research or in other psychological connections? Nobody can fail to note the progress made by university departments of psychology in the past twenty years. But psychology, at any rate for the present, cannot stand by itself. It demands, just as do other biological sciences, connection with and support from other disciplines. A number of our students, some among the best, have missed the opportunity of getting practical grounding in any of the basic scientific disciplines. To an astonishing extent, the better students grasp from reading and lectures the salient points, say, of contemporary neurophysiology or the leading ideas of communication theory. But in doing this they sometimes remain mindful only of the bearing of these subjects upon the psychology which is their chief concern. Sometimes the material is used merely for regurgitation in examinations, or for self-gratifying speculation. Might it not be better to curtail a little the psychological bill of fare and give our students an opportunity of learning the elements of neighbouring scientific fields from teachers, and alongside other students, whose chief concern and enthusiasm lie in them?

Experimental psychology does not lack worthwhile tasks, or the means of carrying them out. The next 100 years promises exciting progress. What the impact on people generally may be it is difficult to foresee. The great majority of human beings give little evidence of really wanting to understand themselves. Or is it just that, in Spinoza's words, 'every excellent thing is as difficult as it is rare'?

NOTES AND REFERENCES

1. Fuller accounts may be found in BORING, E. G., 1929, *A History of Experimental Psychology*, New York: Appleton-Century-Crofts, and FLUGEL, J. C., 1945, *A Hundred Years of Psychology*, London: Duckworth.
2. JAMES, W., 1901, *The Principles of Psychology*, p. 534, London: Macmillan.
3. EBBINGHAUS, H., 1885, *Über das Gedächtniss*, Leipzig: Duncker.
4. BARTLETT, F. C., 1932, *Remembering*, London: Cambridge University Press.
5. OLDFIELD, R. C., and ZANGWILL, O. L., 1942, 1943, 'Head's Concept of the Schema and its Application in Contemporary British Psychology', *Brit. J. Psychol.*, *32*, 267: *33*, 58, 113, 143.
6. The best introductions to the Gestalt school are KÖHLER, W., 1929, *Gestalt Psychology*, London: Bell, and ELLIS, W. D. (ed.), 1950, *A Source Book of Gestalt Psychology*, London: Routledge and Kegan Paul.
7. WATSON, J. B., 1914, *Behaviour, an Introduction to Comparative Psychology*, New York: Holt.

8. LLOYD MORGAN, C., 1900, *Animal Behaviour*, London: Arnold.

9. THORNDIKE, E. L., 1898, 'Animal intelligence; an experimental study of the associative processes in animals', *Psychol. Monog.*, 2, No. 8.

10. FLOURENS, M. J. P., 1824, *Recherches Expérimentales sur les Propriétés et les Fonctions du Système Nerveux dans les animaux vertébrés*, Paris.

11. See e.g. FERRIER, D., 1876, *The Functions of the Brain*, London: Smith and Elder.

12. FRANZ, S. I., 1902, 'On the Functions of the Cerebrum', *Amer. J. Physiol.*, 8, 1.

13. LASHLEY, K. S., 1930, *Brain Mechanisms and Intelligence*, Chicago: Behaviour Research Fund Monographs.

14. MCDOUGALL, W., 1926, *An Introduction to Social Psychology*, (20th edition), London: Methuen.

15. HOWARD, H. E., 1929, *An Introduction to the Study of Bird Behaviour*, London: Cambridge University Press.

    KIRKMAN, F. B., 1937, *Bird Behaviour*, London: Nelson.

16. TINBERGEN, N., 1951, *The Study of Instinct*, Oxford: Clarendon.

17. SHANNON, C. E., and WEAVER, W., 1949, *A Mathematical Theory of Communication*, Urbana, Ill.: University of Ill. Press.

18. BROADBENT, D. E., 1958, *Perception and Communication*, London: Pergamon.

    CHERRY, C., 1957, *On Human Communication*, New York: Wiley.

    OLDFIELD, R. C., 1962, *Proc. XVI Internat. Cong. Psychol.* (Bonn, 1960), p. 55, Amsterdam: North-Holland Publ. Co.

CHAPTER 3

FRANCIS GALTON AND HIS CONTRIBUTIONS TO PSYCHOLOGY*

BY CYRIL BURT

———◆———

I

When I was a boy, my father, who was a country doctor, used to take me on his rounds to visit his patients. Of these by far the most impressive was the squire of a neighbouring village called Claverdon, a small Warwickshire hamlet, lying between Stratford-on-Avon and Birmingham. The squire was an octogenarian named Darwin Galton. On his mother's side he was the grandson of Erasmus Darwin, physician, zoologist, botanist, and poet, and on his father's of a Birmingham Quaker who had made his money by manufacturing rifles. He himself was the eldest son in a family of nine. And, when he was fit, I was sometimes taken up to see him, and so met many other members of the same family, including the youngest, called Frank or Francis.

Francis Galton was one of the most distinguished-looking people I have ever known—tall, slim, neatly dressed, with a forehead like the dome of St Paul's. My father, who was an ardent Darwinian, used to try to inspire me with intellectual ambitions of my own by telling me of the remarkable investigations carried out and published by this exceptionally brilliant member of an exceptionally brilliant family. I met him again as an undergraduate at Oxford, and later in London shortly before his death. He died in January 1911, at Haslemere, in a house he had taken to escape the London winter; and his body now lies in the family vault in Claverdon churchyard.

Francis was the youngest son of Samuel Tertius Galton and Violetta

* An abridged version of 'Francis Galton and his Contributions to Psychology', *Brit. J. Statist. Psychol.*, 1962, *15*, 1.

Darwin. He was born on February 16, 1822, at the Larches—a country house a mile and a half from Birmingham, where his father was partner in a large bank. The year 1822 was by a curious coincidence the year in which another great hereditarian was born—the Abbé Mendel; and it is chiefly as the champion of heredity and the apostle of eugenics that we find Francis Galton depicted in Pearson's biography. He himself presents a most instructive example of inheritance; and the pedigree of his family, which Pearson traces back through a dozen or more generations, must be one of the most thorough genealogical studies in existence.

On the paternal side, the oldest members of the Galton family seem to have been natives of the village of Galton, in the county of Dorset, farming or working on the land around. As commonly happened, the younger sons migrated first to neighbouring villages, and then to the larger towns. In the reign of James II we find a certain Robert Galton starting a modest business as 'haberdasher of small wares' at Bristol—the nearest large city and in those days second in importance only to London. Shortly afterwards, John Galton, Robert's brother, joined him there; and became a member of the Bristol branch of the Society of Friends. In 1703 he married Sarah Button, whose father had been imprisoned as a Quaker; indeed, out of Francis's sixteen great-great-great-grandparents on the paternal side more than a dozen were adherents of this sect. Among the early Galtons, John's grandson, Samuel, was almost the only man of note. He moved from Bristol to Birmingham, and married another Quakeress, Lucy Barclay. There he became a member of the Lunar Society, which included Priestley, Watt, Wedgwood, Baskerville the printer, and Erasmus Darwin. Samuel's hobbies were optics and astronomy; University College now possesses a complicated orrery that he once purchased. Nominated by Joseph Priestley, Samuel was the first of the Galtons to be elected a Fellow of the Royal Society. His mechanical skill made him, like Baskerville, a successful maker of guns. But eventually he determined to concentrate talents that might have made him a leading physicist or mathematician on the problems of finance. He died a wealthy banker, worth £300,000. His son, Samuel Tertius, the oldest surviving son in a family of ten, inherited the business. He was elected High Bailiff of Birmingham, and in 1807 he married Violetta, daughter of Erasmus Darwin, and so became the father of Darwin Galton and of Francis.

The earlier Darwins, like the earlier Galtons, comprise few names of note. The pedigree starts about 1500 with four generations of Lincolnshire yeomen. In 1650 one of the younger members of the family became a London lawyer, a member of Lincoln's Inn, and married the daughter of a still more eminent lawyer, Erasmus Earle, ancestor of the novelist Bulwer Lytton, and Own Serjeant to the Commonwealth. Their great-grandson was Erasmus Darwin, MD, FRS, famous in his day as the author of several philosophical poems on biological subjects.

Erasmus Darwin married twice; and with each of the two families we encounter stocks of entirely different types from those we have met with hitherto. His first wife was Mary Howard, grandmother of Charles Darwin. Their third son, the second Robert Waring Darwin, was, like his father, both a doctor of medicine and a Fellow of the Royal Society: he became the leading physician of Shropshire, accumulated a handsome fortune, and married Susannah Wedgwood, the eldest daughter of Josiah Wedgwood, FRS. Their youngest son was Charles Robert Darwin, the celebrated naturalist. Erasmus Darwin's second wife, the grandmother of Francis Galton, was Elizabeth Collier, widow of Edward Sacheverell Pole (a relative of the famous Dr Sacheverell who was impeached in 1710). Here we encounter a temperamental strain, differing still more widely from that which characterized the Galtons and the Barclays.

The branch begins with two memorable scientists—Sir Henry Savile, tutor to Queen Elizabeth I, and founder of the Savilian professorships of Geometry and Astronomy at Oxford, and Sir William Sedley, founder of the Sedleian Chair in Natural Philosophy. Both were direct ancestors of Francis. Sedley's son John married Savile's only daughter Elizabeth. She was the precocious girl of whom the poet Waller wrote:

> Here lies the learned Savile's heir,
> So early wise and lasting fair
> That none, except her years they told,
> Thought her a child or thought her old.

Their son was the playwright, Sir Charles Sedley, one of the most profligate of Charles II's courtiers, whose lewdness shocked even Pepys. His lyrics—'Phyllis is my only joy', 'Love still has something of the sea'—adorn almost every anthology. His only child was Catherine, Countess of Dorchester, who succeeded Arabella Churchill as mistress of James II. She subsequently married David Colyear, a sagacious officer of foot, who served under William of Orange, and was raised to the peerage as first Earl of Portmore. Their son, Beau Colyear, the second Earl of Portmore, married Juliana, Dowager

Duchess of Leeds. The Duchess engaged a governess for her daughters; and it seems probable that her choice fell on a grandchild of the non-juror, Jeremy Collier (author of *The Ecclesiastical History of Great Britain* and the *Short View of the Profaneness and Immorality of the English Stage*—an attack on the licentiousness of Dryden, Congreve, and Wycherley). A few years later Beau Colyear had by this governess a natural daughter named Elizabeth Collier, 'a lady of great talent and natural charm'; and it was she who eventually became Erasmus Darwin's second wife. It must be, I fancy, to this particular strain in his ancestry that Francis Galton owed his lively humour, vivid imagination, and literary tastes and style, which so sharply distin-guished him from the rest of the Galton and Darwin stock, as well as the wayward behaviour which, in his early youth, occasioned not a little anxiety in the mind of his somewhat Puritanical father.

From this brief survey of his pedigree it is plain that Francis was a mixture of many different breeds. It would be tempting to speculate about the sources of his intellectual and temperamental qualities. But probably almost the only mental characteristic that we can confidently assign to hereditary endowment is the intellectual precocity and high intelligence which Francis showed even more conspicuously than the other members of his family tree. Terman assesses his IQ as approxi-mately 200, and that of Charles Darwin, with less assurance, as between 135 and 140. An exceptional measure of intelligence is trace-able in one or more members of every one of the ten generations for whom we have first-hand information. The steady ascent in social rank of the Galtons, the Barclays, and the Darwins, implies a degree of ability that must have been well above the general average, and suggests a cumulative process of social selection. The later generations include eleven Fellows of the Royal Society—surely a record. Francis himself was elected in 1856, and later was awarded the Gold Medal, the Society's Copley Medal, as well as in 1902 its Darwin Medal. Both his grandfathers were Fellows, two of his cousins, one of his uncles, three of his nephews, and one great-nephew.

II

Right from birth Francis was the little Benjamin of his family. His sister Adèle, who was something of an invalid, devoted herself to his studies. By the time he was $2\frac{1}{2}$ he could read simple fairy tales; and he could sign his name before he was 3. The following is the first of many letters treasured by the family.

My dear Adèle,

I am four years old, and I can read any English book. I can say all the Latin substantives, adjectives, and active verbs, besides fifty-two lines of Latin poetry. I can cast up any sum in addition and multiply by 2, 3, 4, 5, 6, 7, 8, (9), 10, (11). I read French a little and I know the clock.

                                   Francis Galton. Feb(r)uary 15, 1827.*

An aunt who visited the family when he was six describes him as 'a little prodigy, reading Pope and Shakespeare for pleasure. He has only to go over a page a couple of times and he can repeat it by heart.' The next year he was studying Greek; and, when an academic friend kept quizzing him about Homer's *Odyssey*, Francis at length replied, 'Pray, Mr Horner, look at the last line in the twelfth book.' The last line (as Lang translates it) reads: 'All this have I told thee already, and it likes me not to repeat a twice-told tale.'

Both his father and his masters recognized that he was a lad of great ability; but none of them realized *how* great it was. 'The time spent at school', he tells us in his *Memories*, 'was a period of stagnation: I learnt nothing, and chafed at the limitations. I craved for an abundance of good reading, solid science, and well-taught mathematics.' His mother earnestly desired that, since the family business had been wound up, Francis, like her famous father and her brothers, should become a doctor. Accordingly, an uncle by marriage, Dr Booth, agreed to sponsor his entrance as a House Pupil at the General Hospital, Birmingham, 'at the rate of 200 guineas per annum'. And so, after spending a week in London with Charles Darwin for Queen Victoria's coronation, he started at the age of sixteen to 'go the round of the wards with the surgeons and physicians'. 'I begin to understand all the humbug of medicine, which is not a little!' he writes a few weeks later. 'Doctors have the fault of parsons—of being much too positive. . . . Cut a brace of fingers off yesterday, and one the day before. Happy to operate on any one at home!'

The following year, however, he was again in London attending medical lectures at King's College, and in October 1840 he arrived on the top of a stage coach before the famous gateway of Trinity College, Cambridge. Since he had chosen Mathematics, his tutor set him, 'with a sort of grin', to study Conic Sections. In the end, however, he found the work for an Honours degree in Mathematics at once too

* The figures in brackets appear to be insertions and corrections made by Francis himself.

exacting and too dull. His health suffered; and so, like Charles Darwin, he eventually contented himself with a Poll degree.

Galton's adult life may be divided into three main periods; during the first (1844–64) he was chiefly occupied with travel and exploration, and with various geographical and meteorological studies arising out of his adventures; during the second (1865–99) he became more and more engrossed in the theoretical study of individual differences, with the problems of inheritance as the focus of almost all his researches; during the third (1900–11) his interest changed to the more practical aspects of the subject, and he came forward as the champion of eugenics.

III

In October 1844, the year in which Francis left Cambridge, his father died; and the following year he set out alone for Egypt and the Sudan. For a while (he tells us) he 'lived a very oriental life', dressed in Arab costume, and became 'fairly fluent in Arabic'. After a succession of adventures, he at length worked his way home via Jerusalem and the Holy Land, 'escorted by mounted spearmen, and bringing back a couple of monkeys'. His next expedition, to tropical South Africa, had a more serious purpose. Of the territory between the Kalahari Desert and the West Coast practically nothing was then known. This he determined to explore, starting from Walfish Bay. He succeeded in making friends with the 'murderous Damaras' by investing a chieftain with a theatrical crown 'bought in Drury Lane for some such purpose'; and eventually he and his little party worked their way for more than 1,000 miles inland 'through a country never before penetrated by a civilized being'. On his return he published a detailed account of the journey, and an official survey of the area was issued with maps and woodcuts based on his own sketches. Incidentally he relates one curious anecdote which illustrates what later became his ruling maxim—'Whenever you can, measure or count'. In Damaraland he met a typical Hottentot Venus whose buttocks were so immense that he felt they should be accurately measured; and yet any such approach was almost bound to be misinterpreted. He resolved his dilemma by the device employed by Gulliver's Laputan tailor: 'with the aid of navigational instruments', he tells us, he measured the lady's dimensions 'from a distance'.

The following year, 1853, Galton married Louisa Butler, daughter of the Dean of Peterborough and former headmaster of Harrow, and his travels virtually ceased: otherwise it might have been Galton, and not H. M. Stanley, who set out to discover Livingstone. In 1856, however, as Secretary of the Geographical Society, he drafted the instructions for the Burton-Speke Expedition, which led to the discovery of Lake Tanganyika and Lake Victoria Nyanza. He next became interested in the geography of climate; and this led to the construction of meteorological charts for the British Isles—the first weather maps ever to be published. On April 1, 1875, the readers of *The Times* began to see at their breakfast tables diagrammatic maps with isobars and the like, very much in the form with which we are familiar today. It is to Galton and to his meteorological studies that we owe the name and the whole notion of the anticyclone.

IV

Meanwhile, the observations which he made during his travels had turned his thoughts more and more from man's environment to man himself. 'Before the appearance of Darwin's *Origin of Species* in 1859,' he tells us, 'some ideas I had about human heredity were set fermenting; and I then began a book on *Hereditary Genius.*' The leading ideas were embodied in a preliminary paper entitled 'Hereditary Talent and Character', published in *Macmillan s Magazine* in 1865. 'The terms talent and character', he says, 'are meant to include the whole of man's spiritual nature.' In writing *Hereditary Genius* (1869) he appears to have preferred a tripartite to a dual classification of mental characteristics. He now speaks of three main ingredients—an ability to work, an interest in the work, and a power or will to work, corresponding to what Ward and Stout would have called the cognitive, the affective, and the conative aspects of mental activity. It is principally with the first—with ability or talent in its various forms—that his book is concerned.

And here he introduces at the very outset a new and far-reaching distinction—the distinction between *general* ability and *special* abilities. The current faculty psychology recognized only the latter. Galton insists on the superior importance of the former, a doctrine later borrowed by both Binet and Spearman. 'Numerous instances recorded in this book', he says, 'show in how small a degree eminence can be considered as due to purely special powers. People lay too much stress on apparent specialities, thinking that because a man is devoted to some particular pursuit, he would not have succeeded in anything else. They might as well say that, because a youth has fallen in love with a brunette, he could not possibly have fallen in love with a blonde. As

likely as not the affair was mainly or wholly due to a *general* amorous-
ness.' It is just the same, he argues, with mental exploits.

Other writers had considered the possibility that genius might be
inherited, some defending the notion, others attacking it. Galton
claims to be 'the first to treat the subject in a statistical manner and to
arrive at exact numerical results'. He begins by suggesting that people
can be graded for ability in accordance with the normal distribution;
and here, for the first time, we find this famous curve applied to mental
differences, and the use of percentiles and mean deviations as measures
of ability. The term 'genius' is defined as designating the brightest
248 in a million: thus very roughly a genius is the ablest person in a
random sample of 4,000. He points out that, since the distribution is
symmetrical, the same principles could be used to define imbeciles
and idiots: and for these he uses a method of assessment which anti-
cipates the 'mental ratio' or IQ. A person in the lowest grade of
deficiency, he says, is roughly capable of working with the efficiency
of one-third of an average man; a person in the next higher grade of
working like two-thirds of a man.

To demonstrate his theory of inheritance Galton examines the
pedigrees of nearly 1,000 geniuses—judges, generals, statesmen,
scientists, poets, painters, and divines. Among their relatives he
discovers 89 equally eminent fathers, 114 eminent brothers, and 129
eminent sons. If for simplicity we suppose that the number of male
children born to each member of the population, whether a genius or
not, is on an average four, then the chances that the son of a genius
will himself be a genius would be 129 times as great as that of a parent
chosen at random; and, since four is obviously much too high a
figure, our estimate of the chances must be much too low. Galton, of
course, was well aware that the environmental advantages which an
able father could provide for his children might be partly responsible;
and both in this book and in later papers he deals at some length,
though not perhaps quite convincingly, with this complication.

The ideas and methods outlined in *Hereditary Genius* were applied
to a more specialized problem in his book on *English Men of Science:
Their Nature and Nurture* (1874). He calculated that there were in the
British Isles about 300 males between the ages of 50 and 65 who had
achieved recognition as men of the highest scientific ability, but that
this was well below the number we might expect on the assumption
of a normal distribution. He then goes on to ask 'What special qualities
ought we to look for in those who should be encouraged to take up
science?' On the basis of questionnaires addressed to 180 men of

science, chiefly Fellows of the Royal Society, he enumerates the following, in addition to a high degree of general ability: (1) Physical and Mental Energy, (2) Health, (3) Perseverance, (4) Business Habits, (5) Memory, (6) Independence of Character, (7) Mechanical Aptitude.

Of all his books, however, the one of greatest interest to the student of psychology is that published in 1883 under the title *Inquiries into Human Faculty and its Development*. The central problem of the book is the analysis of individual personality as the joint effect of two distinct but complementary factors, 'Nature' and 'Nurture'. The safest mode of approach, he believes, is to start by examining the more important ways in which post-natal experience operates—the effects of 'Nurture'. This he treats under two main headings as consisting of *ideas* and of the *associations* that introduce or suggest them. Ideas, he maintains, are conveyed by means of mental 'images'. These he investigated by means of his well-known questionnaire; and, as he rightly points out, the results reveal, perhaps more clearly than any other field of mental inquiry, the startling differences between the mental processes of different individuals.

In his study of 'associations' he employs an ingenious procedure (what the textbooks now call 'the method of free association') which 'enables us to drag into light thoughts, ideas, and wishes that have lapsed out of ordinary consciousness', and so helps us to unravel the associative processes by which they have been acquired. Once again he gives detailed results from experiments upon himself and others, which he analyses statistically. Of the associations that occur most frequently (that is, at least three or four times), the majority, he finds, are drawn from childhood, and comparatively few from recent experiences. To interpret his results he suggests that we may think of the mind as divided into two or three fairly distinct compartments according to the degree to which the activities taking place are 'lit up by consciousness'. 'There seems to be,' he writes, 'a presence-chamber where full consciousness holds court, and an antechamber just outside, crowded with ideas lying beyond the ken of consciousness; out of this antechamber the ideas most nearly allied to the problem at issue appear to be summoned in a mechanical or a logical way, and so have their turn of audience.' Beyond or below all this there is a darker basement, an underground storehouse from which older and remoter ideas can with greater difficulty be hauled up into consciousness. In all this we detect a remarkable anticipation of the theories and methods adopted later on by psychoanalysts like Freud and Jung.

Galton applies the same hypothesis to account for the achievements of genius. The creativity of successful thinkers—great orators, imaginative writers, and inventive scientists—arises largely from the interplay of their conscious and unconscious processes: a flood of relevant ideas is always streaming through the channels of their fertile mind, usually without deliberate exertion or control; and the associations that bring the right idea at the right moment to explicit utterance operate like some curious logical sorting machine. When they lack this automatic means of selection, such persons are likely to exhibit the phenomena of 'morbid imagination' so characteristic of the neurotic and the insane. The ability to produce this rich flow of ideas he terms 'fluency'—a specific type of ability, which, it may be remembered, Spearman and many of his research students later on subjected to systematic investigation.

One or two further studies of what Galton termed 'morbid imagination' may be mentioned, since they illustrate the ingenious ways in which he sought to combine introspective with experimental techniques. In the hope of gaining some insight into the way the fantasies of the insane are built up, he determined, during the course of a morning's walk, to invest everything he encountered with the attribute of a secret spy. The experiment was only too successful. By the time he had reached Piccadilly, he says, 'every horse on every cab-stand seemed to be watching me either openly or in disguise'. These persecutory delusions, self-induced, lasted for eight or nine hours, and could be easily revived, even two or three months later. On another occasion he hung up a picture of Mr Punch, and treated it as a kind of fetish or idol, mentally ascribing to it all sorts of divine and magical powers. At first these daily rites had no effect, but presently he found himself behaving as though his self-imposed fancies were literally true. An ever-present image stamped itself upon his mind; and round it gathered a set of potent emotional associations—all utterly irrational. For weeks after the experiment was over, he still retained a deep and awe-struck reverence for Punch's grotesque figure.

From Nurture he turns to Nature; and this forms the subject of the rest of the *Inquiries*. After casting about for some practicable means of 'distinguishing between the effects of the tendencies that are implanted at birth and those that are imposed by the special circumstances of the individual's after-life', he finally hit on the happy idea of making a comparative study of the histories and characteristics of twins. This 'new method', he believed, might enable us 'to weigh in the scale the effects of Nature and Nurture, and ascertain their respective shares in framing the dispositions and the intellectual abilities of men.' He notes the importance of discriminating between different types of twin, and particularly the need to secure comparable data for monovular twins who have been reared apart and binovular twins who have been reared together. His own results, largely anecdotal at this preliminary stage, are reported in some detail. His main conclusion is that 'Nature prevails enormously over Nurture when the differences in Nurture do not exceed what is commonly found among persons brought up in the same rank of society.'

There are instructive sections and appendices describing his early attempts to produce standardized tests, such as his calibrated whistle for the upper limit of audible pitch, and his geometric series of weights for measuring the delicacy of weight perception. The principles underlying these methods of measurement, he tells us, are applicable to other senses and to other faculties. He records the interesting observation that, on an average, acuteness of sense-discrimination is 'highest among the intellectually ablest', notably among the Fellows of the Royal Society whom he had tested. It was this and similar findings that led Spearman to put forward his well-known theory that 'general intelligence' and 'general sensory discrimination' are identical and that intelligence itself can best be measured by tests of sensory discrimination. The closing sections of the *Inquiries*, like those of *Hereditary Genius*, are concerned with tentative reflections on 'the ability of nations' and 'the influence of man upon race'—themes which Galton was to elaborate in fuller detail later on. In these early speculations, as Professor Darlington points out, 'Galton foreshadows a genetic interpretation of the history and the structure of society.'

In the early seventies—ten years before the foundation of the Society for Psychical Research—he became interested in spiritualism, and witnessed several demonstrations given by Dunglas Home (the reputed original of 'Mr Sludge the Medium' in Browning's poem) and by other spiritualists. Home's séances were attended by many eminent people of the day—A. R. Wallace and Sir William Barrett (who were convinced), Darwin and Huxley (who considered Home a fraud), George Eliot, Mrs Browning (who was completely swept away), and Browning himself (who was infuriated). In an early letter to Darwin, Galton writes that he has on more than one occasion attended sittings at (Sir William) Crookes' house, and feels 'very disinclined to discredit them: ... I really believe what they allege—that the people who come as men of science are so opinionated and obstructive that the séances rarely succeed with them.' Many of the details reported by Galton (e.g. the alleged communications from Benjamin Franklin) tally closely with the description given in Browning's poem. Later he appears to have become disgusted with the frequent mixture of fraud and evasion and the 'nonsensical twaddle contained in most of the so-called messages'.

This, however, was but one of his many minor interests. The establishment of what he called an 'Anthropometric Laboratory' was something far more momentous. It furnished the starting-point, and to a large extent the model, for the many 'psychological clinics' or 'child guidance centres' subsequently set up in Britain, America, and elsewhere; it formed the birthplace of the whole 'mental testing' movement; and it symbolized the beginning of experimental psychology in this country. The laboratory was opened during the International Health Exhibition in London in 1884. When the Exhibition closed, it was moved first to the Science Museum in South Kensington, and then to University College. The College still preserves a few of the large orange posters which announced that an 'Anthropometric Laboratory for the Measurement of Human Form and Faculty has been instituted, partly for anthropometric experiment and research, partly to familiarize the public with the methods and uses of human measurement, and partly for those who desire to learn what are their bodily and mental powers or those of their children, or to obtain timely warning of remediable faults in development. Charge, threepence each to those who are already on the register, fourpence to those who are not.'

'The leading idea', so Galton explains in his *Memories*, 'was that the measurements should "sample" a man with reasonable completeness: they should measure *absolutely* wherever possible; otherwise *relatively* among his class fellows', i.e. by 'ranks' or 'percentile grades'. Many of the routine measurements were purely physical—tests of bodily strength, measurements of the body and its parts (including the head), observations on hair colour, eye colour, handedness, and the like, and a general note of the examinee's health. The rest of the examination was essentially psychological. This was designed to cover three main levels: first, the simple sensory and motor capacities; secondly, associative processes—memory, habit formation, imagery, reaction time, and the like; and finally, what were designated 'higher mental processes'. For much of his work he had the help of a young American psychologist, J. M. Cattell, who had been studying with Wundt at Leipzig, and acted for a time as Galton's assistant in London. However, in 1888 Cattell was recalled to occupy the first chair of psychology established in the States; and it was principally owing to his introduction of Galton's ideas that mental testing became so popular in that country.

Data collected in this way formed the basis of Galton's next most important work, *Natural Inheritance*, published in 1889. As the title implies, its purpose was to discuss the need for studying the basic principles of biological transmission by scientific methods, and to indicate how this might be done. In an introductory section he observes that 'all living things are in one aspect individual and composite in another. We seem to inherit bit by bit. Inheritance may therefore be described as largely, if not wholly, "particulate"; and as such it will be treated in these pages.' No doubt many human characteristics—height and weight, for instance—exhibit a graded distribution; but each of these, Galton argues, can be regarded as 'a fine mosaic with elements too minute to be distinguished'. Here we have a clear anticipation of the principles of multi-factorial inheritance, where in Galton's phrase 'the multiplicity of quasi-independent elements' combine their effects, and so produce the normal frequency distribution and the varying degrees of family resemblance that we measure by our correlations.

Among statistical psychologists and indeed among statisticians generally Galton's name and reputation are most frequently linked with the concept of correlation. Mendel, it may be remembered, was interested chiefly in discontinuous characteristics, such as flower colour. Galton, on the other hand, devoted his attention mainly to graded characteristics, no doubt because almost all the measurable characteristics of human beings are of that type. The clue to inheritance was to be found, so he believed, in the different amounts of family resemblance exhibited by persons having various degrees of kinship; and accordingly he cast about for some method of measuring the degree of resemblance. His earliest investigations, like those of Mendel, were concerned with inheritance in peas: in Mendel's experiments they were edible peas; in Galton's they were sweet peas. On measuring the size of seeds for both mother and daughter plants, he discovered that, when the mother plants had produced large seeds, the daughter plants likewise produced large seeds, but the 'amount of the increase over the average' proved to be much smaller. The daughter plants in fact tended to revert to the general mean. He reached much the same result when, a few years later, he compared the heights of human parents with their adult offspring. On taking a batch of tall fathers— e.g. those whose heights were three inches above that of the average adult, and then measuring the height of their adult sons, he found that the mean height of the latter was only one inch above the general average. He termed this reduction in the mean height of the second group its 'regression', and the ratio of the two deviations—in this case 1/3—the 'regression coefficient'. His earliest theoretical demonstrations, however, proceeded not by considering resemblances or by calculating correlations, but reasoning along the lines of what Fisher has taught us to call an 'analysis of variance'.

Meanwhile Galton had encountered what seemed at first sight a very different problem. If you want to produce an adequate specification of any particular individual with scientific accuracy the ideal procedure would be, not to seize on his most conspicuous peculiarities after the fashion of the literary biographer, but to measure *all* his distinctively human characteristics. But that is clearly impracticable. How then are the most essential to be selected? In France in order to describe, classify, and identify criminals by their physical characteristics, Alphonse Bertillon had recently put forward a scheme based on twelve body measurements—height, length and breadth of head, length of forearm and of middle finger, and the like, all supplemented by a *portrait parlé*, with photographs and a list of distinguishing marks such as scars and moles. Galton, however, believed that several of Bertillon's measurements would vary so closely with each other that only a few would be really informative. Obviously, if you have measured Arsène Lupin's left leg, you don't need to measure his right leg; and if you measure his height, is it necessary to measure his legs or his arms at all? The question could readily be answered, so Galton argued, if we could only devise some means of assessing the degree of concomitant variation—or, as he termed it, the 'co-relation'—between height, arm-length, head-length, and so on.

However, the problem is of much wider importance than this. As Galton points out, both the term and the concept are of frequent occurrence in biology; yet 'no previous attempt had been made to define it clearly, or to measure its degree'. The method he proposes is to 'transmute' the raw measurements of stature, forearm, weight, and so forth (which will be in inches, pounds, or the like) 'into units determined by their respective scales of variability ... namely, the probable error'. When this is done 'the direct ratio and the converse are identical, viz. for height and forearm about 0·8'. This therefore is the device he proposed to adopt as a measure of the 'co-relation'. In his autobiography he narrates how vividly he recalls the circumstance in which he first grasped this important generalization. 'It was in the grounds of Naworth Castle' (the baronial residence of the Howards, the famous Earls of Carlisle, who were remotely related to him): 'there an invitation had been given to ramble freely; a temporary shower drove me to seek refuge in a reddish recess in the rock by the side of the pathway: here the idea flashed across me, and I forgot everything else for a moment in my great delight'. As Pearson remarks, 'that "recess" deserves a commemorative tablet'.

He found that for nearly all the body measurements advocated by Bertillon the correlations were surprisingly high—ranging from 0·70 (for height and middle finger) to 0·90 (for height and length of lower leg). The correlations furnished by the head measurements, however, both with each other and with the remaining characteristics, proved to be comparatively low (0·35 to 0·45). His statistics thus fully confirmed the ancient maxim, *ex pede Herculem*—if you can measure just one part of a body or a corpse, then you can reconstruct fairly accurately the measurements for the rest—except, significantly enough, for the skull. From the foot alone you can tell whether your man is a giant like Hercules, or a dwarf like Tom Thumb, or what his approximate measurements must be when he is intermediate between the two. In short, underlying all the various measurements of the body lies a 'common cause', or, as we now should say, a 'general factor', more or less modified by certain less influential 'specific factors'.

By this time, however, Galton himself had become convinced that, for mere identification, fingerprints would provide a far surer method than a modified Bertillon scheme of body-measurements, such as that on which Scotland Yard still chiefly relied. In a long series of re-searches, reported in over a dozen memoirs published between 1891 and 1902, he was able to demonstrate the practical superiority of this novel technique. He concludes his argument by reminding the reader that in the story of Jezebel it was said that, besides her skull, only 'the palms of her hands and the soles of her feet were left, so that no man might say: "This is Jezebel".' But, he adds, 'these are the very remains by which her corpse might have been most surely identified'.

V

The later years of Galton's life were devoted more and more to lectures and articles on the practical implications of the views he had thus developed. Since human achievements depend partly on education and partly on hereditary transmission, it is essential, so he maintained, to apply modern scientific techniques to the improvement of both. As a result of the experience gained from his earlier work in schools, Galton, when President of the Anthropological Section of the British

Association, was led to propose an anthropometric survey of the British Isles. The first investigations were confined almost entirely to physical data. However, a quarter of a century later, in 1903, he suggested repeating the survey, and urged that this time it should include mental measurements as well as physical. McDougall was appointed secretary of the Psychological Committee; and for the purpose of the inquiry initiated a series of researches in his laboratory at Oxford. The chief aim was to develop and standardize tests of general intelligence and other abilities for use in the schools through which the surveys were to be carried out. McDougall's research students—William Brown, J. C. Flugel, H. B. English, and myself—set to work on this project with much encouragement from Galton. Spearman, who had just returned from studying experimental psychology under Wundt, also came to Oxford, and joined in the scheme.

During the next ten years or so the researches thus started were continued in London, Liverpool, and elsewhere. Then, after prolonged appeals from Sully and Galton, the London County Council resolved to appoint a school psychologist of its own. Since the post was partly a research post, it was possible to put into execution many of the plans that Galton had long ago proposed. With the help of research students (chiefly teachers) trained in the various University departments, we made regular surveys of typical boroughs; we hunted up identical twins who had been reared apart; we selected large samples of different types of pupil—gifted, backward, dull, defective, and delinquent—with parallel samples of normal children to serve as control groups; and so far as possible, we made studies of their family histories, and followed them up into adult life.

For Galton himself, however, the educational implications of such inquiries were something of a side-issue. More and more he had come to feel that the most urgent need was to arouse public interest in the other aspect of the human problem—the study of heredity. From 1870 onwards governments of both main parties had started introducing revolutionary changes in education, taxation, the health services, the treatment of poverty and crime, all calculated to effect marked improvements in the living conditions of the existing generation, but with little regard to their possible effects on the generations to come. Together with concurrent changes in industry, transport, and the applications of scientific discoveries, they had already produced marked alterations in class structure, in marriage customs, and in the birth-rate. Long ago, during his African travels and later during his pedigree-studies of genius, Galton, as we have seen, had been greatly impressed by 'the frequency with which one race has supplanted others in various geographical areas', and by the rise and decline not only of families, but of communities and of nations. As an anthropologist he was familiar with the practice of endogamy and exogamy among primitive tribes: he had noted how many of the most successful nations—the Greek, the British, the North American—appeared to have started with a long spell of outbreeding and crossbreeding, and that at a later stage many of the more influential clans, castes, sects, and social classes, had practised systematic inbreeding. Again and again in the past the conscious insistence on restrictive matrimonial customs and the deliberate introduction of restrictive marriage laws had shown that civilized man had already vaguely realized that, by controlling the mating system, he might also control his own evolution. And it was Galton's growing conviction, based on a firm belief in the Darwinian creed, that what hitherto had been done in relative ignorance ought in future to be guided by scientific research and rational planning. To the investigation and popularization of this far-reaching project the closing years of his life were almost wholly devoted. He endowed a Record Office, a Research Fellowship, and a journal *(Biometrika)* for the publication of the work carried out at University College. When he died, he bequeathed 'the residue of (his) estate for the establishment of a Laboratory and a Chair of Eugenics in the University of London'.

VI

As this brief retrospect sufficiently shows, Galton, in the course of his long life, made contributions of outstanding importance to many widely different departments of knowledge—geography, meteorology, anthropology, criminology, medicine, statistics, and genetics. He has been hailed as the pioneer of experimental psychology in this country, and the father of statistical psychology as we know it today. But it will, I believe, be for the impetus he gave to the study of individual differences by his ingenious techniques—mental testing, rating scales, standardized questionnaires, coefficients of correlation and regression, and the application of the normal curve—that he will chiefly be remembered. When he took it up, individual psychology was just a speculative topic for the fancies of the poet, the novelist, the biographer, and the quack and charlatan on the seaside pier. By the time he left it and handed it on to others, it had been transformed into a reputable branch of natural science—perhaps for mankind the most important branch there is.

C

CHAPTER 4

MODELS, MEANINGS AND MEN

BY PATRICK MEREDITH

I

Most of us encounter our first models in the cradle before we learn to speak. This is more important than it might seem, for it precludes a 'definitional' approach to the theoretical study of models. From the start we are *shown* models rather than asked to say what a 'model' means. We handle them, squeeze them, bite them, get squeaks out of them, throw them round and use them to establish relations with people. The totality of this experience, for a given model, may be called our 'knowledge' of the model and it quite obviously differs from our knowledge of people or things *not* treated as models. We do not need words to establish this difference. A model is a toy.

Thus when we come to an attempt at *defining* the word 'model', a formal verbal statement which starts from scratch, treating 'model' as if it were a new word with no strings attached will be useless. For we attached the strings in our infancy. The word 'model' can no more be treated as neutral than the word 'mother'. Logicians, mathematicians, semioticians, methodologists, psychologists, epistemologists—all may attempt to appropriate the word to their own use but words are like the atmosphere. When we breathe them out others breathe them in and they are no one's property because they are everyone's.

But a model, whether it is a teddy-bear, a mechanical tortoise, an hydraulic system showing the circulation of money, or a geometrical diagram, is not breathed like a word. It is constructed and it stays put, or it may be carried round. It costs effort, time and money to make and it is owned by somebody. It may or may not have mechanical or electrical working parts but it does have determinate material properties. We cannot do what we like with it as we can with words. Shakespeare can say 'But me no buts' but Grey Walter's tortoise cannot tortoise a tortoise.

This difference between words and models is not, however, altogether decisive. It is true that we can say words, or write them, in any order or arrangement we like. To that extent we are free with them. But we can't make them *work* in any way we like. For 'words at work' means people interpreting them, and if we play fast and loose with accepted conventions the interpretations break down. It is only at the infantile stage of egocentric babbling that we can do what we like with sounds—and at that stage they have not yet become words, and we are not really trying to communicate. Once a sound becomes, for us, a true word, we have lost most of our freedom over it. Society is imposing a patterned inertia on our behaviour. This pattern is the system of objective laws studied by linguistics, the oldest and most precise branch of social psychology though not commonly recognized as such.

Thus we have language constrained to obey social laws, and hardware models constrained to obey physical laws, and this seems a sharp enough contrast. We cannot, however, altogether ignore the physical properties of language, nor can we ignore the social properties of hardware models, and we begin to sense endless ambiguities and difficulties which make the whole subject of 'models' somewhat suspect. Can the rigour of logic come to our rescue? I am not sure that it can, for the 'rigour' is question-begging. The word, after all, means 'stiffness'. We can speak of the rigour of an argument only in so far as the distinctions on which it is based are 'hard-and-fast'. I had better admit that fascinated as I am by logic I do not regard it as the last word in philosophy. Nor is it the first word. It is a middle phase which has to be gone through. The fact that so many models today are described as 'hardware' is consonant with the sudden popularization of logic. It has become an engineering term. It provides a language of rigid components and sharp distinctions with which to reason technologically.

The first models of our acquaintance are not hardware but software. And this is true culturally as well as individually. Most of the requirements for living are made of soft material, of liquid or gas. Only bones, teeth, claws, and horns are hard. The technology of rigidity, of bones and stones, paved the way for hardware logic. Stone walls enabled property to be delimited and so provided models of *definition* (*finis*='a boundary'). Biological membranes are more or less permeable. Only partly do they separate one region from another. The need for civilization to come to terms with the problems of property and power forced the development of hardware and of the logic that goes with it. We are only just beginning to glimpse the possibility of emerging from the logic of hardware mechanism. Hardware had to come as a middle stage between simple software and sophisticated software. But the brain itself has never been happy with mechanical logic, though in an adolescent need for quick control of power it has seized on it with avidity. And without the hardware of laboratory instruments we could never have begun to discover the laws of sophisticated software.

In short, models can be of any material whatever, solid, liquid or gas, and will naturally display the properties of their material whatever vicarious properties we demand of them in their roles as models. And the logic that we need in order to analyse their symbolic behaviour as models must match in subtlety the properties of the materials. Dressing a teddy-bear has none of the metric precision of screwing a nut on a bolt, but it has its own mode of conformation, topological rather than metric. And fitting a political constitution on to a newly liberated territory may also have its own subtle logic.

II

It would be just as misleading to draw an absolute contrast between the mechanical logic of hardware and the subtle, flexible logic of software as it would to suppose that rigid logic is the only kind and that everything must be made to conform to mechanism. The plain technical fact is that hardware is not absolutely hard. It bends, it wobbles, it wears, it tears, it tires, and in time it disintegrates. The engineer can no more afford to rely on rigid logic alone than the nurse or the statesman. But none of these three can afford to ignore logic. The fact is that neither verbal nor symbolic logic has succeeded in formulating the logic actually used in successfully handling software. But the logic is there, tacitly, in the skill with which soft and delicate things are handled. The continuity of soft and hard logic is nowhere more convincingly displayed than in the skill of the eye-surgeon. Without hard logic he could not handle his instruments but without soft logic he would be a butcher.

Logic, then, is our way of getting to grips with matter in all its forms. It is not identical with skill but is the component in skill by which given conditions enable inferences to be made. For skill is utterly and continuously dependent on a sequence of tacit inferences, a cybernetic interchange of 'If I do this then the material will respond thus, and if the material is so-and-so I must behave in such-and-such a manner'. The varieties of logic should, on this view, be classified so as to run parallel with the taxonomy of material forms. But this, of course, would presuppose that our taxonomy was complete. It is precisely because our understanding of matter in all its forms is imperfect that *we construct models in order to force ourselves to modify our logic*. So long as this happens in many different directions, and not solely from hardware outwards, the results can only be for the good. In other words we can afford to explore the mechanical logic of babies if we also sometimes explore the infantile logic of machines. (And 'infantile' is not here a term of disparagement.)

The general principle here is akin to that of Relativity Theory, viz. that no one frame of reference has priority. If it is legitimate to use a construction of material X_1 to make a model of a system made of material X_2 then it is equally legitimate to do the converse. It seems to me that this principle offers a third option to those satisfied with neither the reductionist nor the holistic programmes of explanation. Whenever we explain it is always in terms of something else which itself needs explaining. If we allow one-way explanation only we are committed to an endless regress. The only justification for the claims of the reductionist programme would be the achievement of finality. Without this it is no less metaphysical than the holistic programme. The third option offers reciprocity. We recognize that an explanation posits a model having material properties of some kind (even if we do not physically construct it). But that which we are seeking to explain also has a material basis.

This is not altogether an easy relationship to grasp. We think usually of an 'explanation' as a verbal statement. But it has long been recognized that 'purely verbal' explanation (such as explaining sleeplessness by 'insomnia') explains nothing. We therefore regard the verbal form of a 'true' explanation as only a convenience, an intermediary whereby some *model* is conjured up. It is the latter which constitutes the explanation. We describe a lot of tiny billiard balls dashing about a cylinder, in order to explain the pressure of a gas. The explanation lies not in the words but in the model described. The words are effective only in so far as they call up the kind of behaviour which such a model would physically display if constructed. We may or may not feel called upon actually to construct the model. We may, in fact, find it impossible to construct it. The kinetic theory postulates idealized molecules and although their behaviour can be calculated, it cannot, in fact, be physically demonstrated. And this raises an awkward point of principle. For all such physical models are abstract. And the same is true for most psychological models. (Grey Walter's tortoise, if regarded as a simulator of organic behaviour, and my own Chroma-tropes,[1] as simulators of verbal behaviour, are exceptions in using physical hardware for psychological models, unless computers and teaching-machines are classified as psychological models.) Today the term 'model' is more often used for abstractions than for hardware. This fact prompts three questions:

1. What is the nature of an abstract model?
2. What is its function?
3. How does it work?

What I suspect is happening is that theorists, envious of the com-pelling, demonstrative tangibility of hardware models, have simply appropriated the *word* 'model' for something whose only compulsion is in the (usually unformalized) logic which they themselves apply to it, whose only demonstrativeness arises from the suggestiveness of the vocabulary by which it is described, and which is touched only by their own brains. By this pseudo-realism they pull a fast one on our credulity. A personal note may not be irrelevant here, for the problem of the validity of models has haunted me for forty years. As a student of physics in the early 'twenties I was intrigued by the failure of the 'elastic ether' model to explain all the properties of light and delved into its history. This gave me a life-long critical attitude towards pseudo-mechanical models. In the late 'twenties, as a research student in the Psychology Department at University College, London, I attended Spearman's lectures. I was intrigued by the 'Energy-Engines' hypothesis by which he sought to visualize the distinction between the 'G' and 'S' factors in his theory of intelligence. Much as I admired his 'Noëgenetic Theory',[2] which was quite distinct from his 'Factorial Theory', it was the latter which, regrettably, came to monopolize his attention. And lending itself to ready-made statistical analysis it came to dominate a large sector of modern psychological research and to save many young psychologists the trouble of having to think what they were doing. True, Sir Cyril Burt did much to introduce some degree of logical respectability into the 'Factor' concept, and of course Sir Godfrey Thompson never capitulated to the pseudo-realism of Spearman's doctrine. But this monster was a baby which should never have been born, at any rate not to a psychological father and a statistical mother. Factorialism has made clear thinking in psychology almost an impossibility. It would be flogging a dead horse to go further with this critique, and in any case my own distaste for its pseudo-physical origins (as well as for the social and educational implications of its findings) kept me well away from this muddy mainstream of psychological research. The logic of learning has always seemed to me more important than the statistics of intelligence. But perhaps even more important is the problem of finding a methodology which will allow psychology to grow to full stature, not by borrowing from other sciences but by facing its own problems and finding its own logic.

III

Psychology undoubtedly benefits from a variety of approaches. Any single approach inevitably produces a lop-sided conception of mental phenomena. To attempt to set forth a single all-embracing methodology would not only be pretentiously ambitious but also rather absurd. There is, however, an evident need for methodology, i.e. a study of the rules by which the various games of theorizing are played. Thus we must first ask for a plan by which methodology itself should proceed. The plan is not in the interests of mere formalism. The study of psychology covers an enormous field, and we need a map of the field in order to economize our studies.

Psychology is divided up into a number of conventionalized branches such as Experimental, Social, Physiological, Dynamic, Cognitive, Comparative, etc. It is impossible to make any rational scheme out of the actual material in these various branches, for each branch is nourished by discoveries and hypotheses arising from very diverse approaches such as the psychoanalytic, the behaviourist, the factorial, and the cybernetic approaches. There is no natural unity in any of these branches, even though in some, e.g. child psychology, there is an apparent unity in the object of study.

We must bear in mind that the actual progress of psychological knowledge is carried forward by two classes of psychologists, viz. the pioneers and the textbook writers. (The same individual may attempt both roles, e.g. McDougall and Spearman, but the outcome is generally a bad textbook.) The pioneers do best to confine their writings to the exposition of their own work. Any collation of the work of different schools is best done by text-book writers with no axes to grind.

This point gives us a clue to methodology. In the work of any one pioneer and his followers there is likely to be a certain unity of approach. Thus there are as many methodologies as there are approaches, and it is best to study them singly. But there is also the methodology of collation. When the distinctive features of the separate methodologies are clearly grasped they need to be brought into relation with one another. This is obviously a harder task. And whereas the separate methodologies of the different schools may be worked out with reasonable objectivity by any honest student, the methodology of their interrelation must almost inevitably be governed by criteria and evaluations which are arbitrary and personal to the individual methodologist. This point is made evident again and again in the various attempts at comprehensive surveys of the different schools. Further, whereas in the separate methodologies the scheme of principles is to some extent dictated by the works of the pioneer himself, this integrative methodology has no intrinsic and necessary order. Its pattern must therefore be as arbitrary as its criteria.

The only honest way to set about the exposition of an integrative methodology is therefore to make explicit at the outset the criteria and values of the methodologist himself. Von Bertalanffy[3] sets forth three pairs of alternative characteristics for theoretical models:

1. Static *v.* Dynamic
2. Molecular *v.* Molar
3. Material *v.* Formal

Now different individuals get excited about different issues. Some will become positively apocalyptic at the mention of the word 'Dynamic'. Others have ecstasies over the word 'Molar'. The issue which interests me is the 'material versus formal' one. Bertalanffy says:

'As far as psychology is concerned, little is known about the material counterpart of mental experience in the brain. So it may be useful, instead of elaborating hypothetical neural mechanisms, first to try a formalization of what seem to be the essential laws in this realm.'

In a discussion which merits close consideration Bertalanffy speaks of 'model conceptions' and 'material interpretations'. But we cannot inspect other people's conceptions. They must be *materialized* in verbal or other forms. The 'Formal v. material' dichotomy is very misleading. Every model used for scientific purposes must be made public in a *material form*. Its material components may be words or wires, mathematical symbols or beads, diagrams or diodes. In the model these components are *representative* of certain counterparts in the phenomenon which the model purports to explain. Thus the components constitute a kind of *vocabulary*, and the model represents a complex *proposition*.

IV

It is obvious that we cannot take actual neurones from a living brain and construct a living model. We can only *represent* such a model verbally, mathematically, graphically or electronically. With this proviso we can speak of 'neural models'. Let us contrast these with 'formal models' meaning, by the latter, a model whose components refer not to anatomical forms but to hypothetical forms of organization in the brain. The model then becomes a genuine device for exploring hypotheses without begging physiological questions.

A highly significant fact which proponents of neural models sometimes overlook is that the human brain loses something like 100,000 neurones a day by normal wastage. Having (it is estimated) 27,000,000,000 of them we can afford this loss without much inconvenience, but the designer of a neural model, in which every neurone counts in the functioning, cannot. Thus the units of his construction are too small. He is working at an inappropriate order of magnitude. The neural units needed in a model from which behavioural consequences can be predicted must take, as its typical component, an aggregate of at least some thousands of neurones working in co-operation and not necessarily all located in a single area of the brain—a sort of 'corresponding society' of neurones. Such an aggregate cannot be individually identified by physiological means, as far as I know. Its existence must therefore be *postulated* for the purposes of the model. Its properties represent statistical integrations of the known behaviour of single neurones and must be *predicated* from formal considerations deliberately to make possible the required deductions. The actual process of integration, which necessarily involves not only neurones but neuroglia and other supporting tissues, blood and other fluids, and electromagnetic, osmotic, mechanical and other forces, simply cannot be represented by any known mathematical functions. But each such integration produces a single 'component' in the sort of model we need to throw light on, for example, verbal behaviour.

Since the term 'neural model' could be taken to mean either a model having single neurones as components or a model to which neurones contribute through mass behaviour I prefer a quite different term for these models of postulated functions. Each component may be envisaged as the consolidated outcome of a learning process. Because the neurones are the main active constituents of these components we shall find a relatively stable though highly complex firing-

c*

pattern or 'pulse-spectrum' associated with each component. Segments of this spectrum can activate other components, in a functional
reaching-out process. We thus have a type of *tropism* whose specific
direction is determined by a pulse-spectrum. In my prototype models
(demonstrated to the British Association at York in 1959) the spectra
were simulated by coloured lights, and the models were therefore
called 'Chromatropes'.

My reasons for regarding this as an important issue are as follows:

1. The search for neural models hands the main business of
psychology over to the neurologists. The latter are of necessity pretty
closely tied to the laboratory, the dissecting-room, the clinic and the
operating-theatre. This circumstance precludes them from any adequate grasp of the main phenomena and problems with which psychology deals.

2. Neurology can never be an autonomous science since it is
concerned with a system whose *raison d'être* is to co-ordinate a whole
organism in an environment. The features of the system are meaningless apart from the demands made upon it. Thus the programme for
'material' models implies the admission of 'formal' considerations.

3. The language of neurology is ill-adapted to the description of
psychological phenomena. The properties of even a successful neural
model would have to be translated into psychological terms.

4. The design of neural models is strictly limited by the current
state of neurological knowledge. Formal models are limited only by
the resources of the imagination. Both have eventually to submit to
experimental tests, but the formal model starts from a much richer
range of possibilities. Moreover its design is essentially conditioned by
psychological requirements.

In thus urging the case for the 'formal' model I am not arguing
against the 'material' model, but only against those who would allow
'material' models only. We certainly need 'material' models, but
'formal' models must always lead the way.

We now note that 'formal models' may be of two types, viz. 'hardware' or 'paperware'. Both are symbolic, but whereas the hardware
grinds out its conclusions by physical laws the paperware yields its
conclusions by human operations of interpretation and deduction.
'Hardware' models may be mechanical, chemical, electrical or even
biological (e.g. a shoal of shrimps). They have many obvious
advantages and likewise many disadvantages. Advantages:

1. Their properties are arrived at not by deduction but by direct observation.

2. These properties are of two kinds:

(i) those directly deducible from the known properties of the components and from their mode of combination,

(ii) 'emergent' properties which could not be foreseen, arising from the model as a Gestalt. These latter would never be predicted if the model were not actually constructed.

(iii) we can ring the changes on all possible values of the variables and directly observe the consequences without lengthy and involved calculations.

Against these are the following disadvantages:

(i) We are limited entirely by our powers of construction, by our ingenuity and physical resources, which have little or nothing to do with the level of our theorizing.

(ii) The actual materials used are bound to influence the properties of the model and will, in general, be quite different from the material of the neural structures which the model is designed to explain. The observed properties are those of the model as constructed of other materials.

(iii) The phenomena to be explained occur in biological material. We are as yet nowhere near the possibility of constructing a true biological model. Its mode of functioning would certainly differ widely from that of any physical model.

(iv) Neural structures yielding psychological processes consist of numbers of components enormously exceeding those of even the largest electronic computers. The emergent properties of such large aggregates will mostly not reveal themselves in such comparatively fragmentary models. This is not to deny the suggestiveness of the latter. The point is that the *deducible* properties of the model are inherent in its design, and can therefore be expounded without ever constructing the model. The *emergent* properties, for the reasons given, are likely to differ widely from the emergent properties of a biological model. In particular the actual biological structures to be explained have been developed by phylogenetic and ontogenetic processes whereas the model has been made by deliberate design and construction. This fact must profoundly affect their respective properties.

We most now consider what are the main features of a hypothetical paper model as distinct from a hardware one. The most important feature is that all its deducible properties are logically inherent in its description. This is not so much a truism as a prescription. A model whose consequences are not deducible from its description is logically useless. But we must examine closely the conditions to be satisfied by the description in order that the properties shall, in fact, be deducible. These conditions are more familiar to logicians than to psychologists, but there are certain points liable to be overlooked by both.

Here we move into the realm of abstract geometry. For this is the study of the deduction of the consequences of an axiomatic system. The meanings of the terms used in the axioms do not affect the formal properties of these systems. Thus, for example, formal psychoanalytic theory, if correctly set out, is as much a branch of abstract geometry as the Theory of Relativity. And it is only by making such an effort of abstraction that we can become quite clear in our handling of theoretical models. The danger in failing to adopt the abstractive procedure is seen in the daily writings of many psycho-analysts. For the theoretical model of psychoanalysis as commonly presented resembles a cross between an unstable totalitarian state and a sewage works. The former aspect supplies a connotation of quasi-interpersonal relationships between intra-psychic elements and the latter a connotation of quasi-hydrodynamical motions and forces accompanied by a characteristic aroma. Reasoning out the consequences of such a system the theorist who fails to rely solely on abstract considerations inevitably falls into the trap of allowing the pictorial characteristics of the model to dominate his deductions. Thus an illicit materialization of a model purporting to be formal takes place. For Freud's model was never offered as a neurological model. Although originally a neurologist himself the state of neurological theory at the beginning of his career offered little hope of illumination for the phenomena which interested him. Thus he had to conjure up a purely 'psychic' picture. But he painted this picture in vivid hues of struggle, conflict, censorship, pressure, flow and the like, so in effect materializing the psyche. Posterity has the task of unscrambling the Freudian ego and representing whatever is valid in his conclusions in a form which shall be logically consistent on its formal side and neurologically sound on its material side. This is not intended as a condemnation of Freud. Great pioneers tend to be picture-makers. An obsession with methodology may well be fatal to creativity.

Although formal models are to be regarded as logically identical with axiomatic systems in abstract geometry, we cannot entirely exclude the difference of approach. The geometer is only minimally, if at all, interested in any concrete interpretations of his theorems, and is chiefly concerned with the structure and beauty of his proofs. The scientist, in whatever branch, who is using a formal model is very much concerned with concrete interpretations, and resorts to proofs only to avert the challenge of critics, and then only if verification in the concrete is too difficult to achieve. There may be the same logical connexion between his premises and his conclusions as with the geometer, but as likely as not he jumps to his conclusion intuitively guided not by logic but by intrinsic connexions of *meaning*. This, of course, is precisely the danger. For if the original model is quasi-pictorial it has a dual meaning, and he may be guided by the adventi-tious meaning of the material of the picture instead of by the logical meaning of its form.

This is not the only difference. From any given set of axiomatic propositions an unlimited number of consequential propositions may be deduced. Some policy of selection is imperative. The geometer is likely to select those consequences whose deduction proceeds by way of the most elegant proofs. The scientist uses proof as a means to an end. His criteria are likely to be two:

(i) the interest, importance or utility of the conclusions, or
(ii) their verifiability by empirical test.

The successful verification of conclusions considerably strengthens the acceptability of a hypothetical model, though it can never prove its truth. And as a means of verification the practical interest of a conclusion is irrelevant. The force of such a test in confirming the theory is greatest when the conclusion is unexpected and not evident on other grounds, though the reason for this is psychological rather than logical. Strictly the only logical inference permissible from a confirmed prediction is that the possibility of disproof has been narrowed. The working scientist is rarely as austere in his attitude to his test-results as the logical view would require.

Let us consider now a very concrete conceptual model, viz. Harvey's account of the circulation of the blood.[4]

'First,—the blood is incessantly transmitted by the action of the heart from the vena cava to the arteries in such quantity that it cannot be supplied from the ingesta, and in such a manner that the whole must very quickly pass through the organ; Second,—the blood under the influence of the arterial pulse enters and is impelled in a continuous, equable, and incessant stream through every part and member of the body, in much larger quantity than were sufficient for nutrition, or than the whole mass of fluids could supply; Third,—the veins in like manner return this blood incessantly to the heart from parts and members of the body. These points proved, I conceive it will be manifest that the blood circulates, revolves, propelled and then returning, from the heart to the extremities, from the extremities to the heart, and thus that it performs a kind of circular motion.'

In a model of this type the material referents of the words are not hypothetical—they are observable tissues, many of whose properties are already familiar. The theory is a dynamic model of a process. The theory is worked out in great detail concerning both the pathways of the blood and the amount in circulation. There is an implication of what we now call the law of Conservation of Matter and certain simple topological considerations. Much of Harvey's argument was devoted to the refutation of the existing theory, and is thus not intrinsic to his own model.

The essential point here is that certain properties and laws are stated or implied, and from these certain observable consequences are deduced. A successful model must embody properties and laws which are rich in implications. The more concrete the model, and the more familiar its components, the easier it is to deduce its implications. The more unfamiliar the components or the more abstract the properties and laws the greater is the obligation on the theorist to make explicit the character of the features from which deductions are to be made. The word 'energy' for example, which has very precise physical implications, is used frequently in psychological theory in contexts to which the physical interpretation has no obvious relevance, and without any compensating statement of the exact psychological implications of the term. Thus deductions are made whose logical validity cannot be checked. It may happen that the consequential facts predicted from these deductions can indeed be observed, and the theory is thereby deemed to be experimentally confirmed. But if there is no strict logical chain from the model to the facts the confirmation is illusory. And there can be a chain only if the precise properties and laws of the components are specified.

v

Now this is not merely a matter of giving clear definitions. In fact definitions can give an entirely specious appearance of logical precision, as can be seen in certain texts on Factorial Analysis. A definition merely translates a single term into a verbal formula. Its degree of precision is limited by that of the least precise of the terms used in the definition, and may also be limited by the latter's syntax. In fact syntax is a very vital consideration in psychological methodology. The full exposition of this point would be out of place here,[5] but briefly it relates to the contrast between the ease with which terms are grammatically identified in the sciences dealing with physical processes and the extreme difficulty encountered in psychology. For example, we say 'instinct' (noun), 'instinctive' (adjective), 'instinctively' (adverb). Which of these is primary? Is an action 'instinctive' because it proceeds from an 'instinct', or do we postulate an 'instinct' because actions having certain characteristics which we label 'instinctive' are observed? This is but one of hundreds of grammatical problems which arise in any close scrutiny of psychological theory. These problems, whether explicitly recognized or merely experienced as intellectual discomforts, account in part for the strong temptation to neurologize psychology. For in neurology our concrete nouns refer to localizable entities, our adjectives to verifiable properties, our verbs to ascertainable processes—up to a point. But even here there are terms which defy grammatical identification, e.g. 'integration'.

This stress on grammatical issues is not a matter of pedantry. Words are the stuff of conceptual models. Models stand or fall by the ascertainment of their predicted consequences. The logical deduction of these consequences is possible only by virtue of the logical properties of the terms in the model. A noun is logically a totally different concept from an adjective or a verb. In framing a psychological definition we have to make up our mind exactly what concepts we are using and adopt the appropriate part of speech. The very facility with which, in our language, the adding and subtracting of affixes can change parts of speech, e.g. *cognize, cognition, cognitive*, affords an ever-present temptation to avoid making up our minds on precisely those issues which make a conceptual model logically determinate or indeterminate. Thus grammatical analysis is a central requirement in theoretical methodology.

The grammatical function of a term decides the kind of part which it must play in the logical pattern of deduction. The substantial meanings involved in the deduction are determined by another characteristic of the term. This may be expressed thus: that a term gives rise to determinate consequential meanings only if it can be precisely localized in some initially given conceptual framework. For example, to the non-chemist the term 'iron' carries a certain group of not very precise associations. To a chemist it indicates a certain place in the Periodic Table and an enormous array of precise implications. This is the 'Principle of Entailment'. Every legitimate term, i.e. every term which is so conceived as to satisfy our methodological requirements, has a determinate entailment. The entailment is the conceptual framework in which it is located.

Philosophers today show much less faith than formerly in the immutability of logic, in its total adequacy and in its supremacy over thought. Rightly they have come to regard it as a growing system of technical symbolic instruments, highly efficient for certain specific tasks, and capable of enormous elaboration. If it is to be wisely used it must be interpreted in a wider context in which other constraints set the limits of its application. It is man's policy in the handling of this explosively growing wealth of scientific knowledge which must determine both its constraints and its developments. For this knowledge has itself become almost an environmental threat, certainly an insistent challenge. We need an 'ecology of knowledge' to deal with this challenge, to relate the Psychology of Cognition to the demands of our environment. Such is the concept underlying the Epistemic Theory which I have outlined elsewhere.[5, 6]

VI

Much of the foregoing analysis was written nearly ten years ago as an application of Epistemic Theory to psychological methodology. For, although psychology must find its own method, its *field* is the whole of human experience and this includes the whole of human scientific knowledge. Thus the methodology must be based on a *conspectus* and this is the concern of Epistemics—the taxonomy of man's discoveries, and the promotion of their communication.

In the past ten years, through the industrial stimulus of automation, the theoretical stimulus of computer-science, the bibliographical stimulus of modern documentation, the military stimulus of advanced weapons systems and the astronomical stimulus of space-travel, the whole subject of 'models' has assumed a new look. We have a new science of 'Self-Organizing Systems'. This immensely active and challenging science is changing the face of thought and (in the words of a Foreign Office spokesman in August 1939 after the signing of the Hitler–Stalin pact) "All the 'isms' have become 'wasms'". But when I first formulated the Epistemic programme twelve years ago I was pitching my thoughts twenty years ahead, for the simple reason that at that time mathematical logic was nowhere included in the training of psychologists in this country, as far as I knew (outside Leeds), and it would take a whole generation to build up a degree of sophistication in logic even going no further than the somewhat patchy sophistication in statistics acquired by the last generation.

The problem looks somewhat different today. There are interdisciplinary teams at work, and the respective disciplines of members of these teams are brushing off on one another. But this is not 'discipline' in the traditional sense. It is a combination of osmosis and resonance. It is more fertile, more tolerant of misconceptions (for given free criticism these come out in the wash), more constructive. Further, thanks to Electronics and Bio-chemistry, many models which once were conceivable only in formal terms can now be translated into hardware, software or fluidware. And we can begin to see more clearly now the nature of the relationship between man and his models. May I quote from Uttley's after-dinner speech at the end of the 1959 Interdisciplinary Conference on 'Self-Organizing Systems'?]

'The research covered by this conference raises a number of very important questions in the mind of the average man. Will there be unemployment? Shall we make brains? Are we debunking man?

'As to the first question, machines will slowly take over from men all the tedious thinking which yet must be done without error; all the sorting and checking and counting and repetitive calculation which, frankly, makes machines of us. In less than a century such work will be as unthinkable as the transport of goods on the backs of slaves and man will be released for creative work which will satisfy him and give him joy. Rather than unemployment there will be re-employment in the "clerical revolution" which began ten years ago. But farsighted planning is essential.

'Seondly, we shall not make brains any more than we shall make muscles. The aim, rather, is to understand the manifold functions of the brain and so ourselves. Instead of using the word "mind" we prefer, today, to use the word "thinking". It embraces a large number of activities as yet little understood but already we may venture to resolve the "thinking-matter" problem by suggesting that thinking is a property of matter, matter in its most highly organized state—the nerve cell. And the word "consciousness" may, like "ether", disappear from our scientific language, not by denying obvious facts, but from a deeper understanding of them.'

This brings me back to my three questions on the *nature*, the *function*, and the *operation* of a model. Its physical nature may be a construction of any materials whatever, solids, liquids, or gases, biological organisms, ink and paper, or even groups of human beings. As such it is constrained by its material laws. But it is also constrained by the imposed laws of its construction.

The *function* of a model is not necessarily always to serve as a platform for methodological deductions. It is often more subtle and more varied. Even children do not simply use toys as substitutes for human beings or animals. They use them as probes in the exploration of their own powers and in the dialectic of their intercourse with the world about them. And much of the sophisticated model-building of today owes much less to logic than to curiosity. We make models as intermediary instruments to enrich the dialectic of our interrogation both of Nature and of ourselves. We allow them varying degrees of self-organization deliberately to exclude full predictability. We do this in order to discover new and unsuspected modes of relativity both between the organic and the inorganic and between man and man.

When we talk about the *operation* of a model we may mean *our* operation on *it*, or its own *internal* operations, or its operations on *other things*. We should also not overlook the operations of the latter on the model. In using verbs it is always a good idea to identify the subject of the verb so as to indicate the direction of the process.

We are incurable idolaters. We worship images, we worship toys, and we worship models. We treat images as Gods, toys as persons, and models as scientific truths. But a model is no more than an embodied and articulated question mark, with some life of its own, but used for making a novel impact on our own life.

ADDENDUM TO CHAPTER ON 'MODELS'

BY PATRICK MEREDITH

VII

In 'Models, Meaning and Theories'* May Brodbeck (University of Minnesota) criticizes the vagueness and variety of meanings encountered in the use of the word 'model', and indeed the term has become something of a cliché. But the somewhat dictatorial overtones in Dr Brodbeck's crisp and astringent strictures proceed from a too restricted view of the meaning of science itself. As a commentary on models from the standpoint of mathematical logic her paper is admirable—but scientists do not spend all, or even most, of their time

* In WILLNER, D. (ed.), 1960, *Decisions Values and Groups*, London: Pergamon.

trying to be logical. They are trying to explore. They do not often use models as axiomatic systems but rather as irritants to thought. They are not always fully aware of the logical implications of their models and this fact may be set against Dr Brodbeck's failure to deal with their empirical implications. Her example of the model steam-engine as a *replica* type of model ('not, as such, scientifically interesting' because it gives no new knowledge) illuminates the very point which she overlooks. Being a replica this model is isomorphic, and if it is also steam-propelled 'then the isomorphism is complete'. Now quite apart from the empirical point that if it is structurally isomorphic it cannot work *except* by steam, the actual working would have a certain thermodynamic efficiency. Complete isomorphism would require this to be the same as the efficiency of the large-scale version. But since pressure and cooling depend on areas, and fuel consumption on volumes, the factors determining efficiency are scaled down in different ratios from the linear dimensions. Thus there are internal factors in a model which preclude complete isomorphism, as every engineer knows. Further the engine uses coal and water, and complete iso-morphism would require the lumps of coal to be scaled down too but should it be in linear-ratio or in volume-ratio? And, in principle, the size of the molecules of water should likewise be scaled down, which is the *reductio ad absurdum* of the notion of 'complete isomorphism'. The author would probably agree but would regard the point as trivial, for as she says—'Although social scientists occasionally resort to such pictorial devices, the term "model" is more frequently applied to various kinds of verbal or symbolic systems'. She then proceeds to deal with these in terms of mathematical logic as though they were *purely* symbolic, and as if constructed for the purpose of generating propositions of logic. But as constructed by the scientist it is their *semantic reference* which makes these models valuable and fruitful in suggesting new ways of thinking about empirical facts which baffle him when considered alone. Dr Brodbeck has interesting things to say about models in atomic physics but misses the point that Bohr, in his quantum model of the atom, actually *defied* logic by postulating orbital electrons which did not radiate, contrary to their known properties.

VIII

The point I am making here is that logic cannot legislate for science. For logic itself is not the overriding necessity which some logicians imply. In spite of Wittgenstein's declaration that 'there can be no surprises in logic' there are still controversies among logicians. Logic is no more an absolute than space and time. It is a *skill* which has developed historically into an instrument of great power and subtlety and which has now found its perfect mode of expression in the design and programming of computers. Logic can postulate perfectly self-contained axiomatic systems, devoid of all environmental stress and internal inefficiencies. A sociologist constructing a theoretical model of some phenomenon of group-behaviour will, if he means business, take account both of the fact that his group consists of individuals who are both imperfect and imperfectly understood, and of the fact that they inhabit an environment which imposes conditions which owe nothing to psychology or sociology. His model is not intended as a logical system but as a tentative indicator of relationships which are not obvious in the phenomenon itself but which are worth exploring. If he allows himself to be inhibited by the *hubris* of the logicians he won't dare to think at all.

But although I think that Dr Brodbeck has misconceived the role of models in science I would strongly commend her remarks on reductionism, 'connexion-laws' and 'composition-laws' as valid and important for the methodology of psychology and the social and biological sciences.

REFERENCES

1. MEREDITH, G. PATRICK, 1960, 'The Communication of Scientific Concepts and Models of Semantic Mechanisms', *Advancement of Science, 17*, 110.

2. MEREDITH, G. P., 1949, 'A Revision of Spearman's Noëgenetic Principles', *Proceedings of the Aristotelian Society, 49*, 91.

3. BERTALANFFY, L. VON., 1952, 'Theoretical models in biology and Psychology', in KRECH, D., and KLEIN, G. S., *Theoretical Models and Personality Theory*, Durham N.C.: Duke University Press.

4. HARVEY, W., 1628, *On the Motion of the Heart and Blood in Animals* (trans. WILLIS, R., revised BOWIE, A., 1889), London: Bell.

5. MEREDITH, PATRICK, 1964, *Instruments of Communication*, London: Pergamon, (in the press).

6. MEREDITH, PATRICK, 1951, 'The Transmission of Knowledge', *Brit. J. Psychol., 42*, 322.

7. UTTLEY, D. A. M., 1960, 'The Mechanization of Thinking', in YOVITS, MARSHALL C., and CAMERON, SCOTT, 1960, *Self-Organizing Systems*, Proceedings of an Interdisciplinary Conference, Co-sponsored by the Information Systems Branch of the Office of Naval Research and Armour Research Foundation of Illinois Institute of Technology, London: Pergamon.

CHAPTER 5

SOME ASPECTS OF PIAGET'S GENETIC
APPROACH TO COGNITION

BY BÄRBEL INHELDER

I

Jean Piaget's work must be both baffling and intriguing to Anglo-
Saxon psychologists, particularly to those of the younger generation
who have been brought up in S-R theory and in logical empiricism.
In fact, it goes beyond experimental psychology. Piaget poses his
questions from the point of view of psycho-epistemology; his methods,
in the realm of cognition, are exploratory and flexible; and his methods
of analysis are those of logical symbolism. But the experts in each of
these disciplines tend to consider him as too eclectic, and as something
of an interloper. And yet the interest which has been shown in the
Geneva research seems to suggest that the facts brought to light by
this particular approach shed a new light on the intellectual development of the child.

By way of introduction I would like to outline briefly, first, the
point of view of genetic epistemology which orients our research,
second, the methods, and third, the models we used.

From the very beginning of his career, Piaget has constantly
explored questions of genetic epistemology. It is true that in their most
general terms, such questions as: 'What is knowledge?', can give rise
only to speculative controversy; but if formulated in more restricted
terms and in terms of genesis, questions such as: 'Under what laws
does knowledge develop and change?' can be dealt with scientifically.
Research work in genetic epistemology seeks to analyse the mechanisms
of the growth of knowledge in so far as it pertains to scientific thought,
and to discover the passage from states of least knowledge to those
of the most advanced knowledge. To this end the categories and

concepts of established science—such as those of space, time, causality, number, and logical classes—have been studied as they develop in the life of the child.

Before undergoing formal tuition, the young child progressively elaborates his first logical and mathematical constants, such as logical classes, and the principles of conservation of numerical correspondences, or spatial dimensions, and of physical matter. These constants allow him to handle the transformations of the physical world, in reality and in thought. The laws of this elaboration, while allowing us on the one hand to throw light on epistemological problems, allow us at the same time to analyse more appropriately the active part played by the child in the development of his knowledge of the world. For it does not seem—and I am here anticipating the interpretation of the facts—as if the growth of knowledge in the child were due exclusively to a cumulative stock-piling of information received, or exclusively to the emergence of a sudden 'insight' independent of preliminary preparation. Rather, the development of knowledge seems to result from a process of elaboration that is based essentially on the activity of the child. In effect, two types of activity can be distinguished: first, a logico-mathematical type of activity—the activity of bringing together, of dissociating, of ordering, of counting, and so on—any activity for which objects are no more than a support; and secondly, an activity of a physical type—an activity of exploration aimed at extracting information from objects themselves, such as their colours, form, weight, and so on. It is thus in acting upon the external world that, according to Piaget, the child elaborates a more and more adequate knowledge of reality. It is precisely the successive forms of his activity, in the course of his development, that determine his modes of knowledge.

One is often puzzled about where to place such an epistemological interpretation in the theory of ideas. Konrad Lorenz—with whom Piaget and I had the privilege of partaking for several years in succession in a seminar on the psycho-biological development of the child—expressed, at the end of the third year, his astonished recognition of Piaget's place in the epistemological spectrum: 'All along I have thought that Piaget was one of those tiresome empiricists and only now, after studying Piaget's work on the genesis of the categories of thought, I have come to realize that he is really not so far removed from Kant.' On the other hand, some Russian colleagues, who believed Piaget to be an idealist because he did not admit that knowledge of the external world is simply a reflection of the objects in it, posed to him the following leading question: 'Do you think an object exists prior to any knowledge of it?' Piaget replied: 'As a psychologist, I have no idea; I only know an object to the extent that I act upon it; I can affirm nothing about it prior to such an action.' Then someone offered a more conciliatory formulation: 'For us an object is part of the world. Can *the external world* exist independently of and prior to our knowledge of it?' To this Piaget replied: 'The instruments of our knowledge form part of our organism, which forms part of the external world.' Later Piaget overhead a conversation between these colleagues in which he was able to distinguish the following statement: 'Piaget is not an idealist.' In effect, Piaget is quite willing to label himself a 'relativist'—in the non-sceptical sense of the term—because, for him, that which is knowable and that which changes during the genesis of knowledge is the relation between the knowing subject and the object known. Some commentators go further and refer to him as an 'activist', reflecting Goethe's assertion that 'In the beginning was the deed.'

In studying the formation of concepts and of intellectual operations, we have made use of experimental materials and methods which differ somewhat from those of classical child psychology. In associationist or Gestalt-inspired investigations, the child is confronted with elements or configurations; in our investigations, designed to lay bare the operational mechanisms of thought, the child is brought to grips with physical or spatial transformation of the materials. For instance, he deals with problems related to the pouring of liquids from one container to another or with the spatial displacement of rods. We then observe the manner in which—throughout the course of his development—the child overcomes the conflict presented by the variations and constancies involved.

Since we wish to avoid imposing any preconceived notions on our data, our investigations of the child's thought are always initiated by an exploratory method that is adapted to the child's level of comprehension, both in respect to the nature of the questions and to the order of their presentation. The experimenter does not merely take account of the child's responses, but asks also for the child's explanation of them. And, by modifying the questions and the experimental conditions, the investigator seeks to test the genuineness and the consistency of the child's responses. Proceeding cautiously, one attempts to avoid two evils—one of imposing on the child a point of view which is foreign to him, and the other, of accepting as pure currency each of his responses. By means of this exploratory method—one which calls for both imagination and critical sense—we think that we obtain a truer picture of the child's thought than we would by the use of standardized tests which involve the risk of missing unexpected and often essential aspects of his thought.

It goes without saying that results obtained by such a flexible procedure do not readily lend themselves to statistical treatment. Because of this we have undertaken, with M. Bang, the standardization of some of our procedures, adapting them to diagnosis of the reasoning process. When we have once explored the whole range of reasoning exhibited by children of different ages, then we standardize the procedure of investigation. While standardized procedures increase precision, this method loses, of course, some of the plasticity of the exploratory technique. The analysis of our observations then proceeds by the following steps: (1) a qualitative classification of the different types of reasoning; (2) an analysis in terms of logical models; (3) an analysis of frequencies of responses and distributions by ages; (4) a hierarchical analysis by means of ordinal scales. It is noteworthy and reassuring that this hierarchical and statistical analysis lends broad confirmation to the succession of stages of reasoning which had been established in a preliminary form by qualitative and logical methods.

For the analysis of the operations of thought processes, Piaget has borrowed models from modern mathematics, such as Klein's 'four group' (*Vierergruppe*), and the lattices and structures of Bourbaki (algebraic structures, structures of order, and topological structures). He has himself developed a system of weaker structures, called '*groupements*', which are comparable to semi-lattices. The use of such models in no way implies that the psychologist has succumbed to logicism; that is, has decided in advance that the real thought of the child should conform to the laws which govern logical and mathematical structures. Only the facts can decide whether or not it does so conform—in exactly the same way that facts decide whether a statistical distribution obeys one law or another. These models represent the ideal system of all possible operations, while actual thought makes but one choice amongst them. More than twenty years of research have shown that cognitive development approximates these models without attaining them completely.

The effective operations of the child's concrete thinking and of the formal thinking of the adolescent constitute among themselves closed systems of which the most important characteristic is their reversibility. An operation can be defined psychologically as an action which can be internalized and which is reversible—capable of taking place in both directions. Piaget distinguishes two forms of reversibility: inversion (negation) and reciprocity. At the level of concrete logical thought, negation applies to the classificatory operations, and reciprocity of those involving relations. While the thinking of a child of less than six years (in Switzerland, at least) is still characterized by the absence of reversibility, from six to eleven years the child can already achieve, in given situations, one or the other, but not both, of these forms of reversibility. Those more able adolescents who come to handle formal and propositional operations use the two forms of reversibility simultaneously. These two sets of operations form a unitary system which corresponds to the model of the four trans-formations (IRNC) described by Piaget.* This double reversibility confers a higher degree of mobility and coherence upon formal thought.

II

Like many other authors, Piaget describes cognitive development in terms of stages. Whereas somatic and perceptual development seem to be continuous, intellectual development seems to take place in stages, the criteria of which can be defined as follows:

(*a*) Each stage involves a period of formation (genesis) and a period of attainment. Attainment is characterized by the progressive organization of a composite structure of mental operations.

(*b*) Each structure constitutes at the same time both the attainment of one stage and the starting-point of the next stage, of a new evolu-tionary process.

(*c*) The order of succession of the stages is constant. Ages of attainment can vary within certain limits as a function of factors of motivation, practice, cultural milieu, and so forth.

(*d*) The transition from an earlier to a later stage follows a law of implication analogous to the process of integration, preceding struc-tures becoming a part of later structures.

Some of these hypotheses, advanced in connexion with our previous research, have already found confirmation in the five-year longitudinal study which we have conducted. As we have outlined earlier, on the basis of having seen each child on only one occasion and at a definite moment of its development, the different types of reasoning seem to recur in a stable order of developmental stages.

* I = Identity; R = Reciprocity; N = Negation. C = 'Correlate'; NR = C. CR = N; CN = R: NRC = I.

In certain other respects we have noted certain differences between the 'longitudinal' results now obtained and those obtained by former methods. The elaboration of certain notions and of methods of reasoning was found to be slightly accelerated in the subjects of the longitudinal study, as compared to those of the control (cross-sectional groups. This acceleration, probably resulting from practice, does not seem to be the same at all levels. When the child is given a series of reasoning procedures, we notice a tendency to homogeneity and generalization in his reasoning behaviour, which—though slight in the course of the formation of a structure—manifests itself more clearly once the structure has been achieved.

In certain areas, it now seems possible to distinguish some relatively constant evolutionary processes. For example, at regular intervals, the experimenter confronts the child with the problem of the conservation of a given physical quantity. A liquid is poured from one container into another a different size. In early trials the child is impressed by the change in one of the dimensions of the liquid, neglecting others. With naïve commitment to his position, he refuses to admit any conservation of the liquid quantity. Some months later, however, the same child is beginning to doubt his earlier stand. He tries to put the different changes into perspective, without, however, attaining any understanding of their compensation or inversion. One frequently observes a whole series of attempts to establish relationships, from the simplest to the most complex. Still later, the child finally affirms the constancy of the liquid quantity: 'There is the same amount of liquid to drink.' His justifications become more and more coherent; they indicate that he is beginning to comprehend the changes in the liquid as a reversible system of operations in which the modifications compensate each other. Strangely enough, not only does the child seem to have forgotten his own trials and errors, but he considers their possibility quite absurd. The events seem to suggest that a mental structure is built up through a continuous series of trials, but that once it is established, it becomes relatively independent of the process involved in its formation.

A theory of stages remains incomplete, however, so long as it does not clarify the contradiction between two concepts of development— the one stressing the complete continuity, and the other the absolute discontinuity, of stages. It seems to us, however, that this contradiction is more apparent than real. Our first longitudinal investigations led us to a third notion (as a hypothesis), namely, that in the development of intellectual operations, phases of continuity alternate with phases of discontinuity. Continuity and discontinuity would have to be defined by the relative dependence or independence of newly appearing behaviour with respect to previously established behaviour. Indeed, it seems as if during the formation of a structure of reasoning (characteristic of stage A), each new procedure depends on those that the child has just acquired. Once achieved, this integrated structure serves as a starting-point for new acquisitions (characteristic of stage B). These new acquisitions would then be relatively independent of the formative process of the former structure. It is only in this sense that there would be discontinuity in passing from one stage to another.

If this working hypothesis were confirmed, the theory of developmental stages would take on a new meaning. We would then be inclined to regard it as more than a methodological tool. Rather, it would seem to offer a true picture of the formation of the child's intellectual processes.

Three operational structures can be distinguished in the cognitive development of the child; each one characterizes the attainment of a major stage of development; and within each one, sub-stages can also be distinguished.

The first major stage of sensory-motor operations occupies approximately the first eighteen months. It is characterized by the progressive formation of the schema of the permanent object and by the sensory-motor structuration of one's immediate spatial surroundings. The observations and longitudinal studies carried out by Piaget on his own children indicate that this progression originates in the functional exercising of mechanisms that are reflexive in origin, and leads gradually to a system of movements and of displacements. In this way the child's conception of the permanence of objects is brought about. This sensory-motor system is made up of displacements which, if they are not reversible in the mathematical sense, they are none the less amenable to inversion (*renversables*). The displacements made in one direction can be made in the inverse direction; the child can return to his starting-point; he can attain the same goal by different routes. In the co-ordination of these movements into a system, the child comes to realize that objects have permanence: they can be found again, whatever their displacements (even if these be outside the field of vision). Piaget has compared this sytem, which has the characteristics of a group structure to the structure of Poincaré's model of the geometric 'group of displacements'.

One can distinguish six sub-stages in the course of this first major stage of development; their continuity is assured by 'schemata' of action. These schemata are transposable or generalizable actions. The child establishes relations between similar objects or between objects which are increasingly dissimilar, including relations between those objects and his own body (for instance, the extension of the schema of graspable objects to that of invisible objects). Thus a schema can be defined as the structure common to all those acts which—from the subject's point of view—are equivalent.

The development of sensory-motor schemata is distinguished from habit-family hierarchies by the fact that a new acquisition does not consist merely in the association of a new stimulus or a new movement-response to already existing stimuli or movements. Instead, each fresh acquisition consists in the assimilation of a new object or situation to an existing schema, thus enlarging the latter and co-ordinating it with other schemata. On the other hand, a schema is more than a Gestalt in that it results simultaneously from the action of the subject and from his prior experience of accommodation to the object. The schema is thus the result of a process of assimilation which, at the level of psychological behaviour, is a continuation of biological assimilation.

The second developmental stage of concrete thinking operations extends approximately from the middle of the second year until the eleventh or twelfth year. It is characterized by a long process of elaboration of mental operations. The process is completed by about the age of seven and is then followed by an equally long process of structuration. During their elaboration, concrete thought processes are irreversible. We observe how they gradually become reversible. With reversibility, they form a system of concrete operations. For example, we can establish that although a five-year-old has long since grasped the permanence of objects, he has by no means yet any notion of the elementary physical principle of the conservation of matter.

Let us consider one of many possible examples: Given two equal balls of plasticine, the child is asked to roll one of them into a long sausage form, to flatten it into a pancake, or to break it into small pieces. He is then asked, in language appropriate to his level of under-standing, whether the quantity of matter has increased, decreased, or remained the same. This experiment and others similar to it have shown that most five-year-olds assert without hesitation that each change in form involves a change in the amount of matter. Influenced sometimes by the increase in one dimension, and sometimes by the decrease in the other, the child seems uncritically to accept the dictates of whatever aspect of change he happens to perceive. Errors decrease gradually, as the older child becomes more and more inclined to relate different aspects or dimensions to one another, until he finally comes to a principle of invariance, or constancy. This principle may be expressed somewhat as follows: 'There must be the same amount of plasticine all the time. You only have to make the sausage into a ball again and you can see right away that nothing is added and nothing is taken away.'

After a period of gradual construction, and at about seven years of age, a thought structure is formed; as a structure, it is not yet separated from its concrete content. In contrast with the sensori-motor actions of the first stage—which were executed only in succession—the various thought operations of the second stage are carried out simultaneously, thus forming systems of operations. These systems, however, are still incomplete. They are characterized by two forms of reversibility (a) negation, as expressed in the plasticine experiment, in which a perceived change in form is cancelled by its corresponding negative thought operation; and (b) reciprocity, as expressed in the child's discovery that 'being a foreigner' represents a reciprocal relationship, or that left-right, before-behind spatial relationships are relative. At the concrete level, these forms of reversibility are used independently of one another; while in formal thought, they form one unified system of operations.

The gradual formation of this system of reciprocal relations can be observed most readily in an experiment concerning the relativity of points of view in a system of perspectives. The material for such an experiment—conducted by Piaget and Meyer-Taylor—consists of a landscape of three cardboard mountains, and a series of pictures of landscapes drawn from different points of view. The child remains at a given position, while the experimenter moves from one to another. For each position taken by the experimenter, the child is asked to select the picture which represents what the experimenter sees. It is difficult for five-year-olds to realize that another person may see something different from what he (the child) is seeing. However, during the following years, the increasingly operational character of the child's thought leads to a definite progress in his choice of pictures, until finally he solves the problem.

Thus, during the course of this second period of development, we can follow the genesis of thought processes which—at about seven years of age—issues in the elementary logico-mathematical thought structures. Nevertheless, it still requires years before these structures are brought to bear on all possible concrete contents. It can be shown, for example, that the principle of invariance (constancy, conservation) is applied earlier to the quantity of matter than to weight, and still later to volume. In every case, as earlier schemata are integrated into later ones, they are altered in the process. Thus the process seems indeed to be one of genetic construction—a gradual process of equilibration within a limited system of concrete operations. Equilibrium within this sytem is attained at about eleven or twelve years of age. This operational structure, in turn, forms the basis of the development of the formal thinking operations.

The third stage of formal thinking operations beings, on the average, at about eleven or twelve years of age and is characterized by the development of formal, abstract thought operations. In a rich cultural environment, these operations come to form a stable system of thought structures at about fourteen or fifteen years of age.

In contrast to the child at the second developmental stage whose thought is still bound to the concrete here and now, the adolescent is capable of forming hypotheses and of deducing possible consequences from them. This hypothetico-deductive level of thought expresses itself in linguistic formulations containing propositions and logical constructions (implication, disjunction, etc.). It is also evident in the manner in which experiments are carried out, and proofs provided. The adolescent organizes his experimental procedure in a way that indicates a new sort of thought structure.

The following are two of many possible examples of what we mean, one concerning combinatorial or formal logic, and the other, proportionality. In the experiment on combinatorial logic, the child is presented with five bottles of colourless liquid. The first, third, and fifth bottles, combined together, will produce a brownish colour; the fourth one contains a colour-reducing solution, and the second bottle is neutral. The child's problem is to find out how to produce a coloured solution. The adolescent in this third stage of development gradually discovers the combinatorial method. This method consists in the construction of a table of all the possible combinations and of determining the effectiveness or the ineffectiveness of each factor.

In experiments on proportionality, the adolescent is given a candle, a projection screen, and a series of rings of different diameters; each ring is on a stick which can be stuck into a board with evenly spaced holes. The instructions are to place all the rings along the board between the candle and the screen in such a way that they will produce a single, 'unbroken' shadow on the screen—the shadow of 'a ring'. Gradually, the adolescent discovers that 'There must be some relationship', and he tries to find out what relationship it is by systematic attempts, until finally he becomes aware that it is a matter of proportionality. As one bright fifteen-year-old said, 'The thing is to keep the same proportion between the size of the ring and the distance from the candle; the absolute distance doesn't matter.'

These experimental methods of procedure were not 'taught' in our Geneva schools when our subjects were at this age level. Our subjects, at the point of departure for the formal thought structures, discovered these procedures without specific tuition.

In analysing these thought structures, Piaget found that they come more and more to approximate formal models as the subject's experimental procedures become more and more effective. The combinatorial method, for example, corresponds to a lattice structure and the method of proportionality, to the structure of a group. Above all, the formal thought structure, as compared to the concrete, is marked by a higher degree of reversibility. And in this case, the two forms of reversibility already constituted—negation and reciprocity—are now united in a complete operational system. We can say that the new operational abilities formed during this third stage are the abilities that open up unlimited possibilities for the youth to take a constructive part in the advancement of scientific knowledge—provided that his setting offers him a suitable practice-ground and a favourable intellectual atmosphere.

According to Piaget, the genesis of the mechanisms of knowledge cannot be explained by any of the classical factors of developmental theory; it is not due solely to maturation; (we observe only phenotypes, never genotypes); it does not result solely from learning on the basis of experience; (the capacity to learn is itself tied to development); and it does not result solely from social transmission (a child transforms the elements received while assimilating them). Piaget advances the hypothesis that another factor must be 'put into play' with the above. This is the factor of equilibration. It operates in the sense which von Bertalanffy uses in referring to 'a steady state in an open system'.

Piaget postulates that each organism is an open, active, self-regulating system. Mental development would then be characterized by progressive changes in the processes of active adaptation. The fact that, in healthy children and adolescents in our civilization, this continual mental transformation tends none the less towards order and not towards chaos, would indicate—according to this hypothesis—the influence of self-regulating processes, such as those involved in a principle of equilibrium. Operational structures—both concrete and formal—are a special case of this principle of equilibrium. A change in perception, for instance, can be seen as a disturbance of the equilibrium; operations can restore this equilibrium by compensating or cancelling the change.

The stages of cognitive development thus represent a constant progression from a less to a more complete equilibrium, and manifest therein the organism's steady tendency towards a dynamic integration. This equilibrium is not a static state, but an active system of compensations—not a final conclusion, but a new starting-point to higher forms of mental development.

III

According to a current opinion, spatial notions—particularly the constants of Euclidean metrics (the conservation of dimensions, of distances, and of systems of co-ordinates)—are a direct extension of perception. It is as if the representation of space (which is commonly called geometric intuition) were no more than a mere 'cognition' of perceptual data. But a series of investigations on the child's representation of space and on his spontaneous geometry have indicated to us that spatial notions do not derive directly from perception. On the contrary, they imply a truly operational construction. However, the genetic order of this construction does not follow the historical order of discoveries in geometry; it appears to be more closely related to the system of axioms ordered in terms of complexity. Whereas Euclidean geometry was developed several centuries before projective geometry, and topology (*analysis situs*) has more recently become an independent mathematical discipline, the child's conception of spatial relations begins with the abstraction of certain topological relations, such as homeomorphs, which are then integrated into more specific operations and notions of both Euclidean and projective geometry.

By way of example, here are some illustrative examples of the transition from topological to Euclidean 'space':

When the child has passed the scribbling stage (at about three and a half), he is able both in his drawings and by haptic recognition to establish the distinction between open and closed figures. A cross and a semicircle are represented as open figures while, at the same ages, squares, triangles and diamonds are still drawn as closed and not clearly distinguishable figures. Before the child is able, in his copies, to distinguish between different geometrical forms he is able to draw a figure that is connected with or separated from, another closed figure.

One of the most striking characteristics of the stage of topological representation (from about three to seven years) is the absence of principles of invariance, or constancies, regarding the dimensions of objects when the latter are displaced, for distances between fixed objects, and for the employment of systems of co-ordinates. For the child at the preoperational stage, it is as if empty space as well as occupied space possessed elastic dimensions. And it is as a result of the development of his operational activity that he gradually comes to endow his conception of space with an Euclidean structure:

(*a*) For a young child, the dimensions of objects change with their displacement. If two equal-length rods are placed congruently, and one of them is then displaced in a direction parallel to the other so that their extremities are out of line, we found that 75 per cent of our five-year-old subjects maintained that the one which 'has moved' or which 'passes' the other has changed in length relative to the other. From the age of eight, however, 85 per cent of the children maintained with conviction that the dimensions have not changed in spite of the displacement, thus annulling this displacement by means of the reversibility of their thoughts. Their arguments are more or less as follows: 'The rods are still the same length, we have only moved them; what a rod has gained at one end, it has lost at the other—which leaves it the same.' But it is interesting to note that this phenomenon of non-conservation, or of the conservation of length in the face of displacement, appears to be independent of a perceptual estimation of length. According to Piaget and Taponier, the perceptual estimation of the length of two equal-length but off-set lines is clearly better at the age of five than eight, showing that different mechanisms seem to be involved in perceptual estimates and in conceptual judgments.

(*b*) For a young child, the distance between two fixed objects appears to alter when a third object is inserted between them. In contrast to the well-known perceptual illusion, two dolls are estimated as being closer together when a screen is inserted between them because 'The screen takes up some of the room; if there was an opening in it, the distance between the two dolls would be the same as it was before'. Thus the notion of distance seems to be applied at first only to empty space, and the pre-operational child appears to experience difficulty in combining partly filled and partly empty spaces into one over-all space.

At first the represented dimensions of space exhibit 'privileged' aspects; they are not isomorphic. The pre-operational child readily asserts that the distance to be traversed by a lift is greater when it is ascending than when it is descending: 'It takes more effort to look

D

or to climb up than down.' Spatial representations seem thus to be formed more on the basis of subjective motor experience than on perception, with the result that there is initial non-equivalence in the relation of distances. From the age of seven, in contrast, spatial relations are gradually transformed into a system of symmetrical and reversible relations which ensure the invariance of distance, an invariance which the child expresses as follows: 'The dolls have not moved; they are always the same distance apart', or again, 'The room taken up by the screen counts just as much as the empty space does'.

(c) The use of a co-ordinate system is initially blocked by the child's inability to abstract the horizontal and vertical co-ordinates when they are at variance with other indices—this in spite of the fact that the very young child possesses an adequate kinesthetic knowledge of the orientation of his own body in space (*Lagebewusstsein*). If the child of from four to seven years of age is asked to represent and to draw the level of water hidden in a container which is tipped at different angles, he at first represents it as parallel to the base of the container, whatever its position, or even in one corner of the container. It is only after the age of eight that the child discovers the constant horizontality of the water level. He does so by the use of a system of co-ordinates which permits him to place objects and their inclinations into mutual relationship. Once spatial representation meets those Euclidean (and Cartesian) requirements, the operation of measurement becomes possible.

Contrary to the generally accepted hypothesis that sociolinguistic transmission is the primary mechanism of concept formation, the facts disclosed through our research compel us to conclude that language plays a necessary but not sufficient part in concept formation. It is clear, of course, that language is essential to the subject's attainment of conceptual systems that involve the manipulation of symbols. Nevertheless, language still seems insufficient. This seems due to the fact that the component operations constituting logical classes—as a conceptual system—show evidence of being linked by a markedly continuous progression through such elementary behaviours as 'to bring together', 'to take apart', to anticipatory and retrospective processes that precede and go beyond the use of linguistic associations or connexions.

The children whose classification behaviours we studied ranged from three to eleven years in age. Employing a wide variety of techniques, we engaged them in tasks requiring them to classify objects and pictures. After analysing the protocols of the examination of over 2,000 children, we are led to the following conclusions:

(*a*) The operations of classification originate in essentially active behaviour. In their primitive stages they are framed in the sensory-motor schemata concerned with noting and acting upon resemblances and differences. Long before they are able to handle the verbal counter-parts of these concepts, children of two or three years succeed in bringing objects together in terms of their resemblances—sometimes shouting with the glee of the true classifier, 'Oh—the same! The same!' When small children attempt to classify objects, they tend to construct spatial or figural collections. These figural collections seem to show the child's thinking to lie mid-way between his notion of the object and that of the class.

(*b*) At first, children are unable to distinguish between the two criteria of all logical 'classes'—comprehension and extension. These criteria are: *Comprehension*—all those essential and distinguishing properties which must be possessed by *any* item to be counted as a member of a given class or genus. The comprehension, thus, consists in general and specific properties. *Extension* = the sum-total of all those items which are members of a given class. In other words, the extension is 'the population' of the class. The earliest glimmers of the child's grasp of 'comprehension' are seen in his progressive tendency to assimilate—put together—elements (objects, pictures, etc.) on the basis of their resemblances and differences. The child's first notion of 'extension' appears in the way he begins to make particular spatial arrangements among objects.

Here is an example. When the child of three or four years is given the task to classify counters or tokens of different forms, colours, and sizes—to put together those which are alike—he tends to put them together, one after the other, on the basis of their resemblances. He seems to have no immediate recognition of the whole set of those tokens or objects which are alike, say in form or colour or size. And his successive assimilations of objects into a group seems to be effected on the basis of their spatial proximity and *in terms* of this proximity. Similar objects are placed next to each other in either linear or two-dimensional arrangements. These resemblance relationships, however, are still extremely unstable. At the earliest level of classification pro-cedure, the child loses sight of his criterion—the one with which he began—and ends up, instead, with a complex kind of 'object'; he might call it a 'train' or a 'house'. However, it is the composition of elements—chosen by successive assimilation—into a spatial whole which seems to foreshadow the child's eventual grasp of the notion of the extension of a class.

(c) The child's ability to co-ordinate 'comprehension' and 'extension'—hence truly to classify—depends upon his control of the logical quantifiers 'one', 'some', and 'all'. Such control depends in its own turn upon a progressive elaboration of logical activities of the type: All A's are B's but only B's are A's. To put this in formal terms: $A + A' = B$, provided that A' is not an empty class.

An illustration of how this behaviour progresses is seen in the following example. A row of counters is placed in front of the child. The counters consist of a series of blue and red squares, with a few blue circles among them. The child is asked questions phrased carefully so as to omit the ambiguous word 'some'. We ask him to consider a proposition coming from some other child—say, Tony: 'Tony said all the circles were blue. Now, what do you think? Was Tony right?' A mistaken reply typical among our five-year-olds would be like this: 'No, Tony was wrong, because there are also blue squares.' In fact, the child reasons as if the question has been 'Are all the A's also all the B's?' Among the correct answers,* arguments appear which show the child's understanding of the fact that the A's are some of the B's. 'Yes, Tony is right—all the circles are blue, but not all the blue ones are circles; there are blue squares, too.'

(d) The quantitative aspect of the logical concept of class inclusion, in which if all A is B, then B includes A ($B > A$), depends upon the prior formation—full of snares and pitfalls—of a hierarchical system of classes. And the logic of inclusion arises, moreover, out of the psychological elaboration of two types of operations. (1) The inverse relationship of logical addition and subtraction (different from our conventional arithmetical notions of these operations) is represented as follows: If $(A + A' = B)$, then $(A = B - A')$. (2) The complementarity of A and A' with respect to B is expressed in this way: All A's are B's, and all A's included all those B's which are not A's.

Although the notion of the inclusion of members in a class is foreshadowed in the child's early semantic frame of reference and is learned along with his learning of language, something more is needed before the child masters the operation of logical inclusion. In our experiments with children around six years of age, it has often happened that children who already understand that all ducks are birds, will yet maintain that you could take all the birds away and still there would be ducks. Moreover, while some children maintain that not all birds are ducks, they may go on still to say something like this: 'You can't tell

* Twenty per cent among six-year-olds, 50 per cent at seven years, and 50 per cent at eight years, with 80 per cent at the age of nine.

which kind there are more of in the world. There are too many to count.'

Some children show signs of transition to a higher level, during which the classes A and B are thought to have the same extension: 'Ducks are birds; it's the same thing,' says the child, 'so there are the same number of both.' Everything seems to show that a young child can compare A and A' only while neglecting B. Or else he can only compare A and B while neglecting the complementarity of A and A'. In the end—some years later—the child finally understands that $B > A$. And he expresses his logical reasoning in such statements as: 'There must be more birds than ducks. All those which aren't ducks are birds, and they have to be counted along with them.' The above experiments and many others confirm our hypothesis that operational behaviour and activity makes possible and extends beyond the eventual use of linguistic and other forms of symbolic manipulation.

(e) The psychological development of such conceptual systems as those of logical addition and multiplication of classes is synchronized and proceeds all of a piece. It is during the same period that two other signs of progress appear. On the one hand the child overcomes the obstacles which block his understanding of the fact that classes can be ordered into a system of hierarchies. On the other hand, he gradually learns to classify elements according to two or three criteria at once. And he can be observed to do this in experiments dealing with matrices, or class intersection—in which the common element in a given row and a given column must be found.

(f) The ability to 'shift' criteria, once achieved, allows the subject to consider a collection of objects from several points of view—either in succession or simultaneously. This is a characteristically conceptual activity rather than a perceptual one. The early interplay of the processes of anticipation and retrospection lay the groundwork for this later ability to 'shift'. When the child is able to predict several possible ways in which objects might be classified (at about seven to eight years or older), his mode of expressing anticipation gives evidence of his retrospective processes. For example, he will say: 'Must I first classify them by colour and then by shape or size?' This indicates the child's inclination to reconsider—to look back—and choose a criterion which he had earlier considered only as a possibility. And as we have pointed out before, this process of anticipation and retrospection has their roots in sensory-motor activity, and leads up to operational activity. And it is the essential mobility of operational behaviour—both mental and physical—which allows for every transformation to be cancelled or compensated for by its inverse. And this latter we believe to be one of the main underlying mechanisms forming the systems of logical classification.

The author wishes gratefully to acknowledge the kind help of Mr G. Seagrim and Mrs M. J. Aschner in the translating and editing of this chapter.

REFERENCES

1. PIAGET, JEAN, 1936, *La naissance de l'intelligence chez l'enfant*, Neuchâtel and Paris: Delachaux and Niestlé; 1952, *The Origins of Intelligence in the Child*, New York: Internat. Universities Press.

2. PIAGET, JEAN, 1937, *La construction du réel chez l'enfant*, Neuchâtel and Paris: Delachaux and Niestlé; 1954, *The Construction of Reality in the Child*, New York: Basic Books.

3. PIAGET, JEAN, and SZEMINSKA, ALINA, 1941, *La genèse du nombre chez l'enfant*, Neuchâtel and Paris: Delachaux and Niestlé; 1952, *The Child's Conception of Number*, London: Routledge and Kegan Paul.

4. PIAGET, JEAN, and INHELDER, BÄRBEL, 1941, *La développement des quantités chez l'enfant*, Neuchâtel and Paris: Delachaux and Niestlé; (1962, 2nd edition).

5. PIAGET, JEAN, 1945, *La fonction du symbole chez l'enfant*, Neuchâtel and Paris: Delachaux and Niestlé; 1951, *Play, Dreams, and Imitation*, New York: Norton.

6. PIAGET, JEAN, 1946, *Le développement de la notion de temps chez l'enfant*, Paris: Presses Universitaires de France.

7. PIAGET, JEAN, 1946, *Les notions de mouvements et de vitesse chez l'enfant*, Paris: Presses Universitaires de France.

8. PIAGET, JEAN, and INHELDER, BÄRBEL, 1948, *La représentation de l'espace chez l'enfant*, Paris: Presses Universitaires de France: 1956, *The Child's Conception of Space*, London: Routledge and Kegan Paul.

9. PIAGET, JEAN, INHELDER, BÄRBEL, and SZEMINSKA, ALINA, 1948, *La géométrie spontanée chez l'enfant*, Paris: Presses Universitaires de France; 1960, *The Child's Conception of Geometry*, New York: Basic Books.

10. PIAGET, JEAN, 1949, *Traité de Logique*, Paris: Collin.

11. PIAGET, JEAN, and INHELDER, BÄRBEL, 1951, *La genèse de l'idée de hasard chez l'enfant*, Paris: Presses Universitaires de France.

12. PIAGET, JEAN, 1952, *Essai sur les transformations des opérations logiques*, Paris: Presses Universitaires de France.

13. TANNER, JAMES M., and INHELDER, BÄRBEL, 1956, *Discussions in Child Development*, London: Tavistock.

14. 1956, *Le Problème des stades en psychologie de l'enfant*, Symposium des Psychologues de langue française, Paris: Presses Universitaires de France.

15. PIAGET, JEAN, and TAPONIER, SUZANNE, 1956, 'L'estimation des longueurs de deux droites-horizontales et parallèles à extrémités decalées', *Arch. Psychol.*, No. 32.

16. INHELDER, BÄRBEL, and PIAGET, JEAN, 1955, *De la logique de l'enfant à la logique de l'adolescent*, Paris: Presses Universitaires de France; 1958, *The Growth of Logical Thinking from Childhood to Adolescence*, New York: Basic Books.
17. INHELDER, BÄRBEL, and PIAGET, JEAN, 1959, *La genèse des structures logiques élémentaires, Classification et sériations*, Neuchâtel and Paris: Delachaux and Niestlé.

CHAPTER 6

HOMEOSTASIS, NEEDS AND VALUES

BY C. A. MACE

I

'Science', it is said, 'is not concerned with values. When applied to human affairs it can assist in devising means: it has nothing to do with ends.' These assertions are apt to pass unchallenged, but starkly confronting them are the following facts. Medical science aims at promoting 'health' and preventing 'disease'. Biologists speak of 'survival value', of biological needs, even of biological 'norms'. The social sciences are concerned with the welfare of man in society. But it is in psychology that one meets the sharpest contradiction between practice and profession.

The educational psychologist behaves as if he knows what is good for the child. The psychotherapist behaves as if he knows what is good for the patient. The occupational psychologist conducts himself as though he knows what is good for the workers. *And so in fact they do.* When they say, as they often do when challenged on the point, that their science is not concerned with values, they are merely being inconsistent. This inconsistency is not peculiar to applied psychology. Many of the most general of the theoretical concepts of psychology are evaluative. 'Adjusted' is covertly evaluative. So is 'integration'. So, too, is 'co-ordination'. So, even, is the concept of a 'learned response'. All these concepts require to be defined in terms of adaptation to an end, or of fitness for a purpose. Each of these concepts involves a reference to a 'goal' or purpose; and in most cases the purpose is one which the psychologist implicitly endorses. And the responsibility for clearing up the present confusions in this situation rests upon the theoretical psychologist. It is for him to construct the theory which would make the psychologist's professions consistent with his practice.

Nor should it be difficult to do so. The inconsistency has arisen not from within psychology itself but from an uncritical acceptance by psychologists of one particular reading of the philosopher's distinction between the 'positive' and 'normative' sciences. On this reading of this distinction 'values' are opposed to 'facts'. Within psychology itself another reading is possible, that in which the important distinction is between *what is in fact desired* in the ordinary way and what *would in fact be desired* under conditions more favourable to considered choice. This interpretation need not be restricted to any narrow school. It is all too easy to exaggerate the conflicts between the schools of psychology. But when due allowance is made for the confusion of tongues in the psychologists' tower of Babel there is found to be an impressive measure of agreement concerning the nature of man and the goals of his behaviour.

Man can be usefully described as a collocation of drives, propensities or needs, more or less specific and more or less variable in their modes of satisfaction. Initially, these drives are lacking in coherence, but they tend to fall into a sort of hierarchical system, and by being ordered in this way to attain a measure of consistency. A conception of this sort was first presented in a fairly detailed way in Bishop Butler's *Sermons on Human Nature*. Butler describes human nature as a three-tiered hierarchy. At the base of the pyramid lie the particular impulses; at the second level the two regulative principles of Cool Self-love and Benevolence; and at the apex the supreme controlling agent Conscience. The schema is reproduced with remarkable fidelity in the system of McDougall with his three-tiered hierarchy of instincts, sentiments and the master sentiment of Self-Regard. Nor is the pattern very different in Freud, who has his own three-tiered hierarchy of Id, Ego and Super-Ego. If McDougall may be described as Butler in modern dress, Freud might be described as Butler in fancy dress. But the analogies though instructive must not be pressed too far.

All accounts of this general type would seem to assert or imply that 'the good for man' consists in the mutual adjustment of his needs and in their harmonious satisfaction, in the attainment, that is, of the greatest satisfaction on the whole and in the long run. In principle, the theory is clear and simple, but it requires to be articulated in greater detail. There would appear to be three ingredients in the doctrine: (i) a definition of the primary units in the hierarchical system, (ii) an account of the manner in which these units may be modified and perhaps of the way in which new units may emerge, (iii) an account of their 'integration'.

D*

It does not matter much what we call the basic units—'primary instincts', 'propensities', 'drives', 'needs', 'ergs', 'action potentials' or any of the other names that have been suggested. They can be regarded as functionally equivalent concepts. All enter in the same way into the theoretical systems of this type.

There is some convenience in starting from the concept of a 'need'. It is not a technical term, it is in common use, and it is perhaps less ambiguous than most of the alternatives that might be suggested. We all have many needs, we all experience needs, is there anything odd in that? In point of fact there is something odd in the idea, especially for the natural scientist working within the confines of traditional concepts. The idea carries an aroma of brimstone or what in this connexion is much the same thing, it is suggestive of 'teleology' and evaluation. This indeed is so. 'Need' *is* a teleological concept, and to establish its position in a reputable biology has reopened a number of questions which many had supposed to be closed. This is, of course, a very long story, going back to Aristotle, and his idea of 'final causes'; but a more convenient point of time at which the story may be taken up is that at which the philosopher Spinoza presented to the world his concept of *Conatus*. 'Everything that is in itself', said Spinoza, 'endeavours to persist in its own being.' The suggestion seems to be that everything *whatever* resists change, and if forcibly changed tends to revert to its prior state. Spinoza was mistaken in supposing this to be true of everything whatever, but it would seem that it *is* true of living things. As Broad has observed, 'modern physiology agrees entirely with this doctrine of Spinoza's and its researches have established it in much greater detail than Spinoza could have dreamt of'. Evidence in support of it can in fact be adduced from all the biological sciences. The increasing use by biologists of a principle equivalent to that of Spinoza's *Conatus* means that in effect scientists have now two contrasted models for the description of causality in Nature.

II

The first is the model of the inert body, of a thing that does not move until it is pushed, of a thing that does not change in any way until something else acts upon it. The paradigm of this is the classical billiard ball.

Contrasted with this is the model of the inherently active system— the sort of thing that behaves and continues to behave in a characteristic way until something interferes to change its behaviour. The distinction might be illustrated by reference to the contrast between material things as they appear in ordinary perception and material things as described by physics. The billiard ball sensibly appears to be, in itself, an unchanging, homogeneous inert body, whereas physics describes it as a system of atomic or subatomic elements moving or changing in characteristic ways, and continuing so to move or change until something comes along to change the ways in which they move and change. Both accounts may well be correct since properly stated they are not inconsistent; but it also well may be that the thing as it appears is a perceptual artefact—a perceptual artefact in the sense in which the phi-phenomenon is so. It well may be the case that the second model is *par excellence* the model of all scientific descriptions, and that the first is *par excellence* the model of prescientific thought. Be this as it may, many examples of the use of this second kind of model could be cited. Of greater interest to psychologists is one that is found in contemporary neurology. The traditional conception of the nervous system portrayed it as a structure that remained inert in the absence of stimulation, like a dead electrical circuit before the current is switched on. To this is opposed the idea of the nervous system as an *active* system which continues to tick over in a characteristic way in the absence of stimulation. On this view the function of the stimulus is not to induce activity in a structure previously inert but to modify an activity already in progress. The thesis with which Hebb opens his argument in the *Organization of Behaviour*[1] turns on a distinction of this kind. It is, however, of historical interest to note that a similar function is assigned to peripheral stimulation in Descartes' account of reflex action. The peripheral stimulus merely helps to influence the course of the animal spirits on their way from the heart to the executive organs.

Now, this second type of model would seem to be the more appropriate for the understanding of needs. A system acting under the stress of a need can be described as one which has the following characteristics:

It is a system for which there is a certain possible state such that when the system is in that state it is quiescent (or free from stress or tension). When this state is absent or disturbed the system becomes active and, in a variety of ways, accidents apart, it continues to be active until that state is established or restored.

We may say of such a system that its activity is 'goal directed', and that the state in which it would be quiescent or free from tension is its end or goal. This is a definition of the expression 'goal directed'. Alternatively, we may say that the system has a *need*, and that what it needs is defined as the 'goal' of its activity.

This formula defines the abstract and limiting case of a system with a single need. We can conceive a more complex system for which there are *n* such states; and if that system were a living thing we could say that those *n* states were the ends or goals of its life. If the system in question could introspect and by introspection could define its goals prior to their attainment then we could say of such a system that it 'knows what it wants'. This, too, is *only* a definition, but it is a definition which may have some importance, since it implies conditions under which an introspective report might be validated. If, for example, the System says 'I want *x*' and then giving it *x* does not produce the appropriate kind of quiescence, this is evidence that the system does not really know what it wants. The system does not *really* want *x*. It merely *'thinks it wants x'*.

This account of a need is much too abstract. It can, however, be put much more concretely. Take first a simple, hypothetical case of a system under the stress of a need. Suppose that you had a billiard ball that behaved like a rabbit. Suppose, that is to say, that when you placed this billiard ball in the middle of a perfectly level billiard table it rolled into one of the corner pockets. When you replaced it in the middle of the table and tilted the table so as to raise the level of the pocket, the ball rolled *uphill* into the pocket. When you placed an obstacle in its way it made a detour round the obstacle and again into the pocket. You then put it in the centre of a complicated maze, and after a certain amount of apparently random rolling in and out of blind alleys it escaped from the maze and away again into the pocket. And so for all other variations. The ball is inert or quiescent only when it is in its pocket. Under all other conditions it is 'spontaneously' active, variously active, and it continues to be spontaneously active except when it occupies its pocket. What in these circumstances would we be inclined to say? We should say, shouldn't we, that the ball behaves as though for all the world it were alive, and that it had 'an instinct' or drive impelling it to its pocket. In the terminology here adopted it behaves as if it acted under the stress of a need to occupy a pocket.

Of course, billiard balls do not behave like that. But the importance of this ridiculous hypothetical case is that it draws attention to the fact that we can properly say that a system is active under the stress of a need without introspective evidence, and without any evidence regarding the internal constitution of the system in question. We say this solely on the evidence of its observed molar or macroscopic behaviour. It was McDougall, the arch anti-behaviourist, who was the first to give (without perhaps fully realising what he was doing) a 'behaviourist' analysis of purposive behaviour. The marks of behaviour set out in his *Outline of Psychology*[2] are broadly those contained in the above description of a system under the stress of a need.

A billiard ball does not behave like a rabbit, but the rabbit does. So consider the rabbit. The point of special interest in the rabbit or other organism is the great variety of its activities which are goal directed in the sense defined and the great variety in the ways in which any particular goal may be attained. An impressive survey of the varieties of goal-directed behaviour has been given in E. S. Russell's *Directiveness of Organic Activities*.[3] This survey is impressive not only for its range but also for the generality with which the principle is displayed. Three types of goal-directedness are distinguished by Russell—the behavioural, the physiological and the morpho-plastic. The need for warmth, for example, can be satisfied by increased vigour of bodily activity, by the physiological mechanism for the regulation of body temperature or, as a longer term policy, by the growth of hair. If we extend the survey further to cover the relevant facts of psychology and the social sciences, other forms of behaviour directed to the maintenance of an optimum temperature can be distinguished—such as the making of clothes and the construction of thermally insulated buildings.

III

The most familiar form of physiological goal-directed activity is that which has come to be described as 'homeostasis'. Of outstanding importance in the development of this concept is that in it we begin to pass from mere description to explanation, and the sort of explanation that can be given in terms of—to use Sherrington's expression—'understandable chemistry'. In fact the explanation of the behaviour of the simplest form of homeostat can be given in terms of understandable physics. It is not surprising, then, that homeostasis has tended to become the model for the interpretation of every kind of goal-directedness.

But homeostasis is not enough. This concept is of its greatest value when it is restricted to the case in which (1) the norm is defined in terms of some internal condition of the organism, (2) this norm is merely maintained or restored and (3) it relates to some specific need as contrasted with the general welfare of the body or the personality as a whole.

In this statement the term 'norm' is used in the sense in which it is strictly synonymous with that of the term 'end' or 'goal' as above defined. But at this point it is convenient to mention a point on which misunderstanding might arise. A norm or end state need not be conceived as a *static* or *unchanging* condition of the organism. On the contrary, we may here again prefer the model of the *inherently active system* to the model of the *inherently inert system*. When a homeostat restores the normal state that state *may itself be a state of change*. The cycle is: the system ticks over in a normal way, it is disturbed, and it changes its activity until it has restored the condition of ticking over in its normal way. And even to describe the normal state as one of ticking over may be to write down the complexity of the normal activity presupposed. Certainly as we pass from the simpler so-called 'biological' needs to the more complex 'psychological' and social needs the more frequently shall we describe the so-called end *states* in terms of optimal rates and forms of change. There is a very old dictum to the effect that 'All consciousness is consciousness of change'. It might be paralleled by the dictum 'All life is living through change.' Neither psychology nor biology nor sociology can find much use for the concept of an inert substance or system in a static state. With this general understanding we can continue to use the expressions 'end state' and 'norm'. And using these expressions with this understanding we can proceed to extend or generalize the concept of homeostasis in three ways.

(*a*) The first extension would cover the case in which what is maintained or restored is not so much an internal state of the organism as some relation of the organism to its environment. This would take care of the facts of adaptation and adjustment, including adjustment to the social environment. This would go part of the way towards a clearer and more precise analysis of the vital concept of a 'well-adjusted personality'.

Among the simplest examples of homeostatic maintenance of a relation to the environment is that of the 'following response' (studied by the ethologists) either in its normal form or the variants which arise through 'imprinting'. The activity is such as to maintain a constant relation to a leader in the field of perception, be the leader a hen, a man or a clockwork toy. Incidentally, the case is instructive in indicating a necessary correction of the odd Freudian theory of the Death Wish. Freud's Death Wish is essentially a homeostatic process directed to the restoration and maintenance of an inorganic, lifeless state. The theory of the Death Wish is tied up with another of Freud's odd theories—that every response to a stimulus is directed to the removal of the stimulus. It is not clear why Freud rejected the traditional doctrine that this is true only of responses to nocive or painful stimuli. On traditional accounts the law is: responses to nocive or painful stimulation are directed to the removal of the stimulus; the response to beneficial, pleasurable stimuli is directed to the maintenance of the stimulation. Normally the 'Death Wish' is kept under control by a 'Life Wish'. The 'will to live' or wish to live is directed to the maintenance of certain forms of stimulation and activities for their own sake. This traditional doctrine is surely not just psychology: it is common sense.

(b) The second extension of the concept of homeostasis would cover the case in which the goal, end or norm is some state or relation which has never previously been experienced. There is clearly no reason to suppose that every process of the homeostatic type consists in the maintenance or restoration of a norm. There is no reason whatever to suppose that the process always begins in a state of equilibrium which is then disturbed. Life may *start* in disequilibrium and in maladjustment, so that when the goal-directed process reaches its destination a state or relation is established that has never obtained before. There are, at any rate, many cases in which we require the concept of homeostasis to be extended so that it may apply not only to the *restoration* of an equilibrium but also to the discovery of new equilibrial states.

In social processes the two forms of homeostasis correspond to the two main forms of Utopianism—the nostalgic and the prospective—the one longing for the restoration of a golden age of the past, the other living in hope of a New Jerusalem.

Growth or maturation is an interesting case. Maturation would seem to be a goal-directed process in a sense in which senescence is not. The child has a *need* to grow up, a need in the sense defined. Peter Pan, the mythological exception, was a deviant from the norm. The organism is an active system displaying a characteristic cycle of activity which comes to its characteristic termination in maturity. There is thus a homeostatic theory, in the extended sense, of the process of maturation. It might be supposed that maturation is genetically the restoration or reproduction of a prior state—the state of the parent. But even this is not quite correct. Later generations do not merely reproduce the characteristics of earlier generations. We are most like our parents not at maturity but in old age. This is not a fact of maturation, but falls under the very different concept of 'regression'.

Senescence, in contrast with maturation, is not a homeostatic process unless we are to agree that the process is one which occurs when the Death Wish overcomes the Life Wish. And to explain how this could happen we must add that in part it comes about through a 'mechanical' physio-chemical process. The machine wears out.

Then there are the facts of learning. Three sorts of cases may be noted under this general rubric in which, in the end state of a goal-directed process, something is discovered that has never been experienced before or in which new goals are created. The first is the simple case of cognitive discovery. Observational search by means of the senses is a goal-directed process. So, too, is the process of thought. The facts are set out in the textbooks in the chapter on attention, the chapter which deals with curiosity and the chapter entitled 'The Higher Processes of Thought'. The central facts are that tensions are set up when we are presented with something incomplete, unclear or unfamiliar. A task is prescribed, a problem presented or a question posed. Processes ensue which terminate in the completion of the task, the solving of the problem or the answering of the question. Something is discovered and in discovery tension is relieved. A generalized theory of homeostasis would then cover the perceptual tensions, and by the same token there could be a homeostatic theory of thought. Plato's theory that what we seem to 'discover' is in fact reminiscence or rediscovery is of interest in that, if it were true, discovery could be described as a homeostatic process of the simple type. But, of course, this is most unplausible.

It is clear that in the course of evolution, as in the course of individual development, new goal-directed systems come into being. Man is continually finding new things to go for. Goals emerge through sensory and through motor differentiation. The development of vision and hearing has created the possibility of the major arts. Every sense has in principle its art. For every modality of sense there is a modality of need. So, too, with the development of skills. Movements and activities can be satisfying in themselves and irrespective of their more remote effects. There is clearly a need for movement as such and many needs for specific types of bodily activity. These are paralleled by the needs for what we call 'activity of mind'.

New goals emerge through the well-known mechanisms of 'association', 'conditioning' and the 'transference of affect'. These, too, may be regarded as functionally equivalent concepts. They do corresponding jobs in the several types of learning theory. For the study of values the most important branch of learning theory is that which accounts for acquired tastes. The child dislikes, say, spinach. Skilfully handled, he agrees to eat it 'because it is good for him'. The miracle happens. After a time he likes spinach. Other miracles may occur. He may in the same way acquire a taste for Latin or a need for commendation. These are acquired needs. He becomes, to so speak, homeostatic in respect of his intake of spinach, and homeostatic in respect of his output of good behaviour, which maintains a constant level of the stimulus of commendation.

The principle would seem to be, formally stated: If a system is goal-directed (in the sense defined) to a state E and this state is attained (in greater or less degree) in the setting of, or with the concomitance of, a state C, then the system will become goal-directed to C, and under certain conditions may cease to be goal-directed to E. The operation of this principle is elucidated in detail by studies of conditioning, canalization, studies of acquired tastes and of other ways in which men come to like and to want the things they do like and want.

The study of how men come to like the things they do raises a curious methodological problem—a problem for 'the philosophy of science'. 'Science', it is often said, 'is prediction'. This is plausible in the case of physics and engineering. Physicists and engineers predict how a cantilever bridge will stand up to certain stresses and strains and how a space ship will behave in circling the moon. The criterion of prediction is less plausible in its application to the biological sciences. Theoretically it is possible that the development of the appropriate sense organs should make possible the *visual* perception of non-spectral colours, e.g. colours corresponding to infra-red and ultra-violet rays, but it is *in principle* impossible to predict what these colours would look like. Even less predictable are future tastes and aesthetic preferences. Methodologically market research and psychological aesthetics are the same thing. Market researches find out what sort of flavours people like in their chocolate centres and (if possible) *why* they prefer these flavours. Students of psychological aesthetics find out what sort of pictures people like and why they prefer some pictures to others. If 'science is prediction' market researchers should be able to say what flavours in chocolate centres people will like in the future, and psychological aestheticians should be able to make similar predictions. They should have been able to predict at the time when people liked Landseers that people would come to prefer Picassos, and to predict now what sorts of pictures people would like in fifty or in a hundred years' time. This is a curious consequence of the thesis that science is prediction. For a scientist of the Landseer age to have predicted the preference for Picasso he would have had to have imagined a Picasso —to have produced a Picasso before Picasso did. Few things can be said to be impossible but a simpler hypothesis is that in the biological sciences generally and in psychology in particular prediction is not possible. It is in principle impossible to extrapolate the curves of evolutionary trends. The scientist must be content to be wise after the event: to wait for things to happen and then try to explain why they have happened.

(c) The third way in which the concept of homeostasis can be extended is that in which it would cover second and higher order needs. The various original and acquired needs tend to become mutually adjusted. To this, education and therapy make their distinctive contributions, but it would appear that the mutual adjustment of goal-directed tendencies is in some degree spontaneous. It is found at levels of life below those at which formal education and therapy can operate. An organism, said Aristotle, is a system of organs mutually adjusted to the ends of the organism as a whole. The modern biologist might say that an organism is a system of directed activities mutually adjusted to the goals of the organism as a whole—survival, growth, reproduction, etc. And the psychologist might make a similar statement concerning the nature of a personality.

Freud's 'Reality Principle' is a concept in the same class. Like the 'Pleasure Principle' it is a statement about how people actually behave. Unlike the Pleasure Principle it is not only a statement of how people actually behave under certain conditions; it is also a statement about the way Freud would like people to behave, about the behaviour of which he approved, behaviour which all reasonable and moral men approve. Some psychologists have made the mistake of supposing that the Super-Ego (as described by Freud) is to be identified with 'Conscience' or the supreme ethical control. This was not Freud's view. The Super-Ego is the *primitive unconscious* conscience, the introjected parent; and the conduct prescribed by the Super-Ego is often conduct of which Freud took a dim view. The Reality Principle is the nearest counterpart in Freudian theory to Conscience as conceived by Bishop Butler and other moral philosophers. The Reality Principle is the chief normative concept in Freud's psychology.

This, then, in the sketchiest of outline, is one psychological approach to the theory of values. It rests upon: (i) a generalized concept of a goal-directed tendency provisionally described as a 'need'; (ii) the recognition of the ever-expanding nature of the system of needs and the orientation of learning theory under the paradigm of the acquired taste; (iii) a concept of 'the integration of personality' defined in terms of the mutual adjustment of needs.

IV

This is not the place in which to discuss the relations of the approach here outlined to the traditional philosophical theories, but neither can these relations be entirely ignored. One of the larger issues as philosophers state it is sufficiently familiar:

When we make a value judgment, for example that 'This is good', it has seemed to some that there is being attributed to whatever is judged to have that value a certain distinctive property that it would possess regardless of the emotions, the desires, the needs of those who pass this judgment or the emotions, desires or needs of anybody else. On the other hand, it has seemed to others that the judgment states or expresses a fact about the emotions, desires or needs either of the person making the judgment or the emotions, desires or needs of the members of some 'reference group'. On the first view, value is 'absolute' and 'objective'; on the second, it is relative and subjective. The issue is in part, of course, 'a question of words', a 'semantic' question or a question of 'conceptual analysis'; but this is the sort of 'philosophical' question in which the scientist, whether he likes it or not, has to take some interest. If he talks at all, he must be prepared to say what he means when he uses a word the meaning of which may be ambiguous. 'Good' is a word with many meanings, some are trivial, others important. In some of these meanings whether a thing is or is not good is not a question of empirical fact. In other senses it is. There are senses of 'good' in which whether a thing is or is not good can only be decided by reference to the observable facts.

We may note a certain difference between the philosopher's reaction, and the scientists' reaction to ambiguity and plurality of meanings. There are philosophers of many different kinds. There is the sort of philosopher who scans the heavens for archetypal meanings; as Plato did. There is in contrast the sort of philosopher who is more interested in the ordinary meanings of words as used by ordinary people in the ordinary way. Gilbert Ryle for example has playfully reminded psychologists that 'mental' can mean 'to be queer in the head'. Plato was concerned with aristocratic meanings, Ryle with the egalitarian classless society of meanings. There are philosophers who are interested in meanings for which no suitable words are available. Some invent new words, others take up familiar words and use them in unfamiliar senses. So do scientists.

The scientist is not especially interested in actual uses of a term or with archetypal meanings, but with uses, actual or possible that can be turned to scientific account. He claims too the right to use familiar words in special senses and to invent new words. Meanings can be distinguished as we distinguish, say, beetles, divided into genera and species; or they can be considered as values of a variable. 'Good' is a word in point. It is clearly a word of very many meanings. This is not a matter of ordinary ambiguity. It is not just a matter of six or seven meanings but rather of six or seven hundred.

We can start, for example, with the simple degenerate but actual case in which 'This is good' means what is meant by 'This is what I like here and now'. In a judgment of this form there are three constants other than the thing or situation judged to be good. There is 'I' the agent, 'like' the psychological function that is exercised and the 'here and now' which defines the conditions under which the agent exercises the function in relation to the thing judged to be good. Replacing the constants by variables we obtain a formula of the form 'x exercises the function y under conditions z' in relation to the object upon which the judgment is passed. We may then assign any of a large number of values to each of the variables and obtain an indefinitely extensive series of possible meanings to the judgment of value. Of these a very considerable number may be of scientific interest and importance. Thus, substituting values for the *agent variable* we obtain judgments of the type 'This is what I should like, what *all members of my social class* would like, what *all members of my culture* would like, what *all men* would like, what all *sentient beings* would like'. For the *function variable* we may substitute liking, approving, needing and so forth. From variations of the *conditions variable* we obtain judgments of the form: This is what x would like under *all ordinary* conditions, or what x would like under an immense variety of other specifiable conditions.

There are possible, and interesting, theories of value which would take 'needs' as the constant for the *function* variable. Many possibilities are left open in regard to the *agent* and the *conditions* variable. The following, for example, are two interpretations of the meaning of 'This is good' derived from the basic formula in the way described:

(*a*) This is what would give satisfaction to the needs of any individual on the whole and in the long run.

(*b*) This is what would give satisfaction to the needs of any human social group on the whole and in the long run.

The first interpretation gives meaning to the statement that the good for the individual lies in the 'integration' of his personality. The second gives meaning to the statement that the good for a society consists in an analogous sense in the integrated satisfaction of social needs. On both interpretations the question whether this or that is or is not good becomes an issue of fact—to be decided by observations of actual needs under particular conditions and by inferences from these observations to the needs that would arise under other conditions.

The procedure here consists not in selecting from common usage one particular meaning but in suggesting or prescribing a meaning. This is common scientific practice, but there is nothing arbitrary in this. Meanings are defined and prescribed in accordance with principles. The term as defined must have application, and its applicability must be determinable in any given case by objective tests. Psychologists have not been quite so good in the use of these techniques as other natural scientists, but examples can be cited also from psychology.

V

This can be usefully done for the slippery concept of value. It has already been done, in a sort of way, by the biologists in their discussion of biological needs, biological norms and in their treatment of 'survival values', but as commonly employed these are poverty stricken and basically unscientific concepts. They are poverty stricken in their limitation to the more elementary needs, for food, the avoidance of injury, reproduction, etc., and they are unscientific in that they do not correspond to any natural grouping of the facts. The expression 'biological needs' can in fact be defined only as denoting those needs in which, up to the present, biologists have happened to take an interest. The restriction arises from the accidents of history. There is no logic in a principle which includes the need for food, but excludes the need for change or variety of food, or if it includes these and excludes the more specific food needs of the gourmet. There is no logic in a concept which allows the study of the food choices of rats in an experimental cafeteria but forbids the study of food choices of human beings in a restaurant. There is no logic in a conception of biological needs which covers the case of a bird building a nest but excludes the case of a community building a cathedral. There is no logic in a concept which covers the interest of a cat in a mouse, but excludes the interest of the scientist in the cat's interest in the mouse.

Psychologists have taken over from nineteenth-century biologists these poverty-stricken concepts of *biological needs* and *survival values*. They have interpreted food-seeking behaviour in terms of bodily self-maintenance, and mating in terms of race or species perpetuation. In point of psychological fact it requires some degree of sophistication or hypochondria to make the maintenance and culture of the body a conscious goal. Most men and all of the lower animals eat and drink not in order to maintain or to improve the health of their bodies, but because the food and the drink taste good. Providentially much of what they eat and drink is good for their bodily health, but often what they are impelled to eat and drink does them no good. Most human beings and all of the lower animals mate not because they feel a need to perpetuate their species, but because they find mating a pleasurable experience. In civilized human societies elaborate measures are taken, in mating, to *avoid* the perpetuation of the species. In general, human beings are activated not so much by the so-called 'biological needs' as by *psychological* needs—the needs for certain kinds of conscious experience. This becomes obvious if we consider certain hypotheses.

Suppose (*a*) that the life of man could be prolonged to, say, two hundred years if everyone were trained to sleep for twenty hours out of every twenty-four (there is a little evidence which makes this hypothesis not entirely implausible). Suppose (*b*) that mental processes can be more efficient in sleep or in hypnotic trances than in normal waking life (there is not *much* but there is *some* evidence for this idea). Suppose that sufficient evidence was adduced for these two hypotheses to make it worth while to carry out a study of the opinion survey or market research type asking the subjects in the selected population: Given that you could live for two hundred years five-sixths of your life in which you would be asleep or in a hypnotic trance during which time you would work more efficiently as a sort of physiological computer than as a normal conscious person which would you choose: that sort of life or the usual sort of life? The choice is between two hundred years of life (of which about thirty-three years would be normal waking life) and about seventy years (of which about forty-six would be normal waking life). An opinion survey with only a small but representative sample gives a significant difference in favour of the shorter but gayer life. There is, it would seem, a felt need for consciousness, subject, of course, to the proviso that certain forms of conscious experience should preponderate—certain sensuous experiences, certain forms of mental activity, certain conscious human relations. These are *psychological* needs. Survival value is at least a two-dimensional variable. The life that any living thing endeavours to prolong is *life of a certain kind*. An adaptation can be said to have survival value for any creature when it either prolongs or increases the quality of the life that is characteristic of the creature in question. In general the quality of life characteristic of any creature must be defined mainly in psychological terms.

VI

To redefine the evaluative concepts of biology in terms of 'psychological needs' reduces the gulf that divides these evaluative concepts from those of traditional philosophy and the gulf is reduced to the extent to which the good for man is defined in terms of the fulfilling of his needs. The concept of this good as that which would give satisfaction on the whole and in the long run satisfies some at least of the scientific requirements. It has application and its applicability is subject to observational tests.

The concept is of course subjective in the sense that it refers to 'needs', but is objective in the sense that what a man *would* desire under specified conditions, like what he *does* desire under specified conditions, is an issue of fact. In a sense 'good' is a matter of taste, but it is not a matter of taste to say what a man's tastes are or would be.

There remains an ultimate relativity. What is good for man may not be good for other creatures. The moralist has said that he would rather be a dissatisfied philosopher than a contented pig. The pig's comment has not been reported.

The pig might say that he would much rather be a discontented pig than any self-satisfied philosopher. Even the pig has its own distinctive good, needs which it would satisfy, if it could, on the whole and in the long run. Each kind of creature endeavours to persist in its own being, and in so persisting to enjoy its own distinctive quality of life.

So, too, perhaps with cultures, so too with human types. The colour blind may have little need for pictorial art, the tone deaf little need for music. The satisfactions of mathematics are not for the mentally defective. And in the last analysis so it may be for individuals. What is one man's meat may be another's poison. But this is not a matter for the throwing up of hands or the shrugging of shoulders. What is good for Peter may be different from what is good for Paul. The good for Peter may perhaps need to be tailored to his individuality. But what this good will be, like his individuality, will be a matter of fact. What a man *would* desire if he were consistent, if he were reasonable, if he took into account all the things that he desires and their compatibilities, what he *would* desire if he took a long view, what he would desire if he took into account the fact that some satisfactions pall more rapidly than others, what he would desire if he had developed to maturity: all these and many other possibilities are matters of fact, grounded in his nature. We cannot of course directly observe what he would desire under conditions that do not in fact obtain as we observe what he actually desires under conditions obtaining, but statements concerning the former are derivative from empirical observations concerning the latter. In this sense values are objective. It is in this sense and in this sense only that psychology is a normative as well as a positive science. Hence, normative science is a *kind* of positive science. There need be nothing disturbing in the fact that values are relative to a *given* nature, or relative to a level of maturation or to a level of culture. It is to be expected that new values will emerge, new goods discovered with experience and with the acquisition of new powers. Though 'goods' may be in principle predicted it may well be that no man can know for certain what he wants until he gets it, and that when he gets what he wants he will want something else.

There need accordingly be nothing disturbing in the fact that it is for each individual to discover for himself his own distinctive principle for the harmonization of his goals. To make this discovery calls for the exercise of his highest faculties of imagination, intelligence and reason. It is by reason and the resources of science that that issue of fact will be decided—what is it that a man would desire on the whole and in the long run if he were consistent?

To *reduce* the gulf between psychological concepts of value and those of philosophy is not however to close that gap. Why should anyone wish to close it? It is not the job of the psychologist to attempt to settle issues in ethical philosophy. It can be agreed that the uses of the term 'good' are a 'family' of uses, some of which can be arranged in a simple serial or hierarchical order. But most families have eccentric members. In the family of uses of the word 'good' there may well be members which have no obvious relation to other members of the family. This would be so, for example, if there is a use of the word 'good' for reference to some simple indefinable and unanalysable 'non-natural' quality entirely unrelated to what people want—a use in which it would not be self-contradictory to say 'x' is good but no sentient being could possibly want it. There may be categorical imperatives (e.g. 'Love your neighbour as yourself') to which men might respond 'I won't, I can't and I wouldn't even if I could'. To pass judgment on such ideas is quite outside the psychologist's terms of reference.

The possibility explored in this chapter is simply that there are value concepts implicit not only in the various branches of applied psychology but also in general theories of motivation which (like, for example, Freud's Reality Principle) incorporate a judgment to the effect that it would be a good thing if primitive impulses were controlled by reflective and rational consideration of the question: What action will on the whole and in the long run give the greatest satisfaction? To such rational reflection the psychologist can contribute relevant factual data. Such reflection could take the form of a sort of sophisticated hedonic calculus.

REFERENCES

1. HEBB, D. O., 1949, *The Organization of Behaviour*, New York: Wiley.
2. MCDOUGALL, W., 1923, *An Outline of Psychology*, London: Methuen.
3. RUSSELL, E. S., 1946, *The Directiveness of Organic Activities*, London: Cambridge University Press.

Note: This chapter is based upon the author's Presidential Address to the British Psychological Society published in the *British Journal of Psychology*, 1953, 44, pp. 200–210. As revised for this volume it incorporates some themes developed in later publications:

(i) 'Human Motivation in an Affluent Society' in Farber, S. M., and Wilson, R. J. L. (eds.) *Man and Civilization: Control of the Mind*, New York: McGraw-Hill, 1962;

(ii) 'Psychology and Aesthetics', a paper read to the British Society of Aesthetics published in the journal of that Society (1962, Vol. II, 1).

CHAPTER 7

PHYSIOLOGICAL AND EXPERIMENTAL PSYCHOLOGY*

BY OLIVER ZANGWILL

I

In the present chapter, a selection will be given from among the many loosely-related 'inquiries and techniques' which together compose modern psychology. This selection makes no claim to be authoritative, nor even wholly representative of present-day interests and pre-occupations. It is governed first, by the relevance of the studies described to a biological conception of conduct; secondly, by their probable significance as 'growing-points' for future research; and thirdly, by the personal interest which they happen to hold for the writer.

The study of animal behaviour has for long been dominated by two opposing dogmas. The first, commonly called *mechanism*, has sought to account for all behaviour in terms of the quasi-automatic activities of the central nervous system. Its units have been the tropism, the reflex and, more recently, the conditioned reflex. The second, commonly called *vitalism*, has sought to explain behaviour in terms of non-material principles, commonly equated with life or mind. This dichotomy has obviously sprung from the traditional dualism of mind and matter and betrays all the gloomier tints of the Cartesian picture. It has provoked vigorous polemics, dictated by prejudice rather than by evidence, but no agreed method of resolving the dilemma.[1] In quite recent years, however, a fresh point of view has gradually been evolved by behaviour students. This is bound up with the emergence of a new type of behaviour study which endeavours to combine the

* A revised version of the author's chapter, 'Psychology', in PRYCE-JONES, A., 1956, *The New Outline of Modern Knowledge*, London: Gollancz.

rigours of scientific materialism with genuine understanding of the ways of animals. This branch of study, which is associated especially with the names of K. Lorenz and N. Tinbergen, has been christened *ethology*.[2] Although it has arisen under the auspices of zoology rather than of psychology, its obvious importance would seem to justify some short account in the present context.

Ethology is concerned with field-observations of behaviour and their systematic interpretation. Special attention has been paid to the study of inborn (instinctive) behaviour patterns in the lower verte-brates and a serious theoretical attempt made to relate them to the activity of preformed nervous mechanisms. Although it has not yet proved possible to isolate the latter from a strictly neurological point of view, it has already become clear that instinctive behaviour cannot be reduced to a simple combination of reflexes and chain-reflexes of the kind so beloved of an earlier generation of animal psychologists. It is probable, indeed, that reflex action in the traditional sense plays but a small and insignificant part in instinctive activity and that the latter is predominantly subserved by nervous mechanisms of a non-reflex type. At all events, ethologists favour a view of instinct regarded not as a complex reflex system but as a hierarchy of directed activities, motivated from within, and susceptible to priming and release at a variety of levels.[2] Although this conception is open to objection, and is by no means generally accepted by scientists, it provides a con-venient framework within which to group the observed facts.

Some of the most interesting work carried out by the ethologists is concerned with the external factors, or stimuli, that provoke instinctive responses in the lower animals. As McDougall clearly saw, effective action presupposes effective recognition, and if the action is unlearnt so also must be the recognition.[3] But McDougall undertook no systematic analysis of the perceptual factors which evoke innate behaviour and it is only in quite recent years that a genuine start has been made. In the first place, it is clear that the effective stimulus to any particular response is by no means necessarily the 'biologically appropriate object', as McDougall supposed. For instance, gulls 'instinctively' retrieve their eggs if they are removed a short distance from the nest. But they will also retrieve pebbles, potatoes and billiard balls. Hence it cannot be the egg *as such* that elicits the response but some aspect of it common to all objects within a certain range of size, shape and brightness. In the same way, a male robin will attack not only another male intruding into its territory but also a small tuft of red feathers mounted on a wire.[4] In this case, it is the stimulus of the red breast with which the bird's aggressive responses are innately linked. It would therefore appear that the instinctive behaviour is set off by the perception of a limited feature of the environment which acts as a signal to the immediate performance of appropriate action. To these signals the name *sign-stimuli* has been given. Their significance must clearly depend in some way not yet understood upon inborn constitution.

An amusing observation which has been made in certain birds is that the 'sign-stimulus' which evokes a particular action in the natural state is not always optimal for this purpose. Thus the oyster-catcher actually prefers to incubate a model egg very much larger than its own and if given a choice of several eggs of varying size will always select the largest.[5] It is possible that the tenderness shown by many birds towards the cuckoo at the expense of their own young is likewise due to the 'supernormal' stimulus value of the lusty intruder.

Another class of actions to which ethologists have drawn attention are those known as *displacement activities*. It is not uncommonly observed that an animal will pause while performing some coherent sequence of actions and do something totally at variance with the actual needs of the moment. 'For instance, fighting domestic cocks may suddenly pick at the ground, as if they were feeding. Fighting European starlings may vigorously preen their feathers. . . . Herring-gulls, while engaged in deadly combat, may all at once pluck nesting material.'[6] These activities occur principally under two types of condition. First, when there is an element of conflict in the situation confronting the animal; and secondly, when there is a 'surplus of motivation'. As an example of the first type may be mentioned 'displacement sand-digging' in the stickleback, studied by Tinbergen. When male sticklebacks meet on the border of their respective breeding territories, one or both of them may be observed to 'stand on its head'. This posture is in fact part of the nesting pattern, and is normally adopted to dig a pit for the nest. Under present circumstances, however, it is seen as the outcome of a conflict between the tendency to attack, activated by the presence of a male within the territory, and a tendency to flee, evoked by the presence of a male outside the territory. One may suppose that this conflict becomes acute at the territorial border and issues in a response which ordinarily forms part of an entirely different behaviour pattern. Interestingly enough, Tinbergen has been able to show that certain displacement activities may come to acquire fresh significance in the course of evolution.[7] Thus 'displacement sand-digging' in the stickleback appears to possess the secondary significance of a threat. This further evolution of a displacement activity is known as 'ritualization' and would well repay more detailed study.[8]

The second type of situation under which displacement activities may arise are those in which a highly motivated animal is unable to undertake the appropriate consummatory response. In many species, for instance, the male is unable to perform coition until the necessary sign-stimulus is displayed by the female. If for any reason she should fail to do so, displacement activities derived from a variety of non-sexual behaviour patterns may be observed. It would appear, then, that displacement activity is in general a response either to conflict or frustration. Although it has been studied in detail only in the lower vertebrates, it almost certainly occurs in the mammals as well, and possibly even in man. In particular, striking parallels have been drawn between displacement activities of the kind described and many non-adjustive human actions, more especially those studied by the psycho-pathologist.[9] Although inferences from animal behaviour to that of man are always somewhat risky, it is at least possible that closer studies of the innate activities of animals will throw light on the vexed question of instinct in man.

II

The history of physiology shows how activities ascribed to 'vital forces' by one generation have been resolved into 'mechanical activities' by the next. In psychology, we may discern a somewhat similar trend: Activities ascribed to 'mental forces' by one generation are interpreted in terms of neural mechanisms by its successor. Although this does not necessarily mean that mental processes can be identified with brain processes, it does suggest that many aspects of behaviour formerly attributed to mind may now be more profitably viewed as the outcome of nervous integration. At all events, a body of knowledge is steadily being asssembled which relates the facts of behaviour to the nervous and glandular activities of the body. To this body of knowledge the term 'physiological psychology' is commonly applied. In the present section, some illustrative recent work based principally on animal experiment will be briefly considered. Evidence from human neuro-logical study will be reviewed in the following section.

A very old problem in psychology is that of the perception of spatial relationships. Is this function innate? Or is it, on the other hand, a skill acquired by experience? This issue has been debated at very great length by philosophers and psychologists, but their arguments have failed to produce a clear-cut solution.[10] Recently, however, important light has been thrown on the question by the experiments of Sperry and his co-workers at Chicago.[11] These research workers, approaching the problem from the anatomical standpoint, have been able to show that in amphibians such as the frog or newt it is entirely possible to rotate the eye on its optic axis through 180 degrees, leaving the optic nerve intact. The eye heals readily in its new position but the animal thereafter shows *a complete reversal of all its visual responses*. In attempting to catch a fly, the animal will invariably strike at a point in the visual field diametrically opposite to the actual position of its prey. A similar result is obtained if rotation of the eye is actually combined with section of the optic nerve. Although the severed nerve fibres regenerate, the new connexions preserve the old spatial relationships so that there is again systematic reversal of visual-motor reaction. These reversals, moreover, *never undergo correction*. It may be concluded, then, that in the amphibian at least accuracy of visual localization depends upon inborn nervous arrangements. Individual experience would appear to play a negligible role.

In a further series of experiments, Sperry has shown that localization on the skin is likewise governed by considerations of anatomical pattern. If skin-flaps with their original innervation intact are transplanted across the mid-line of the frog's back, the animal is found to misdirect its reaction to the opposite side of the body. If, for instance, a point on the transplanted areas is gently touched, the frog will perform a 'wiping reaction' with the hind-limb falsely aimed at the *original* site of the skin-flap. Even more striking, perhaps, is the following experiment: The sensory roots of the nerves serving the hind limbs of a tadpole are severed and cross-connected to the opposite sides of the spinal cord. After metamorphosis, a touch applied to (say) the *left* hind foot of the animal is found to produce reflex withdrawal of the *right* hind limb—i.e. the 'wrong' foot is withdrawn. As in the case of vision, these maladaptive actions are never corrected. Although it would be unwise to generalize too freely from these admittedly artificial preparations, it is at least clear that control of adaptive behaviour is very largely vested in preformed nervous arrangements. To this extent, at least, Sperry's findings lend support to nativist theories of space perception.

The physiological psychologist has also given much attention to the bodily factors governing instinctive activity. Whereas the ethologist, as we have seen, is principally engaged in defining the external factors, or sign-stimuli, upon which such activity depends, the psychologist has concentrated his research mainly on the internal conditions necessary for its display. Of these, the most essential are of course the nervous system and certain chemical substances (hormones) secreted into the blood by the endocrine glands. As a rule, though not invariably, nervous and chemical factors co-operate closely in the control of innate behaviour. In the case of fear and rage, for instance, the hormone adrenalin, released through the activity of the sympathetic nervous system, works closely in 'sympathy' with the latter to promote effective bodily action. In the case of sex, testicular hormones in the male and ovarian hormones in the female appear essential to mating behaviour in all classes of vertebrates below the level of the primates. Although the precise mode of action of hormones in relation to behaviour is not clearly understood, it is at least clear that no theory of instinct which fails to take account of their significance can be regarded as complete.

The nervous mechanisms subserving certain forms of instinctive activity, in particular those concerned with reproduction, have been closely studied in recent years and a clearer conception of their nature is beginning to emerge.[12] It has already become evident that the sequence of actions composing an instinctive response, despite its apparently unitary character, results from the integration of activities organized at very different levels in the central nervous system. In the male frog, for example, the 'sexual clasp' is a spinal reflex; the spawning movements are controlled by the mid-brain; whereas release of the female by the male depends on the posterior areas of the forebrain. It follows that at least three component mechanisms, governed by the spinal cord, the mid-brain and the forebrain respectively, are concerned in the total mating pattern. From the neurological point of view, therefore, the simplicity and coherence of the total pattern is somewhat deceptive. As knowledge advances, one may hope that the descriptive schemes of instinct based on the observations of the ethologists will be brought into fruitful relation with the data of direct neurological study.

There is good evidence that the part played by the higher brain centres in instinctive activity becomes progressively more important as we ascend the phylogenetic scale. This is shown first by the progressive liberation of sexual behaviour from the strict control which, in the lowlier animals, is exercised by the sex hormones; and secondly, by the ever-increasing responsibility of the cerebral cortex for the control of sexual activity. In the male, especially, the cortex comes to play a most important part in governing sexual responsiveness. In the male rat, sexual activity is markedly depressed by extensive cortical injury. In the female, on the other hand, mating behaviour survives total decortication. In male cats, sexual activity is even more disrupted by cortical injury than in the rat, but here again the female may continue to mate after extensive injury to the forebrain. It is not yet known whether a sex difference of this kind is likewise characteristic of the primates. It is possible, however, that sexual arousal in the female primate is less dependent on the cortex than is the case in the male. Apart from these sex differences, however, it may be said that sexual mechanisms which, in the lower animals, are subserved by subcortical nervous mechanisms, are represented in the cerebral cortex in the higher mammals and man.

Beach has further shown that parental behaviour in mammals depends on the integrity of the cerebral cortex. In the rat, cortical injury disrupts all aspects of maternal behaviour, the degree of deterioration being roughly proportional to the extent of the injury. Thus normal females begin nest-building several days before the birth of the litter. Animals on whom the operation has been performed, on the other hand, may delay this essential duty until just before the young are born; if the injury is severe, indeed, no nest at all may be constructed. Care of the young is likewise affected by cerebral injuries: thus removal of more than 30 per cent of the cortex renders the mother unable to collect and clean her young in an efficient fashion, and she may fail to retrieve them should they stray from the nest. Although no single element of the maternal behaviour pattern is completely lost, the over-all efficiency of the latter is gravely reduced. It is probable, then, that the coherence of maternal behaviour reflects the integrative activity of the cerebral cortex.

The effects of cortical lesions upon inborn and acquired behaviour patterns are by no means wholly dissimilar. In a long series of admirable researches, K. S. Lashley[13] has shown that maze-habits and kindred skills acquired by training in the rat are significantly impaired by cortical lesions, the degree of impairment being broadly proportional to the extent of the lesion and independent of its locality. Again, we find that no specific component of the behaviour sequence is totally lost, but the various reactions involved become harder to evoke and their over-all integration is significantly weakened. It is also notable that the more complex the habit, the greater the impairment produced by a cortical lesion of given extent. The results of these experiments have led Lashley to the view that complex behaviour patterns, whether inborn or acquired, are not laid down in any very specific fashion in the brain cortex, e.g. in the form of anatomically discrete 'traces' or systems of neuronal connexions, but in some more generalized fashion involving large areas, if not the whole, of the cerebral cortex.

Although no very precise localization of function appears to exist in the cortex of the lower mammals (except with regard to the central representation of the special sense fields), it is likely that a greater degree of cortical segregation occurs in the primates and man. In monkeys, there is good evidence to suggest that skills depending upon immediate memory for their execution are selectively impaired by lesions of the frontal lobes. On the other hand, skills involving fine discrimination, visual or tactual, are affected solely by lesions involving the posterior areas of the brain cortex. In man, as we shall see below, there is evidence that intellectual activity, though in some respects dependent on the cortex as a whole, is almost certainly bound up in its more specialized aspects with the integrity of particular regions of the brain. This task of unravelling the functions of the brain, which a distinguished physicist has dubbed as 'not only one of the tasks, but *the* task, of science', is of course still in its infancy. Yet it may be hoped that the physiological psychologist, along with his colleagues in neurology and neurophysiology, biochemistry and genetics, will play a not unworthy part in its eventual elucidation.

III

The general plan of the central nervous system undergoes no fundamental change as we ascend the vertebrate scale. It follows, therefore, that much information derived from experimental work on animals, especially the higher primates, throws light on the functions of the human brain. In experimental physiology, much use has been made of techniques of electrical stimulation, especially in the study of movement, and the results of this work have taught us a great deal about the organization of motor function in the human cerebral cortex. At the same time, it is often perilous to base theories of human behaviour upon the results of animal experiment. The extraordinary development of the human intellect creates at least a *prima facie* case for a corresponding advance in human cerebral organization, even if the factors upon which it depends are invisible under the microscope. The only method open to us, therefore, is to turn directly to the human nervous system and to inquire whether it has yielded up any of its secrets to the probes of the neurologist.

Neorological inquiry in man cannot, by its very nature, be prosecuted by strictly experimental methods of study. Its place lies within

E

medicine, its *raison d'être* being the relief of nervous afflictions. The experiments with which it is concerned are experiments of nature, unplanned and undesired, but none the less an incidental source of invaluable scientific evidence. In recent years, it is noteworthy that neurologists and neurosurgeons have not only concerned themselves increasingly with the scientific implications of their work but have given constant encouragement to the psychologist to associate himself with their inquiries. It is indeed not too much to suggest that the neurology of today may well provide the psychology of tomorrow with its basic principles.

Among the many lines of neurological inquiry at the present day few have attracted more widespread interest than the experiments of Penfield on the direct electrical stimulation of the human brain cortex.[14] This procedure is of course carried out only in the course of essential brain operations, where it is often of great value in the location of abnormal cerebral tissue. But in view of the fact that the patient is conscious, suffers no pain, and can report freely on his experiences when his brain is stimulated, the method obviously holds great promise as a method of psychological research.

The first important result of this work has been to confirm, in man, the existence of discrete areas of the cortex, stimulation of which produces either discrete movements of the various muscle groups (e.g. fingers, wrist, elbow, shoulder, neck, eyelids) or specific sensations referred to particular regions of the body surface. Although the cortical areas devoted to sensation and motion respectively overlap to a very considerable extent, the general pattern of representation agrees closely with that established in sub-human primates by purely physiological methods. The sensations evoked by cortical stimulation are often described by the patient himself as a numbness, tingling or 'feeling of electricity'. Rarely is the sensory experience identified with a particular modality of sensation, e.g. heat, pain or touch. It is also noteworthy that patients may on occasion report a sense of movement in a particular part of the body without the latter being actually observed to move. Occasionally, too, the 'desire to move' an arm or leg may be reported, again without actual movement taking place. Very rarely, the patient may report a sense of inability to carry out a particular movement. In all these experiments, however, the phenomena induced by stimulation have a distinctly 'intrusive' character. When movements occur, they are experienced as coerced rather than as the outcome of the patient's own intention. Although these phenomena are of great interest, it must be borne in mind that they represent extremely crude and unorganized responses. In Penfield's own words, the movements produced by cortical stimulation '... are not more complicated than those the newborn infant is able to perform'.

A second finding of great interest is Penfield's recent success in inducing both *vocalization* and *arrest of speech* by cortical stimulation.[15] The vocalization is usually a vowel sound and bears more resemblance to the cry of an infant than to true speech. This cry may be intermittent or continuous, depending on the region stimulated, and is often associated with some involuntary lip-movement. Arrest of speech may be regarded as the negative counterpart of vocalization. It is generally evoked by stimulation within the same regions as produce vocalization and is clearly an inhibitory phenomenon. If, for instance, the patient is instructed to count, application of the stimulus causes his counting first to slow down and then to cease altogether. If it is applied before counting begins, the patient is unable to start and is apt to say that he could not think of the numbers. On tests of naming objects, stimulation may provoke temporary forgetfulness of the required names and even some confusion of words, closely parallel to what is often observed in cases of aphasia. Although these phenomena of vocalization and its arrest are evidently primitive, it may be hoped that their further elucidation will throw important light on the neurological basis of language.

Among other interesting findings reported by Penfield are crude visual and auditory phenomena evoked by stimulation of the occipital and temporal areas respectively. The visual effects are generally described as whirling lights, balls of colour, or crudely coloured forms— never, be it noted, as formed visual experiences. Their localization in the visual field is not very precise, but does appear to bear some relation to the area of cortex stimulated. It is also noteworthy that colours are more frequently seen when the stimulus is applied to the primary visual cortex rather than to its immediate vicinity. As regards auditory phenomena, these are likewise crude—being generally described as buzzing or whistling noises. They are usually referred to the contra-lateral ear. No case of elaborate auditory hallucination has been reported to follow stimulation of the particular area of the temporal lobe from which these crude auditory responses may be evoked.

The most dramatic effects of cortical stimulation are to be seen in certain cases of epilepsy in which the pathological disturbance involves the temporal lobe. In these cases, the epileptic seizure typically consists in a curious alteration of consciousness, in which the patient is liable to experience feelings of misplaced familiarity (*déjà vu*), apparent changes in visual or auditory experience, and occasionally dream-like trains of visual imagery. Now in cases in which surgical treatment is expedient in relieving the symptoms, electrical exploration of the brain cortex is often carried out prior to operation. In such cases, Penfield has been able to show that *the characteristic mental features of the seizure pattern can be duplicated, in part or in whole, by direct stimulation of the temporal cortex.* Perceptual illusions, *déjà vu*, alterations in mood, elaborate memory images, and even fragments of dreams, have all been artificially evoked by stimulation in fully conscious subjects. Sometimes, too, elements of past experience which do not normally form part of the seizure pattern are similarly revived. These remarkable findings have led Penfield to the view that 'memory patterns' are actually 'stored in the temporal lobes and are reactivated by the electrical stimulus'.[16] At the same time, it must be borne in mind that such phenomena have been elicited only in cases of temporal lobe epilepsy and no comparable evidence exists regarding the location of 'memory patterns' in the healthy individual. None the less, Penfield's brilliant work has given fresh hope to those who seek the basis of perception, memory and thought in the physical machinery of the human brain.

A complementary approach to the study of cerebral function in man is by way of the changes brought about by injury, disease or surgical removal of circumscribed areas of the brain. The advent of neurosurgery has made possible the study of a large number of human beings who have undergone extensive removals of brain tissue, and careful study of the resulting psychological deficits (if any) might be expected to throw valuable light on the functions of the parts removed at operation. Unfortunately, this type of study is less easy than is often supposed. No two patients, no two brains, and no two operations are exactly alike. Further, the effects of a brain operation on mental capacity depend upon many factors other than the precise locus and extent of the removal. The age of the patient, the nature of the pathological condition, and the time that has elapsed since operation all play an important part in determining the final picture. None the less, the psychological study of neurosurgical cases is an interesting and provocative field and a number of important psycho-physical correlations have already been established.

It has been found by neurologists that lesions of the frontal lobes, if severe, are liable to produce some impairment of thought in its conceptual aspects, often accompanied by deterioration of character. In some cases, however, unilateral removal of a frontal lobe (lobectomy) gives rise to surprisingly little alteration in the psychological sphere. Lesions of the parietal lobes commonly cause a variety of defects in perception and orientation which are of great interest to the psychologist. Difficulties in spatial judgment, in fine manipulation, in route finding and topographical memory, and in awareness of certain aspects of one's own body, are often prominent and have been subjected to detailed analysis.[17] Lesions involving certain regions of the frontal and temporal lobes of the left hemisphere commonly cause the disorder of language known as *aphasia*, in which speech may be disturbed in its expressive aspects, its receptive aspects, or in both. Reading and writing may also be affected, though not always in association with speech disorders. Although these various conditions have been known to neurologists for many years, it is only quite recently that attempts have been made to subject them to more refined methods of psychological examination. Thus the methods of mental testing have made possible a quantitative assessment of intellectual deterioration that is often of value to the neurologist. More refined tests of spatial judgment and mechanical skill are proving of great value in analysing the effects of brain injury, more especially of the parietal lobes. Tests of scholastic attainment are useful in the study of aphasia and kindred disorders of language. Although test methods have to be adapted with some care for use in neurology, and despite certain limitations which they carry in the clinical setting, it may be said that the analysis of brain damage is rapidly becoming a major concern of modern experimental psychology.

It may be objected that neurological study in man has given us no new theory regarding the relation of body and mind. While it remains true that this essential gap in our knowledge remains as large as ever, it may none the less be argued that we are approaching a view of the brain envisaged as the instrument of behaviour rather than as the 'seat of the soul'. Hence the body-mind problem in its traditional form ceases to exercise us. By analysis of the modes of breakdown of human psychological performance, data essential to a proper understanding of its structure and development are beginning to emerge. To give but one example: It is clear from the findings of neurology that human orientation in space is a complex affair dependent above all upon the integrity of the parietal lobes. No theory of orientation which neglects the role of parietal mechanisms is likely to meet with enduring success. In consequence, theories based solely upon observations of behaviour in healthy individuals are unlikely to prove acceptable to the neurologist. The study of neurological symptoms is thus no mere psychological sideline: it is an essential method, comparable to the ablation method of the physiologist, without which data indispensable to psychological theory will be for ever wanting. The neurological approach, while no royal road to psychological truth, is at least a well-worn track not wholly destitute of sign-posts.

IV

The idea of experiment as a method of systematic exploration of human reactions grew up in Germany in the latter half of the nineteenth century. By observing human behaviour under conditions open to systematic variation and control, it was hoped to establish more or less exact relationships between physical stimuli and at least the simpler forms of human experience and reaction. In the sphere of sensation, for example, it proved possible to establish a fairly constant relationship between the intensity of a physical stimulus and the increment necessary for a just perceptible difference in sensation to result. This relationship, known as the Weber–Fechner law, has proved to be an empirical generalization of some value in the study of the human senses. In the sphere of reaction, systematic attempts were made to measure the time required for movements of various types to occur in response to sensory signals of varying complexity. The 'reaction times' thus determined were of some importance in relation to our understanding of movement and its central control and proved relevant to a variety of practical issues involving speedy decision and action. In the field of memory, a large number of experiments were performed in the learning, retention and forgetting of material memorized under set conditions. This led to the formulation of the 'curve of forgetting' and other empirical generalizations concerning memory. Attempts were even made to study thought processes experimentally but the outcome in the opinion of many was meagre. Although it is often said that nothing of the first importance emerged from experimental psychology, it at least set an example of method hitherto unknown in mental science. The pioneers of experimental psychology made it their business to evolve standards of evidence and control in no way inferior to those prevailing in the established sciences. Every student of psychology today stands in their debt.[18]

It has already been pointed out that experimental psychology has not wholly justified the earlier confidence placed in it as a department of science. It soon becomes apparent that human reactions are influenced by internal no less than by external circumstances, and that experimental control of the former is difficult, if not impossible, to achieve. Thus although the stimulus applied to an individual may be controlled with the utmost precision, we cannot so readily control or determine the mental attitude which he brings to its interpretation. It follows that an attempt to make psychology fully objective is unlikely to succeed unless we confine ourselves wholly to the study of behaviour. This, of course, is the answer of the Behaviourists, but it has failed to appeal to those whose interest lies in experience rather than in conduct. In consequence, psychologists who wished to preserve experiment, but at the same time to study experience, have been obliged to reconsider the whole structure of their science. Some, like Bartlett, have taken the position that it is folly for the psychologist to stick to the ideal of constant objective conditions and have attempted to introduce a less rigid conception of experiment in psychology.[19] Others, like the Gestalt-psychologists, have limited their studies to aspects of experience in regard to which variations in mental attitude are of minor importance.[20] Although both approaches have proved fertile, it remains true that the whole conception of experiment in psychology awaits clarification.

The contemporary use of experiment in human psychology is perhaps best illustrated by reference to two lines of inquiry which have developed independently within recent years. The first, which we owe almost exclusively to Michotte, of Louvain, has endeavoured to define the conditions under which various types of causal connexion occur in visual experience. The second, associated especially with Sir Frederic Bartlett, of Cambridge, has been concerned with the experimental analysis of human skills and their breakdown under conditions of stress. Although no really satisfactory theoretical system has evolved from either set of findings, the results well bring out the gain to psychology of an experimental approach to its problems.

Michotte's work has been principally concerned with the conditions under which particular constellations of sensory events give rise to experiences (or implicit judgments) of causal relationship.[21] In a series of elegant experiments, Michotte has been able to show that *mere proximity* of two objects may, under certain specified conditions, be sufficient to produce the impression of a causal relationship. For instance, a disk A may be arranged to move horizontally towards a second disk B, and to remain in contact with it for about half a second. If, then, B is independently set in motion at about the same speed as A, the observer unfailingly reports that *its motion has been caused by the impact of A*. This propulsion effect is reported by all subjects and is considered by Michotte to be largely, if not wholly, independent of past experience. He regards it as a primary phenomenon narrowly bound up with the time-relations and other intrinsic conditions of the experimental setting. If, for instance, the period of contact between the disks is too long, or their respective sizes and speeds too diverse, the impression is partly or wholly lost. Variations in direction of motion may also modify the effect. The regularity of 'apparent propulsion' and its close dependence upon spatio-temporal aspects of the visual field have led Michotte to the view that the impression of causation is given in, or coerced by, the objective conditions of stimulation. Although this strongly nativistic interpretation has been disputed, the empirical value of Michotte's observations is evidently considerable.

In a second series of experiments, Michotte endeavoured to specify the physical conditions that determine our impressions of the permanence and reality of perceived objects. His results indicate that there is a strong tendency for a perceived object to retain its identity even under conditions in which, objectively regarded, it ceases to exist. If, for instance, a rectangular patch of light is moved horizontally on a plain ground towards a large black square, and is then caused to shorten as soon as contact is made, the observer invariably perceives it as *sliding behind* the black square. If, then, the rectangle is reconstituted on the opposite side of the latter, the observer perceives it as if emerging from a tunnel. Thus the patch of light appears to preserve its identity whilst concealed from view. From these and many other ingenious experiments Michotte concludes that the normal appearance of objects as real and permanent can be related to the objective structure of the stimulus field. The orderly character of the perceptual world depends less, he believes, upon inference and judgment than upon certain preformed perceptual reactions to particular constellations of sensory events. In particular, the role of past experience in perceptual organization may be somewhat less central than is often supposed. Although Michotte's interpretations are both tentative and controversial, his work holds great promise for the fuller understanding of the origins of experience.

The work of Bartlett and his school has been predominantly concerned with the analysis of skill in highly trained adult personnel. This work differs principally from earlier studies in so far as the skills under inquiry are relatively complex and studied under conditions as lifelike as laboratory conditions permit. Thus some of the factors involved in flying an aeroplane were investigated by constructing a dummy cockpit in which all the instruments responded to controls in very much the same way as they do in a real machine and all movements made by the pilot were systematically recorded. In this way, 'instrument flying' over a period of several hours could be intensively studied. In other experiments, the conditions obtaining in a variety of industrial skills have been systematically duplicated in the laboratory. Although it can be objected that such experiments must inevitably be artificial, it is none the less true that they permit the study of a great many factors which cannot be isolated under natural conditions of performance. At the sensori-motor level, at least, the propriety of this form of human experiment has been abundantly justified by results.[22]

In the Cambridge experiments, particular attention has been given to the breakdown of skilled performance under conditions of stress and fatigue. In the first place, it is commonly found that well-established skills display a remarkable resistance to adverse conditions and may be sustained without appreciable loss over a wide range of variation in the environment. If, however, the range specific to any particular skill is exceeded, performance rapidly deteriorates. For instance, Mackworth[23] has shown that the skills involved in wireless telegraphy are maintained without significant change if the room temperature is increased from a dry bulb/wet bulb reading of 85°/75° to one of 100°/90°. A further increase to 105°/95°, however, leads to an enormous increase in mistakes, particularly marked among the less skilled operators. It is therefore probable that every skill displays a certain 'range of tolerance' to adverse conditions, depending both on the nature of the skill itself and the proficiency with which it is executed. The neurological basis of this 'tolerance range' is at present unknown.

Secondly, it has been shown that the breakdown of skill is seldom a matter of simple muscular fatigue. It is above all an affair of defective sensori-motor co-ordination. In the cockpit experiment, for instance, the fatigued operator tends to make more—and less appropriate—movements, to time his movements less precisely, to react to unduly limited aspects of his perceptual field (e.g. the information conveyed by a single instrument), and to become increasingly irritable and dissatisfied with his performance. It is clear that some of these indications of breakdown arise from failure of interpretation, others from a narrowed capacity to co-ordinate the incoming pattern of signals with effective action. Yet others may reflect temperamental changes. Here again, an analysis of these fatigue effects from the neurological standpoint may be awaited with lively anticipation.

An interesting development of this work on skill is the link that is being forged with the general field of self-regulating machines and with the concept of the operator as an element in a control system. This line of thinking, which arose in part from the work of the late K. J. W.

E*

Craik at Cambridge,[24] is at present being widely developed both in this country and in America. Although the relation of psychology to engineering might appear somewhat tenuous, it is likely that the subject has much to gain from exposure to the fresh ideas recently marshalled under the banner of Cybernetics.[25]

In conclusion, it may be said that the idea of experiment is firmly established in psychology, although its use is no longer restricted to the study of human consciousness. Apart from its application to the study of animal behaviour, and to the nervous mechanisms whereby it is sustained, experiment has a valuable part to play in specifying the conditions of human experience and behaviour. In the hands of Michotte, experimental psychology may be said to have thrown light on some thorny problems in the theory of knowledge. In the hands of Bartlett, experimental psychology has helped us to master, in a manner loyal to scientific evidence, the technological demands with which modern man is increasingly confronted. Although we have far to go before the outcome of human experimental psychology can be linked with the simpler nervous reactions discussed in earlier sections, its place in scientific endeavour is already secure.

V

Experimental psychology has produced many facts, a few generalizations, and even an occasional 'law'. But it has so far failed to produce anything resembling a coherent and generally accepted body of scientific theory. Why is this so?

The first reason that springs to mind is scientific immaturity: certainly psychology, in its experimental aspects at least, has a short history, but so also have biochemistry and genetics, in both of which progress has been astonishingly rapid over the past fifty years. A second reason, advanced by a leading psychological historian,[26] is that psychology has yet to discover its own man of genius. Although this may well be true, it seems hardly sufficient to account for the meagre outcome of the toil of innumerable lesser men. More fundamental, perhaps, is the reason put forward by Ryle.[27] Psychology, he suggests, has been founded on the assumption that there exists a distinct order of phenomena—mental events—open to study by the methods of natural science. This assumption he believes to be wholly gratuitous. Although Ryle's position is based largely on philosophical considerations, there would seem no doubt that many psychologists have independently come to recognize its strength. As Ryle himself has said, the Cartesian picture left no place for Mendel or Darwin, and psychology as we know it today finds its main inspiration in the biological sciences. During the past fifty years, there has been a steady shift of interest within psychology from the traditional analysis of mind to the broader study of the behaviour of organisms in their relation with the environment. No longer does psychology aspire to become the science complementary to physics; it is content to claim modest recognition as one of the many disciplines of which modern biology is composed.

POSTSCRIPT: 1963

This article is condensed from a chapter originally written for *The New Outline of Modern Knowledge*, which appeared in 1956. Since that time, there has been a good deal of development in the fields of psychology under review and very substantial revision would be necessary to take proper account of them. In particular, recent applications of information theory to problems in experimental psychology, especially in regard to choice and decision processes, have transformed large areas of the subject. In physiological psychology, although there has been no comparable revolution in method, there have been many new directions of research interest. For example, the discovery that electrical stimulation applied to certain areas of the brain in mammals may have effects analogous to 'reward' or 'punishment' in learning has given fresh impetus to explanation of motivation and reinforcement in physiological terms. Again, recent neurophysiological work on 'arousal mechanisms' has interested experimental psychologists considerably and has stimulated important research on the neural basis of attention. Much interest has also been aroused by experiments on 'split brain' preparations in which input is limited by surgical means to one hemisphere of the brain only, resulting in a virtual restriction of what is learned to one side of the body. This technique, due largely to R. W. Sperry, has important implications for our understanding of the relative parts played by the two hemispheres in the control of skilled action.

There is no single text which brings together recent work in all these fields of inquiry. For developments in ethology, W. H. Thorpe's *Learning and Instinct in Animals* (London: Cambridge University Press, 2nd edition 1963) is extremely useful. For physiological psychology, the symposium on *Biological and Biochemical Bases of Behaviour*, edited by H. F. Harlow and C. N. Woolsey (Wisconsin: University of Wisconsin Press, 1958) is recommended. Problems of inter-hemispheric relations are fully discussed in *Interhemispheric*

Relations and Cerebral Dominance, edited by Vernon Mountcastle (Baltimore: Johns Hopkins, 1962), in which work on 'split-brain' preparations is extensively reported. Some problems of arousal and its physiological basis are outlined in *Sleeping and Waking*, by I. Oswald (Amsterdam: Elsevier, 1962). D. E. Broadbent's *Perception and Communication* (London: Pergamon, 1958) well reflects the impact of information theory on current thinking in experimental psychology.

NOTES AND REFERENCES

1. The opposing viewpoints have been hotly debated by WATSON, J. B., and MCDOUGALL, W., 1928, *The Battle of Behaviourism*, London: Kegan Paul, Trench, Trubner. This battle clearly resulted in stalemate.
2. This term was originally introduced by John Stuart Mill to denote what he was pleased to call the 'science of Character'. Its present-day usage is entirely confined to the study of animal behaviour as it is observed in the natural state. A full account of modern ethological work is given by TINBERGEN, N., 1951, *The Study of Instinct*, Oxford: Clarendon.
3. MCDOUGALL, W., 1923, *An Outline of Psychology*, London: Methuen.
4. LACK, D., 1946, *The Life of the Robin*, London: Witherby.
5. See TINBERGEN, N., Ref. 2, p. 45.
6. See TINBERGEN, N., Ref. 2, p. 113.
7. See TINBERGEN, N., Ref. 2, p. 191.
8. This has been well discussed by BLEST, A. D., 1961, 'The Concept of Ritualisation', in THORPE, W. H., and ZANGWILL, O. L. (ed.), in *Current Problems of Animal Behaviour*, London: Cambridge University Press. It should be added that more recent work on displacement activities strongly suggests that the interpretation given here will require modification. It now seems likely that such activities represent normal reactions to stimuli which become effective only if other and hitherto prepotent stimuli become temporarily less intense. If this is the case, it is incorrect to treat displacement activity in terms of conflict.
9. DAVIS, D. RUSSELL, 1954, 'Some Applications of Behaviour Theory in Psychopathology', *Brit. J. med. Psychol.*, *27*, 216.
10. A good account of this celebrated controversy is given by MCDOUGALL, W., see ref. 3, p. 235.
11. For an introductory account of Sperry's work, see WILKIE, J. S., 1953, *The Science of Brain and Mind*, London: Hutchinson. For an advanced review, see SPERRY, R. W., 1951, 'Mechanisms of Neural Maturation', in STEVENS, S. S. (ed.), *Handbook of Experimental Psychology*, London: Chapman and Hall.
12. Recent advances in this field are largely due to the work of F. A. Beach and colleagues at Yale. See FORD, C. S., and BEACH, F. A., 1952, *Patterns of Sexual Behaviour*, London: Eyre and Spottiswoode, for an over-all review of modern work.
13. K. S. Lashley's earlier work is reported in LASHLEY, K. S., 1929, *Brain Mechanisms and Intelligence*, Chicago: University of Chicago Press. For more

recent work in this field, see MORGAN, C. T., and STELLAR, E., 1950, *Physiological Psychology*, New York: McGraw-Hill.

14. PENFIELD, W., and RASMUSSEN, T., 1950, *The Cerebral Cortex of Man: A Clinical Study of Localization of Function*, London: Macmillan.

15. See PENFIELD, W., and RASMUSSEN, T., ref. 14, p. 87.

16. PENFIELD, W., 1952, 'Memory Mechanisms', *Arch. Neurol. Psychiat.*, *67*, 178.

17. An exhaustive account of these syndromes is given by CRITCHLEY, M., 1953, *The Parietal Lobes*, London: Arnold.

18. The aims and methods of experimental psychology have been well described by MYERS, C. S., 1925, *Textbook of Experimental Psychology*, London: Macmillan.

19. BARTLETT, F. C., 1932, *Remembering*, London: Cambridge University Press.

20. KOFFKA, K., 1935, *Principles of Gestalt Psychology*, London: Kegan Paul.

21. MICHOTTE, A., 1963, *The Perception of Causality*, London: Methuen, (originally published in 1946 under the title *La Perception de la Causalité*, Paris: Louvain).

22. An outline of this line of work has been given by OLDFIELD, R. C., 1959, 'The Analysis of Human Skill', in HALMOS, P., and ILIFFE, A. (ed.), *Readings in Modern Psychology*, London: Kegan Paul. For more detailed accounts, see BARTLETT, F. C., 1947, 'The Measurement of Human Skill', *Brit. med. J.*, *1*, 835, 877; WELFORD, A. T., 1951, *Skill and Age*, Oxford: Oxford Clarendon Press; MACKWORTH, N. H., 1950, 'Researches on the Measurement of Human Performance', *Medical Research Council Special Report Series, No. 268.*

23. See MACKWORTH, N. H., ref. 22, p. 134.

24. The posthumous papers of K. J. W. Craik on 'The Theory of the Human Operator in Control Systems' were published in 1947, *Brit. J. Psychol.*, *38*, 56, 142. See also HICK, W. E., and BATES, J. A. V., 'The Human Operator of Control Mechanisms', *Ministry of Supply Monograph No. 17*, 204.

25. WIENER, N., 1952, *Cybernetics*, New York: Wiley.

26. BORING, E. G., 1929, *A History of Experimental Psychology*, New York: Appleton-Century Crofts.

27. RYLE, G., 1949, *The Concept of Mind*, London: Hutchinson.

CHAPTER 8

ASPECTS OF PSYCHOPHARMACOLOGY: DRUG-INDUCED CHANGES IN EMOTIONS AND PERSONALITY*

BY HANNAH STEINBERG

————◆————

I

Interest in drugs which have psychological effects is of course very ancient and substances like alcohol and opium have long been known. In the last ten years or so there has been intense research activity among psychologists, psychiatrists, pharmacologists, neurophysiologists and biochemists which has been especially concerned with drugs which might be useful in psychiatry. Many new substances have been introduced as 'tranquillizers', 'anti-depressants' or 'hallucinogens', and this has also led to renewed study of older well-known drugs.

Investigations of psychological effects can be roughly classified according to their predominating point of view: either (*a*) drugs are used as tools to analyse behaviour, or (*b*) behaviour is used to analyse the action of drugs. Psychologists naturally are apt to be more interested in the first of these, and for this they need drugs which act on the nervous system in ways which are relatively specific and well understood. Such knowledge is beginning to become available in some cases already, e.g. for curare and for some drugs which act primarily on the autonomic system; but for most drugs which act on

* This chapter is based on the author's paper 'Methods and Problems of Measuring Drug-Induced Changes in Emotions and Personality', *Rev. Psychol. Appl.*, 1961, *11*, 361, and on her contribution to a Symposium on Drugs as Research Tools in Psychology, Proceedings of the XVIth International Congress of Psychology (Bonn, 1960), *Acta Psychol.*, *1961*, *19*, 771. Its preparation was supported by research grant MY-3313 from the National Institute of Mental Health, Public Health Service, U.S.A.

the central nervous system modes of action are still unclear. A better understanding will depend in part on a more effective grasp of the very behaviour phenomena which psychologists would like the drugs to illuminate, that is, on the validity of the behaviour tests used in investigations of type (b).

In practice it is therefore sometimes necessary to go through a process of successive approximation: one can take for granted neither the validity of one's methods for measuring behaviour nor the validity of available accounts of the action of drugs, and in the course of the same series of experiments one may find confirmatory evidence for aspects of both these, or one may come to conclude that views on either or both need modifying. The study of emotions which is discussed in this paper illustrates this dual approach: for example, drugs which are supposed to be useful clinically as 'tranquillizers' should also be able to mitigate emotional responses which have been induced experimentally in the laboratory if the methods of the laboratory have anything in common with real life emotions.

In the course of studying the effects of drugs on behaviour many individual differences and other apparent inconsistencies are often observed. The factors underlying some of these have recently been much studied and as a result the important part played by personality, past experience, set and similar factors in determining drug-behaviour interactions is increasingly being recognized; the second part of this paper briefly deals with this.

II

Some time ago Arthur Koestler[1] wrote in the London newspaper *The Observer* about a symposium on 'Control of the Mind' which he had just attended in San Francisco. One of the things that specially impressed him was the emphasis he heard placed on the role of personality and environment in determining how drugs affect behaviour. For example one speaker pointed out that in experiments with drugs like mescaline and lysergic acid diethylamide (LSD-25) it had been found that the same drug seemed to produce 'one kind of effect on the sober East Coast and another in eccentric California'. On the East Coast experimental subjects suffered some distortions in the visual field, but otherwise they mentioned few dramatic subjective effects. Investigators in Los Angeles on the other hand 'seemed to be able to induce most subjects to experience cosmic events such as union with the sun or death and rebirth with comparative ease'.

On the basis of evidence of this kind Koestler, as one or two others have done before him, seemed to come to the conclusion that the effects of drugs were unreliable and that drugs were not much good for influencing the mind.

One might have drawn the opposite conclusion, it is partly *because* of such interactions that drugs are interesting and versatile tools and allow much room for manoeuvre. By coming to understand how aspects of environment and of personality and the drug and the dose are related to each other one might eventually learn to control and manipulate these factors in appropriate ways and so to tailor the exact combination to fit each particular purpose. Another consequence of these interactions, of course, is that the planning and interpretation of experiments must be correspondingly careful and sensitive; and this has indeed increasingly been the trend in psychopharmacological research during the last few years.

In order to give these complexities their due weight, Professor Pichot[2] has adopted a distinction between two kinds of effects of drugs on behaviour: 'specific' effects, which are a function of the drug itself, and 'non-specific' effects which are functions of the personality of the recipient.[3, 4, 5]

I wonder whether one ought not to go even further than that. All that any drug can do is to act upon *ongoing behaviour* and modify it; hence its effects must always to some extent be dependent upon the nature of the behaviour which is going on at the time, and this in turn depends on the subject's personality, his current emotions, his past experience, the setting in which the drug is administered and so forth.[6] Since it is therefore always the results of drug-personality-environment interactions which are actually observed, I wonder whether one ought not, regretfully, to give up the idea of a separate 'drug-specific' effect in Professor Pichot's sense altogether. (The term 'specific' in relation to the action of drugs has in any case an established and somewhat different meaning in pharmacology: a drug is usually said to have a specific effect on a particular organ or function if it affects it in lower doses than other organs or functions.) It seems preferable to go on using non-committal terms like the 'predominant', 'typical' or 'characteristic' effects of a particular drug or group of drugs, and then to specify in what kinds of circumstance these effects are liable to be modified. For example, barbiturates depress most forms of activity in most people and animals and in most situations, and their effects can accordingly be described as predominantly depressant. But in some circumstances, e.g. if motivation is exceptionally high[7] or if environments are novel[8] doses which normally somewhat depress activity can do the opposite and behave like stimulants, and in very small doses the effects of barbiturates seem actually to be *predominantly* stimulant, though whether this is detected probably depends on the experimental technique used.[9, 10, 11]

It seems probable that the effects of modifying factors are most easily demonstrated and most dramatic when relatively small doses are used, but they are not limited to them. Thus with anaesthetic doses experience has shown[12] that less anaesthetic is apt to be needed to induce unconsciousness if patients or animals are calm than if they are frightened or excited. And as is now well known the lethal dose of amphetamine in mice is much smaller if the animals are crowded together than when they are singly housed;[13] recently similar effects with lethal doses have been demonstrated when animals were given repeated electric shocks.[14]

Considerations of this kind are a special feature of research on the psychological effects of drugs, and they are implicit in the brief review of methods for studying effects on emotions and personality which forms the third part of this paper. I shall come back to them explicitly at the end.

III

A great deal of research has been carried out on the effects of drugs on emotions and personality. Almost any existing technique of assessment which shows promise has been tried; which is not surprising since, apart from special problems like those just discussed, such research can be regarded merely as the application of general principles to a particular subject matter. The terms 'emotions' and 'personality' are here being used in the widest possible sense to include for example moods, motivation and attitudes; they are in effect mainly intended as convenient labels to indicate that a distinction is being made between them and the more cognitive aspects of behaviour (perception, learning and memory, reasoning, motor performance); cognitive changes can however be very relevant to the study of emotions and personality under the influence of drugs, and this will be discussed. 'Emotion' is being used to refer to relatively transient characteristics and 'personality' to more permanent ones. I shall give as examples chiefly experiments carried out on 'normal' volunteers, but the methods apply equally of course to research with psychiatric patients.

There are various ways of classifying such methods, and the following three kinds include most of the methods which have been widely used with drugs. General reviews of such methods can be found in many textbooks of psychology,[15, 16, 17] and there are many recent reviews specially concerned with the study of drugs.[18, 19, 20, 21, 22, 23]

Descriptive methods are based on introspection; the aim is to get the subject to observe and report on what he experiences. They are the most direct methods and they are also the most difficult to use in a quantitative and systematic way. Drugs can induce a great variety of interesting experiences; the most exciting occur with 'hallucinogens' like mescaline and LSD-25, though relatively homely substances like alcohol, anaesthetics and amphetamine can be more productive than is sometimes realized.[24]

Descriptive methods can be refined in various ways, for example by training the subjects or by using standardized questionnaires, rating scales or check lists. Assessments made by others, as distinct from self-observation, are another extension of these methods. Sometimes it is possible to extend descriptive methods by experiments which aim at directly translating subjective phenomena into objective measurements. For example, individuals under the influence of a drug often report that 'things feel remote', and this can be tested by actually asking them to estimate the size of objects they see around them; it may then be found that they make estimates which correspond to estimates which normal subjects make when objects really are further away[25]—though if the test fails it does not of course prove that the drugged subjects were lying when they reported the experience.

Descriptive methods are essential in the early exploratory stages of research when one wants to select from a great many phenomena those which seem to deserve further study; and unsuspected psychological effects of drugs have sometimes been discovered through simple and almost accidental observations. How far descriptive methods should be refined and how far they should be retained in later stages depends on the purpose of the investigation. They can be especially useful where the aim is to throw light on a particular problem by comparing broad patterns of effects. Examples are studies of the influence of group behaviour on reactions to drugs,[26] of the features of 'drug-induced' psychoses and their modification by other drugs,[27, 28, 29, 30, 31] and the growing number of investigations of links between individual differences in reactions to drugs and aspects of personality.[32, 33, 24, 34, 35, 36, 37] Probably it is a good idea to retain some method of eliciting introspections, however quick and simple, in even the most 'objective' kinds of investigation.

The emphasis with *methods depending on efficiency of performance* is not on how the subject feels but on what he can do. There is much evidence that the two are related—though the relations can be complex—but in practice it is apt to be easier to assess in objective and quantitative ways what a person can do. A great variety of performances has been used. The effects of 'stress' or 'anxiety' on efficiency have been particularly studied, both by comparing different diagnostic groups and by experiment; the weight of the evidence probably favours an inverted U-shaped relation, though much depends on the nature of the task and on the conditions under which it is carried out. As one would expect, the majority of experiments involving drugs has been with 'tranquillizing' or similar substances. The usual procedure is first to disrupt performance in some way and then to administer drugs in the hope that they will restore the performance to normal. Performances have been disrupted by various means, e.g. by first presenting an unsolvable task,[38] by punishing errors,[39] by making subjects read the instructions under 'delayed auditory feedback',[40] or by giving them electric shocks in the course of testing their reaction times.[41] Drugs have indeed been found able to mitigate or abolish the effects of such disrupting stimuli, though further experiments may sometimes be needed to investigate whether efficiency improved because the drug directly reduced anxiety or because it acted in some other way.[42]

It has long been known that various *bodily changes accompany emotion*, and a very large literature exists on this topic. Many kinds of physiological characteristic have been investigated for this purpose, including heart rate, blood pressure, respiration, electrical activity in the skin and in muscles and the composition of body fluids, and changes have been studied in response to a great variety of stimuli. Characteristics of this kind can, like the efficiency of performances, be measured objectively and quantitatively, and sometimes they can be more sensitive than the subject's own introspections.[43, 44] But in spite of intensive research and modern apparatus, and in spite of much suggestive evidence[45] it is not yet established how far one can differentiate between different kinds of emotion or personality on the basis of such physiological characteristics alone. Similar physiological reactions can, moreover, be elicited by stimuli which seem to have little emotional significance but which merely increase a person's alertness or his concentration on a task. Furthermore, variation between individuals is very great, though there is evidence that individuals may be somewhat self-consistent in their response patterns.[46]

Drugs which are used in psychiatry can often modify physiological characteristics in various ways; for example 'tranquillizing' and similar drugs can mitigate rises in autonomic and muscle activity which have been induced by many kinds of stimuli in the laboratory.[47, 48, 49, 50] Effects of this kind may be partly responsible for the clinical efficacy of these drugs, and they also have theoretical implications for the role played by physiological factors in emotion.

IV

Sometimes it is possible to combine several kinds of method in the same investigation and so to examine how far results derived in different ways tally with and mutually support each other.

For example, some time ago Dr S. E. Dicker and I were studying the effects of one of the newer hypnotics, methylpentynol ('Oblivon'), which has also been recommended as a sedative and 'tranquillizer' and has been reported to allay anxiety before ordeals like dental operations and childbirth. We found that in the recommended clinical dose of 500 mg. the drug made subjects report a feeling of being relaxed and calm, and also that it reduced autonomic reactions when they performed a difficult motor task. But the subjects' efficiency at carrying out the task was reduced as well, and so was their 'level of aspiration' which depended on the improvement they expected to make on repetition of the task.[49] In a later investigation[21] with a different and more prolonged task, it was found that subjects given methylpentynol performed as accurately as control subjects, but only if they were given 'knowledge of results' and were therefore probably highly motivated to do well; if, however, 'knowledge of results' was withheld drugged subjects made more errors than did control subjects under similar conditions. This suggested that the main effect of the drug was not on the ability to perform but on the *inclination*—which fitted in with our conclusion from the earlier experiments that the effect of methylpentynol was to make subjects 'do worse but mind less'.

My last example is also about relations between performance and feeling, and in addition it illustrates aspects of the complexity of drug-behaviour interactions, which were discussed at the beginning of this paper. Most of the results to be described form part of a larger investigation which has been reported in detail elsewhere.[51]

The performance involved was the very simple one of tapping a key as often as possible with a finger of the preferred hand for 1 minute at a time, the drugs were cyclobarbitone 300 mg. and amphetamine sulphate 15 mg., and the subjects were a class of medical students. Figure 1 shows the results obtained with three groups of students in successive trials made at 20-minute intervals. The performance of the control subjects remained fairly stable throughout, while amphetamine produced a marked improvement and cyclobarbitone produced a marked worsening of performance; compared with their initial scores these changes were of the order of 10–15 per cent in each direction. Figure 2 shows results for a later experiment with different subjects in which the procedure was similar except in one important respect: whereas in the first experiment the subjects had been told nothing about their own or anyone else's scores until after the whole experimental session was over, in the second experiment they were told their scores after each trial and could discuss them with one another. In the second experiment the students were thus under competitive conditions and, as was also confirmed by introspections, their motivation to do well was much higher than among the subjects in the first experiment. They were therefore probably working near the limits of their capacity—the scores of the controls were consistently higher than the scores of the controls in the first experiment—and under such circumstances one would not expect amphetamine to produce much further improvement;[*][52] which is what happened here, as is shown in the figure. In other words, under the special conditions of experiment 2, only cyclobarbitone still produced its usual effects, impairment, but amphetamine was practically inactive. And this would have been our final conclusion if we had not also tested a fourth group of subjects. This fourth group was given a combination of amphetamine and cyclobarbitone in the same doses as had been given separately. We used the mixture partly because in animal experiments a mixture had produced effects which could not be obtained with either drug separately,[54, 55] and partly because similar mixtures are used in psychiatry, especially for treating anxious patients. It has been suggested that mixtures produce more marked and favourable effects on mood than either drug alone, and that they do this without making patients drowsy or inefficient as is apt to happen with barbiturates or 'jittery' as can happen with amphetamine. As is seen from Figure 2, efficiency of tapping with the mixture was in fact no worse than among

* Recently, however, Smith and Beecher[53] have shown that amphetamine can improve the speed of trained swimmers who were already working near the peak of their ability; the improvement was only a small percentage but large enough to be decisive in contests.

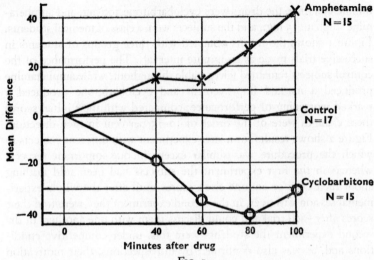

FIG. 1

Experiment 1, tapping scores of three groups of subjects, expressed as mean differences from pre-drug scores ('O' minutes after drug). Throughout subjects were not allowed to know their scores. It can be seen that amphetamine produced a marked improvement in performance.

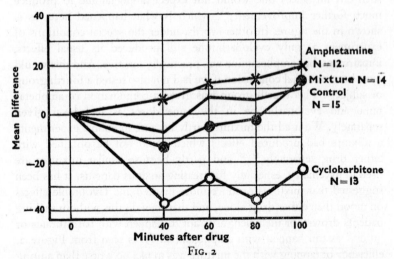

FIG. 2

Experiment 2; tapping scores of four groups of subjects, expressed as for experiment 1. In contrast with experiment 1, subjects were told their scores after each trial; it can be seen that amphetamine on its own hardly improved performance, but was nevertheless able to counteract the deleterious effects of cyclobarbitone.

the controls. Thus even under conditions where amphetamine on its own could produce no significant improvement in performance it was still able to counteract the deleterious effects of cyclobarbitone. This is an example of a 'hidden' effect which might perhaps have been suspected but could not have been confidently predicted from the results obtained with the separate drugs.

In the course of these experiments the subjects were also encouraged to describe their feelings and sensations. Reports of 'jitteriness' were hardly made by any group, and drowsiness was reported by the three drug groups about equally. The incidence of reports of 'elation', expressed as percentages, has been plotted in Figure 3: elation was

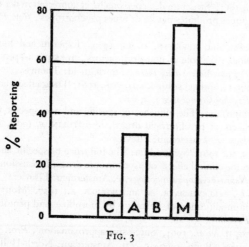

FIG. 3

The incidence of 'elation', expressed as the percentage of subjects who reported symptoms of elation in each or four groups. C = Control group (n = 14), A = Amphetamine group (n = 12), B = Cyclobarbitone group (n = 12), M = Mixture of A + B (n = 12). The groups were the same as in Fig. 2. The mixture produced significantly more reports of elation than either drug alone.

reported by a significantly greater proportion of subjects in the mixture group than in the groups given the separate drugs. Thus, although on one aspect of behaviour, speed of tapping, the effects of the two drugs when given in combination seemed to be in opposite directions and virtually cancelled each other out, on another aspect, feelings of elation, their effects were in the same direction and seemed to augment each other.

Although one cannot generalize much from such simple laboratory experiments, these findings do suggest that amphetamine/barbiturate mixtures might in appropriate dose combinations and environmental circumstances produce various and useful patterns of effects, and that these possibilities deserve further study. More generally, the results illustrate yet another aspect of the complex relations which determine how the effects of drugs on behaviour manifest themselves.

REFERENCES

1. KOESTLER, A., 1961, 'A new look at the mind, I. Pavlov in retreat', *The Observer (Weekend Review)*, April 23rd, 21.
2. PICHOT, P., 1961, 'Structure de la personalité et appréciation des modifications psychologiques produites par les drogues psychotropes', *Rev. Psychol. Appl.*, *11*, 353.
3. DIMASCIO, A., and KLERMAN, G. L., 1960, 'Experimental human psychopharmacology; the role of non-drug factors', in SARWER-FONER, G. J. (ed.), *Dynamics of psychiatric drug therapy*, Springfield: Thomas.
4. LINDEMANN, E., and FELSINGER, J. M. VON, 1961, 'Drug effects and personality theory', *Psychopharmacologia*, 2, 69.
5. 1961, 'Symposium: The influence of specific and non-specific factors on the clinical effects of psychotropic drugs', in ROTHLIN, E. (ed.), *Neuro-psychopharmacology*, 2, Amsterdam: Elsevier.
6. HAMILTON, M., 1961, 'Symposium: The influence of specific and non-specific factors on the clinical effects of psychotropic drugs, Discussion', in ROTHLIN, E. (ed.), *Neuro-psychopharmacology*, 2, Amsterdam: Elsevier.
7. HILL, H. E., BELLEVILLE, R. E., and WIKLER, A., 1957, 'Motivational determinants in modification of behavior by morphine and pentobarbital', *Arch. Neurol. Psychiat.*, *77*, 28.
8. STEINBERG, H., *et al.*, 1961, 'Successive approximation', *Proc. XVI Internat. Cong. Psychol.* (Bonn, 1960), p. 771, Amsterdam: North-Holland Publ. Co.
9. BROWN, B. B., 1960, 'CNS actions and interaction in mice', *Arch. int. Pharmacodyn, 78*, 391.
10. KINNARD, W. J., and CARR, C. J., 1957, 'A preliminary procedure for the evaluation of central nervous system depressants', *J. Pharmacol.*, *121*, 354.
11. READ, G. W., CUTTING, W., and FURST, A., 1960, 'Comparison of excited phases after sedatives and tranquilizers', *Psychopharmacologia*, *1*, 346.
12. BOVARD, E. W., 1959, 'The effects of social stimuli on the response to stress', *Psychol. Rev.*, *66*, 267.
13. CHANCE, M. R. A., 1946, 'Aggregation as a factor influencing the toxity of sympathomimetic amines in mice', *J. Pharmacol.*, *87*, 214.
14. WEISS, B., LATIES, V. G., and BLANTON, F. L., 1961, 'Amphetamine toxicity in rats and mice subjected to stress', *J. Pharmacol.*, *132*, 366.
15. STEVENS, S. S. (ed.), 1951, *Handbook of Experimental psychology*, New York: Wiley.
16. WOODWORTH, R. S., and SCHLOSBERG, H., 1954, *Experimental Psychology*, New York: Holt.

17. EYSENCK, H. J. (ed.), 1960, *Handbook of abnormal psychology*, London: Pitman.
18. HAMILTON, M., 1957, 'Methodological problems in investigating psychotropic drugs', Report to Study Group on Ataraxics and Hallucinogenics, World Health Organisation.
19. BEECHER, H. K., 1959, *Measurement of subjective responses. Quantitative effects of drugs*, New York: Oxford University Press.
20. LEHMANN, H. E., 1959, 'Methods of evaluation of drug effects on the human central nervous system', in BRACELAND, F. J. (ed.), *The effect of pharmacologic agents on the nervous system*, Baltimore: Williams and Wilkins.
21. STEINBERG, H., 1959, 'Effects of drugs on performance and incentives', in LAURENCE, D. R. (ed.), *Quantitative methods in human pharmacology and therapeutics*, London: Pergamon.
22. UHR, L., and MILLER, J. G. (ed.), 1960, *Drugs and Behaviour*, New York: Wiley.
23. PICHOT, P., 1961, 'L'évaluation des modifications du comportement humain sous l'influence des drogues psychotropes', in ROTHLIN, E. (ed.), *Neuropsychopharmacology*, 2, Amsterdam: Elsevier.
24. STEINBERG, H., 1956, 'Abnormal behaviour induced by nitrous oxide', *Brit. J. Psychol.*, *47*, 183.
25. STEINBERG, H., RUSHTON, R., and TINSON, C., 1961, 'Modification of the effect of an amphetamine/barbiturate mixture by the past experience of rats', *Nature*, *192*, 533.
26. NOWLIS, V., and NOWLIS, H. H., 1956, 'The description and analysis of mood', *Ann. New York Acad. Sci.*, *65*, 345.
27. OSMOND, H., and SMYTHIES, J., 1952, 'Schizophrenia; a new approach', *J. ment. Sci.*, *98*, 309.
28. MCKELLAR, P., 1957, *Imagination and thinking* (chap. 6), London: Cohen and West.
29. ISBELL, H., 1959, 'Comparison of the reactions induced by psilocybin and LSD–25 in man', *Psychopharmacologia*, *1*, 29.
30. ISBELL, H., MINER, E. J., and LOGAN, C. R., 1959, 'Cross tolerance between D-2-Brom-Lysergic acid diethylamide (BOL-148) and the D-Diethylamide lysergic acid (LSD-25)', *Psychopharmacologia*, *1*, 109.
31. 1958, 'Symposium: Comparison of drug-induced and endogenous psychoses in man', in BRADLEY, P. B., DENIKER, P., and RADOUCO-THOMAS, C. (ed.), *Neuro-psychopharmacology*, Amsterdam: Elsevier.
32. MALAMUD, W., and LINDEMANN, E., 1934, 'Experimental analysis of psychopathological effects of intoxicating drugs', *Amer. J. Psychiat.*, *90*, 853.
33. FELSINGER, J. M. VON., LASAGNA, L., and BEECHER, H. K., 1955, 'Drug-induced mood changes in man. II. Personality and reactions to drugs', *J. Amer. med. Ass.*, *157*, 1113.
34. EYSENCK, H. J., 1957, 'Drugs and personality. I. Theory and methodology', *J. ment. Sci.*, *103*, 119.
35. BARTHOLOMEW, A. A., and MARLEY, E., 1959, 'Susceptibility to methylpentynol: personality and other variables', *J. ment. Sci.*, *105*, 957.
36. KORNETSKY, C., 1960, 'Alterations in psychomotor functions and individual differences in responses produced by psychoactive drugs', in UHR, L., and MILLER, J. G. (ed.), *Drugs and behavior*, New York: Wiley.

37. RINKEL, M., DIMASCIO, A., ROBEY, A., and ATWELL, C., 1961, 'Personality patterns and reaction to psilocybine', in ROTHLIN, E. (ed.), *Neuro-psychopharmacology*, 2, Amsterdam: Elsevier.

38. RUSSELL, R. W., and STEINBERG, H., 1955, 'Effects of nitrous oxide on reactions to "stress"', *Quart. J. Exper. Psychol.*, 6, 67.

39. HOLLIDAY, A. R., and DILLE, J. M., 1958, 'The effects of meprobamate, chlorpromazine, pentobarbital and a placebo on a behavioural task performed under stress conditions, *J. Compar. physiol. Psychol.*, 1, 51, 811.

40. PRONKO, H. N., and KENYON, G. Y., 1959, 'Meprobamate and laboratory-induced anxiety', *Psychol. Rep.*, 5, 217.

41. HILL, H. E., KORNETSKY, C., FLANARY, H., and WIKLER, A., 1952, 'Effects of anxiety and morphine on discrimination of intensities of painful stimuli', *J. clin. Invest.*, 31, 473.

42. STEINBERG, H., and RUSSELL, R. W., 1957, 'Transfer effects in reactions to "stress"', *Quart. J. Exper. Psychol.*, 9, 215.

43. LACEY, J. I., and SMITH, R. L., 1954, 'Conditioning and generalization of unconscious anxiety', *Science*, 120, 1045.

44. LURIA, A. R., and VINOGRADOVA, O. S., 1959, 'An objective investigation of the dynamics of semantic systems', *Brit. J. Psychol.*, 50, 89.

45. MALMO, R. B., 1957, 'Anxiety and behavioral arousal', *Psychol. Rev.*, 64, 276.

46. LACEY, J. I., and LACEY, B. C., 1958, 'Verification and extension of the principle of autonomic response-stereotopy', *Amer. J. Psychol.*, 71, 50.

47. JACOBSEN, E., KEHLET, H., LARSEN, V., MUNKVAD, I., and SKINHOJ, K., 1955, 'The autonomic reaction of psycho-neurotics to a new sedative: benactyzine nfn, suavitil (R)', *Acta psychiat. neurol. scand.*, 30, 627.

48. DICKEL, H. A., WOOD, J. A., and DIXON, H. H., 1957, 'Electromyographic studies on meprobamate and the working, anxious patient', *Ann. New York Acad. Sci.*, 67, 780.

49. DICKER, S. E., and STEINBERG, H., 1957, 'The effect of methylpentynol in man', *Brit. J. Pharmacol.*, 12, 479.

50. LATIES, V. G., 1959, 'Effects of meprobamate on fear and palmar sweating', *J. Abn. Soc. Psychol.*, 59, 156.

51. LEGGE, D., and STEINBERG, H., 1962, 'Actions of a mixture of amphetamine and barbiturate in man', *Brit. J. Pharmacol.*, 18, 490.

52. HAUTY, G. T., and PAYNE, R. B., 1958, 'Effects of analeptic and depressant drugs upon psychological behaviour', *Am. J. Pub. Health*, 48, 571.

53. SMITH, G. M., and BEECHER, H. K., 1960, 'Amphetamine, secobarbital and athletic performance', *J. Am. Med. Assoc.*, 172, 1632.

54. STEINBERG, H., RUSHTON, R., and TINSON, C., 1961, 'Modification of the effects of an amphetamine-barbiturate mixture by the past experience of rats', *Nature*, 192, 533.

55. STEINBERG, H., and RUSHTON, R., 1963, 'Mutual potentiation of amphetamine and amylbarbitone measured by activity in rats', *Brit. J. Pharmacol.*, 21, 295.

CHAPTER 9

ATTENTION AND VISUAL PERCEPTION*

BY M. D. VERNON

I

We may consider attention in the first place as a direction of perception to some particular aspect of the environment. Although we tend to think that our ability to perceive what lies in front of us is so great that we can see the whole of it at a glance, this in fact is not so. Its detail and complexity are too great for simultaneous registration by the visual mechanisms of the eye and the brain; thus only a part of what is present is actually perceived. At any one moment we may perceive and be fully aware of only a small selection of the objects and events in the world around us. Some we may overlook altogether; others we perceive dimly. At some times we attend maximally to only a small section of the field of view, as when looking down a micro-scope, and notice little outside that area. At other times, we perceive a wider field; we look to and fro, noticing first one thing and then another. Sometimes this is done rather inattentively; but on other occasions we may search the field of view eagerly and expectantly for a particular object or event.

In general we attend more closely to that part of the visual field which is imaged on the centre of the retina, the fovea, than to the surrounding areas. In the first place, in daylight visual acuity is highest in the fovea. But in very dim light the area surrounding the fovea has greater sensitivity than the fovea, since the former contains rods, which are capable of a high degree of dark adaptation, while the

* Based on a presidential address delivered to Section J (Psychology), on September 4, 1959, at the York meeting of the British Association for the Advancement of Science, published as 'Perception, Attention and Conscious-ness', in *Advancement of Science*, 16, 111.

latter is made up of cones, which are not. In spite of this, it is difficult to attend to a light projected on to this surrounding area, since we possess a habitual tendency to rotate the eyes, the head and even the body, until that part of the field to which we are attending is imaged on the fovea. Thus attention is not determined solely by the sensitivity of the eye. However, in daylight we can perceive more, and more clearly and accurately, at the centre of fixation than elsewhere, as can be shown by presenting objects momentarily at different points in the field of vision. As regards the central field, if a random arrangement of black dots on a white background is exposed by a tachistoscope for a fraction of a second, the observer having concentrated his attention upon this point, he can as a rule perceive the number of dots correctly provided that it does not exceed six.[1] With a larger number, he begins to guess, and is often incorrect. He is particularly likely to overlook dots which are farthest from the centre of the field.[2] But if the dots are arranged in groups or patterns, he may perceive a larger number. If he is shown, instead of simple dots, more complex forms which he is required to describe or identify, then the number which he can perceive is reduced. But it is difficult to estimate this number exactly, since in order to report them he must remember their identity for a short period of time; and experiment has shown that immediate short-term memory decays very rapidly.[3] But again if the complex forms can be related together in some way or 'coded'—if they can be combined together like the parts of a pattern or like letters in a word—they may together produce corroborative or 'redundant' information, and they will be perceived more readily.

If instead of concentrating solely upon the centre of the field, the observer endeavours to attend also to what is happening in the periphery, then what is perceived there depends considerably upon the direction of attention. If an object is exposed momentarily in that part of the field to which the observer is instructed beforehand to look, it will be perceived more readily and accurately than if his attention is directed elsewhere, or not directed at all but diffused widely over the field.[4,5] Moreover, perception of any one object exposed in the peripheral field will be less accurate the larger the number of objects shown simultaneously elsewhere, because they distract attention even when it is initially directed towards a particular point.[6]

It is extremely difficult to perceive two or more events occurring at the same moment for only a short period of time, unless they can be combined in some manner. Thus when two pieces of information were presented simultaneously, one visually and the other aurally, it was impossible to perceive more than one of them.[7] However, when observers were required to make appropriate responses to simultaneously presented pairs of visual and auditory signals, the responses were as rapid to those pairs of signals which they knew would be linked together as to the auditory signal alone.[8] But if they did not know what combination of visual and auditory signals would occur, the responses were slower, again through diffusion or distraction of attention. Again, if different events occur in close succession, attention may alternate between them. This alternation can be very rapid if there is a rhythmical sequence of events,[4] or if the observer is able to anticipate their occurrence.[9] If he has some knowledge as to what is going to happen, he can switch his attention from one event to another in about 1/5th of a second; but if he is uncertain, the period may be longer.

Thus we see that the number of pieces of isolated information which can be dealt with at any one time or place is strictly limited; but that by means of switches of attention and by coding, the individual is able to integrate these together to gain a coherent knowledge of his environment.

II

But we do not ordinarily fix our eyes for any length of time upon a small area of the field of view. Indeed, it has been shown that even when an individual thinks that he is fixating steadily, his eyes are in fact oscillating continuously, and also drifting away from the point of fixation and then flicking rapidly back again.[10] The function of these movements appears to be the avoidance of continuous homogeneous stimulation of the retina. But it is possible to cause the optical image to fall continuously upon the same area of the retina by means of the 'stabilized retinal image' technique. A minute figure is attached by a thin glass stalk to a contact lens covering the cornea; the figure then moves as the eye moves, and its image, focused by a lens, remains stationary on the retina.[11] It is then found that the stabilized image fades from view after about five seconds, and then continues to fade and regenerate periodically. The fading is due in part to adaptation in the retina, and is less with brighter figures. But it is also affected by the shape of the figure, notably its Gestalt qualities, and even by its meaning.[12] These findings have not been fully confirmed by later work (not yet published), but it seems clear that some central factor, in the nature of fluctuation of attention, must be operative.

Other evidence as to the fluctuation of attention when it is concentrated upon a single area is afforded by the phenomena of alternating perspective figures and alternating 'figure' and 'ground'. Here the fluctuation is between two aspects of the same sensory data. The alternation may be affected to some extent by the nature of the figures employed, and controlled by voluntary efforts of attention—but only up to a point.

It seems, therefore, that prolonged concentration of attention is difficult, and that our more usual mode of perceiving is that of successive fixation of different parts of the field. It is possible to gain some idea of the manner in which this occurs by recording the movements of the eyes.* In looking at a picture, they may follow the main lines of the design.[15] In searching for an object in the field, the movements tend to be quite irregular, and to differ in different people. The eyes may move in circular paths,[16] or concentrate in the centre, or explore one quadrant of the field more than others.[17] It is in fact quite difficult to scan the field regularly and systematically. During the war it was necessary to train aircraft spotters to do this; otherwise they tended to scan certain regions of the sky more extensively than others.

Piaget[18] has shown that the capacity to scan systematically is even more deficient in young children than in older people, and that this considerably affects their ability to attend to and perceive important aspects of the field. They tend to 'centrate' upon certain parts of the field, especially the upper part, or upon certain salient parts of a figure, and ignore the remainder. But from the age of six or seven years they increase in 'perceptual activity', and explore the field more exhaustively and systematically. Even adults vary in their capacity to scan, as we shall consider on p. 162 below.

III

It is clear that, whether we are concentrating upon a small area or viewing a wider field, we select certain parts or certain objects for

---

* The two methods most commonly used nowadays for recording eye movements are: (1) photographing the reflection of a beam of light from a contact lens covering the cornea; the reflected beam moves as the cornea moves;[10] (2) recording the electro-oculograph;[13, 14] the changes in electrical potential difference between the front and back of the eyeball which occur as the eye moves are recorded by means of electrodes attached to the face surrounding the eye.

perception, and that our selection operates through the direction of attention. We must now consider what it is that determines the direction of attention. In the first place, certain objects and events appear to be of great significance to us; they automatically attract attention and stimulate us to make what have been called 'orienting' responses in order to examine them and to react as rapidly and as appropriately as possible, even though we have not expected them before they occurred. Thus when we suddenly hear a loud noise, see a bright light or receive a blow or other painful stimulus, we not only seek to perceive what has caused these events, but also take action immediately, by starting, jumping aside, shielding the eyes or ears. Now it might be argued that it is the great intensity of these stimuli which ensures that they shall blot out everything else. Intensity may indeed be one of the factors concerned, but there is evidence to show that these stimuli are significant also because they constitute a potential threat of danger or hurt. Thus intense stimuli, if repeated and prolonged, may cease to be consciously perceived. It is possible to ignore the loud noise of traffic in the street outside, and even sleep in spite of it, but to awake immediately at the sound of someone opening the bedroom door. Therefore it appears that suddenness, unexpectedness and potential threat may be the important factors in attracting attention. Again, we may quickly notice a sudden change in the visual field, and especially a rapid movement, without perceiving at first *what* is changing or moving. But once it is realized that there is something unexpected or incongruous in the field, then the tendency is to devote more attention to that part of the field than to its more familiar and humdrum aspects.[19, 20]

But although we may very rapidly attend to the sudden and unexpected, on other occasions attention may be directed by expectation of the familiar; that is to say, we tend to anticipate that events will occur in a manner to which we have become accustomed, and to perceive them accordingly. Indeed, we may assume that we have actually perceived what we expected to see, and only a considerable environmental change or a deliberate voluntary alteration in expectation will enable us to perceive differently. The effects of anticipation in determining what the observer perceives are particularly noticeable when the actual sensory data are inadequate—when the field or view is unclear or ambiguous. This is clearly illustrated by a demonstration by Ames of what has been called the 'distorted room', in which walls, floor and ceiling were slanted at various angles to one another.[21] But if viewed with one eye through a small hole in a screen, the sensory impressions were similar to those produced by a normal rectilinear room, and that was what the observer perceived. The ambiguous sensory data resulted in perception of a rectilinear room, presumably because such a room is more commonly encountered and is more familiar than is a distorted room.

Many experiments have been carried out to demonstrate the effects of 'set', the manner in which the observer's expectations can be moulded or modified by the experimental instructions, and hence what he perceives. Thus it has been shown repeatedly in experiments on the 'constancies' that observers can be instructed to judge the 'real' shape or size of an object presented to them; or to estimate the size or shape it projects on the retina; or to relate its size or shape to surrounding objects. In the first case, the perceived size or shape will approximate to that of an object seen at a short distance, perpendicular to the line of sight; while in the second and third cases, percepts will be more similar to the size or shape of the retinal projection. Different people tend naturally to adopt one or other of these procedures, although their judgments can be influenced by instructions.[22]

The direction of attention can be affected also by the experimental procedure, in the absence of any conscious intention to perceive some aspects of the field rather than others. This was shown in one experiment when observers were given a problem-solving task in which they had to select certain cards to obtain a correct solution.[23] In fact, correct solutions were given only by green and blue cards, and incorrect ones by red and yellow cards. Subsequently, in trying to find simple figures obscured by more complex multicoloured ones, of the Gottschaldt type,[24] they tended to look in the green and blue areas rather than in the red and yellow, though no one was aware of the tendency.

People may be trained to attend to and perceive certain aspects of the field which previously they had not noticed or failed to discriminate. Thus observers were trained to perceive that the Ames' room was distorted, by requiring them to bounce a ball against its sides or touch them with a pointer.[25] Other people merely observed the experimenter performing these actions, and they were slower to perceive the distortion than the observers who had acted themselves. Thus attention to appropriate aspects of the environment is aroused most readily by the actions of the observer who explores these for himself.

In everyday life, this type of perceptual learning commonly occurs when people are interested or encouraged to learn to perceive what they have hitherto overlooked. Thus a scientific training enables people to observe characteristics of plants, animals, etc., more accurately. In industry, operatives may be taught to perceive the qualities of materials which they grade, or to find the flaws in faulty products. Commonly there is no general improvement in visual acuity or perceptual sensitivity. But the trainer draws the attention of the learner to particular aspects of his task, and he acquires the ability to notice these himself. Thus in learning to identify aircraft, observers improved most quickly when they were shown the significant points of difference in the shapes of different aircraft.[26]

It has been postulated that observers may be trained to attend to certain aspects of the visual field by rewarding them directly when they are shown these aspects, and to avoid these aspects by punishing them. In one experiment,[27] one part of an alternating 'figure-ground' figure was presented alone accompanied by a money reward, and the other part was presented alone together with punishment-taking money away. When the whole 'figure-ground' figure was shown subsequently, there was a tendency to attend to and perceive the rewarded part and ignore the punished, although the observers were unaware of this. Again, when observers were required to find simple Gottschaldt forms obscured in more complex ones, simple ones which had previously been presented to the accompaniment of a loud unpleasant screeching noise were discovered more slowly than those which had not.[28]

In everyday life, attention may be directed by desires and emotions towards certain characteristics of other people. We attend to and perceive most clearly the details of faces of those in whom we are interested. A group of White American students who were favourably disposed towards Negroes perceived and recognised photographs of different Negroes more correctly than did students whose attitudes were unfavourable. The former perceived them as individuals; the latter lumped them together as 'niggers' and perceived little difference between them.[29] On the other hand, other investigators[30] showed that a group of people prejudiced against Negroes perceived the difference between Negroes and white people in accentuated form—the width of the nose, the fullness of the lips, etc.—by comparison with those who were not prejudiced.

It has often been claimed that individuals may perceive more readily situations, events or pictures of events which appeal to their inherent desires; but that if these desires are repressed, they may fail to perceive. Some evidence for this was produced, in connection with sex

F

and aggression.[31, 32] However, it has been shown recently that pictures of scenes related to fully conscious motives, such as achievement, were more fully and correctly described than were others, but not necessarily more readily perceived; neither was there any failure to perceive pictures of scenes related to repressed needs.[33] And indeed in much work on the relation of motivation to attention and perception, it seems to be the verbal responses which are principally affected.

The studies which have been described of the effect on perception of motivation and training suggest an explanation for the many differences which occur between the percepts of different people, who are differently motivated and have had different training. Recent work[34, 35] at the Menninger Clinic has indicated that individuals may differ consistently in specific modes of attending, for instance, in the tendency to scan attentively a wide visual field, or to concentrate upon a narrow area ('centration'); and in the ability to direct attention selectively and appropriately towards the significant features of the field and ignore irrelevancies, as against registering passively what is presented to them. Moreover, it has been postulated that these characteristics of attending are related to certain inherent personality qualities, for instance, methods of 'ego defence'. Unfortunately it is impossible in this chapter to do justice to the range of experimental work carried out by these psychologists, or to the hypotheses they have derived from it. Undoubtedly the work opens up many interesting possibilities as to the nature of differences in attending, though the hypotheses cannot yet be accepted as proven.

There is some evidence to show that direction of attention to events which are not consciously perceived may nevertheless cause these events to influence an observer's thoughts and actions. There is little to support the notion that people can be affected by 'subliminal stimulation', that is to say, by the presentation of stimuli just below threshold intensity, when they are in no way prepared for such stimulation. But in an extensive inquiry into the effects of subliminal stimulation, the observers were instructed beforehand that some event was likely to occur, and that they were to respond at a given moment.[36] When a word was presented to them subliminally, they were to say the first word that came into their heads, although they saw nothing. Often they responded with words which had meaningful associations with the stimulus words. With sexual words, these sometimes had a Freudian character, and they were accompanied by psychogalvanic reflex responses of the kind which appear in reaction to conscious emotional experiences. Again, the observers were frequently able to associate their responses to the corresponding stimulus words when these were shown them subsequently. In other experiments it was found that such associations occurred only when they had been long established by use and familiarity, and when the observers knew they were to receive subliminal stimulation. Hence we may infer that direction of attention can produce effects other than conscious perception.

IV

We have so far considered mainly the functions of attention in directing perception towards a particular aspect of the environment, and hence facilitating this perception. But it appears that in some circumstances attention may also have an energizing effect, as for instance when we say that we are able to concentrate upon a task by making an effort of attention. However, we know that unless the task is itself interesting, or we are highly motivated to perform it, this effort becomes more and more difficult to make, and in time we may cease to attend or perceive. These effects have been investigated in a long series of experiments on 'vigilance'—the capacity to continue perceiving and responding appropriately to a prolonged series of events. In the 'clock test'[37] a pointer rotated in successive small jumps, one every second, round a dial like that of a clock; and at irregular and comparatively infrequent intervals it made a double jump. Observers had to notice and signal each of these double jumps by depressing a key. After only about half an hour they began to miss the double jumps; and the number missed increased, throughout a two-hour period. Efficiency could be maintained, however, by increasing motivation; and by informing the observer every time a double jump had occurred whether or not he had responded to it. Subsequent experiments with similar situations showed that making signals brighter and lengthening the time over which they were visible emphasized them and prevented decline. So also did increasing their frequency and regularity, because the observer knew when to expect them, and could be more certain of noticing them.[38] On the other hand, a continuous loud noise enhanced the decline in vigilance. It seems probable, therefore, that the more homogeneous and unvarying the situation, the less easy it is to maintain attention, which tends to fluctuate or to lapse altogether. The effect is perhaps even greater when fatigue is incurred, as in long spells of work by aircraft pilots, in which attention wandered to an increasing extent from the signals on instrument dials.[39]

The effects of prolonged unvarying sensory stimulation have been demonstrated in a startling manner in the now well-known MacGill experiments on 'sensory deprivation'.[40, 41] The experimenters induced observers by paying them considerable sums of money to remain over a period of 2–5 days in an environment in which almost all sensory stimulation was kept constant. Each observer lay on a bed; he wore translucent goggles over his eyes so that he could see nothing but a blur of light; he could hear only an unvarying buzz; and he was prevented from touching anything by cuffs which came down over his hands. Although at first most of the observers slept a great deal, after about twenty-four hours they could sleep only in snatches. They became bored and restless, and several were unable to endure the conditions any longer. Their tested intelligence deteriorated, they could not concentrate, and they experienced visual and auditory hallucinations. When they emerged from their incarceration, their perception of the visual field was distorted, spatial orientation was impaired, and objects sometimes appeared blurred and unstable.

Many repetitions and variations of these experiments have been carried out since, the results of which can only be summarized here.[42] Constriction of movement seemed to aggravate the effects, facilitating hallucinations and producing feelings of depersonalization and in some cases of anxiety and even of acute panic. But hallucinations did develop when visual perception alone was restricted. In some experiments darkness and silence were employed instead of constant light and sound, on the whole with less severe effects. But other investigators[43] found that an irregularly flashing light gave the same effects as constant light, and they therefore attributed these to lack of meaningful stimulation rather than to lack of variation. A number of different visual disturbances has been reported to occur after release, including a more rapid decline of vigilance. But there are considerable individual differences in the effects. Those who could endure the situation longest seemed on the whole to be less impulsive and more passive in personality,[44] whereas those prone to anxiety could not tolerate it.[45] Although it does not seem clear what aspect of the homogeneous environment was most important in producing these effects, it may be concluded that attention is normally geared to a continuously changing environment, and that inhibitory processes may occur in the central nervous system when there is no change. We shall now consider the physiological evidence as to the nature of these processes.

V

There has been in recent years a very large volume of neurophysiological investigation relating the psychological processes of attention and perception to certain processes occurring in the central nervous system; and particularly to the functions of nerve tissue in the subcortical region of the brain called the 'reticular formation'. The activities of this appear to be associated with the arousal of awareness, the maintenance of vigilance and the direction of attention to specific events.[46, 47] The functions of the reticular formation seem to be twofold. In the first place, one part of it appears to be concerned with general arousal and wakefulness. Impulses from it inhibit the spontaneous activity of the cortex which is shown in long slow rhythmical discharges in the electroencephalogram during sleep; and these discharges are replaced by the more rapid alpha rhythm which characterizes waking states in which attention is relatively relaxed, and which in turn is blocked by direct sensory stimulation, or when attention is aroused. The reticular formation is itself stimulated to action by impulses arriving through collateral fibres from the sensory nerve tracts, and also by impulses from the cortex. The latter arise particularly in sudden and unexpected stimulation of the cortex, and their effect appears to be relatively temporary. After partial arousal to wakefulness, repetition of stimulation produces habituation, arousal is inhibited and sleep restored. A similar type of habituation may occur in 'sensory deprivation'. Injuries to the reticular formation result in a condition of lethargy or coma in animals, which cannot then be aroused.

But another part of the reticular formation appears to be concerned with more specific alerting to particular sensory stimuli. Impulses from this may interrupt and re-set the general pattern of cortical excitation; enhance or recruit discharges in some areas of the cortex; and inhibit discharges in other areas. In visual stimulation, they block the alpha rhythm of the visual areas. This part of the reticular formation is also stimulated by impulses through collaterals from the specific sensory pathways. It is affected to the greatest extent by pain impulses; and auditory impulses produce more effect than do visual ones. These differences seem to reflect the relative degree of attention paid to these different sensory modes.

The activities of this part of the reticular formation are also closely geared to and dependent upon impulses from the cortex. Sensory impulses passing up the direct pathways to the cortex travel at higher speeds than those proceeding through the collaterals to the reticular formation. Thus there is time for the cortex to evaluate the former and to discharge downwards to the reticular formation, regulating its reactions to the sensory impulses it receives through collaterals. Its facilitatory activities may then be directed towards percepts significant to the individual, and its inhibitory activities towards irrelevant percepts, producing an enhancement of discrimination. Such enhancement has been demonstrated in an experiment by Lindsley in which people were required to distinguish between two successive flashes of light.[46] It was found that the temporal interval necessary for discrimination between the flashes was shortened by direct stimulation of the reticular formation. Again, it was found that rhesus monkeys could discriminate more quickly and more correctly between two differently shaped solids, exposed tachistoscopically, when the reticular formation was directly stimulated by a weak electrical current.[48]

It appears that impulses from the reticular formation also pass down efferent fibres associated with the sensory nerve tracts to relay stations in the latter, controlling the sensory impulses which are conducted from these to the cortex. Thus in a well-known experiment, impulses produced in response to a series of clicks were recorded from the cochlear nucleus of the auditory nerve of the cat.[49] These impulses ceased to occur when the cat saw a mouse or smelt fish. Similar effects have been recorded for visual impulses, when the cat attended to auditory or olfactory stimuli. Again sensory impulses aroused by stimuli to which the animal is specifically attending will tend to be facilitated. But if a long series of similar stimuli is presented, in time the animal tends to become habituated to these, and the sensory impulses will decrease even when there is no interference from something more attractive.[50]

Thus we may infer that information transmitted to the cortex and the manner in which it is discriminated depend on the activities of the reticular formation. This is demonstrated by the effects of stimulation by barbiturate drugs. The activities of the reticular formation are depressed and inhibited by concentrations of these drugs which are insufficient to affect direct responses of the sensory areas of the cortex. Thus an individual may continue to be aware of sensory stimulation after he has lost the power to attend or discriminate. The functions of the reticular formation have also been shown to be affected by impulses from the limbic cortex which is concerned with motivation and emotion. General arousal, specific anticipatory 'set' and attentive searching with the eyes ('orienting responses'), followed by exploratory behaviour, are set up through the activity of the reticular formation in response to impulses from the limbic cortex.

VI

The above is a very brief and much over-simplified account of very complex neurological functions which are as yet imperfectly understood. However, it does suggest that there are two mechanisms involved in perception, the first which responds perceptually to some part of those sensory impulses which reach it, and the second which regulates both the input to the cortex and the nature and extent of the response. The operations of the latter correspond in many ways to the psychological functions of attention, and to this extent the use of that concept is justified. Activity in the reticular formation appears to determine whether the cortex shall be aroused to respond at all, and to regulate the response in accordance with the information received and the significance of that information to the individual. Significance is a function of novelty and variability; of expectation and anticipation; of emotion and need; and it fails when there is a lack of interest or of variation. Attention and orienting responses tend to occur on reception of significant information, together with some form of adaptive behaviour; and these also may be mediated by the reticular formation. However, in some circumstances these attentive processes are to a considerable extent under voluntary control, in that they may be set in motion and directed by the individual from deliberate intention and without prior stimulation. It has been suggested that the function of the frontal cortex is to plan and set in action such intentional activities;[51] and this hypothesis receives some support from the work of Pribram on the effects of frontal lesions in monkeys. But this also lies outside the scope of this chapter.

REFERENCES

1. KAUFMAN, E. L., *et. al.*, 1949, 'The discrimination of visual number', *Amer. J. Psychol.*, *62*, 498.
2. BAKER, C. H., 1958, 'Attention to visual displays during a vigilance task, 1, Biasing attention', *Brit. J. Psychol.*, *49*, 279.
3. SPERLING, G., 1960, 'The information available in brief visual presentations', *Psychol. Monog.*, *74*, No. 11.
4. HYLAN, J. P., 1903, 'The distribution of attention', *Psychol. Rev.*, *10*, 373.
5. MEISENHEIMER, J., 1929, 'Experimente im peripheren Sehen von Gestalten', *Arch. f. d. ges. Psychol.*, *67*, 1.

6. GRINDLEY, G. C., 1931, 'Psychological factors in peripheral vision', *Medical Research Council Special Report Series*, No. 163.

7. MOWBRAY, G. H., 1954, 'The perception of short phrases presented simultanously for visual and auditory reception', *Quart. J. Exper. Psychol.*, 6, 86.

8. ADAMS, J. A., and CHAMBERS, R. W., 1962, 'Response to simultaneous stimulation of two sense modalities', *J. Exper. Psychol.*, 63, 198.

9. POULTON, E. C., 1950, 'Perceptual anticipation and reaction time', *Quart. J. Exper. Psychol.*, 2, 99.

10. DITCHBURN, R. W., and GINSBORG, B. L., 1953, 'Involuntary eye movements during fixation', *J. Physiol.*, 119, 1.

11. CLOWES, M. B., and DITCHBURN, R. W., 1959, 'An improved apparatus for producing a stabilized retinal image', *Optica Acta*, 6, 252.

12. PRITCHARD, R. M., *et. al.*, 1960, 'Visual perception approached by the method of stabilized images', *Canad. J. Psychol.*, 14, 67.

13. CARMICHAEL, L., and DEARBORN, W. F., 1947, *Reading and Visual Fatigue*, Boston: Houghton Mifflin.

14. SHACKEL, B., 1960, 'Pilot study in electro-oculography', *Brit. J. Ophthal.*, 44, 89.

15. GIBSON, J. J., 1950, *The Perception of the Visual World*, p. 155, Boston: Houghton Mifflin.

16. FORD, A., *et al.*, 1959, 'Analysis of eye movements during free search', *J. Opt. Soc. Amer.*, 49, 287.

17. ENOCH, J. M., 1959, 'Effect of the size of a complex visual display upon visual search', *J. Opt. Soc. Amer.*, 49, 280.

18. PIAGET, J., 1961, *Les Mécanismes Perceptifs*, Paris: Presses Universitaires de France.

19. BERLYNE, D. E., 1957, 'Conflict and information-theory variables as determinants of human perceptual curiosity', *J. Exper. Psychol.*, 53, 399.

20. BERLYNE, D. E., 1958, 'The influence of complexity and novelty in visual figures on orienting responses', *J. Exper. Psychol.*, 55, 289.

21. AMES, A., 1946, *Some Demonstrations Concerned With the Origin and Nature of Our Sensations: A Laboratory Manual*, Dartmouth Eye Institute.

22. JOYNSON, R. B., 1958, 'An experimental synthesis of the Associationist and Gestalt accounts of the perception of size', *Quart. J. Exper. Psychol.*, 10, 65, 142.

23. WALTERS, R. H., 1958, 'Conditioning of attention as a source of autistic effects in perception', *J. Abn. Soc. Psychol.*, 57, 197.

24. GOTTSCHALDT, K., 1926, 'Über den Einfluss der Erfahrung auf die Wahrnehmung von Figuren', *Psychol. Forsch.*, 8, 261.

25. KILPATRICK, F. P., 1954, 'Two processes in perceptual learning', *J. Exper. Psychol.*, 47, 362.

26. GIBSON, J. J. (ed.), 1947, *Motion Picture Testing and Research*, Army Air Forces Aviation Psychology Program Research Reports, No. 7.

27. SCHAFER, R., and MURPHY, G., 1943, 'The role of autism in a visual figure-ground relationship', *J. Exper. Psychol.*, 32, 335.

28. HOCHBERG, J. E., and BROOKS, V., 1958, 'Effects of previously associated annoying stimuli (auditory) on visual recognition thresholds', *J. Exper. Psychol.*, 55, 490.

29. SEELEMAN, V., 1940, 'The influence of attitude upon the remembering of pictorial material', *Arch. Psychol.*, No. 258.

30. SECORD, P. F., *et al.*, 1956, 'The negro stereotype and perceptual accentuation', *J. Abn. Soc. Psychol.*, *53*, 78.

31. ERIKSEN, C. W., 1951, 'Perceptual defense as a function of unacceptable needs', *J. Abn. Soc. Psychol.*, *46*, 557.

32. LINDNER, H., 1953, 'Sexual responsiveness to perceptual tests in a group of sexual offenders', *J. Person.*, *21*, 364.

33. FORREST, D. W., and LEE, S. G., 1962, 'Mechanisms of defense and readiness in perception and recall', *Psychol. Monog.*, *76*, No. 4.

34. GARDNER, R. W., 1961, 'Cognitive controls of attention deployment as determinants of visual illusions', *J. Abn. Soc. Psychol.*, *62*, 120.

35. GARDNER, R. W., and LONG, R. I., 1962, 'Control, defence and centration effect; a study of scanning behaviour', *Brit. J. Psychol.*, *53*, 129.

36. DIXON, N. F., 1955, *The Effect of Subliminal Stimulation upon Cognitive and other Processes*, Unpublished Ph.D. thesis, University of Reading.

37. MACKWORTH, N. H., 1950, 'Researches on the measurement of human performance', *Medical Research Council Special Report Series*, No. 268.

38. BROADBENT, D. E., 1958, *Perception and Communication*, London: Pergamon.

39. BARTLETT, F. C., 1943, 'Fatigue following highly skilled work', *Proc. Roy. Soc. B.*, *131*, 247.

40. BEXTON, W. H., *et al.*, 1954, 'Effects of decreased variation in the sensory environment', *Canad. J. Psychol.*, *8*, 70.

41. HERON, W., *et al.*, 1956, 'Visual disturbances after prolonged perceptual isolation', *Canad. J. Psychol.*, *10*, 13.

42. SOLOMON, P., *et al.* (ed.), 1961, *Sensory Deprivation*, Cambridge, Mass.: Harvard University Press (for a recent discussion).

43. DAVIS, J. M., *et al.*, 1960, 'Effects of visual stimulation on hallucinations and other mental experience during sensory deprivation', *Amer. J. Psychiat.*, *116*, 889.

44. HULL, J., and ZUBEK, J. P., 1962, 'Personality characteristics of successful and unsuccessful sensory isolation subjects', *Percept. Motor Skills*, *14*, 231.

45. SMITH, S., and LEWTY, W., 1959, 'Perceptual isolation using a silent room', *Lancet*, ii, 342.

46. JASPER, H. H., *et al.* (ed.), 1957, *Reticular Formation of the Brain*, Henry Ford Hospital International Symposium, London: Churchill.

47. SAMUELS, I., 1959, 'Reticular mechanisms and behaviour', *Psychol. Bull.*, *56*, 1.

48. FUSTER, J. M., 1958, 'Effects of stimulation of brain stem on tachistoscopic perception', *Science*, *127*, 150.

49. HERNÁNDEZ-PEÓN, R., *et al.*, 1956, 'Modification of electric activity in cochlear nucleus during "attention" in unanaesthetised cats', *Science*, *123*, 331.

50. HERNÁNDEZ-PEÓN, R., 1961, chap. 26 in ROSENBLITH, W. A. (ed.), *Sensory Communication*, New York: Wiley.

51. MILLER, G. A., GALANTER, E., and PRIBRAM, K. H., 1960, *Plans and the Structure of Behavior*, New York: Holt.

F*

CHAPTER 10

PERCEPTUAL ORGANIZATION AND ACTION*

BY JAMES DREVER

I

The suggestion has been made[1] that the years between 1930 and 1960 might fittingly be called the Age of Theory in psychology. It is the age of S and R, of intervening variables, of operational definitions, and of the hypothetico-deductive method. It is an age that is passing. This is no judgment of an outsider but is implicit in the present views of many psychologists to whom the Age of Theory owes its existence. Some may be unwilling to recognize the signs. Hullians, Eysenckians and others, formidable in their singleness of purpose, may march on like mammoths across the icy wastes. Their bones will endure to puzzle the archaeologists of our science. As for the rest of us we must think again. Scientistic rituals are getting us nowhere.

Rightly regarded, this is a liberation, not a catastrophe. It frees us to go back to our data with that puzzled humility which is the only frame of mind appropriate in the biological field. Nor have the years been entirely wasted. We have at our disposal techniques and equipment which we lacked in 1930, and a much better idea than we had then of how to design experiments. So we can ask old questions in the hope of new answers: and take a second look at problems whose complexity may once have scared us into denying their existence.

The problem to be dealt with in this paper is perceptual organization, and particularly the basic kind of organization which enables us to perceive objects in space. During much of the nineteenth century this

---

* Based on a Presidential address, delivered at Liverpool, at the 1961 Annual Conference of the British Psychological Society, published as 'Perception and Action', in *Bull. Brit. Psychol. Soc.*, 1962, *No. 45*, 1.

was a matter for debate rather than experiment. Nativist and empiricist refuted one another, each to his own satisfaction, until reactive inhibition set in and attention was directed elsewhere. During the first few decades of the present century the question was raised again by the Gestalt psychologists, and this time there was some factual evidence behind the nativist arguments which they used. The evidence has since been eroded, but enough remains to require some theoretical provision. Just what provision is not altogether clear. 'Certainly', said Bruner[2] a few years ago, 'Hebb is correct in asserting, like Immanuel Kant, that certain primitive unities and identities within perception must be innate or autochthonous and not learned.' 'Certainly' is a strong word in this context, even with Kant's blessing. What 'primitive unities and identities' are referred to here? Are Bruner, Hebb, and Kant supposed to be saying the same thing, or are they merely agreeing in principle that an innate basis is needed to give experience its starting-point?

Kant is much the most explicit of the three. The sensory manifold, he says, cannot be apprehended as such, but must be structured by the forms of space and time, and by the categories; that is to say such basic relationships as substance and attribute and cause and effect. It is unlikely that if Bruner and Hebb were to be asked what they had in mind that they would formulate it in just this way. We can, however, use a more modern idiom. Kant is saying that if the sensory input were to be coded merely in terms of qualitative characteristics, i.e. colours, tones, pressures and so on, this would be of no use to us. The qualitative characteristics must be ordered and related in various ways. Further, this order cannot itself be sensed: there are no sensations of proximity, enclosures, or succession, though our most elementary visual experiences seem to involve, and indeed to require, these relationships. To go on from this and say that they must be innate is another matter. In this context the word seems to do little more than stand for the fact that the perceptual field, wherever it is studied, in young children or in patients operated on for congenital cataract, always shows some degree of organization. Thus Bruner's statement really calls attention to a problem, though it may seem at first glance to be suggesting a solution. The sources of perceptual organization are still obscure.

Let us stay with Kant for a little; he may still have something to say to psychologists. It will be remembered that he published three Critiques, of Pure Reason, of Practical Reason, and of Judgment. In the second of these his preoccupations were moral and theological, and he made great use of a distinction between the Self as knower and the

Self as agent. Various forms of this distinction are to be found in recent writing in the philosophical,[3] the physical,[4] and the psychological fields.[5] Unfortunately Kant never looked back and asked himself whether the self as agent through its activity might not have something to do with the structure of the world apprehended by the self as knower. Perhaps if he had he would have dismissed the question as unanswerable, for it is difficult to see how philosophical analysis could proceed. But when the question is raised in psychological terms it seems to make sense, even when we phrase it in old-fashioned terms, and ask about the influence of an organism's activity or conation upon its cognition. To get an answer we should have to use what the organism is doing as our independent variable, and try to hold the stimulus conditions constant. This is rather a difficult enterprise, and there are historical reasons which made it seem unnecessary. Introspection did not produce conative variables, only the attributes of sensation and feeling. Even though the Würzburg school seemed to be looking in the right direction when they attempted to study thinking they were only successful to the extent that *Bewusstseinslage* joined the solemn group of teutonic abstractions that stand around the cradle of psychology.

II

There is a widespread belief that the introspection which was discredited by the early Behaviourists was simply the verbal report of the subject on what he was aware of in the course of a psychological experiment. In point of fact it was rather a special kind of report which had to do with the attributes and dimensions of the subject's immediate experience. Such a report was necessitated by a particular, and probably mistaken, idea of what consciousness is, put forward originally by Wundt. Dissatisfaction with this kind of report and the theory behind it, was generalized to include the running commentary on his own actions by the agent, and the reflective analysis of mental processes practised by the philosophical psychologists. The running commentary has been coming back of recent years, as part of a renewed interest in perceiving and thinking, but the reflective analysis is still regarded with suspicion as 'armchair psychology'. It could be argued that so long as the armchair is near a laboratory, it is a very desirable piece of research equipment. Consider the problem of perceptual organization: it raises at once the question of what sort of psychological entities correspond to the words 'space' and 'time'. Are they concepts like 'colour' for example, or something different? This seems to be an armchair rather than a laboratory question, but the answer to it will do something towards determining what laboratory studies are undertaken.

But when psychology redefined itself as the study of behaviour, the oddest thing about the new programme was not so much its rejection of any reference to mental phenomena but rather the very limited view it took of its new subject-matter. Human behaviour is an astoundingly rich and various phenomenon. Anthropologists have given us some account of its diversity, as, in another context, have clinicians. Experimental psychologists, however, have shown little interest in behaviour as such, and have used a few limited and stereotyped varieties of it to study such processes as discrimination or the acquisition of simple habits. So it comes about that in a psychological laboratory very little behaviour occurs; maze-running, bar-pressing, saying 'yes' or 'no' cover a large proportion of it. Even where there is variety it is mostly ignored. I remember this being brought home to me very forcibly during my first visit to the United States. I had never seen a rat experiment before, and a graduate student showed two of his subjects perform. They had to seize the end of a string attached to one of two food containers some ten feet away and pull it into the cage. The correct container was indicated by a geometrical figure displayed above it. One rat stood up boldly and pulled the string in paw over paw while the other picked the string up in its mouth, walked to the back of the cage, laid it down, and so on until the container was on the right side of the bars. All that was recorded was whether or not the correct string was chosen. There is nothing wrong with this procedure: it is used because the choices can be related to the stimulus variables, that is to the figures displayed above the containers. The string-pulling idiosyncrasies might have a long and complicated history whose investigation would require quite a different kind of approach, but they too are behaviour.

The preoccupation of most experimental psychologists with matters other than behaviour is so pervasive that it is taken for granted, and only seldom does it become explicit. 'In a sense,' says Stevens, 'there is only one problem of psychophysics, namely the definition of the stimulus. In this sense there is only one problem in the whole of psychology—and it is the same problem.'[6] True, he defines the stimulus very widely as something which 'involves the specification of all the transformations of the environment, both internal and external, that leave the response invariant'. But notice here the question-begging use of 'environment'. It means every possible condition of the behaviour, including the state of the organism, which by some curious juggling becomes part of its own environment. Notice also that 'stimulus for behaviour' and 'cause of behaviour' have become synonymous phrases.

Though this position is vulnerable enough when stated as Stevens has stated it, it is generally taken to mean something even more limited. After all the so-called 'internal stimuli' are very difficult to get at, even if we know what we are looking for. So that when Gibson says, 'It is still true that the stimulus is the prime independent variable of a psychological experiment',[7] he is talking about the external stimuli, molar, molecular, pictorial, or symbolic, which the experimenter can control and manipulate.

It is not the aim of this paper to deny that the exploration of stimulus variables is an important part of the psychologist's task. He is better at this than anything else. But if he takes it to be his whole task, he is sure to run into trouble. He finds that there are some events he cannot account for in terms of the variables he has been using, and he is tempted to fall back upon 'primitive unities and identities' that have been obscurely present from the beginning.

III

The need for an alternative starting point has been apparent for some time. More than twenty years ago it was pointed out[8] that 'Analysis of the properties of stimuli which determine reaction shows that in every case there is a functional equivalence between a rather wide range of objects which have in common only certain general or relational characters which cannot be reduced to stimulation of identical nervous elements.' This has been termed the 'intersubstitutability of cue systems',[9] and points to the wide range of inputs that can be used to produce the same output. If we study behaviour over time so that processes like adaptation, learning and maturation could occur, it would also be easy to show that the same input can produce a wide range of outputs. We have abandoned the notion that the perceptual process is almost entirely determined from outside, that a stimulus acts through a receptor upon a more or less inert nervous system and somehow causes it to produce a response. We think rather of the input interacting with a continuous stream of ongoing activity. In these circumstances what a stimulus does is clearly as important as where it comes from. In other words, as well as starting with the stimulus and describing it in terms of its physical characteristics, and the route by which it enters the central nervous system, it might be a good idea to start with the response and work back to a stimulus classification which, instead of using physical characteristics anchored to the various sensory modalities, bases itself upon the different ways in which stimuli act upon behaviour.

Perhaps an example will make this point clearer. It has been reported[10] that young thrushes are unable to see during the first week or so after hatching, and the characteristic wide open, gaping response is released by jolting or vibration. Once the nestlings become sensitive to visual stimulation, any object of sufficient size appearing in the upper half of the visual field is also effective as a releaser, though it does not replace vibration in this respect. Visual discrimination of shape, direction, and distance soon become possible, but there is a short period during which visual stimuli act only as releasers, and the young birds gape blindly towards the sky as they did before they could see at all. Gaping, that is to say, is released by visual stimuli, but directed by gravity. Only after some days does vision assume a directing as well as a releasing function, and make it possible for the bird to turn its head towards an approaching object.

Thus a classification of stimuli according to whether they release or direct would not be identical with one based upon sensory modes. Three stages in the early development of the young thrushes can be identified. In the first the releasing stimuli are tactile-kinaesthetic and the directing stimuli are vestibular. In the second both tactile-kinaesthetic and visual stimuli have releasing functions, but the gaping is still under vestibular direction. Finally, the visual stimuli become capable of directing as well as releasing the response. This does not mean that vestibular stimuli are no longer relevant. Directed behaviour is only possible against a postural background, mainly proprioceptive and vestibular in origin. So we have in this very simple situation at least one more functional mode, which may be termed 'supporting'.

One important point emerges at this stage, namely, that very diverse stimuli in the physical sense may be functionally equivalent: a shaking nest has the same effect as a birdwatcher's head. The term 'intersubstitutability' will clearly have to cross sensory modal boundaries.

A second point requires another example. Remaining within the context of early avian behaviour, we find that the innate releasing stimulus for the alarm response in jackdaws is 'any living being that carries a black thing, dangling or fluttering'.[11] In sensory or physical terms this is quite complex, yet behaviourally it is simple, and one may not be able to break it down further without depriving it of its functional characteristics.

Evidence of the importance of supporting stimuli in general may appear when we consider the effects of minor changes in familiar situations. With familiarity the cues needed to direct behaviour are reduced, and so a good deal of the sensory input must have merely a supporting function. It has been shown repeatedly[12] that an unexpected change, even a small one, in part of this input can be extremely disturbing. The change need not involve anything in itself new. A familiar attendant, for example, wearing the equally familiar coat of another attendant disturbs young chimpanzees. Lorenz calls this 'false recognition'[13] and states that animals may react to the change of single characteristics in familiar situations with escape reactions of extreme intensity. In fact we have clearly identified another functional class of stimuli, which might be called 'disrupting'. This would include unexpected absence of supporting stimuli, along with pain and various types of stress.

IV

Since it is the aim of the argument to do no more than suggest the possibility of an approach to the stimulus which does not base itself upon the sensory modalities, there is no need to carry it further. One point that is worth underlining is that any classification in functional terms must have neuro-physiological implications. There is evidence that this may be so. For example, in studies of what has been called 'habituation', and its effects in the central nervous system, it has been shown[14] that, as a task becomes familiar, characteristic changes in the electrical activity in different parts of the cortex can be demonstrated. Sokolov[15] has suggested that when placed in a continuing or slowly changing situation the organism sets up some pattern in the central nervous system which matches the input. While this is going on we may think of the stimuli as directive. When successful matching has been achieved the stimuli are no longer needed to direct and come to play a supporting part. Corresponding to this change there is a reduction in the extent to which cortical activity is related to input. When the stimulus changes the earlier and more widespread pattern of cortical activity reappears. Subjectively we would say that the organism starts attending once more to what is going on around about it instead of relying on internal processes with minimal external support. Work of this kind is at an early stage, but it is already clear that the difference between the two states that have just been described is at least as important physiologically as the fact that the stimuli in question happened to be visual or auditory.

This kind of development was foreshadowed more than a dozen years ago by Hebb. 'When the detailed evidence of neuro-physiology and histology are considered, the conclusion becomes inevitable that the non-sensory factor in cerebral action must be consistently present, and of more dominating importance than reluctant psychological theory has ever recognized.'[12] Sensory physiology itself, now that it can move in from the periphery, is providing evidence which will bring about its own transformation. Apparently just as an organism searches, manipulates, and turns its back on parts of its environment, so the nervous system scans, filters, matches and guesses in dealing with the input from the sense organs. In fact input and output are involved with one another to an extent which makes the older type of peripheral theory very difficult to maintain. Consider another experiment on habituation, this time one which concentrates on the input stage rather than on central processes.[16] If a cat is sitting listening to something rather unrewarding, and a mouse runs by, the cat reaches out, as it were, by efferent pathways, and switches off its ears at the cochlear nuclei. At one time this might have been called 'afferent neural (or stimulus) interaction',[17] but the phrase is a little misleading. It seems to imply that the mouse switches off the cat's ears on the way in from the cat's eyes. Certainly it implies a functional and anatomical separation of output and input which neuro-physiology does not seem able to confirm.

Perhaps by now there are enough straws in the wind to make a modest bale. It is clear that the simple input-output system of classical S–R theory has become very complicated. What should we do? There are three current proposals. (1) Get rid of S–R theory entirely.[18] (2) Carry on with S–R thinking, but do it better.[19] (3) Escape all these troubles by relating environmental variables to overt behaviour changes without asking questions about what goes on in the organism.[20] It may be that a chastening process of avoidance learning will eventually drive us into this last position, with reduced anxiety and some helpful rationalizations, but the time for this has not yet come. Among the avenues, or should one say alleys, still to be explored, are those that have been already indicated at the R end of the S–R formulation.

V

Reassured by the neurophysiological and other evidence that has been cited we may return to the Kantian problems without feeling, as some may have done, that in raising it at this stage we were being antiquarian or merely whimsical. The problem is one which has to do with the spatio-temporal and other structural features of the perceptual world. This same problem is tackled by Piaget,[21] only his approach is developmental and psychological, not epistemological. Like Kant, Piaget finds himself unable to derive the ordered space of the perceptual world from the stimuli reaching us through our sense organs. It is true that such stimuli carry an immense amount of spatial information. The trouble is that the information is coded, and we need some sort of schema to enable us to break the code. However we do it we are in fact able to use qualitative and discontinuous data to reach an ordered and extended continuity. As an alternative to the suggestion that here we depend upon 'primitive unities and identities' which are innate is Piaget's claim that awareness of space is based upon action in space. 'The intuition of space', he says, 'is not a "reading" or apprehension of the properties of objects, but, from the very beginning, an action performed on them. It is precisely because it enriches and develops physical reality instead of extracting from it a set of ready-made structures, that action is eventually able to transcend physical limitations and create operational schemata which can be formalized and made to function in a purely abstract deductive fashion.' This is a psychological answer to the question, How is synthetic *a priori* knowledge possible? An 'empirical deduction' as Kant would have called it. By action Piaget means in the first instance motor activity. 'The fact of its continuous existence through all stages renders motor activity of enormous importance for the understanding of spatial thinking.' This gives us quite a concrete starting-point. Piaget's theory of 'operations' has troubled some as being rather abstract and philosophical, but when he says that motor activity is 'the fountainhead of the operations' he brings his position within the boundaries of empirical science.

The principal advantage of starting with motor activity in considering perceptual organization is that we may find it possible to substitute known reflexes for hypothetical 'unities and identities'. For example, we know that the neonate has a two-dimensional space implicit in his head-mouth reflex. A light touch on the face will elicit a movement of the head up, down, or sideways, which will bring the mouth towards the point touched. Similarly there seem to be protective reflexes which produce a brushing movement of the hand across an area subjected to continuous pressure. Visual pursuit also seems to be present at a very early age. Thus we seem to have a directionally structured space of action, and a discriminative locating response within that space. It has been suggested[22] that something of this sort is all that we need as a starting-point for a self-organizing system to control spatial behaviour generally. Just because the responses at the beginning are few and crude, goal directed trial and error learning will be quite fast. We may not be able to do just what we want, but we shall find out quickly how to make the best of our simple response repertoire. This means that the basic or structural characteristics of environmental events will impose quite early some degree of corresponding organisation upon the internal system upon which the responses depend.

At this point it will be helpful to draw a distinction between motor activity on the one hand and its sensory consequences on the other. The stimulus bias of psychological theory has often tended to make it appear that motor activity makes its contribution to perception in and through tactile-kinaesthetic feedback, or through the augmentation of exteroceptive information, as when we explore or manipulate. The word 'feedback' as used here is much wider than anything engineers had in mind when they invented the term. For them it is simply the amount by which an output is greater or less than some target value applied negatively or positively as a correction. Perhaps when we are thinking of the more complex perceptual situation we might use the term 'backput' for those changes which result from our own behaviour. Backput, then, in this sense, is usually treated as though it were just a particular kind of source of input. It seems possible that a rather fundamental error is being made here because backput implies output in a way that input does not: indeed backput can only be defined in terms of output. Furthermore, the fact that we can always, in ordinary perception, discriminate backput from input seems to require that output must be cognitively present in its own right, and not merely as a derivative of change in input. In other words, action, intention, conation, or whatever word one uses for this part of the perceptual process, is as basic as any other, even though we cannot point to some conscious content corresponding to these terms.

There is a good deal of empirical evidence pointing in the same direction. A number of statements have been quoted[23] made by patients while various parts of the motor cortex, mainly in the first pre-central gyrus, were being stimulated. 'You made me move', 'My hands want to tremble a little', 'I have a twisting-around feeling of the eyes', are typical remarks. One patient reported a desire to move her hand but in this case no movement in fact took place. Whatever did happen seemed distinguishable from voluntary movement, or indeed from any other kind of normal output. Consequently under these circumstances the proprioceptive backput is responded to as though it were input. In fact it is input, since the patient has not done anything. Even though some of his muscles have contracted there has been no output.

VI

We can approach the same position from another direction. Nothing that has been said is intended to detract from the basic importance of backput in the control of motor activity. Apart from a few reflexes the movements of the neonate are random and unco-ordinated. Even the spatial reflexes that have already been discussed are poorly executed at first. Control depends upon proprioceptive and exteroceptive coding. Perhaps the notion of exteroceptive backput may seem a little odd. Surely, it may be said, exteroceptive stimulation is input. I disagree. Nothing seems to be gained by relating a functional distinction such as that between backput and input to anatomical differences. Consider the case of vision. When I move my head or my eyes I generate proprioceptive and exteroceptive information. Both kinds are related closely to my motor activity, and in much the same way. Neither is responded to as a signal which indicates a change in the environment. It is worth while looking at this familiar example rather closely. Voluntary movement, it has been suggested,[24] leads to no input in the functional sense, because the visual signal is informationally redundant in a stable environment. If retinal changes did *not* take place, then there would be an output-backput mismatch and input would occur, that is, we should see movement. When I am lecturing I can raise and lower my eyes and nothing seems to happen in spite of the way the faces of the students must be moving on my retinae. If, however, the retinal patterns did remain constant under these conditions then they would appear to bounce up and down in the most fantastic fashion, rendered even more puzzling by the absence of an audible thud as they hit their seats again. The very slightest output-backput mismatch can produce input. One of them has only to yawn or scratch his head, and the movement shows up at once whether my own eyes are still or not.

Considered in this light input has clearly become something which can only be specified in relation to the ongoing motor activity of the organism, and it has already been pointed out that motor activity is not reducible to its proprioceptive consequences. The evidence from stimulation of the motor cortex can be supplemented in simple and familiar ways. If eye movements are produced abnormally by pressing the finger on the eyeball or by vestibular disturbance, then an apparent movement of the visual world is seen. Similar consequences follow when we change the output-backput coding. For instance when we reverse the direction of retinal movement either in the horizontal or the vertical axis by means of prisms or mirrors worn in front of the eyes, the visual world becomes unstable until the new code has been learned.[25]

Going back for a moment to the question of early spatial learning, it would seem that the relationship between proprioceptive and extero-ceptive, especially visual, backputs is very important. It is the means whereby a sequential space, which has a temporal component, becomes purified, a topological space becomes Euclidean. The learning of this relationship may well have an instinctive basis. Those familiar with the behaviour of young blind children claim that they often behave like sighted children, turning their eyes or heads towards an actively mov-ing hand. It is said too that a child who goes blind before the age of four or five can never really understand school geometry. The writer has examined two such children in the course of an investigation into the effects of early blindness.[26] Both were very intelligent and later passed matriculation level mathematics. In each case rote-learning seems to have been necessary.

VII

Let us now return to more general considerations. Most people, when they came across the reference to Kant, in the remark by Bruner quoted at the beginning of this paper, probably did not realize the extent to which we have been considering an old problem in a new context. Kant, it will be remembered, undertook the task of showing that Hume's atomistic associationism was not enough. He proceeded in the more mature parts of the First Critique, by drawing implications from demonstrable facts of everyday experience. In the Second Analogy, where he was concerned with the status of causal relationships he used an example which is almost exactly the same as the one to be found on page 180. If we look at a house our eyes can look from roof to foundation and back again as we choose, whereas when we see a ship sailing down a river the sequence of impressions is to some extent imposed upon us. There is a mismatch between output and backput which has to be accounted for; we see an event not just as an object. Kant developed his argument epistemologically not psychologically, but at least he saw the problem in essentially psychological terms. In many ways our position today is very like Kant's. Some feel, as he did, the need for a Copernican revolution which will shift the centre of gravity in psychology from the outside to the inside, from the safe, familiar stimuli to the shifting complexities of action. But the Copernican revolution was not what Copernicus took it to be, and even if it had been, it would have done no more than allow us to look at old data in a new way. We cannot, as some might wish, jettison the results of several generations of laborious research. Psychological experiment is always difficult, and often frustrating, so that the rumbling wheels of the latest bandwaggon have sometimes seemed a welcome distraction from our necessary tasks. The trouble is that we cannot always distinguish between a bandwaggon and a tumbril. There can be no doubt that as a result of our preoccupation with the periphery we have limited ourselves to what may turn out to be only a small part of our problem. Confronted as we are with an incredibly complex and versatile organism we have, for the most part, to use computer jargon, programmed our subjects in perceptual experiments to transmit, and have studied the characteristics and limitations of their performance in this task only. The results of our inquiries have consequently been restricted to discriminations, channel capacities, and things of that sort. But they are valid results, and the the job that has been done would have had to be done whatever our starting-point. Though we are now becoming more interested in what our subjects are doing than in what is happening to them, the stimulus is still an essential element in the total sequence of events of which we are trying to give an account. Organisms do not behave *in vacuo*. All that is being suggested is that we might make better progress if we were to stop acting as though stimuli were genuinely independent variables and provided the only possible starting-point for psychological experiment. There seems to be evidence that the 'primitive unities and identities' which were mentioned earlier, as well as other characteristics of perception of which we know very little at present, are due to the fact that perceiving grows out of and remains part of action. This means that the manipulation of stimulus variables, no matter how extensive or precise, cannot by itself lead to an explanation of behaviour. We must take into account the programme as well as the data being processed. Even although any organism complicated enough to be interesting has an immense variety of programmes available to it we can exercise some control by instructions, by learning, by deprivation, by habituation, and so on. This is being done already, and not only in the work of Piaget that has been mentioned. There is also the rapidly growing volume of research on the strategies and tactics of thinking. Neurophysiology and cybernetics too are giving some stimulating leads.

So far as perceptual organization is concerned we may tentatively sum up along the following lines. We are dealing in perception with a coding process whereby stimulus energies are brought into relation with the ongoing activity of the organism. The nature of the coding will never be independent of the activity which it serves.[27] In the beginning, since activity precedes perception, there is available to us a rather basic or primitive coding, for which the term 'innate' has been loosely used. In studying the adult human subject psychologists have in the past tended to restrict the scope of their work by concentrating too much on what is being coded, and not enough on what it is being coded for. It would seem that in a number of ways we are beginning to escape from this limitation.

REFERENCES

1. KOCH, S., 1959, 'Epilogue', in KOCH, S. (ed.), *Psychology: A Study of a Science*, Vol. 3, New York: McGraw-Hill.
2. BRUNER, J. S., 1957, 'On perceptual readiness', *Psychol. Rev.*, *64*, 123.
3. MACMURRAY, J., 1957, *The Self as Agent*, London: Faber.
4. BRIDGMAN, P. W., 1959, *The Way Things Are*, Cambridge, Mass.: Harvard University Press.
5. AMES, A., JR., 1953, 'Reconsideration of the origin and nature of perception', in RATNER, S. (ed.), *Vision and Action*, New Brunswick: Batgers University Press.
6. STEVENS, S. S., 1951, 'Mathematics, Measurement and Psychophysics', in STEVENS, S. S. (ed.), *Handbook of Experimental Psychology*, New York: Wiley.
7. GIBSON, J. J., 1960, 'The concept of stimulus in psychology', *Amer. Psychologist*, *15*, 694.
8. LASHLEY, K. S., 1942, 'The problem of cerebral organization in vision', in KLÜVER, H. (ed.), *Biological Symposia*, Vol. 7, Lancaster: Cattell.
9. BRUNSWICK, E., 1956, *Perception and the Representative Design of Psychological Experiments*, Berkeley: University of California Press.
10. TINBERGEN, N., 1951, *The Study of Instinct*, London: Oxford University Press.
11. LORENZ, K., 1952, *King Solomon's Ring*, London: Methuen.
12. HEBB, D. O., 1949, *The Organization of Behaviour*, New York: Wiley.
13. LORENZ, K., 1956, 'Comments on Piaget's paper', in TANNER, J. M., and INHELDER, B. (ed.), *Discussions on Child Development*, London: Tavistock Publications.
14. PRIBRAM, K. H., 1962, 'Psychology and the neurological disciplines', in KOCH, S. (ed.), *Psychology; The Study of a Science*, Vol. 4, New York: McGraw-Hill.
15. SOKOLOV, E. N., 1960, in BRAZIER, M. A. B. (ed.), *The Central Nervous System and Behaviour, Transactions of the Third Conference*, New York: Josiah Macy, Jr. Foundation.

16. HERNÁNDEZ-PEÓN, R., SCHERRER, H., and JOUVET, M., 1956, 'Modification of electric activity in the cochlear nucleus during "attention" in unanaesthetized cats', *Science, 123,* 331.
17. HULL, C. L., 1943, *Principles of Behaviour,* New York: Appleton-Century.
18. MILLER, G. A., GALANTER, E., and PRIBRAM, K. H., 1960, *Plans and the Structure of Behaviour,* New York: Holt.
19. HEBB, D. O., 1960, Review of MILLER, G. A., GALANTER, E., and PRIBRAM, K. H., 'Plans and the Structure of Behaviour', *Contemp. Psychol., 5,* 209.
20. SKINNER, B. F., 1959, 'A case history in scientific method', in KOCH, S. (ed.), *Psychology: A study of a Science,* Vol. 2, New York: McGraw-Hill.
21. PIAGET, J., and INHELDER, B., 1956, *The Child's Conception of Space,* London: Routledge and Kegan Paul.
22. MACKAY, D. M., 1956, 'Towards an information-flow model of human behaviour', *Brit. J. Psychol., 47,* 30.
23. PENFIELD, W., and RASMUSSEN, T., 1952, *The Cerebral Cortex of Man,* New York: Macmillan.
24. MACKAY, D. M., 1957, 'The stabilization of perception during voluntary activity', *Proc. XV Internat. Cong. Psychol.,* p. 284, Amsterdam: North-Holland Publ. Co.
25. KÖHLER, I., 1951, *Über Aufbau und Wandlungen der Wahrnehmungswelt,* Vienna: Rohrer.
26. DREVER, J., 1955, 'Early learning and the perception of space', *Amer. J. Psychol., 68,* 605.
27. SUMMERFIELD, A., and LEGGE, D., 1960, 'Perception and information theory', *Bull. Brit. Psychol. Soc., 42,* 23.

CHAPTER II

FIFTY YEARS' EXPERIMENT ON THINKING:* 1900–1950

BY GEORGE HUMPHREY

I

Fifty years' experiment on the psychology of thinking or reasoning has not brought us very far, but it has at least shown the kind of road which must be traversed. Looking over the immense mass of literature which has now accumulated, several persistent problems or perhaps groups of problems seem to obtrude themselves. There is first the problem of the 'motor' of thought, as the late Professor Lewin might have called it. Thinking or reasoning does not happen by itself. At the least, some term corresponding to 'motivation' is necessary in order to describe what takes place, the word being used without any implication that it corresponds to a separate psychological process, but for experimental and theoretical convenience.[1] Inheriting the doctrine from their predecessors, the earlier experimentalists took it almost for granted that the 'law of association' provided the necessary motor, although there were some dissentients; and the classical work of Pavlov enabled the behaviourists to translate association into their own language. The experimental attack on associationism[2] developed in three stages. The first was reached by the Würzburgers, who found the 'reproductive tendencies' of the time inadequate to explain thinking, and postulated the determining tendencies and the *Aufgabe* as epicyclic mechanisms. Following their lead, Selz argued with telling effect against the whole associational structure, and experimentally demonstrated the integrative nature of at least one stage of the thought process, thus putting forward a principle basically opposed to that of

* Originally published as Chapter X, 'Summary and Conclusions', in the author's book, *Thinking*, 1951, London: Methuen.

classical associationism. Finally a concerted attack was made by the Gestalt psychologists, who claimed to have shown experimentally that habit, identified with association, is never the motor of a psychic event, and developed the theory of the unitary system-under-stress.[3] But the theory is by no means dead. Thorndike's theory of 'connectionism' was professedly associational. The *Foundations of Psychology*[4] devotes the first six pages of the chapter on *Learning*[5] (Hovland) to what is called a 'simple type, associative learning', that is, to conditioned-reflex learning, and ends the section with a formulation of the *law of contiguity*, which, the writer says, must be supplemented by other principles, especially by motivation. There are many other psychologists of the first rank who hold some kind of associational theory today.

The fact is that in spite of many serious criticisms from both the experimental and the analytical side the theory is still of undoubted value in providing a formulation of relatively complex events. At the same time, many feel with Hovland that it must be supplemented, at least by the concept of motive. Using the hypothesis of need-reduction, Clark Hull[6] has made an impressive attempt to combine both principles, that of association and that of motive. There are, however, great difficulties in the equation which he makes of need-reduction with motive.[7] In addition the notion of motive is itself vague, and, as Woodworth once remarked, there are doubts whether it can ever be made scientific. It certainly holds many dangers, of which not the least is that of begetting a new Faculty psychology; but its use by psychologists of the highest competence testifies to its convenience and value. And as giving recognition to what Lewin called the 'motor' for physical or mental events and recognizing the part played by the larger integrations of the organism, larger, that is to say, than what might be called the 'quick fire' of associationism, the modern doctrine of motive does seem to have justified itself. But the theory of thinking thus finds itself in the paradoxical position of being forced to employ two concepts or hypotheses one of which experiment seems largely to have refuted, while theory has but uneasily digested, if indeed it has digested, the other.

In addition, the psychology of thinking must deal not only with conscious but also with unconscious processes and motivation. It was of course Freud that first taught us to recognize the existence of 'wishes' of which we are not conscious, and it has been seen that the *Aufgabe* and the *Determining Tendencies* were claimed to function unconsciously. It has been seen that Messer also postulated an unconscious machinery underlying the conscious process of thought, and that, of the modern experimentalists, Maier showed that what he calls 'direction' can be given unconsciously.[8] There is ostensible evidence from other sources that what would ordinarily be called thought-processes may occur without the consciousness of the thinker, who may 'lay the problem aside'.[9] It appears fairly certain that scientific and artistic invention may be consciously initiated, laid aside for a while and suddenly completed with full consciousness after an interval which may in some cases amount to years. In all probability some form of working that is unconscious must be postulated to explain these cases.[10] The question of whether unconscious steps occur corresponding to those of conscious reasoning has yet to be decided experimentally. If such unconscious thought processes do occur we do not know whether they are of the same general nature as ordinary conscious reasoning, or as Freud claims for the workings of his Unconscious, radically different. The necessary experiments should not be impossible to devise.

There are thus many problems clustering round the concept of the motor of thinking. Only experiment can solve and probably in some cases even formulate them. It seems likely that both problems and their solutions will ultimately be found to belong not to the psychology of thinking alone but to the broad field of Psychology itself.

II

Another salient group of problems centres on the fact that thinking involves not only 'covert' processes, those of experience, of the kind the Würzburgers treated, but also 'overt' activities, the existence of which they did indeed notice but only incidentally. The most obvious of these is speech, but clearly other activities are in many cases involved. It is fair to say that in general while a human being thinks his problem out, an animal acts it out, though there are many exceptions to be found. Probably here again there is a continuum from, as far as we know, a complete 'acting out' in the more primitive organisms to a nearly complete 'thinking-out' in human beings engaged in certain problems. It may be shown that one form of action namely speech, is of great assistance to human thinking, and reason has been given to believe that the elementary activity known as muscular tonus is in all probability of assistance also. We still lack any intimate knowledge of the relationship of the two terms in the Thought-in-Action complex. Except for a very few experiments we do not know the nature of the dazzling advantages conferred on our thinking by language. We do not know exactly what it means to say that different series of activities, verbal and otherwise, may result from processes which in a genuine sense of the word are prior to them. Lashley's and Dashiell's experiments, as well as everyday experience, have shown us the fact beyond doubt. A hundred years of psychologizing have shown only what statements to avoid, such as the 'idea results in action', or 'the idea (or image) precedes thought'.

III

One other problem seems to be worth noting which does not seem to be related directly to the other two. During the 'trial and error' activity which may be found in much thinking and perhaps at every level of psychological activity, nobody has yet asked the question how the thinker recognizes the (correct) solution when it occurs to him. For overt trial and error the question answers itself—at least we assume that it does. That is to say the conventional statement is that the cat in the puzzle makes a number of movements until it obtains food. There is 'need-reduction' in Hull's language, and activity stops. But what of a man thinking out a way to earn food? All sorts of solutions come to mind. Some are rejected, but on what principle? We do not know at present. It is, of course, conceivable that 'motive' is again involved.

IV

After fifty years of experiment the following skeletal account may then be tentatively given. The intention is, in the main, to include experimentally derived fact, with only such analytical statement as is necessary to provide a framework for it.

(a) *Thinking as the term is understood in this discussion may be provisionally defined as what occurs in experience when an organism, human or animal, meets, recognizes, and solves a problem.*[11] (The term reasoning is preferred by some writers.) It is thus part of the total process of organic interaction with the environment. On the side of the organism this total process includes many levels of organized activity, of which thinking itself should possibly be considered one, as apparently by Bentley[12] and the later Würzburgers. Those considered here generally facilitate the total process, but there is some evidence that they may on occasion be a hindrance to it. (See paragraphs 10, 12, 13 to follow.) One may compare the popular belief that if thought itself is over-elaborated it may hinder 'action'. There is probably no hard-and-fast distinction between learning and thinking, though the former term if generally used when there is repetition of the total organism-environment complex, and when certain other conditions are complied with.

(b) *A problem is a situation which for some reason appreciably holds up an organism in its efforts to reach a goal.* In practice the problem often though not always contains contradictory factors, which have to be reconciled.[13] Duncker[14] has drawn attention to what he calls 'constraint' which is often found in problem situations.

(c) *The process of thinking involves an active combination of features which as part of the problem situation were originally discrete.* (Selz, Maier, Gestalt, Herrick, many philosophers.) This process is the culmination of the organic process of integration described and examined minutely by such writers as Sherrington.[15] The delay characteristic of reaction to a problem is often due to the fact that the necessary integration begins to approach the limit of organic capacity.

(d) *It involves the use of past experience. The fact is obvious, but the method by which it comes about is still not decided.* The early experimentalists thought that a replica of past experience was produced by association ('reproductive tendencies'). Various alternatives have been proposed, such as the 'actualization' of (stereotyped) knowledge (Selz); a (more or less) inert and modifiable 'memory-trace' (Gestalt); a Schema,[16, 17] the 'conditioned response', and so on. It is possible that more than one of these suggested mechanisms may actually operate.

(e) *Not only the method but also the form of the ingression of the past into the present is under dispute.* One school maintains that the relation between past and present is particular (Hull: the 'continuity theory'), an opposing school that it is general (Lashley). This divergence of opinion has had its counterpart among philosophers. Paragraphs (d) and (e) involve problems which are being attacked in the field of learning. The problems belong equally to the field of thinking, as so many others.

(f) *There is ubiquitous 'Trial and error' during thought-activity, whether animal or human, overt or covert.* This has been noted in verbal (Würzburg, Selz, Willwoll) problems, puzzle-solving by human beings (Ruger[18]) generalization and abstraction, mechanical and practical problem-solving by human beings, and so on.

Such behaviour may be found in the descriptions of the Gestalt experiments. The mechanism by which the 'wrong' solutions are rejected in overt learning is obscure; it is doubly obscure in thinking. Trial and error or its counterpart is a general principle of adaptive behaviour, and may be found in organisms of many grades.

(g) *For purposes of psychological analysis, motive (motor) may be distinguished as an aspect of thinking.* This distinction seems to be made necessary by the pioneer work of Watt and Ach, and it was sharpened by the work of Lewin. The motivation of thought has received little experimental attention, though much attention has been paid to motivation in learning. Motive implies a goal. It might thus be said that for the thinker the problem-field becomes polarized towards the goal.[19] The polarization disappears when the problem is finally solved. Although the present concern with problems of motivation is a healthy one, it is entirely possible that further developments will render the dichotomy no longer useful.[20]

(h) In addition there must be postulated some principle to account for the 'direction' of thinking; that is, to account for the fact that thinking keeps more or less to the point. The fact was long ago noticed, and many explanations have been given for it.[21] The assumption is generally made that the motive performs this function, but it is not necessarily correct. (Distinguish this use of the term 'direction' from Maier's.)

(i) *The Würzburg group, under the direction of Külpe, developed the doctrine that thought-as-experienced is free from sensory content of any kind.* Thus they contradicted the conventional (structural) theory of the time which claimed that experience comprised only sensation, images and effects. The Würzburg results were confirmed by many, notably by Binet,[22] who indeed claimed priority for them. They were contradicted by the results of the Cornell experiments,[23] which resolved the imageless thoughts into kinaesthetic sensations. It is maintained that the position of the Cornell group is untenable.[24] Since they are stated in demoded terms the Wurzburg results are unacceptable in their original form to many modern psychologists. An alternative statement is possible.

(j) *The Würzburg psychologists were inclined to underestimate the importance of the image. The image is a form of organization which is part of the more inclusive process of response.* It seems undoubtedly to be of value in certain contexts, though there is evidence that it may be valueless at times and even a hindrance to the total process. Individual and group differences may be important here, and also the nature of the problem.[25]

(k) *The Gestalt theorists, and in particular, Kohler, Koffka, Wertheimer, and Duncker, have stressed production as against (associative) reproduction in thinking. At the same time they have developed the notion of the organism under stress to account for the motor of thought.* Certain experimentalists allied to this school, such as Luchins[26] and Maier[27] seem to admit also a principle akin to association, which according to their experiments may be detrimental to productive thinking. The latter is accompanied by the restructuring of the perceptual field, which gives 'insight' into the problem.

(l) *Even when the thinker is overtly still, traces of the matrix of activity in which thought has grown up still remain in the changes of muscular tonus observed by many experimentalists.* There is an optimal range of tonus, above or below which any particular process of thinking is impeded. Thus tonus, like muscular activity in general, may under the right conditions help and under the wrong conditions hinder solution. (That is, trial here, as in every case, presupposes error.[27]) 'Thinking out' may clearly prevent a disaster that would have been precipitated by 'acting out'. That is why the 'thinking' method has won its evolutionary place.

(m) *A specialized form of activity is speech, which at least in its derivatives, such as writing and mathematics, is peculiar to human beings. Clinical, experimental, and factorial results agree that language cannot be equated with thinking.* Language is ordinarily of great assistance in thinking. It may also be a hindrance, as pointed out by Woodworth,[28] and many others. This is probably because speech, too, is so highly organized. Should then talking decide important issues?

(n) *Generalization may be defined as the activity whereby an organism comes to effect a constant modification towards an invariable feature or set of features occurring in a variable context.* Since all learning involves a context which is to some extent variable, the process is common to both learning and thinking. Like all kinds of thinking, *generalization does not necessarily involve language, though it is often improved by language.* (Query: Is it ever impeded by language?)

(o) Thus a number of different grades and kinds of organization are involved in the total response to a problem-situation; of these (1) images of various modalities; (2) muscular action, including, in particular (3) speech, have been mentioned as such; to this list there should perhaps be added (4) concepts. The total process is in general facilitated by these organizations, but, apparently, cases occur where it is hindered by at least (1), (2), and (3).

(p) An artificial problem of 'meaning' has been created by treating the *image* and *speech-activity* apart from their total context. (Conceivably the same kind of confusion has been created by treating the 'concept' apart from its environmental context, thus invoking the 'problem of the Universal'.)

(q) To paraphrase a great man, the position as analysed above may be said to be the 'end of the beginning'. Later developments may well follow an entirely different direction. For one of many possibilities see note 29.

NOTES AND REFERENCES

1. By his experimental demonstration of the formation of the *Gesamtaufgabe*, Selz has shown that in the type of thinking he is examining there is a recognizable unification of motivational and non-motivational processes. *Thereafter* only, the process of thinking is unitary and motivation is an aspect of it. It is from this unitary stage that the Gestalt psychologists begin. Ach recognizes a similar stage of unification. The rapid descent of many maze-learning curves for the rat possibly corresponds to a similar unification also.

2. Associationism presupposes simultaneous (or nearly so) mental events. One, under certain conditions, tends on recurrence to reinstate the other.

3. Lewin himself spoke on the 'pressure of will or of a need' and apparently approved of this formulation in 1935. (LEWIN, K., 1935, *A Dynamic Theory of Personality*, p. 44, New York: McGraw-Hill.)

4. BORING, E. G., LANGFELD, H. S., and WELD, H. P., 1948, *Foundations of Psychology*, New York: Wiley.

5. HOVLAND, C. I., 1948, 'Learning', in BORING, LANGFELD, and WELD (*op. cit.*).

6. HULL, C. L., 1943, *Principles of Behaviour*, New York: Appleton-Century.

7. See HILGARD, E. R., 1948, *Theories of Learning*, pp. 106 ff., New York: Appleton-Century-Crofts.

8. It is conceivable, of course, that the cue was immediately forgotten in Maier's experiment.

9. PLATT, W., and BAKER, B. A. (1931, 'The relation of the scientific "hunch" to research', *J. Chemical Educ.*, *8*, 1977), and ROSSMANN, J. (1931, *The Psychology of the Inventor*, Washington, D.C.; Inventors Publ. Co.), give many interesting examples; as does HADAMARD, J. (1945, *The Psychology of Invention in the Mathematical Field*, Princeton, N.J.: Princeton University Press). Some of these are collected by HUMPHREY, G. (1948, *Directed Thinking*, pp. 116, 128 ff., New York: Dodd, Mead). PATRICK, C. (1935, 'Creative Thought in Poets', *Arch. Psychol.*, *78*, 74 and 1937, 'Creative Thought in Artists', *J. Psychol.*, *4*, 35) reports the same kind of thing for creative artists. WOODWORTH, R. S., quotes MEINECKE, G. (1934, 'Ein Beitrag zur Theorie des intuitiv-produktiven Denkens', *Arch. des. Psychol.*, *92*, 249) who set problems to an inventor and obtained reports from him. Again one finds the process of 'laying the problem aside'. CARPENTER, W. B. (1874, *Mental Physiology*, London: King), who believes that 'a large part of our intellectual activity is essentially automatic', has a most interesting and properly famous

chapter on 'Unconscious Cerebration'. He traces the notion to Hamilton and Leibnitz, and gives some excellent non-experimental examples of what seems to be the unconscious reorganization of data.

10. It is possible that removal of fatigue, fresh stimulation, etc., may account for at least part of what happens in some cases.

11. The term *problem* is used with some hesitation. Since problem and non-problem situations shade imperceptibly into each other, the term must necessarily be indefinite. It should be noted that there is no qualitative difference between problem and non-problem situations, that 'thinking' occurs during, perhaps is 'released by', the period of delay, that a given situation will or will not be a problem according to the experience and capacities of the particular organism concerned. To borrow Woodworth's remark about motive, it is perhaps doubtful whether the term problem can ever be made scientific. Nevertheless it has been and still is of value in psychology. Woodworth's definition in terms of 'novelty' cannot be accepted (see HUMPHREY, G., 1951, *Thinking* (Chap. VI), London: Methuen). A first attempt is made in this general statement to combine Woodworth's 'problem solving' with his 'Thinking'. (1938, *Experimental Psychology* (Chaps. XXIX, XXX), New York: Holt). Madison Bentley's excellent article: 'Where does Thinking come in?' (1943, see ref. 11) discusses with great acumen the definition of thinking. He makes it a single, *distinctive* resource of the organism. When he says that it 'integrates ... simpler and more primitive operations', the conclusion reached here fully confirms and perhaps elaborates on his conclusion. CHRISTOF, C., a pupil of Bentley's (1939, 'The Formulation and Elaboration of Thought-Problems', *Amer. J. Psychol.*, *52*, 161), collects the more common definitions of thinking.

12. BENTLEY, M., 1943, 'Where does Thinking come in?', *Amer. J. Psychol.*, *56*, 354.

13. E.g. Maier's rats were motivated to traverse a certain path, but the path was impassable (MAIER, N. R. F., 1938, see ref. 26). One of Bühler's problems was; 'Is this true? The smaller the woman's foot, the larger the bill for the shoes.'

14. DUNCKER, K., 1926, 'A qualitative study of productive thinking', *Ped. Sem. (J. genet. Psychol.)*, *33*, 642, and 1935, *Zur Psychologie des Produktiven Denkens*, Berlin: Springer.

15. SHERRINGTON, C. S., 1906, *The Integrative Action of the Nervous System*, New York: Yale University Press. BÜHLER, C. (1918, *Über Gedankenentstehung*, *Z. Psychol.*, *80*, 129) found that her subjects were unable to apprehend two meaningful words *without* relating them.

16. BARTLETT, F. C., 1938, *Remembering*, Chap. X, London: Cambridge University Press.

17. OLDFIELD, R. C., and ZANGWILL, O. L., 1942, 1943, 'Head's Concept of the Schema and its applications in Contemporary British Psychology', *Brit. J. Psychol.*, *32*, 267; *33*, 58.

18. RUGER, H. A., 1926 (1910), *The Psychology of Efficiency*, New York: The Science Press.

19. Conceivably this is the process of 'seeing the problem'. The problem is perhaps a problem because of the incomplete polarization.

20. HEBB, D. O., 1949, in his book *Organization of Behaviour*, New York: Wiley, has pointed the way in this direction.

G

21. HUMPHREY, G., 1940, 'The Problem of the Direction of Thought', *Brit. J. Psychol.*, *30*, 183.

22. BINET, A., 1909, 'L'Intelligence des Imbéciles', *Année Psychol.*, *15*, 1, and 'Les Signes Physiques de L'Intelligence chez les enfants', *Année Psychol.*, *16*, 1.

23. PYLE, W. H., 1909, 'An Experimental Study of Expectation', *Amer. J. Psychol.*, *20*, 530; OKABE, T., 1910, 'An Experimental Study of Belief', *Amer. J. Psychol.*, *21*, 563; CLARKE, H. M., 1911, 'Conscious Attitudes', *Amer. J. Psychol.*, *22*, 214; JACOBSON, E., 1911, 'Consciousness under Anaesthetics' and 'On Meaning and Understanding', *Amer. J. Psychol.*, *22*, 338, 553, and others.

24. See HUMPHREY, G., 1951, *Thinking* (Chap. IV), pp. 119–31, London: Methuen.

25. BOWERS, H. (1931, 'Memory and Mental Imagery', *Brit. J. Psychol.*, *21*, 271, and 1935, 'The Role of Visual Imagery in Reasoning', *Brit. J. Psychol.*, *25*, 436), found images of use in some tasks but not in others; Willwoll found images generally a help but sometimes a hindrance: Galton gives some anecdotal cases which tend towards the hindrance conclusion; KULVER, H. (1931, in MURCHISON, C. A. (ed.), *A Handbook of Child Psychology*, London: Milford) states that eidetic images may sometimes be a hindrance, and believes it is difficult to distinguish them from ordinary memory images, an opinion shared by MORSH, J. E., and ABBOTT, H. D. (1945, 'An Investigation of after-images', *J. Compar. Psychol.*, *38*, 47). COMSTOCK, C. (1921, 'On the Relevancy of Imagery to the Process of Thought', *Amer. J. Psychol.*, *32*, 196), gives good evidence for this as finding that images are of value.

26. LUCHINS, A. S., 1942, 'Mechanization in problem solving; the effect of Einstellung', *Psychol. Monog.*, *54*, No. 6.

27. MAIER, N. R. F., 1938, 'A Further Analysis of Reasoning in Rats', *Compar. Psychol. Monog.*, *15*, 1, and ref. 19, p. 41.

28. WOODWORTH, R. S., 1938, *Experimental Psychology*, New York: Holt ('often we have to get away from speech in order to think clearly'—p. 809).

29. See the monograph by HUMPHREY, G., and COXON, R. V., 1962, *Chemistry of Thinking*, Springfield; Ohio: Thomas.

For more detailed references see HUMPHREY, G., 1951, *Thinking*, London: Methuen.

CHAPTER 12

THOUGHT AND MACHINE PROCESSES*

BY B. V. BOWDEN

Cogito, ergo sum—DESCARTES
I do not think, therefore I am not—DR STRABISMUS (whom God preserve) of Utrecht. President of the Anti-Cartesian Society.

I

I propose, in this chapter, to compare some properties of electronic computers with human thought processes and, at the same time, try to assess the limitations of the machines we can build today as well as of those which may be built in the future. Let me begin by describing some of the feats of mental arithmetic accomplished by calculating prodigies.

At rare intervals there have appeared men and boys who display extraordinary powers of mental arithmetic. In a few seconds they can give the answer to questions which an expert mathematician could obtain only in a much longer time with the aid of pencil and paper. Some of them have remained otherwise illiterate; others, such as Gauss and Ampere, have risen to positions of eminence as mathematicians, physicists, or engineers. Many of them seem to have taught themselves the rules of arithmetic in their childhood, and to have learnt the multiplication table by playing with pebbles.

Few of them have been able to describe in detail how their minds work but I have been fortunate enough to have received a description at first hand from two of the most remarkable among them, Professor A. C. Aitken of Edinburgh University and Mr William Klein of the Mathematisch Centrum at Amsterdam.

As far as I can judge, Professor Aitken and Mr Klein use very similar methods in their mental computations; their speeds are quite

* An abridged version of Chapter 26, 'Thought and Machine Processes', in BOWDEN, B. V. (ed.), 1953, *Faster Than Thought*, London: Pitman.

comparable, and they are at least as fast as, and probably faster than, any of the prodigies whose performances have been described in the past.

Both men have most remarkable memories—they know by heart the multiplication table up to 100 × 100, all squares up to 1000 × 1000, and an enormous number of odd facts, such as 3937 × 127 = 499999, which are very useful to them, and seem to arise instantaneously in their minds when they are needed. In addition Mr Klein knows by heart the logarithms of all numbers less than 100, and of all prime numbers less than 10,000 (to twenty decimal places) so that he can work out sums like compound interest by 'looking up' the logs in his head, after factorizing the numbers he is using, if need be. He has also learnt enough about the calendar to be able to give the day of the week corresponding to any specified date in history; he learnt most of the Amsterdam telephone directory for fun. Professor Aitken has neglected logarithms in favour of mathematical formulae and the piano music and violin sonatas of Bach and Beethoven, but nevertheless he learnt 802 places of Π by heart in about fifteen minutes, an operation which to him was comparable in difficulty to learning a Bach fugue. If one realizes that in addition to their phenomenal memories both men possess an equally phenomenal ability at mental arithmetic, one can begin to understand some of the feats which they perform every day. Mr Klein, for instance, multiplies together numbers of up to six digits by six digits faster in his head than an ordinary man can do by using a desk calculating machine.

Professor Aitken was once asked to multiply 123456789 by 987654321; he immediately remarked to himself that 987654321 is 80000000001/81, thereby converting a tedious sum into a 'gift'. Asked for the recurring decimal form of 41/67, he multiplied numerator and denominator by 597, obtaining 24477/39999, and writing down immediately 0.611940298507462686567164179104477.

Even as a schoolboy he was able to astonish his fellows by squaring 57586 in his head in two seconds. He worked it out as follows, using $a^2 = (a - b)(a + b) + b^2$.

$$57586^2 = 57500 \times 57672 + 86^2$$
$$= 23 \times 144180000 + 86^2$$
$$= 3316147396.$$

These short cuts, which are an essential part of the repertoire of all mental prodigies, are quite beyond the scope of a machine, which makes much better time by using straightforward methods once the problem has been explained to it; but it is in this sort of way that Mr Klein performs a type of computation in which he has a most unusual skill. He can express prime numbers of the form $4n + 1$ as the sum of two squares; if they can be expressed as $8n + 1$, in the form $2c^2 + d^2$, etc. For example:—

$$5881 = 75^2 + 16^2$$
$$= 2 \times 54^2 + 7^2$$
$$= 3 \times 32^2 + 53^2$$
$$= 5 \times 9^2 + 74^2$$
$$= 7 \times 24^2 + 43^2$$

all of which he did in 100 seconds. Any machine would take a relatively long time to do such a computation, as it would have to work by a tedious process of trial and error. A mathematician would probably take an hour or so to prepare a tape of instructions for a machine which was to handle the general case, a second or so to feed in the particular number which he wanted to investigate, and the machine would take two or three seconds at most to produce the whole series of squares once it had started to work. The point is, of course, that the machine has to be told everything it needs to know for this particular problem, and even when it knows how to proceed it may well take so long for a man to pose a problem to the machine that a human calculator may have done the sum long before his colleague has had time to punch a tape with which to feed the numbers into the machine.

'The numbers', says Professor Aitken, 'come into view as one needs them, but even to say that they come into "view" gives a false impression. It is not "seeing" in the ordinary sense; it is a compound faculty that has never yet been accurately described. The analogy of music will throw light on calculation. The violinist (unless he is momentarily in a difficulty) does not need to visualize the notes on the stave, or the fingering or the bowing; the melody is everything— he is caught up in what he is playing. So it is with the mental calculator; visualizing occurs last of all, and only as required when all else has been done.'

Mr William Klein's brother Leo, who died at the hands of the Gestapo during the war, was almost as good a computer as William, and a better mathematician. Dr Stokvis, of Amsterdam, made a psychological study of the brothers;[1] he found that although their performances were very similar, their methods of operation were quite different. For example, Mr William Klein remembers numbers 'audibly'; he mutters to himself as he computes, he can be interrupted by loud noises, and if he ever does make a mistake it is by confusing two numbers which sound alike. Leo, on the other hand, remembered things 'visually'; and if he made a mistake it was by confusing digits which look alike. Both brothers were fascinated by numbers from their earliest childhood; William practised arithmetic almost all the time, but Leo hardly ever. Leo studied mathematics at the university, but William read medicine, took a medical degree, and had 'walked the hospitals' before he finally decided to earn his living as a computer. Dr Stokvis investigated the effect of drugs and of hypnosis on Mr William Klein, and found that neither improved his performance as a computer if he was using methods in which he was experienced and in which he had already achieved an 'optimum' performance.

II

The reader may feel that he is overwhelmed by the possibility of this kind of calculation, but before he decides to take up farming instead of arithmetic let us for one moment consider the mental arithmetic which is sometimes done by a certain Lakeland shepherd. During the course of a day his dog may drive past him a flock of perhaps 2,000 sheep. At the end of the day he knows not only *how many* sheep are missing, but *which* sheep are missing. Now even if one assumes for purposes of argument that a man can learn to tell the difference between one sheep and another, one must admit that even a shepherd requires and can exploit a skill in mental arithmetic which few of us could ever hope to achieve.

We have seen how skilfully some fortunate men can do arithmetic, and it is impossible for us to evade any longer a discussion of the interesting but not perhaps very important question: 'Can these new machines think, and if not, will it ever be possible to build machines which do?'

Anyone who has watched an automatic pilot controlling a giant air liner, and bringing it almost all the way across the Atlantic with no help from the human beings on board, may have wondered whether it is not reasonable to imagine that 'George' is thinking for himself. Instruments of this type have 'grown up' gradually stage by stage, they perform 'calculations' of a fairly simple type which can be done almost instinctively after long practice by the human beings whom they so ably assist, and, perhaps most important of all, these machines are quite unoriginal. Each type is capable of only one sort of computation—for example, 'George' cannot drive a car. Few people have seriously insisted that an automatic pilot 'thinks' for itself in the sense that its designer thought when he was making it.

Turing[2] has analysed the problem from another point of view, and suggests that in a few years' time it may be possible to make a machine which will answer almost any question asked of it in the same sort of way as a human being would do, so much so, in fact, that it would be difficult for anyone who posed the questions simultaneously to a machine and to a human being to discover from the answers which was which (or who was who). When he is playing this 'imitation game' the inquisitor must be able to see neither of his victims and all communications must take place in code. Turing assumes, of course, that the machine would be trying to 'pass itself off' as human and that it would for example type out a statement that it has blue eyes and blond hair and likes strawberries and cream, if asked the appropriate questions. The machine might make a few 'mistakes' in arithmetic from time to time so that the inquisitor would not be able to identify it because of its infallibility. Turing thinks that in ten or twenty years' time it should be possible to build a machine which would in this 'imitation game' leave more than half its inquisitors in doubt of its 'humanity' for five minutes or so.

To build a machine that would write something like *Ulysses* in sonnet form might tax the ability of several generations of Babbages, and as Watson-Watt[3] put it, the life-long efforts of a potential Shakespeare might be devoted to the construction of a mechanized Martin Tupper. It is easy, however, to make this point too strongly. We know of no potential Shakespeare who is devoting his efforts to digital computers at the moment, nor do we think it likely that such a man would do so if the opportunity were given to him. He would make far more money in Hollywood. (We must confess that we cannot be so certain about potential Bacons.) We must point out, furthermore, that the efforts of computer engineers have already produced a mechanized Briggs (who spent his lifetime computing logarithms) and a mechanized Barlow (whose famous Tables were his life's work) but no one has ever conceived of a mechanized Napier (for he *invented* logarithms). It will be better to devote ourselves to the development of machines which can handle problems of a type more suited to their abilities, and to remember that calculating prodigies are less important than original thinkers.

It already appears that over a limited range of types of intellectual activity the differences between the operations of the machines and those of a human being are of degree rather than of kind, so let us for a moment contemplate the structure rather than the functions of the human brain. The average brain contains about ten thousand million individual cells, or approximately three times as many cells as there are human beings in the world. Each cell is connected, directly or indirectly, to every other, and small electrical impulses flow through the nerve fibre connecting them at a speed of between fifty and two hundred miles an hour. A modern digital computer may perhaps use three or four thousand valves. It is doubtful if all the valves that have been made since Lee de Forrest's time amount to a fifth of the number of cells in the brain of an idiot child. If they could be assembled together in one place they would require all the buildings in Whitehall to house them, several Battersea power stations to drive them and the Thames to cool them. Even if they were of the best modern type about a 1,000 would fail and need replacing every minute. Moreover, the problem of interconnecting them would daunt the imagination of the most stout-hearted engineer.

III

Machines are in a very early stage of development; their structure, by comparison with that of a human brain, is exceedingly simple; nevertheless they can perform operations which tax the abilities of a thinking human being to the utmost. It already appears that the difference in complexity between man and machine is greater than the difference in ability. The structure of the brain of an ordinary earthworm is as complicated as that of a modern computer. The computer achieves its success because the whole of its 'abilities', limited though they are, are directed by a mathematician to some particular end. This fact, of course, is the measure of the skill and ability of the programmer, and it is a pity not to reverse the argument and speculate for a moment on the potentialities of a human brain if it were efficiently organized by some 'programme' or other. It is well known that, when he has been hypnotized, a man can often recall in detail all kinds of incidents that completely escape him when he is in his normal conscious state. The extent of this power of recall is very surprising. It is easy enough to store information in our own minds, in a library, in a filing system or in a computing machine, but it always seems to be exasperatingly difficult to get it out again. It is most frustrating to discover that one really possesses an infallible memory, but that one can only explore it properly if one submits to hypnosis by someone else, who doesn't really know what is inside it. It is difficult for a hypnotist to improve the reasoning powers of his patient, though every schoolmaster claims to do so, but there does unfortunately seem to be a limit to the improvement to be expected in a man's mental powers, however well his thoughts are programmed.

Let us now consider the astonishing rate at which a human being can absorb 'information' through his senses. A trained musician, for example, can appreciate the overall effect of a gramophone record and simultaneously detect very small imperfections in it. It by no means follows, however, that this 'information' in all its detail ever reaches the level of consciousness. It is possible to reduce the 'information' in a recording channel a hundredfold before the listener fails to recognize a simple tune. The truth is, apparently, that the senses make great use of 'redundancy' as a method of assuring that the final result which reaches the brain is correct, in much the same way as (but to a much greater extent than) a digital computer.[4] The UNIVAC consists of two complete machines, one of which constantly checks the operations of the other. There are scores of such channels in the human brain which filter the incoming information before presenting it to consciousness, thereby avoiding error at the expense of the loss of the greater part of the incoming information to which the senses are exposed. Moreover, some part of the analysis seems to take place unconsciously; a good musician can fill in the rest if the record gives him a hint of the music, and he may be quite unaware of the extent to which his mind is supplementing his senses. A musically illiterate engineer is far more likely to detect the onset of distortion in the reproducing system. Most people can understand snatches of conversation in their own language, but lose the thread of a conversation in a foreign language unless they hear everything very distinctly. It is presumably for this reason that so many Englishmen and Americans shout at French porters, on the assumption that if it is loud enough anyone can understand English. I once heard an English officer at Ostend shouting in Hindustani, but he was producing no visible results.

After the senses have dealt with the incoming information the brain proceeds to interpret it in the light of long experience. It is quite true that an acute and well-trained ear can detect the degradation in musical quality if the reproducing channel is capable (in theory) of handling much less than 200,000 digits per second, but this phenomenal amount of information is really necessary only because the gramophone has no musical intelligence whatever; it could with equal fidelity handle any sort of noise; music is subject to certain rules. Most European music is written in subdivisions no finer than semi-

G*

tones, almost all within a compass of seven octaves, or eighty-four semitones in all. A note can therefore be expressed by seven binary digits. Assume as a reasonable average one bar per second, eight chords to the bar, and four notes per chord, if there are more they can certainly be constructed by the mechanical rules of harmony. This gives $7 \times 8 \times 4 = 224$ binary digits per second for the specification of piano music. There is no need to count changes of tempo or loudness as they only occur relatively infrequently. In fact we have already a factor of perhaps two too much, as a musician could guess half the information from the rules of harmony, so that 200 digits per second is more than enough for piano music, and may be enough for orchestral music. Suppose that a conductor such as Toscanini knows by heart a couple of hundred hours of music; on these assumptions his whole musical memory contains about 150,000,000 binary digits, or as many as the gramophone handles in twelve minutes. Toscanini will notice if the oboe is a quarter-tone out, but even theoretically it will take him anything up to a tenth of a second to do so; it follows that he cannot detect many such errors per second, and if several similar errors occur at once he will probably give up in despair. The point is, once again, that one learns to ignore everything except the one thing on which one is concentrating at the moment.

IV

This question is so interesting that we must study it in a little more detail. An ordinary telephone line can be used to transmit words in the standard teleprinter code, and it can be shown that if a line is used in this way it will handle about two hundred times as much information as can be passed through it if it is being used to transmit conversation. This estimate is made on the assumption that the tone of voice of the speaker and what one may call the 'emotional content' of the message are unimportant. The redundancy in speech is in fact so great that the most hideous distortion of the wave form does not make it unintelligible. For example, the waves can be 'clipped' or 'limited', and the resultant series of square waves differentiated. This operation completely changes the shape and frequency spectrum of the message, but although one would be hard put to to discover any point of similarity between the input and output, the signal remains quite comprehensible although it sounds like a talking buzz-saw. All that has been preserved are the points at which the wave crosses the axis, yet these convey the meaning. The transmission of 'start-stop' signals which modulate half a dozen oscillators will also suffice to transmit intelligence. In this case the distortions are quite different, but still inadequate to destroy the meaning. We are now beginning to understand how fortunate the pioneer telephone companies were, it didn't matter very much how bad their system was, it was still bound to work.

There is a considerable amount of redundancy in written language too. One can usually guess a word in its proper context even if a few letters are missing, and one can usually understand a message if a few words have been lost. It is this sort of thing which makes crossword puzzles possible. The idea of redundancy is very widely exploited; for example, the navigating officer of a ship or an aircraft never depends entirely on one method of position fixing, but he ensures the safety of his vessel by comparing the results of two or three quite different methods of navigation. Commercial accountancy makes extensive use of redundancy as a method of assuring accuracy. All items are entered into the books of account twice, and the totals are then determined by two different addition sums in which the numbers are usually written in a different order. This process, which is known as Book-keeping by Double Entry, has acquired a status and even a Mystique of its own. The fact that the books balance, which simply means that the mechanical operations of accountancy have been performed without error is held to be of major importance in itself, and it is presumably for this reason that we have become accustomed to the idea that a company should express its balance sheet to eight or nine significant figures although in fact the total value of its assets is probably in doubt by at least twenty per cent.

It is important to realize that, in all the different examples we have considered, the redundant information conveys the same message in several different ways. This is far better than mere repetition of the same sort of information. For this reason it is much better to 'difference' a set of tables than it is to repeat the computation of each entry; on a much humbler plane, this is why it is so useful to 'cast out nines'. A mathematician will feel much more confident if a formula can be verified in a particular case by a simple argument than he will be if he repeats his analysis and gets the same answer. Unfortunately, in a computing machine it is very difficult to devise many simple uses of the principle of redundancy. Much of the arid beauty of mathematics stems from its unambiguous and non-redundant symbolism, but it is at least arguable that a type of mathematics which had something comparable to the redundancy of English prose would be much more easy to handle. Even more useful would be a method of incorporating the redundancy of functional parts by which an organ such as, for example, the brain is able to carry on apparently unharmed if quite a large part of it has been damaged—the healing process is quite automatic. The best a machine can do is to say where the pain is which is something a man cannot do if the fault is within his own brain.

We can make effective use of redundancy in the storage of information. When we record music we can pack the equivalent of ten thousand digits on an inch of magnetic tape; but when we do this we are quite content if we can be reasonably sure of most of the information we have recorded. We have to be much more conservative if we are recording numbers. We can, for example, write about a hundred digits to the inch, and find that the recording process then introduces an error once in every ten thousand digits. By writing everything in triplicate on tracks which are far enough apart to ensure that a single blemish on the tape cannot affect all three tracks one can reduce the chance of errors occurring simultaneously in two tracks, and thereby introducing a mistake in the final result, to about one in a hundred million. This is tolerable if one can then apply a check such as 'casting out nines'.

v

It is remarkable that a phenomenon which one might at first think to be evidence of the relative inefficiency of our senses, which never fully load the information channels which they use, turns out in fact to be of fundamental importance to us all in avoiding errors; and that systems which exploit redundancy in much the same way will have to be introduced into our great computing machines, in spite of the complexity of the special equipment which will be needed.

The human eye can absorb information even faster than the ear—the information passes between eye and brain on more than a million separate fibres. A good television channel will handle the equivalent of more than 20,000,000 binary digits per second, but it is capable of transmitting a meaningless pattern of dots. It has been shown that only about five per cent of the channel is really needed to transmit an ordinary picture, owing to the fact that most of it consists of large featureless areas,[5] and no one seems yet to have estimated how much of this five per cent is concerned with movement. The eye has a remarkable ability to select the significant item and to ignore the rest; think for a moment what must be involved in looking at a tree, ignoring the detail of leaves and branches, and concentrating on a small bird.

The extent of visual memory is immense and almost impossible to estimate. Half an hour ago the writer was walking down a busy street and recognized from behind a friend whom he hadn't seen for twenty years, a man who had lost all his hair and gained sixty pounds in the meantime. What does this type of memory involve?

It has recently been shown that blind people whose sight is first given to them when they are grown up have to undergo a prolonged and difficult period of training before they can make use of their eyes in a way which most people regard as instinctive and automatic; for example, it may take such a person years to learn to appreciate the fact that a yellow square, the sides of which are horizontal and vertical, is the same shape as a red square, half its size and inclined at an angle. In other words, for an individual to learn to appreciate the *Gestalt* or squareness of a square in various orientations is very difficult and such an ability is acquired only (if at all) after years of experience, which usually take place before the period of conscious memory, at the same time as the child is learning to understand its mother tongue.

Ehrenfels called attention to man's ability to appreciate certain phenomena which are related to *sets* of stimuli, for example, such qualities as 'slenderness', 'regularity', 'roundness', 'angularity', or the characteristic appearance of a circle, a triangle, or other geometric shapes. In German the word *Gestalt* is often used as a synonym for form or shape and Ehrenfels used the name *Gestaltqualitäten* for all of them. Animals with much simpler brain structures than man have this sense of *Gestalt*; as Adrian has pointed out, even a rat can be trained to recognize a circle or a triangle or the more abstract 'triangularity'.

It appears that an appreciation of the meaning or the *Gestalt* of sounds or shapes is often derived by the brain by the analysis of redundant information. The processes which are involved in the analysis are beyond our present understanding, but we know that they often depend upon reference to enormous quantities of stored information which, however imperfectly remembered, may represent the essence of a lifetime's experience. We no more understand how we recognize a square when we see it than we know how we recognize the word 'square' when we hear it on a bad telephone circuit. Now, as we have seen, machines have only the most rudimentary ability (with which they have been endowed with great difficulty) to exploit the simplest type of redundancy to ensure the accuracy of their calculations; furthermore their memories are of limited capacity, and it is certain that no one can programme a machine to solve a problem he doesn't understand himself, so it is not surprising that it is precisely in this mysterious ability to take an overall view which human beings find so difficult to learn that the machine at the moment seems to be weak by comparison with any human brain.

No one has yet devised a method by which a machine could recognize the 'threeness' of a figure 3 in any handwriting, and it would probably be difficult to make it copy instructions from dictation. Nevertheless, the success of Bell Telephone Laboratories in producing 'visible-speech' patterns by displaying the Fourier spectrum of speech on a cathode-ray tube in such a manner as to allow a deaf man to interpret it, and the production by the British Post Office of the Vocoder which compresses the total spectrum required for intelligible speech transmission, make it clear that a machine could be taught to listen intelligently to spoken numbers if it is necessary to do so. In particular it should not be hard to make a machine recognize perhaps a couple of dozen different sounds, which might for convenience include most of the numbers from 0 to 9, so that it could understand the relatively few symbols that are needed to encode numbers and instructions. It would not be asking too much of human beings that they should learn to speak these sounds distinctly and use them when they were talking to the machine (for example, when they were preparing an inventory) so that it could understand them whoever spoke them.

Aesthetic judgments, which usually involve the consideration of the total effects of sounds or shapes, will be outside the proper province of computing machines for many years to come. It seems most improbable that a machine will ever be able to give an answer to a general question of the type: 'Is this picture likely to have been painted by Vermeer, or could van Meegeren have done it?' This question was answered confidently (though incorrectly) by the art critics over a period of several years. The machine would, of course, be able to remember the date of Vermeer's birth and the titles of all his known paintings, which is more than some critics could do.

VI

Some people can size up a most complicated situation almost instantaneously, far too quickly for any logical analysis to have been possible, and their first appreciation is more reliable than the results of conscious thought. This is in fact the argument for the reality of that rarest of human abilities, usually described as 'common sense'. The entire judicial system of this country is based upon the supposition that ordinary men can make decisions in this 'common sense' sort of way. For consider: a jury consists of men who are ignorant of law, unaccustomed to hearing and interpreting evidence, lacking the experience and mental agility of professional lawyers, and usually destitute of scientific training. All reason suggests, therefore, that they must be quite unable in a complicated case to weigh the evidence properly and arrive at a reasonable verdict. Nevertheless, said Lord Chancellor Halsbury (who sat on the Woolsack longer than any other man), 'As a rule, juries are in my opinion more generally right than judges'. The great Lord Mansfield advised an inexperienced judge to announce his decisions but never to give his reasons, for, he said, 'Your judgments will probably be right, but your reasons will certainly be wrong'. The judge did very well as long as he followed this advice, but some years later he was accused of gross incompetence, and Mansfield had to sit on a commission which was to decide whether to remove him from office. It turned out that his judgments had in fact been uniformly correct, but his continued success had made him over-confident, he had taken to announcing his reasons, and they were palpably absurd.

Since we do not know ourselves how we do this sort of thing and few of us ever learn to do it well, and since decisions of this type do in fact seem to demand the subconscious evaluation of a situation with a background of a lifetime's experience, there is little wonder that the problem of giving such an ability to a machine has baffled everyone since Babbage who was well aware of the problem and remarked that men who can effectively base their decisions on a proper appreciation of a complicated situation are very rare. It is, he said, the quality which is most needed by a successful general, and he added that the Duke of Wellington, whom he knew well, possessed this ability to an outstanding degree. The most difficult of a general's problems are due to never-ending changes in his data as the battle progresses. Very different is the problem of a composer who has to appreciate the *Gestalt* of a whole piece of music. Mozart has told us that he conceived the whole of a piano concerto at once before he wrote any of it down.

Babbage's own judgment often seems to have been unreliable when he dealt with practical matters, and this letter, which he wrote to

Lord Tennyson, suggests that even his aesthetic opinions had a quantitative bias—

Sir,

   In your otherwise beautiful poem ('The Vision of Sin') there is a verse which reads—

> Every moment dies a man,
> Every moment one is born.

It must be manifest that if this were true, the population of the world would be at a standstill. In truth the rate of birth is slightly in excess of that of death. I would suggest that in the next edition of your poem you have it read—

> Every moment dies a man,
> Every moment $\frac{1}{16}$ is born.

Strictly speaking, this is not correct, the actual figure is so long that I cannot get it into a line, but I believe that the figure $\frac{1}{16}$ will be sufficiently accurate for poetry.

I am, Sir, yours, etc.

   A machine might well have inspired this, for it is reasonable and logical, apparently serious—and quite irrelevant.

   Yet we must not assume too hastily that a machine cannot cope with a situation merely because it is complicated. Once the complexities become too great for one man to handle, the difficulties of communication between man and man may be such that the machine begins to show up favourably by comparison. This is why we feel that it ought to pay to mechanize a big office. Let us consider for a moment a more straightforward problem: all large airlines have great difficulty in handling their seat reservations. They lose money unless two-thirds of all seats are sold, so they cannot use the same system as a bus line; and they find themselves saddled with a huge organization which may cost more than the petrol which the aeroplanes use (in some cases nearly twice as much). Trunk telephones connect all the booking offices in the country to a central office in which scores of girls look at flight information written on a series of blackboards. There are so many blackboards, and the girls have to sit so far away (there are so many girls too) that they have to use telescopes to read the blackboards and the system tends to be limited by the power of available telescopes. One cannot but feel that any attempt to improve such a system in its present form holds about as much promise for the airlines as would a long-term research programme to improve the thermodynamical efficiency of horses. It is clearly a job for a computer. A memory of a few million digits, some computing circuits and a series of teleprinter lines should make it possible for any booking office to reserve space on any flight, or to offer alternative space if need be. Machines which solve at least part of this problem are, in fact, now in use.

VII

It is pertinent to ask ourselves what, if anything, distinguishes the processes which take place in these machines from some which go on in the brains of human beings. We shall give the game away completely if we try to restrict the use of the verb 'to think' to those mental operations which we do not understand ourselves, which we cannot control, which take place subconsciously and which we strongly suspect are illogical into the bargain. One cannot dismiss the question by saying that the machine is merely a 'complicated abacus'—it is the very complexity which poses the problem. To ask 'How complicated must a machine be before this question arises?' is as pointless as to ask 'How many hairs can a man lose before he becomes bald?'

Three hundred years ago, Thomas Hobbes considered the philosophical implications of Pascal's invention of a simple calculating machine. The mental effort which its development cost Pascal was so great that his health never recovered from the resulting breakdown. His contemporaries thought that his machine was much less important than his mathematics, his philosophy and his theology, but posterity is even more indebted to him for his invention of the ordinary wheelbarrow. Pascal had written 'La machine arithmetique fait des effets qui approchent plus de la pensée que tout ce que font des animaux'. Hobbes commented that 'Brass and iron have been invested with the functions of brain, and instructed to perform some of the most difficult operations of mind. . . . In what manner so ever there is place for addition and subtraction, there also is place for reason, and where these have no place, there reason has nothing at all to do; for reason is nothing but reckoning (that is the adding and subtracting) of the consequences. . . . When a man reasoneth, he does nothing else but conceive a sum total from addition of the partials. . . .' It is difficult not to agree with him, although we have to admit that many of these mental 'additions' must take place unconsciously.

VIII

Before we conclude this discussion of the current and potential applications of digital computers, it is worth considering for a moment whether machines of this type can assist research work in fields other than mathematics. In particular, is it possible to exploit the fact that a few hundred thousand feet of cine-film would contain a significant fraction of all the 'information' which has ever been reduced to print?

Vannevar Bush (who, during World War II, was scientific adviser to President Roosevelt) has recently concerned himself with the problem of storing and correlating the information which is constantly being prepared and published in books all over the world. He points out that, on an average, the number of books in a large library such as the Library of Congress doubles every sixteen years.[6] Most libraries are already full and it is clear that in about another hundred years' time there will be no buildings in the world large enough if they continue as at present to store all the books which are offered to them. The obvious proposal has been made that books should be stored in microfilm form, but this is only a very partial answer to the fundamental problem, which is how the information contained in them can be made available to people who are engaged in research work and wish to familiarize themselves with the work already done. It is true even now to say that it is often much quicker to repeat a simple piece of research work than to look through the literature to find out if it has been done before—the system of disseminating information seems likely within a foreseeable time to break down under its own weight.

Mendel's views on genetics were lost to the world for a generation because his publication did not reach the few who were capable of grasping and extending it; and this sort of catastrophe is undoubtedly being repeated all about us, as truly significant attainments become lost in the mass of the inconsequential.

'The difficulty seems to be, not so much that we publish unduly in view of the extent and variety of present-day interests, but rather that publication has been extended far beyond our present ability to make real use of the record. The summation of human experience is being expanded at a prodigious rate, and the means we use for threading through the consequent maze to the momentarily important item is the same as was used in the days of square-rigged ships.'

Bush proposed that all incoming literature should be classified and docketed, and that the equivalents of the card indexes should be stored in such a way that a research worker would be able, by dialling a number or two, to obtain access to all the data which existed on the subject in which he is interested. The greater part of the literature which any normal individual would want could, if it were photographed on microfilm, be contained in a single room. It may be possible to solve the problem of storing information in this way and, if the major difficulty of classifying the information adequately could be solved with a machine of the type which Bush proposes, it would assist research workers by giving them access to information very quickly. Furthermore, by drawing their attention to similarities between topics which have hitherto been regarded as totally disconnected, such a machine may perform one of those operations which is now thought of as peculiarly that of the original thinker. Nevertheless, this argument can be pushed too far, as it would be most unlikely for example that in any index an apple and the moon would both have been included under the general heading of 'falling' before the idea had occurred to Newton, and it is improbable that any machine would produce its best 'ideas' about any subject when it was not 'thinking' about it, or even more important, that it would recognize them for what they were if it did.

Bush discussed the problems which would confront a man who was investigating the developments of the composite bow which was used by the cavalry of Ghenghis Khan and the effect of its introduction on world history. The would-be author would need to know something about the mechanical properties of the materials of which the bow is made, the aerodynamics of arrow flight, and the history of archery, as well as the campaigns of the Mongols, and no one individual could ever be expected to have an acquaintance with such a wide variety of topics. It is, moreover, far from clear that he would have sufficient familiarity with the index of published literature to know which buttons to press. All one can say is that the production and development of machines of this kind would be of great assistance to human thought, that they might mechanize many of the more humdrum operations involved in thinking, and might even be of importance to original thinkers in the development of their own ideas by making it possible for them to do things which they would never achieve without assistance. One would not normally describe such an operation as one of 'thought' in the accepted sense of the word, but it is not easy to define the word in such a way as to exclude these operations if one imagines that they may be performed equally by a machine or by an assistant librarian.

At this stage, the connection between the Vannevar Bush machine and the ordinary digital computer is not particularly obvious, but we have mentioned it, first, because it is one of the outstanding proposals for mechanizing processes of storing and using information; secondly, because the process of selection would inevitably be performed according to some numerical criteria; and thirdly, because it is possible that a combination of a digital computer with a memory of the type proposed by Bush is the next step in the development of computing machinery.

It is interesting to speculate on the possibility of using such a machine to help a lawyer in his judgment of a case which was presented to him in such a way as to allow him to decide it entirely by a logical interpretation of statutes and by reference to a well-indexed library of leading cases. If the findings of the machine seemed to lack something of the spontaneity and variety of current legal verdicts, the careful and judicious use of the random number generator might help to mitigate the harshness of pure logic. It has been argued for example that a decision of the House of Lords might be likened to an Act of God, being something unexpected and unpredictable which no 'reasonable man' would expect (unfortunately the argument was rejected by the court). Of course, in England 'the law has never recognized the existence of a reasonable woman, whose existence must therefore be regarded as impossible' (Lord Chief Justice Hewart).[7]

IX

What then are we to conclude from this discussion? It is hard to deny that many of the activities of a digital computer are such as would normally be regarded as evidence of conscious thought were they to be undertaken by a human being. If a distinction is to be made it will require a redefinition of the verb 'to think' which has so far not been faced by the lexicographers, and it will be hard to exclude the performance of the machine and admit that the ordinary man ever thinks at all. We have no doubt that the metaphysicians, who understand the manipulation of words much better than that of machines, will find a way out of the impasse in the end, even if they have to use a machine to do it. It is certain that in a few years time they will, like the rest of us, be using machines to help them in all kinds of ways in their everyday lives.

If it is true to say that a machine can do the work of several hundred ordinary men, it is equally true to say that no machine is ever likely to undertake the work of those few extraordinary men whose dreams and whose efforts are responsible for the growth and the flowering of our civilization.

NOTES AND REFERENCES

1. STOKVIS, B., 1952, 'A medical-psychological account followed by a demonstration of a case of super-normal aptitude', in *Proceedings of the International Congress on Orthopedagogics* (July 1949), Amsterdam: Systemen Keesing.

2. TURING, A. M., 1950, 'Computing Machinery and Intelligence', *Mind*, *59*, 433.

3. WATSON-WATT, SIR R., 1949, 'Electronics and Free-Will', *The Hibbert Journal*, *48*, 8.

4. JEFFRESS, L. A. (ed.), 1950, *Cerebral Mechanisms in Behaviour*, London: Chapman and Hall.

5. This means in practice that the whole of the frequency spectrum allotted to a television channel is not filled with useful information. In fact the radiated energy is concentrated into a series of narrow bands which have gaps between them. It has been found possible to exploit this fact, and to radiate the extra information which is needed to provide 'colour' in the gaps which occur in the spectrum of an ordinary black and white picture.

6. BUSH, V., 1945, 'As We May Think', *The Atlantic Monthly*, *176*, 101.

7. HERBERT, SIR A. P., 1927, *Misleading Cases in the Common Law*, London: Methuen.

CHAPTER 13

INFORMATION THEORY IN THE STUDY OF MAN *

BY D. M. MACKAY

I

The organization of the human body and of human society depends almost entirely on the flow and exchange of information. In these days of radio, television, the press, the telephone, such a statement is trite enough. It is all the more remarkable that until a few decades ago no science of 'information systems' was in existence. Fifty years ago anyone who thought of information as something scientifically measurable would have been greeted with a smile, as if he had been misled by a metaphorical usage. Yet today, largely through the work of communication engineers and physicists, a whole subject of 'Information Theory' has come into being, giving us a new and powerful scientific tool for the study of all kinds of systems in which 'information' is a basic commodity. Communication systems (television, radio, telephone), automatic-control systems (in factories or aircraft, for example), economic systems, the human body and the brain itself—all these and many others can be analysed in remarkably similar terms, and our understanding of them enriched by a recognition of the same fundamental principles operating in the most diverse cases.

This is not to say that the methods appropriate to one such system should or can be transferred wholesale to another. A certain amount of harm has been done to the good name of Information System Theory by over-precipitate generalization of its simpler principles to psychological situations without regard to their greater complexity. The

* An abridged and revised version of 'Information Theory and Human Information Systems', first published in 1957 in the *Impact of Science on Society*, a Unesco Publication.

purpose of this chapter is not, of course, to expound the theory in any detail; but the insights it offers are so fundamental that it seems important that some of its basic principles should be more generally known and their implications worked out by those competent to do so in other fields.

II

The new theory has two main branches, or we might say two levels. One is concerned with the structure and measurable properties of information itself. The other might be called the study of systems organized by information flow.

(a) The first deals mainly with questions of *amount* of information: how much information have I gained from this experiment? How much information can be sent through this radio channel, or through this man's visual system, in one minute? What is the most economical way of encoding a given item of information? How can I best safeguard a message against loss of information through disturbances? How can a filing system be designed to yield the maximum of information in a given searching-time?

(b) The second is concerned chiefly with analysis of the paths along which information flows in an organized system, with information-map making, so to say, and with questions of the stability and efficiency of such systems. What 'division of labour' is possible in mechanisms of pattern-recognition? How can an unstable control system be made stable, and at what cost? What are the effects of delay in an information channel? What happens if predictive information about a system (e.g. the human brain) is fed back into the system itself?

It is the second of these branches that seems to hold the greater promise for our understanding of the nervous system and of human social organizations, but a brief look at the first may serve to show how essentially simple and down-to-earth the basic notions really are.

III

The newcomer to information theory will have to cope with a persistent confusion in the literature between the concept of information *per se*, and various formulae used in calculating its *amount*. The distinction is both elementary and necessary. The central concern of information theory is with the process of *determination of form*. Information is said to flow from A to B when an event or situation at A determines the form (in space and/or time) of one at B, regardless of the flow of energy involved. Thus a short definition of information (as distinct from *amount* of information) would be simply 'that which determines form'. Very often, the form in question is a *representation* of some state of affairs. In this case our short definition becomes 'that which logically validates representational activity'.

In all cases, information is operationally defined (like energy), by what it *does*. But whereas the work done by energy is physical in character, the work done by information is 'logical work'. Always, in talk about information there is a suppressed reference to a 'third party'. Rather as in the physical theory of relativity, we have to relate our definitions to an observer before they become operationally precise.

Now a form can be determined in one of two ways: (*a*) by a process of *construction*; (*b*) by a process of *selection*. An example of (*a*) would be the determination of the form of a photographic image by a microscope or telescope, or of a graphical record by an amplifier and recording pen. An example of (*b*) would be the selection of a standard message from a pre-established set by a telegraph operator, in response to a code number.

In each case, the process of form-determination has one or more quantifiable aspects. Thus in (*a*) we can ask (i) *how many degrees of freedom* of form were determined—how many optically independent areas of photographic plate, or independent ordinates of graph; (ii) *how much evidence* (in the statistical sense) the process has supplied for the resulting form—how *reliable* is the optical image, or the graph.

In (*b*) we can ask from *how many equally likely possibilities* the form was selected—how *improbable* was the selection.

By fastening on these quantities, we can derive from them various numerical measures (useful for different purposes) of the *size* of the process of form-determination—the magnitude of the constructive or selective process concerned. It is these measures of size that have been given the name of 'amount of information' or 'information-content', and that are often confused with the notion of information itself. Their multiplicity does not, of course, betoken any rivalry between them, any more than length, area and volume are rival measures of spatial extent.

It is true, of course, that the message selected in (*b*) must at one time have been constructed. Conversely, the result of the constructive process in (*a*) can always be regarded as one of a set of possible forms, so that its determination is logically equivalent to a selection from that set. Both types of measure can always (at least formally) be applied; the question is only one of appropriateness to the purpose in hand.

IV

A good example of the need for a 'constructive' measure comes in studies of visual acuity, where R. A. Fisher's[1] 'measure of information' in the sense of *weight of evidence* turns out to be appropriate.[2] Another is in the analysis of optical images,[3] where the *number of degrees of freedom* may be the most important measure. Recent studies[4] on perceptual capacity also suggest the need for 'constructive' measures of the form-determining processes involved in recognition and recall.

On the other hand, the most general way of measuring 'amount of information', due in its most highly developed form to C. E. Shannon,[5] is undoubtedly to look at the event in question as one of a *range of possible alternatives*, and to derive an additive index of the extent to which that range has been *narrowed* by the event.

Thus, suppose that we are standing at a road-fork, and are equally uncertain whether to go to left or right. The 'amount of selective information' we need, in order to identify one out of two equally-likely possibilities of this kind, is defined to be one binary unit, or *'BIT'*. The unit of selective information is that which enables one simple choice to be determined, between two *equally-likely* alternatives: left or right? yes or no? If the range is reduced by $\frac{1}{2}$, we say we have gained one unit. If it is reduced by $1/4$ ($\frac{1}{2} \times \frac{1}{2}$), we say we have gained two units; if by $1/8$ ($\frac{1}{2} \times \frac{1}{2} \times \frac{1}{2}$), three units; if by $1/16$ ($\frac{1}{2} \times \frac{1}{2} \times \frac{1}{2} \times \frac{1}{2}$), four units; and so on.

This is just the same arithmetic as in calculating the number of rounds required in a knock-out tennis tournament, in which half of the competitors are eliminated at each round. The total number of rounds measures (roughly) the 'amount of selective information' gained when the winner is identified (assuming that we had no prior knowledge of the competitors' chances).

To put it in another way, the task of measuring the 'amount of selective information' gained from an item (a message, an experiment, the result of a competition) is approached by asking 'Out of how many *equally-likely competitors* has this item been selected? How many *equally-likely alternatives* were there? How unlikely was it?' In other words, for the purposes of this particular measure we are not now interested in the *nature* of the item, but essentially in its *unexpectedness*. The greater the 'unexpectedness' of an item, the greater the 'gain of information' when it is received. As we have seen, the number of units of information is not *proportional* to the reduction in the number of competitive possibilities. If they are equally likely, it increases by one unit for every *halving* of that number—increasing 'as the logarithm of that number', the mathematician would say.

Clearly this definition enables us to measure the amount of information gained even when that information is incomplete. If we were faced for example with four equally-likely roads, and were told only that the road we wanted was one of two left-hand roads, this would narrow the range from 4 to 2, and so give us one unit of information, just as would the identification of one road out of two.

But what, one may ask, is the point of measuring information in this way? The answer is severely practical. This is the measure which tells a communication engineer how much a message should cost him to transmit. The 'amount of information' of a message determines the minimum number of code-signals it will require to represent it in an ideally efficient system. So by comparing this theoretical cost with the actual cost of a particular method, we have a solid mathematical measure of *informational efficiency* which is as vital in the design of competitive communication systems as power efficiency is in the design of electrical supplies.

'Information' in fact is to the communication engineer what 'energy' is to the power engineer. It has come to be recognized as one of the basic commodities* of our civilization.

v

So far, we have made the assumption that all selections are equally likely, and occur equally often on an average; but there are very few communicative processes in real life where the assumption of 'equal likelihood' holds good. Think for example of the code symbols with which we are most familiar, the letters of the alphabet. These letters are 26 in number (27 if we include the space) but they are certainly not used equally frequently. Some are much commoner than others, and we would probably agree that in some sense or other they give us 'less information' than the ones that turn up rather rarely, which would have been harder to guess. By a piece of straightforward mathematics, the communication theorist is able to justify our intuitive feeling here, and to show quite precisely that the only way to get the most out of a given code is to use all the possibilities equally often. Samuel Morse, as we all know, recognized this principle when devising his code

---

* This does not, of course, mean that 'information' is a kind of (intangible) 'stuff', like water or gas, but only that as a 'measurable' it has a similar economic importance.

(without the help of Information Theory!) by making the symbols for common letters shorter than those for the rarer ones, so that different possible *long sequences* of dots and dashes tend to occur with equal frequency.

This brings us to another of the basic notions of communication theory: the notion of *redundancy*. 'Redundancy' has a somewhat pejorative flavour, and in a sense it is indeed a measure of waste. Redundancy may be defined as the percentage inefficiency with which the selective power of a sequence of symbols is being used. Loosely, we might think of it as the percentage that need not have been sent, because they could have been guessed from their context. If it is possible to guess any of the symbols, with even slightly better than chance success, then to a certain extent they are redundant, and we are using the code wastefully.

Redundancy, however, is not all pure loss, for alongside of this notion we have to set another, which in the jargon is termed *noise*. 'Noise' is used loosely to refer to any uncorrelated disturbance which upsets the system by making it perform selections that were not intended; and the point is that in the presence of noise, redundancy is a help. Indeed, noise is tolerable at all only if the signals have some redundancy. One can see why by remembering that redundancy is a measure of the dependence of text on context; and it is only context-dependence that enables an error in transmission to be recognized as such, let alone corrected.

If we were to rely on correcting errors by guesswork, of course, the life of the professional communicator would be hard; but it turns out to be possible to devise codes which are 'self-checking' and 'self-correcting'. These are codes so designed that at the end of a given run of text one can for example add up numbers of dots and of dashes, and with the help of some arithmetic, deduce whether there has been a mistake, and even which symbol is wrong. The price of this is, of course, redundancy—we have to be content not to use the whole range of code-sequences with maximum efficiency.

VI

Because the notion of a selective process is such a general one, the ideas and theorems of information theory have already found a wide range of application. Take for example the theorem that efficiency is maximal when all the outcomes are equally likely. This has repercussions in such diverse fields as the design of experiments and the playing of guessing games. If one is designing a research programme in which hypotheses are to be tested on a trial basis, then according to this theorem one's programme will not be running as informatively as it might unless the various outcomes of each experiment are equally likely.* This applies of course in such games as '20 questions', as every skilled 20-questioner knows. At each stage in the questioning process, you have to try to divide the remaining range of possibilities into two roughly *equal* portions, one indicated by 'yes', the other by 'no'. If you do not do this, then other people who do will beat you at the game.

The usefulness of redundancy, on the other hand, can be illustrated rather well in connection with the English language, which turns out to be about 50 per cent redundant. This means that roughly half the letters in an average English text can be deleted at random without depriving the reader of the bulk of the sense. Figure 1 shows the result of an interesting experiment by C. E. Shannon,[6] to discover the extent to which each letter in English text can be guessed from the preceding letters only. Below each letter is shown the number of guesses required by a subject who started 'from scratch' and guessed his way along. We note the large number of 1's indicating 'right first time'. Note also the steady increase in efficiency of guessing—showing that the redundancy depends considerably on the effects of 'long-range' context.

Now at first sight this discovery by the theorists might have seemed to indicate a serious defect of our language. The theory shows undeniably that if English were re-designed or re-coded to use the alphabet more efficiently, our books could be half their present length, our telegrams could be transmitted (though not delivered!) at half the cost, and so forth. But here once again the pejorative flavour of the term 'redundancy' is misleading. For the very tests by which it is measured indicate that it is very far from being undesirable in practice. It is only the redundancy of English that enables us to spot misprints and to restore texts mutilated by disturbances in transmission or printing. A similar redundancy in spoken English helps us to listen to one conversation against a background of a dozen others, and to understand a telephone message half drowned by extraneous crackles and buzzes. An ideally non-redundant language would be one in which every single symbol was of equal importance and entirely independent of its context. It would be satisfactory enough for communication between perfect machines: many telegraphic codes indeed

* Of course if the cost of redesigning, so as to equalize the likelihoods, is significant, then the amount of information per unit of cost may be a more important index than the amount per experiment.

are of this kind. But in a world of imperfections and disturbances in both the transmitting channel and the receiver, redundancy is something for which to give thanks. Indeed, as every schoolteacher knows, it may often pay us to increase redundancy artificially by repeating the same information in as many different ways as possible. *Any reduction of redundancy brings a corresponding risk of failure to communicate.*

Information theory thus suggests some much-needed criteria by which to evaluate proposals for linguistic reform. Some changes that make words easier to spell for example, might show up badly in terms of informational efficiency. Objective measures of this kind are still at an early stage of development, and the necessary statistical data are hard to accumulate; but at least some mathematical principles of evaluation may help to supplement and discipline intuitive judgment.

```
(1) THERE IS NO REVERSE ON A MOTORCYCLE A
(2) 1 1 1 5 1 1211 2 1115117 1 1 1 213 21227 1 1 1  14 1 1 1 1131
(1) FRIEND OF MINE FOUND THIS OUT
(2) 8 6 1 3 1  111 1 111 1 1 116 2 11 1111 12 111 1 1 1
(1) RATHER DRAMATICALLY THE OTHER DAY
(2) 4 1 1 1  1 1 1115 1 1 1 1 1 1  111 1 116 1 1111 1 1 111 1 1 1
```

FIG. I

The 'guessability' of English text (after Shannon[6])

VII

Let us now try to make more precise the notion of a system organized by the 'flow of information'. When the front-door button (A) is pressed and the bell (B) rings in the kitchen we have seen that it makes sense in terms of information theory to say that 'information flows' from door to kitchen, even although the energy to ring the bell comes from a transformer which is in the kitchen. We can draw a simple map showing a line from A to B, and say that information flows from A to B, no matter what may be the flow of energy involved—where it comes from, or how much is required.

In the same way we can draw a map showing the lines of information flow (or communication) between the units of an army and headquarters, regardless of whether the messages are conveyed by radio or telephone or signal lamp. The lines of our map are not meant to show what happens to the *energy* transmitted, but to depict the flow of *information*, in the sense which information theory has found for the term.

Drawing an information-flow map, then, amounts to singling out one particular aspect of a situation for attention, concentrating on what specifies the *form* of activity, rather than its material embodiment.

Now the power of this method of studying situations lies in its great generality. Simplified though a flow map undoubtedly is as a model of what goes on, it allows us to ask questions and apply principles which are far from trivial, and which cover a number of particular cases that have hitherto been studied as separate problems.

VIII

A simple example of an information-flow map which is familiar in many forms is shown in Fig. 2. It represents the informational 'skeleton' of automatic regulators such as the thermostat, the ball cock and the steam governor, as well as various human situations which we shall consider later. In each of these there are two essential parts.

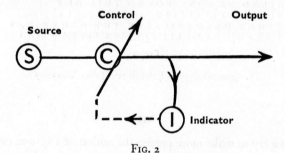

FIG. 2

The essentials of automatic regulation.

The control C determines the form of the output drawn from the source S. An indicator I shows how the output differs from the goal or standard which is required to be attained, and calculates the adjustment required in the control.

(*a*) There is a control, C, by which the output drawn from the repertoire of a source S can be selected.

(*b*) There is an indicator, I, which shows the difference between the current state of affairs and some 'goal state', and calculates the corrective action required. In a domestic oven, for example, C may be a gas valve, and I a mechanical thermometer. In the water cistern, C is a water cock and I a ball floating on the water. In the steam governor, C is a throttle and I is a speed-indicator.

In every case, the system is made self-regulating by *making the Indicator work the Control*, in such a way that any deviation from the goal state is *self-correcting*. Information from I is 'fed back', as we say, to C, in such a way that it selects automatically the required form of output from C.

Thus in the domestic oven the thermometer is mechanically linked to the internal gas valve so as to turn up the gas when the temperature is below standard, and *vice versa*. In the water cistern the ball is linked by a metal arm to the water cock, so that the cock opens when the water level is below standard. In the steam governor the speed-indicator is linked to the throttle so that the flow of steam is increased when the speed is below standard.

In every case the information fed back specifies action to *oppose* the change which has given rise to it. In technical jargon this is known as 'negative feedback'.

Suppose, however, that by some mistake the thermometer in the oven were connected to the gas valve in such a way as to turn up the gas when the temperature rose *above* the 'goal', and *vice versa*. This would be called '*positive* feedback', and it would obviously cause the system to become *unstable*. Any slight rise in output would cause the control to open farther and so accelerate the rise indefinitely. Conversely, a slight fall would shut down the control and so initiate a cumulative drop in output. This would be an example of 'goal-avoidance' rather than 'goal-pursuit'.

IX

We shall have more to say later about the conditions under which systems of the type of Fig. 2 are stable and properly behaved. But first let us see how the same information map may be used to depict situations involving human beings.

In the days before thermostats were available, if a housewife wanted to hold her oven-temperature constant, she had to read the thermometer herself, *calculate* the adjustment needed, and turn the gas up or down by hand. The situation could then be depicted by Fig. 3, where C represents the tap and I the thermometer as before, and the only difference is that the information from I is fed back to C not directly, but via the housewife H. The thermostat was invented when someone realized that in this function the calculation was so simple that the housewife could quite well be replaced by a mechanical connection!

If now instead of an oven we think of a house with central heating,

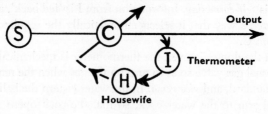

FIG. 3

A simple information-flow map in which one element is a human being

C is a heat regulator controlling the temperature of an oven. The difference between the actual and required temperatures is indicated by a thermometer I. The housewife calculates and makes the corrective adjustment required in C.

our picture of the situation becomes further simplified, for the housewife now can become her own temperature-indicator, and the function of I and H are combined (Fig. 4).

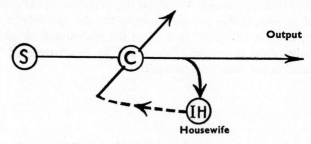

FIG. 4

Central heating

In regulating the temperature of an artificially heated room the occupant can combine the functions of indicator and calculator of adjustment.

We have reached an example in which one of the units of this basic flow map is a human being. It is not difficult to think of examples where the other units are also human. The relation of a rowing eight to their coxswain, for instance, can be depicted by the same basic diagram where the team combine the functions of S and C, and the coxswain acts as the indicator and calculator, I. Again in a factory C could represent a production team and I their manager. Examples are manifold; what we have been drawing is in fact the basic skeleton information map for *goal-directed activity* or self-regulation of any kind, whether human or mechanical.

The difference between human and mechanical situations—and it is a major one—lies not in the validity of these flow maps, but in the complexity of the information-channels they must represent. The richness and variety of interconnections between human beings make most realistic flow maps of social situations enormously more complicated than anything we have discussed. But when all this has been said by way of warning, it is still possible for many purposes to simplify the maps of human situations to manageable proportions and apply general principles with profit. This is particularly true of those in which questions of stability arise. Indeed, it is the qualitative maxims of information-system theory, rather than the quantitative calculations, which have the greater relevance to human affairs.

X

Let us then turn to the central question of the theory of information-systems. Under what conditions is an active self-governing system stable? We have seen that instability arises when information is 'fed back' in such a way as to reinforce the changes giving rise to it, instead of damping them down. Unfortunately, it does not follow that an unstable system can always be made stable merely by reversing the 'sign' of the feedback—even assuming we have the power to do so. The problem is complicated by questions of the *time* taken for information to flow around the closed path of our map.

Suppose, for example, that we take a simple speed-regulator of the sort we have discussed, and introduce *delay* in the connection between the indicator and the control, so that when the speed falls below standard it can go on dropping for some time before the trend is corrected, then go on rising above the standard for some time before it is brought back again, and so on. There is obviously a risk of this process building up into a continual succession of wild swings of speed, first in one direction and then in the other—a process known in the jargon as 'hunting'. It is in fact a common disease of self-regulating systems, and the diagnosis has by now been quite thoroughly worked out. *Sluggishness* in any part of a closed information-flow path is one of the chief causes of instability of this sort. In other words, if a system is *disproportionately insensitive to rates of change* of output, it is more liable to instability.

Oddly enough, the opposite fault can also lead to the same sort of behaviour, though this is not quite so easy to show in non-mathematical terms. *Either too little or too much sensitivity to the rate of change of*

H

output—to the trend of its own activity—is a menace to the stability of any self-guided system. The details of the theory show that a single stage with 'inertia' can often be tolerated in the chain of self-regulation without disastrous results, but that three or more such stages in a closed information-path will always set up an unstable oscillation unless the sensitivity of the indicator is reduced below a certain figure.

XI

Now the upshot of all this in practical terms is seen when we ask how such instability may be remedied. Broadly, there are four prescriptions:

(*a*) Keep the *number of stages* to a minimum.

(*b*) If instability is from the first cause, *reduce delays* and increase sensitivity to rates of change; i.e. make feedback 'anticipatory'.

(*c*) If the second cause is operative, *reduce sensitivity to rates of change* and *increase sensitivity to average levels*.

(*d*) If all else fails, *reduce overall sensitivity*.

A common example of the last remedy is the replacement of a hard washer in a ball cock by a softer one to stop the continual oscillation known as 'hammering'. The softer washer makes the cock less sensitive.

Examples of (*b*) and (*c*) are numerous in the design of automatic control systems, but may be less familiar. The question for us is whether any *human* information systems show similar instabilities, and if so, what form the analogous remedies might take. It may be emphasized again that this is not a question of applying the same mathematical methods of analysis, but only a matter of interpreting the same qualitative principles in the human context.

XII

Perhaps the example that leaps first to mind is the economic system, with its notorious trade cycles of boom and slump. A considerable amount of work has been done to elucidate the details of this particular flow-map, and it now seems clear that these fluctuations were largely of the type we have been considering, being caused by certain defects of the complex informational feedback system through which most societies regulate their production and consumption. The difficulty is that this system comprises not just one closed information-path but many; and it is not always obvious at what points adjustments in sensitivity would help. Electronic analogue computers have recently been pressed into service to simulate such a system and enable experiments on this point to be carried out.

Only a brief indication can be given of other fields open to similar investigation. Systems of popular representation offer another obvious example, in which a comparison of the stability of different national systems is full of suggestive material for the information-system theorist. The implications of principles (*a*), (*b*), (*c*), and (*d*) are more obvious in this field—the role of the Press in providing anticipatory feedback and enhancing overall sensitivity is particularly clear and significant—but (for good or ill) their simplest practical expression would not always be compatible with democratic ideas of freedom of speech

Other obvious examples are offered by the activities of trade unions, by the phenomena of advertising, and by competitive business practice. Here the allied subject of Games Theory has its contribution to make; but to discuss it would take us too far; enough may now have been said to indicate the possible impact of these new disciplines on the theory of group behaviour.

XIII

One theoretical topic remains to be raised before we discuss the human organism itself as our final example. This is the question of the extent to which the activity of an information system can be predicted if the prediction is to be fed back into it.

There are two kinds of fundamental limitation on prediction in these circumstances. The first arises in the social sciences even when the predictor is content just to keep his prediction to himself. It is simply the familiar fact that in order to collect enough data for a detailed prediction, one must disturb the system one is studying. Unreflecting people who have been quizzed for a public opinion poll, for example, are no longer typical, for they have been forced to reflect. Thus although this need not invalidate one's calculations, it does mean that the answer in part is coloured by one's own action in sampling. The more closely one seeks to observe an information system, the more significantly one's action shares in determining rather than merely predicting it.

The second limitation may be less familiar but it is still more fundamental. It arises when the predictor wishes to *react* upon the basis of his prediction: when he plays an active part in the situation he wants to predict. In this case the information-flow map may develop a kind of vicious circle.

Consider for example the dilemma of Mrs Brown, whose husband habitually asks for prunes when he sees her cooking porridge and porridge when he sees her cooking prunes. Given sufficient psychological and other data, she might conceivably be able to predict perfectly accurately what his genuine preference will be tomorrow morning, as long as she keeps her prediction to herself and does not do any cooking. What is more, she knows precisely (we may assume) the laws according to which her husband's preference will be determined, if she does do some cooking. And yet, no matter how long or how carefully she calculates, she is forever precluded from forestalling her husband's demand, for she herself is irreducibly part of the system which she wishes to predict.

This may seem a rather artificial example, but it is closely parallel to the dilemma of the large-scale speculator on the Stock Exchange, and indeed of any administrator who has to make a decision which will affect *conflicting* interests. It may not be much consolation to him, but it seems important to recognize that no scientific discoveries in social psychology or anything else can be expected to remedy this fundamental unpredictability of an information system to a sufficiently participant observer.

XIV

This leads to our final question. To what extent is it possible to analyse and understand the human organism itself as an information system? Be it said at once that our knowledge of the details of the human nervous system is far too slender to allow the kind of direct map-making that we have so far considered, except in such peripheral problems as the control of muscle contraction. With something like 10,000 million nerve cells, the human information system is unlikely ever to be analysed in this way. Our approach must be indirect, by way of hypothesis and test; and at best we may hope to arrive at only a kind of 'main trunk-route map' of the system.

This hypothetical 'model-making' is as yet in its infancy, but already it promises to serve a useful function as a kind of working link between the concepts of psychology on the one hand and physiology on the other, especially in the understanding of mental disorder. The language of information theory has a foot, as it were, in both camps, so that evidence expressed in psychological terms can be interpreted in terms of information flow so as to suggest a correlate in physiological terms, and *vice versa*. At the same time the information-flow model can find itself tested and refined and re-defined as a result of clues gleaned from both fields.[7, 8]

It will be realized that this is quite a different matter from drawing analogies between brains and digital computing machines, which are in fact deliberately designed not to show most of the characteristics typical of a human being. It is not even a matter of building machines to imitate human behaviour, for imitations can be produced in many ways which would be quite unrealistic as models of brain-processes. It is really the development of a new theoretical tool of research, intended only to grow and develop on paper so as to approximate progressively to the informational 'blueprint' of the brain.

To take one example which I have discussed elsewhere,[9] the information-flow type of model proves useful when discussing such puzzles as the stability of the perceptual world—why our surroundings do not normally seem to jump about when we move our eyes or our bodies voluntarily, although they generally do if the motion is involuntary. Here various hypotheses can be summarized and their consequences readily analysed in terms of their different information-flow maps; and in this 'intermediary' language it turns out to be possible to apply both psychological and neurological data to the task of narrowing the range of possibilities.[10]

Again, consideration of even an elementary information-flow model[11] can enable us to test the informational feasibility of some theories of 'concept-formation' and can suggest the principles of maturation that would lead to maximal efficiency in a given process. These principles, which amount to a strategy for keeping the complexity of the adaptive task matched to the degree of internal organization attained, are of course applicable in a wider context of human learning.[12]

In all such semi-quantitative discussions, however, the presuppositions behind our notions of 'efficiency' must be carefully defined. An engineer, for example, tends to measure the 'cost' of his models by the number of units required to build them; whereas the nervous system (presumably) could grow a million units almost as readily as a hundred. There are other ways, too, in which the over-simple application of notions drawn from communication engineering can be treacherous.[13] Here, as in any field, numerical techniques are no substitute for understanding.

xv

Needless to say, conclusions from such theoretical studies are tentative at best. The most one can say as yet is that the barrier to our understanding of the brain is not any *impossibility* of reproducing human behaviour in a suitable information system. The difficulty is rather to decide which of a great range of eligible candidates is the right model.

What then, one might ask, would become of human responsibility, if information-system theory were able to demonstrate eventually that all human behaviour could be accounted for in physical terms? It is often assumed that this would prove human freedom to be 'illusory'; but I believe this conclusion itself to be fallacious. It is reasonable that if you were about to make a choice, and if I could tell you with certainty what your choice would be before you made up your mind, you should excuse yourself from responsibility for that choice (suspecting perhaps that you had been hypnotized). If, on the other hand, you can defy anyone to tell you with certainty the outcome of the choice you have yet to make, and you make it, then you cannot escape responsibility, and you may claim to have chosen freely.

Now the fallacy to which I referred lies in supposing that a complete knowledge of the physical basis of behaviour, however mechanical, *could* enable anyone to give you an irrefutable advance prediction of a normal choice that you have yet to make. This, as I have shown elsewhere,[14] is irreducibly impossible, not on physical but on logical grounds. To be a man is to have an information system of a particular kind, which without defying any physical laws enables you to defy anyone to tell you your decisions in advance. Mr Brown's freedom to upset Mrs Brown's calculations does not arise because his brain is physically 'queer'. The simple fact is that no prediction of a decision could be embodied in his information system as a *belief* without falsifying itself. To try to embody such a belief would be to try to set up in advance the state of organization which (according to that belief) *has yet to be* set up when the future decision is made. This is simply the mechanical counterpart of the logical impossibility of believing *both* that the outcome of a decision will be X *and* that one has still to decide that outcome.

Clearly this leaves open the possibility that someone who keeps quiet about it might successfully predict your decision in advance. I believe there are serious practical barriers to such prediction, but I see no objection to the possibility from an ethical standpoint. The bulk of our normal choices are predictable, in this sense, to anyone who knows us well, without his even having to look inside our heads. But the question of your responsibility turns on whether you have the *power* to falsify a prediction. A predictor who conceals his prediction is not demonstrating that you lack the power; he is only withholding the opportunity to show that you have it.

It is important to realize that in its mechanical aspect this criterion of responsibility is not in principle a *behavioural* but a *structural* one. It is not a matter of offering a prediction and then watching to see whether the man falsifies it. He might prefer not to (if for example he is hungry and we predict to him that he will eat). The basic question could be settled in principle by inspection of the 'wiring diagram' of his brain. All we need to verify is that no prediction of his future choice could be *accepted* by his information system without altering it in such a way as to invalidate the assumption on which the prediction was based. If we can show that his believing the prediction would nullify it, then of course it is invalid for him; he would be in *error* if he were to believe it; and he is not in error to believe that he is free, in the sense that *no universally-valid prediction exists* (in the common language of himself and his observers). In this vitally important sense, his freedom to choose is not an illusion, but a matter of simple fact.

Our criterion thus reduces in essence to a question of the unity or 'wholeness' of the man's information-flow system. If the sub-system embodying his beliefs is rationally integrated in the normal way with the sub-system that is active in decision, so that they function as a single whole, his responsibility for his actions is assured. If, however —as may well be the case in some mental disorders—the flow system is broken up into sufficiently detached sub-systems, it is entirely possible that the subject could accept predictions of some of his actions without *ipso facto* being able to invalidate them. In such a case we would not then hold him responsible.

XVI

It will be realized that the criterion just suggested, which seems to accord with our normal ideas of responsibility, would apply equally well whether the brain were a physically determinate system or not. It thus cuts across any view that would hang moral responsibility on theories of physical indeterminacy in the brain. I venture to suggest in fact that a view of responsibility as conditional on physical indeterminacy is both *misguided* and *immoral*; *misguided*, because my responsibility is adequately nailed to my door if my choice is *logically* indeterminate until I make it—which we have seen to be true irrespective of any physical discontinuities there may or may not be in my brain; *immoral,* because a reliance on physical indeterminacy would deny my responsibility for any choices which did not entail some physical discontinuity in my brain, even although I made them deliberately, and could have defied anyone to describe them to me with certainty beforehand.

Physical indeterminacy has often been invoked in order to make room for the action of the mind 'on' the brain. I have no wish to 'debunk' the mind—on the contrary, I believe most seriously in the spiritual as well as the physical aspect of our human nature. But I believe that mental activity and brain activity are not to be pictured as *two* activities in quasi-physical interaction, but as two complementary aspects of one and the same activity, which in its full nature is richer— has more significance—than can be expressed in either mental or physical language alone.

I am not suggesting that mental activity is 'nothing but' an aspect of brain activity: this would be the attitude which I call 'nothing buttery', and one might equally fallaciously maintain the converse. The idea is rather that each is a descriptive projection, so to say, from different logical standpoints, of a single complex unity which we can call simply human activity.

It would follow from this view that there is no need—indeed it would be fallacious—to look for a *causal mechanism* by which mind and brain could act 'on' one another, any more than an equation requires a mechanism in order to act 'on' the electronic computer that embodies it. Mind acts not *on* but *in* brain. Their unity is already a closer (and a more mysterious) one than if they were pictured as separate interactive activities, one visible and the other invisible. Yet this is a unity which safeguards rather than threatens human responsibility; for it makes nonsense of any suggestion that my *body,* rather than I myself, could be held responsible for my choices. This would be simply to muddle up two languages—rather like asserting (or denying)—that when a *man* feels in love, his brain-cells feel in love.[15]

XVII

The discovery of an informational criterion which in principle distinguishes responsible choices from other actions, irrespective of the degree of physical determinacy involved, seems to call for some rethinking of popular ideas with regard to the penal code. It is too often presupposed that an action is *either* free *or* the result of physical causes. If a physical cause could be found, it is popularly taken as axiomatic that the man could not then be held responsible. It would seem to be strongly arguable that this view, despite its humane intentions, is a menace to human dignity; for it would, if pressed to its logical conclusion, deny responsibility for choices (whether good or bad) for which I have argued that a man has a *right* to claim responsibility.

The informational criterion on the other hand provides all the safeguards required to excuse those whose information-systems are sufficiently disorganized, while rescuing the responsibility of a normal human being from any dependence on our ignorance of physiology or psychology. It would excuse the schizophrenic or the hypnotized subject, not on any grounds of 'physical causation' as such, but on the ground (and to the extent) that an advance description of his action would *not* be logically indeterminate for him.

It would classify a normal subject as responsible, not because of any absence of 'physical causation', but on the ground (and to the extent) that an advance description of his action *would* be logically indeterminate for him, and for us if we are in dialogue with him.

In each case the corresponding neurological or psychological criterion would be in principle a structural one, concerned with the organization of the subject's information system rather than its observable behaviour. This might have to be inferred in practice from past observations of behaviour; but the criterion avoids the difficulty of some purely behavioural tests, which could be applied only by disturbing the subject in the act of choosing.

XVIII

This survey has ranged rather widely and somewhat cursorily over the ramifications of information theory, and it may be well to draw some threads together in conclusion.

Before the advent of information theory, the notion of physical explanation had been restricted almost entirely to the reduction of phenomena in terms of energy-flow, or the action of force upon force. Remarkably fruitful in the inanimate sphere, this approach has proved disappointingly sterile in the analysis of complex biological behaviour, and most of all in the study of man himself.

The emergence of 'information' as a basic scientific concept has provided a new tool with a function complementary to that of classical energetics. Though still in its infancy, the science of information-flow systems, framed in terms of the action of form upon form, seems likely

H*

to revolutionize the study of living organism and particularly the science of man.

The detailed working out of this new approach lies still in the future; the purpose of this chapter has been to bring out some principles, new and powerful, whose application is wide and general and independent of the particularities of human nature which remain to be discovered.

Finally, we have considered some fundamental limitations on the predictability of all such systems. We have seen in particular how an active member of an information system (e.g. an administrator) may be unable to make, or even to accept as certain, a prediction which is public, or has sufficiently large public consequences. This is true irrespective of the degree of 'physical causality' in the system. Turning to man himself as an information system, we saw that the same principle offered a fundamental distinction between actions for which responsibility might be attributed and those which might be excused—again on grounds independent of theories of physical causality in the brain. The implications for penal theory require more detailed discussion than could be given here; but the impropriety of treating 'physical causality' as an excuse from responsibility seems clear.

Man is, indeed, a mystery; but we shall serve no purpose, moral or spiritual, by confounding this mystery with the purely scientific puzzles presented by the human information system.

REFERENCES

1. FISHER, R. A., 1935, *The Design of Experiments*, p. 188, London: Oliver and Boyd.
2. MACKAY, D. M., 1960, 'Interactive Processes in Visual Perception', in ROSEN-BLITH, W. A. (ed.), *Sensory Communication*, New York: M.I.T. and Wiley.
3. MACKAY, D. M., 1950, 'Quantal Aspects of Scientific Information', *Phil. Mag.*, *41*, 289.
   MACKAY, D. M., 1958, 'The Structural Information Capacity of Optical Instruments', *Information and Control*, *1*, 148.
4. MILLER, G. A., 1956, 'The magical number 7: plus or minus 2', *Psychol. Rev.*, *63*, 81.
5. SHANNON, C. E., 1948, 'Mathematical Theory of Communication', *Bell Syst. Tech. J.*, *27*, 397 and 623.
6. SHANNON, C. E., 1951, 'Prediction and Entropy of Printed English', *Bell Syst. Tech. J.*, *30*, 50.
7. MACKAY, D. M., 1954, 'On Comparing the Brain with Machines', *Advancement of Science*, *40*, 402.
   1954, *American Scientist*, *42*, 261.
   1954, *Ann. Rept. of Smithsonian Inst.*, 231.

8. ROSENBLITH, W. A. (ed.), 1961, *Sensory Communication*, New York: M.I.T. and Wiley.

9. MACKAY, D. M., 1962, 'Theoretical Models of Space Perception', in MUSES, C. A. (ed.), *Aspects of the Theory of Artificial Intelligence: Proceedings, Locarno Symposium on Biosimulation*, New York: Plenum Press.

10. See for example the Symposium, 1962, *Information Processing in the Nervous System*, Leiden, to be published by Excerpta Medica Foundation.

11. MACKAY, D. M., 1956, 'Towards an Information-Flow Model of Human Behaviour', *Brit. J. Psychol.*, *47*, 30.

12. MACKAY, D. M., 1961, 'Information and Learning', *Proceedings of the N.T.G. Symposium on Learning Automata*, Karlsruhe: Oldenburg.

13. ATTNEAVE, F., 1959, *Applications of Information Theory to Psychology*, New York: Holt-Dryden.

14. MACKAY, D. M., 1960, 'On the Logical Indeterminacy of a Free Choice', *Mind.* *62*, 31.

15. MACKAY, D. M., 1958, 'Complementarity', *Proceedings of the Aristotelean Society Supplement*, *32*, 105.

CHAPTER 14

INFORMATION THEORY AND PERCEPTION*

BY ARTHUR SUMMERFIELD AND DAVID LEGGE

I

Information theory is a mathematical theory of the behaviour of communication systems. It has been used by psychologists to investigate the efficiency of some aspects of human behaviour. To apply information theory it is necessary to regard the subject of an experiment as a communication channel. No direct observation of the channel is possible; but it is possible to relate the way in which the output of the channel varies with the input to the channel, that is, how a sequence of responses made by the subject varies with the sequence of stimuli which is used. The efficiency with which the subject reacts to stimulation can then be measured by an informational analysis. To put it another way, what is measured is the efficiency with which the input information is transmitted and coded in the channel into an output of responses.

The average amount of information in a signal (or stimulus) is defined as the logarithm of the number of different signals. It is customary to use logarithms to base 2, but the theory does not necessarily require this base. If logarithms to base 2 are used, the unit of information is the BIT or Binary Digit. If there are as many signals of one kind as of any other in a sequence, the signals are said to be 'equiprobable'. For equiprobable signals the average information per signal is one bit if there are two possible signals, two bits if four

* This chapter originally appeared in a more condensed form under the title 'Perception and Information Theory', in the *Bull. Brit. Psychol. Soc.*, 1960, No. 42, 32, the Editor of which has kindly agreed that we might extend it. Its preparation was supported in part by a research grant MH-03313 from the National Institute of Mental Health, Public Health Service, U.S.A.

($=2^2$), three bits if eight ($=2^3$) and so on. To be more precise, the average amount of information in an input is:

$$H_{(x)} = \sum_{i=1}^{n} p_i \log_2 \frac{1}{p_i},$$

where n is the total number of possible signals and p_i is the probability of occurrence of the ith signal. It may be shown that the average information content of a signal is highest when all the possible signals are equiprobable, i.e. $H_{(x)}$ is a maximum when $p = 1/n$. When signals are not equiprobable the formula gives a properly weighted average, but we shall only be concerned here with situations in which all signals are equiprobable.

The measure of information may be interpreted as a measure of the *uncertainty* of the signal. Thus the information content of a signal which is one of eight equiprobable signals is higher than that of a signal which is only one of two. The information values in these two cases would actually be three bits and one bit respectively. An introduction to the calculation of information values is to be found in Attneave;[10] more advanced discussions are given by Brillouin[14] and in relation to psychology by Frick,[36] Garner[38] and Luce;[54] and the source for the mathematical principles is Shannon and Weaver.[65] 'Information theory and human information systems' are discussed generally elsewhere in this book,[55] and this account of basic ideas, particularly of information and its measurement and of the informational efficiency of communication systems, extends and supplements what is given here. The rest of this chapter is confined to applications of information theory in studies of perception.

II

For this dicussion perception is conveniently defined as the coding of inputs (signals or stimuli) into responses when the demand on *immediate* memory is minimal and new learning is not involved; i.e. when inputs do not have to be 'stored' in the channel and the channel is not being modified to adopt a new 'programme' for coding inputs into outputs. The subject is a simple channel transmitting information. We have also confined ourselves to investigations in which the mathematics of information theory have been used to analyse the results. This necessarily means that we have not discussed a number of studies which have been based more generally on the concepts of information theory.

Experiments which meet our criteria have all been concerned with assessing the performance of subjects on tasks which require stimuli to be coded into some kind of response, with the subject acting as the communication channel. For instance, a subject may be instructed to respond so that whenever he is shown the figure '7' he is to say 'seven', whenever he is shown '3' he is to say 'three', and so on. When responses have been made to a random sequence of stimuli, informational analysis supplies a method for measuring how much information has been transmitted by the channel. This *transmitted information* is defined by the following formula:

$$T_{(x;y)} = H_{(x)} + H_{(y)} - H_{(x,y)}$$

In words, the amount of transmitted information equals the sum of the average input information and the average output information minus the average information in the joint occurrence of input and output. If the channel is transmitting perfectly the amount of transmitted information will be the same as the amount of input information; but if the channel is imperfect the amount of transmitted information per signal will be less than the input information per signal.

The calculation may be illustrated by a simple example. A rat is being taught a simple discrimination between two stimuli, A and B. The rat must learn to make response a to stimulus A and response b to stimulus B. The stimuli, A and B, might be lights of different

TABLE I

(A)	Responses			(B)		
	a	b	Total	p_{ij}		p_i
Stimuli A	35	15	50	0·35	0·15	0·50
B	20	30	50	0·20	0·30	0·50
Total	55	45	100	p_j 0·55	0·45	1·00

(A) Frequencies of responses a and b made by a rat in discriminating two stimuli A and B presented an equal number of times in a random sequence of 100 trials. (B) The corresponding proportions, p.

brightness in a 'Skinner' box. When the stimulus is A the rat is rewarded if it presses Lever A (response a); when the stimulus is B it must press a different Lever B (response b) for reward. A and B occur equally often in a long random sequence, part of which might be:

... $A, B, B, A, A, A, B, A, B, B, ...$

The discrimination is a difficult one for the rat; massed practice is used and 100 trials are given each day. Table 1(A) summarizes the rat's performance on the tenth day after the beginning of training.

The degree to which the rat has learned the discrimination can be assessed by calculating the average amount of information it is transmitting. If the discrimination has been learned perfectly all of the input information will be transmitted—the rat will make no mistakes. If the rat is responding randomly to the stimuli, no information will be transmitted at all. In order to calculate the average amount of transmitted information three basic calculations are necessary. They are made on the proportions, p, shown in Table 1(B), derived from the frequencies in Table 1(A). Tables of $p \log_2 (1/p)$ have been prepared.[10,38,61] They help considerably.

1. *Average Input Information*

$$\begin{aligned} H_{(x)} &= \Sigma p_i \log_2(1/p_i) \\ &= 0 \cdot 5 \log_2(1/0 \cdot 5) + 0 \cdot 5 \log_2(1/0 \cdot 5) \\ &= 0 \cdot 5 + 0 \cdot 5 \\ &= 1 \cdot 00 \text{ bit} \end{aligned}$$

2. *Average Output Information*

$$\begin{aligned} H_{(y)} &= \Sigma p_j \log_2(1/p_j) \\ &= 0 \cdot 55 \log_2(1/0 \cdot 55) + 0 \cdot 45 \log_2(1/0 \cdot 45) \\ &= 0 \cdot 4744 + 0 \cdot 5184 \\ &= 0 \cdot 9928 \text{ bits} \end{aligned}$$

3. *Average Information in Joint Occurrence of Input and Output*

$$\begin{aligned} H_{(x,y)} &= \Sigma p_{ij} \log_2(1/p_{ij}) \\ &= 0 \cdot 35 \log_2(1/0 \cdot 35) + 0 \cdot 15 \log_2(1/0 \cdot 15) + 0 \cdot 2 \log_2 (1/0 \cdot 2) + 0 \cdot 3 \log_2(1/0 \cdot 3) \\ &= 0 \cdot 5301 + 0 \cdot 4105 + 0 \cdot 4644 + 0 \cdot 5211 \\ &= 1 \cdot 9261 \text{ bits} \end{aligned}$$

It may be seen that very little information is transmitted by our rat:

$$\begin{aligned} T_{(x;y)} &= H_{(x)} + H_{(y)} - H_{(x,y)} \\ &= 1 \cdot 000 + 0 \cdot 9928 - 1 \cdot 9261 \\ &= 0 \cdot 0667 \text{ bits per stimulus.} \end{aligned}$$

Clearly our rat will have to have much more training before it will approach being able to transmit all of the information in the stimulus sequence, 1·0 bit per stimulus.

III

Capacity to code information has been investigated in a variety of experiments. The maximum information transmission achieved has been called the *channel capacity*. There are in fact two kinds of channel capacity. The first is an index of the maximum number of stimuli of a particular type which can be distinguished without error and is measured in bits per stimulus. The second is an index of the maximum rate at which stimuli can be coded without error and is measured in bits per second.

The first kind of channel capacity is a measure of subjects' ability to identify stimuli absolutely. Experiments have been carried out to investigate the accuracy with which subjects make absolute judgments of various kinds as a function of the number of equiprobable stimuli and there are several reviews of their results.[1, 38, 56] A particular example will illustrate the principle of them all.

A subject is required to make absolute judgments of hue. He is instructed to respond to each colour shown to him by calling out a number; for instance, *one* for *red* and *two* for *blue*. In this simple case there are two response categories. He is then shown, say, a hundred 'reds' and a hundred 'blues' in random order, and the numbers he calls out are recorded. Analysis of his responses over a sequence like this will probably show that, unlike the rat above, he has made no errors; all the information in the input has been transmitted into the output and $T = 1$ bit. This procedure may be repeated with more than two hues, and thus more input information, and with correspondingly more different responses to be made, e.g. four hues and four responses, eight hues and eight responses, and so on. For four hues identified without error the transmitted information would be 2 bits and for eight the largest possible value of T would similarly be 3 bits per stimulus. The information actually transmitted for each amount of input information can be calculated. It may be found that the subject makes more errors as the number of stimulus categories (hues) is increased, and that eventually no further increase in input information will increase the amount of information transmitted. This maximum information transmission is the channel capacity. The process is illustrated in the figure opposite.

Investigations of this kind have included determinations of channel capacities for hue,[22, 32] brightness,[32, 40] pitch,[62, 63] loudness,[37] touch,[39, 44, 45] saltiness,[12] points-on-a-line[41] and size.[33] Table 2 shows that the channel capacities calculated from these experiments vary from 1·9 bits per signal for saltiness to 3·25 bits per signal for points-on-a-line; they are equivalent to perfect identification of about four and ten different stimuli of each kind respectively. This variation in calculated channel capacity for judgments on a single stimulus dimension may

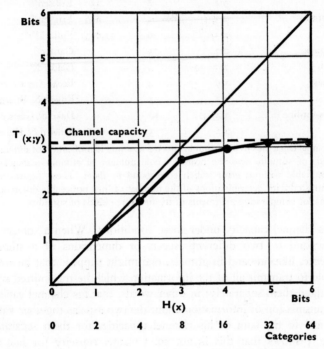

Channel capacity for the absolute identification of hues as the limiting value of transmitted information, $T_{(x;y)}$, for increasing amounts of average input information per stimulus, $H_{(x)}$. The diagonal line, $T_{(x;y)} = H_{(x)}$, is the relation for perfect, errorless transmission, and the numbers of equiprobable categories which correspond to values of $H_{(x)}$ are also shown.

have been due to a number of factors. First, different subjects were used and the amount of training the subjects received probably varied from one experiment to another. Secondly, the range of stimulus values used may have been different for the different dimensions. Or it may indeed be the case that absolute judgments can be made more efficiently for some stimulus dimensions than for others.

So far we have considered the case of a subject judging just one aspect of a stimulus. However, it is possible to ask him to make judgments simultaneously about more than one aspect. What happens

TABLE 2

Kind of Stimulus	Channel Capacity (bits/stimulus)	Categories	j.n.d. steps	Investigator
Hue	3·1	8	150	Eriksen[32]
Brightness	2·3	5	696	Eriksen[32]
Pitch	2·5	6	11,063	Pollack[62,63]
Loudness	2·3	5		Garner[37]
Touch	2·0	4		Geldard[39]
Saltiness	1·9	4		Beebe-Centre et al.[12]
Smell	2·2	5		Engen & Pfaffman[31]
Points-on-line	3.25	10		Hake & Garner[41]
Size	2·2	5		Eriksen & Hake[33]

Channel capacities in bits/stimulus for the absolute identification of different kinds of stimulus and the nearest whole number of stimulus categories identifiable without error which correspond to them. These figures are contrasted with determinations of the number of 'just noticeable difference' steps for comparative judgments of the first three kinds of stimulus.

to his channel capacity under these conditions? When a subject has to respond to two different aspects or dimensions of a stimulus sequence, like hue and brightness, one might suppose that he would be able to transmit all of the information which he transmitted when he judged them separately; in other words, that his channel capacity for transmission of information about the two aspects together would be equal to the sum of his channel capacities for them separately. Table 3 shows that this is not so. Channel capacity for hue and brightness together for example was found to be only 3·6 bits per signal.[42] It was not the 5·4 bits to be expected from the findings that channel capacities for hue and brightness separately are about 3·1 and 2·3 bits per signal respectively. The channel capacity for the two dimensions together is, however, higher than for either alone. Similar results have been reported for up to six auditory dimensions[64] and for eight spatial dimensions.[50]

There have been a number of studies of the effect of the range of input values on channel capacity. For instance, one might present eight hues between red and violet or eight between red and green. In the latter case the eight stimuli cover a narrower range of the visible spectrum and the intervals between the adjacent hues are smaller. Channel capacity for tones has been found to be directly proportional to the 'interstimulus interval';[43] but the effect is small. The same investigation also showed that although practice effects are

TABLE 3

Stimulus Dimensions	Channel Capacity (bits/stimulus)				Investigator
	No. of 'dimensions'				
	1	*2*	*3*	*6*	
Hue	3·1	} 3·6			Halsey & Chapanis[42]
Brightness	2·3		} 4·1		Eriksen[32]
Size	2·2				
Pitch	2·5	} 3·1			Pollack[63]
Loudness	2·3				
Rate of Interruption				} 7·2	Pollack & Ficks[64]
On-time fraction					
Total duration					
Spatial location					
Saltiness	1·9	} 3·6			Beebe-Center et al.[12]
Sweetness	2·3				
Points-on-line	3·25	} 4·6			Klemmer & Frick[50]
Points-in-Square	3·25				

Channel capacities in bits/stimulus for absolute identifications of more than one aspect or dimension of a stimulus contrasted with unidimensional channel capacities.

small, they are greater the larger the interstimulus interval. A similar effect of interstimulus interval on channel capacity has also been found for judgments of the size of circles of light.[4] Factors which decrease the probability of confusing adjacent stimuli do therefore appear to increase channel capacity; they do so reliably but only by small amounts. In judgments of pitch, a twentyfold increase in the range of frequencies only resulted in about a 10 per cent increase in the information transmitted per tone.[62]

So far we have only considered channel capacity in terms of the information transmitted per signal. However, channel capacity in terms of the average information transmitted per second may be calculated if signals are presented at a known and constant rate. The procedure is similar to that outlined above, but the subject is now paced. In one experiment of this kind the ten numbers 0 to 9 were shown to the subject.[3] He either simply had to say the number which he saw, or, in a different series of trials, to press one of ten numbered keys. The results showed that when subjects simply had to say the number they made no errors up to the maximum signal input which was used: 6 bits per second. However, the maximum rate of information transmission for the manual response was found to be only a little more than 3 bits per second. In another experiment with hues, the verbal response (naming colours) was once again found to result in a higher maximum transmission rate than a manual response, but both rates were lower than those for numbers. Evidently the kind of stimulus, the kind of response and the relation between particular stimuli and particular responses limit channel capacity. One might say that they limit the coding efficiency of the channel. These phenomena have been extensively studied in investigations of 'Stimulus-Response compatibility'.[29, 34] The main findings are that while the physical and physiological attributes of stimulus and response limit the degree of S-R compatibility which can be attained, practice produces wide variation within these limits.[13,16,28,47] These results therefore support earlier demonstrations that practice may increase channel capacity.[43]

IV

Informational analysis is by no means free from drawbacks. The following are examples. Transmitted information has been used as a measure of channel efficiency. This measure of efficiency is inversely related to the number of errors made. However, it does not take into account either the direction or the size of errors and thus disregards potential information about subjects' performance. Moreover, the subjective probability of the occurrence of any event may not be the same as the objective probability.[23] In an extensive series of experiments on ways in which subjective probabilities affect behaviour, a lack of correspondence between subjective and objective probabilities has indeed repeatedly been found.[17,18,19,20,21] The objection is unimportant if the information measure is used as an overall estimate of performance, but it is crucial if one entertains particular hypotheses about the factors determining performance. For instance, an electronic technician may fail to discover a fault in the least possible time for two reasons. He may be aware of the objective probabilities of faults in different parts of the system, but not search for them in the most efficient way; or he may search efficiently, but on the basis of incorrect subjective estimates of the probabilities.[25,26,27]

V

This discussion has been restricted to experiments in which the mathematical structure of information theory has been used to analyse the results. It has not included an account of all the direct and indirect influences which information theory has had on studies of perception.

Many of them have been reviewed elsewhere.[2,10,15,38] There are perhaps two main groups of investigations which have not been considered. The first is of experiments in which the framework of information theory has been used to give some kind of specification of a class of stimuli, but not to analyse efficiency of transmission. In some cases the basis in information theory has been fairly specific;[5,6,8 35,57,60] in others it has been much less so.[7,9,11,30,66,67] The second group is of experiments on the relation between choice time and information content of the signal.[24,46,48,49,51,52,53,58,59,68] These experiments are more concerned with speed of coding; and the analyses which have been used do not depend on information theory.

VI

The experiments which have been considered in some detail have been studies of channel capacity. The data from these experiments have been analysed in terms of the input and output of information. Major factors which affect efficiency of coding or channel capacity are S-R compatibility, stimulus discriminability and degree of practice in the task. Information theory has given a new impetus to studies of perception. It has provided a new way of analysing relations between stimuli and responses to supplement, rather than supplant, older methods. In doing so it emphasizes the notion of perception as a coding process and so directs attention in a new way upon an old idea: when there are no responses into which inputs can be coded, there is no perceptual organization.

REFERENCES

1. ALLUISI, E. A., 1957, 'Conditions affecting the amount of information in absolute judgements', *Psychol. Rev.*, *64*, 97.
2. ALLUISI, E. A., 1960, 'On the use of information measures in studies of form perception', *Percept. Motor Skills*, *11*, 195.
3. ALLUISI, E. A., and MULLER, P. F., 1958, 'Verbal and motor responses to seven symbolic visual codes; a study in S-R compatibility', *J. Exper. Psychol.*, *55*, 247.
4. ALLUISI, E. A., and SIDORSKY, R. C., 1958, 'The empirical validity of equal discriminability scaling', *J. Exper. Psychol.*, *55*, 86.
5. ANDERSON, N. S., and FITTS, P. M., 1958, 'Amount of information gained during brief exposures of numerals and colours', *J. Exper. Psychol.*, *56*, 362.
6. ARNOULT, M. D., and PRICE, C. W., 1961, 'Pattern matching in the presence of visual noise', *J. Exper. Psychol.*, *62*, 372.
7. ATTNEAVE, F., 1954, 'Some informational aspects of visual perception', *Psychol. Rev.*, *61*, 183.

8. ATTNEAVE, F., 1955, 'Symmetry, information and memory for patterns', *Amer. J. Psychol.*, *68*, 209.

9. ATTNEAVE, F., 1957, 'Physical determinants of the judged complexity of shapes', *J. Exper. Psychol.*, *53*, 221.

10. ATTNEAVE, F., 1959, *Applications of Information Theory to Psychology*, New York: Holt-Dryden.

11. ATTNEAVE, F., and ARNOULT, M. D., 1956, 'The quantitative study of shape and pattern perception', *Psychol. Bull.*, *53*, 452.

12. BEEBE-CENTRE, J. C., ROGERS, M. S., and O'CONNELL, D. N., 1955, 'Transmission of information about sucrose and saline solutions through the sense of taste', *J. Psychol.*, *39*, 157.

13. BRAINARD, R. W., IRBY, T. S., FITTS, P. M., and ALLUISI, E. A., 1962, 'Some variables influencing the rate of gain of information', *J. Exper. Psychol.*, *63*, 105.

14. BRILLOUIN, L., 1962, *Science and Information Theory*, New York: Wiley.

15. BROADBENT, D. E., 1958, *Perception and Communication*, London: Pergamon.

16. BROADBENT, D. E., and GREGORY, M., 1962, 'Donder's B- & C- Reaction and S-R Compatibility', *J. Exper. Psychol.*, *63*, 575.

17. COHEN, J., 1960, *Chance, Skill and Luck*, Harmondsworth: Pelican.

18. COHEN, J., and COOPER, P., 1962, 'Subjective value of a "bit" of information', *Nature*, *196*, 360.

19. COHEN, J., DEARNALEY, E. J., and HANSEL, C. E. M., 1956, 'The addition of subjective probabilities; the summation of estimates of success and failure', *Acta Psychol.*, *12*, 371.

20. COHEN, J., DEARNALEY, E. J., and HANSEL, C. E. M., 1958, 'The mutual effect of two uncertainties', *Durham Res. Rev.*, *2*, 215.

21. COHEN, J., and HANSEL, C. E. M., 1958, 'Subjective probability, gambling and intelligence', *Nature*, *181*, 1160.

22. CONOVER, D. W., 1959, 'The amount of information in the absolute judgement of Munsel hues', *USAF WADC Tech. Note* No. 58-262.

23. CRONBACH, L. J., 1955, 'On the non-rational application of information measures in psychology', in QUASTLER, H. (ed.), *Information Theory in Psychology*, Glencoe, Ill.: Free Press.

24. CROSSMAN, E. R. F. W., 1953, 'Entropy and choice time; the effect of frequency unbalance on choice-response', *Quart. J. Exper. Psychol.*, *5*, 41.

25. DALE, H. C. A., 1958, 'Fault-finding in electronic equipment', *Ergonomics*, *1*, 356.

26. DALE, H. C. A., 1959, 'Strategies of searching in two simple systems', *Amer. J. Psychol.*, *72*, 539.

27. DALE, H. C. A., 1960, 'Study of subjective probability', *Brit. J. Statist. Psychol.*, *13*, 19.

28. DAVIS, R., MORAY, N., and TREISMAN, A., 1961, 'Imitative responses and the rate of gain of information', *Quart. J. Exper. Psychol.*, *13*, 78.

29. DEININGER, R. L., and FITTS, P. M., 1955, 'Stimulus-response compatibility, information theory, and perceptual-motor performance', in QUASTLER, H. (ed), *Information Theory in Psychology*, Glencoe, Ill.: Free Press.

30. ELLIOTT, L. L., 1958, 'Reliability of judgements of figural complexity', *J. Exper. Psychol.*, *56*, 335.

31. ENGEN, T., and PFAFFMAN, C., 1959, 'Absolute judgments of odor intensity', *J. Exper. Psychol.*, *58*, 23.

32. ERIKSEN, C. W., 1954, 'Multi-dimensional stimulus differences and accuracy of discrimination', *USAF WADC Tech. Report*, 54.

33. ERIKSEN, C. W., and HAKE, H. W., 1955, 'Absolute judgements as a function of the stimulus range and the number of stimulus and response categories', *J. Exper. Psychol.*, *49*, 323.

34. FITTS, P. M., and SEEGER, C. M., 1953, 'S-R compatibility: spatial characteristics of stimulus and response codes', *J. Exper. Psychol.*, *46*, 199.

35. FITTS, P. M., WEINSTEIN, M., RAPPAPORT, M., ANDERSON, N., and LEONARD, A. J., 1956, 'Stimulus correlates of visual pattern perception', *J. Exper. Psychol.*, *51*, 1.

36. FRICK, F. C., 1959, 'Information theory', in KOCH, S. (ed.), *Psychology; A Study of a Science*, Vol. II, New York; McGraw-Hill.

37. GARNER, W. R., 1953, 'An informational analysis of absolute judgements of loudness', *J. Exper. Psychol*, *46*, 373.

38. GARNER, W. R., 1962, *Uncertainty and Structure as Psychological Concepts*, New York: Wiley.

39. GELDARD, F. A., 1956, Personal communication reported by MILLER, G. A. 1956 (see Ref. 56).

40. GLEZER, V. D., TSUKKERMAN, I. I., and TSYKUNOVA, T. M., 1961, 'O zavisimosti propusknoi sposobnosti zrenia ot iorkosti' (On the dependence of transmission capacity of vision on brightness), *Dokl. Akad. Nauk. SSSR*, *136*, 721.

41. HAKE, H. W., and GARNER, W. R., 1951, 'The effect of presenting various numbers of discrete stages on scale reading accuracy', *J. Exper. Psychol.*, *42*, 358.

42. HALSEY, R. H., and CHAPANIS, A., 1954, 'Chromaticity-confusion contours in a complex receiving situation', *J. Opt. Soc. Amer.*, *44*, 442.

43. HARTMAN, E. B., 1954, 'The influence of practice and pitch-distance between tones on the absolute identification of pitch', *Amer. J. Psychol*, *67*, 1.

44. HAWKES, GLENN R., and WARM, JOEL S., 1959, 'Communication by electrical stimulation of the skin; I. Absolute identification of stimulus intensity level', *USA Med. Res. Lab. Report*, No. 400, ii.

45. HAWKES, GLENN R., and WARM, JOEL S., 1959, 'Communication by electrical stimulation of the skin; II. Maximum I, for absolute identification of current intensity level', *USA Med. Res. Lab. Report*, 410, ii.

46. HICK, W. E., 1952, 'On the rate of gain of information', *Quart. J. Exper. Psychol.*, *4*, 11.

47. HOWELL, W. C., 1962, 'On the heterogeneity of stimulus and response elements in the processing of information', *J. Exper. Psychol.*, *63*, 235.

48. HOWELL, W. C., and KREIDLER, D. L., 1963, 'Information processing under contradictory instructional sets', *J. Exper. Psychol.*, *65*, 39.

49. HYMAN, R., 1953, 'Stimulus information as a determinant of reaction times', *J. Exper. Psychol.*, *45*, 188.

50. KLEMMER, E. T., and FRICK, F. C., 1953, 'Assimilation of information from dot and matrix patterns', *J. Exper. Psychol.*, *45*, 15.

51. LAMING, D. R. J., 1962, 'A statistical test of a prediction from information theory in a card-sorting situation', *Quart. J. Exper. Psychol.*, *14*, 38.

52. LEONARD, J. A., 1959, 'Tactual choice reactions, I.', *Quart. J. Exper. Psychol.*, *11*, 76.

53. LEONARD, J. A., 1960, 'Choice reaction time experiments and information theory', *Proc. Lond. Symp. Inform. Theory*, 4.

54. LUCE, D. R., 1960, 'The theory of selective information and some of its behavioural applications', in LUCE, D. R. (ed.), *Development in Mathematical Psychology*, Glencoe, Ill.: Free Press.

55. MACKAY, D. M., 1964, 'Information theory and human information systems', in COHEN, J. (ed.), *Readings in Psychology* (this book).

56. MILLER, G. A., 1956, 'The magical number seven, plus or minus two; some limits on our capacity for processing information', *Psychol. Rev.*, *63*, 81.

57. MILLER, G. A., 1958, 'Free recall of redundant strings of letters', *J. Exper. Psychol.*, *56*, 485.

58. MORIN, R. E., FORRIN, B., and ARCHER, W., 1961, 'Information processing behaviour; the role of irrelevant stimulus information', *J. Exper. Psychol.*, 61, 89.

59. MOWBRAY, G. H., and RHOADES, M. V., 1959, 'On the reduction of choice reaction time with practice', *Quart. J. Exper. Psychol.*, *11*, 16.

60. NEWBROUGH, J. R., 1958, 'Interaction between total stimulus information and specific stimulus information in visual recognition', *J. Exper. Psychol.*, *55*, 297.

61. NEWMAN, E. B., 1951, 'Computational methods useful in analyzing series of binary data', *Amer. J. Psychol.*, *64*, 252.

62. POLLACK, I., 1952, 'The information of elementary auditory displays', *J. acoust. Soc. Amer.*, *24*, 745.

63. POLLACK, I., 1953, 'The information of elementary auditory displays, II', *J. acoust. Soc. Amer.*, *25*, 765.

64. POLLACK, I., and FICKS, L., 1954, 'Information of multi-dimensional displays', *J. acoust. Soc. Amer.*, *26*, 155.

65. SHANNON, C. E., and WEAVER, W., 1949, *The Mathematical Theory of Communication*, Urbana; University of Illinois Press.

66. VANDERPLAS, J. M., and GARVIN, E. A., 1959, 'The association value of random shapes', *J. Exper. Psychol.*, *57*, 147.

67. VANDERPLAS, J. M., and GARVIN, E. A., 1959, 'Complexity association value and practice as factors in shape recognition following paired-associates training', *J. Exper. Psychol.*, *57*, 155.

68. WELFORD, A. T., 1960, 'The measurement of sensory motor performance; survey and reappraisal of twelve years progress', *Ergonomics*, *3*, 189.

Note. To meet the author's wishes the references have been listed in alphabetical order.

CHAPTER 15

CONTACT BETWEEN MINDS*

BY JOHN COHEN

I

'Who would expect originality from a committee or commission or board or that sort of thing?'[1] Let us consider whether the answer to this question, posed by Schrödinger, should be 'No one!'

Recent decades have seen a rapid growth in collective 'thinking' and decision-making, for the sheer size and complexity of social problems have shifted control from individuals to groups. In central and local government, in industry, in the professions and in institutions of one kind or another, the number of committees must run into hundreds of thousands in Britain alone. It was the prestige of committees in the West which prompted a Chinese mandarin to ask whether the Trinity was a device for 'religion by committee'. Consider, for example, the committees in the scientific world, bustling with Research Councils and Institutes, Foundations and Trusts, learned societies and universities. These are often concerned with the tactics as well as with the strategy of research, with planning and directing and with deciding who should do what, when and where. If these committees were to be dissolved, would the activities of scientists grind to a halt? Or would scientists breathe with relief as if a dead hand had been lifted from the conduct of their affairs? Is the change from individual to group control conducive to greater effectiveness? Are the enormous number of hours spent at the committee table necessarily devoid of inventiveness?

Committees and other such groups vary in many ways which may have a bearing on their capacity for original achievement; they vary, for instance, in the manner in which they come into being. Some are self-generating. Others are appointed, and the choice of members will determine the character and degree of novelty of their deliberations;

* An abridged version of Chapter 7, *Humanistic Psychology*, London: Allen & Unwin, 1958.

if someone is chosen because he is said to be impartial, this may only mean that he shares the prejudices of those who have selected him.

Institutions which engage in collective thinking vary in the extent to which ideas are allowed to disseminate within them. In research laboratories, innovation is normally encouraged and information flows freely. In government departments, on the other hand, ideas tend to travel a hierarchical route, and anyone who suggests a new way of doing things is looked at with suspicion, for he implies that the existing state of affairs is not the best. Such organizations perpetuate themselves by reshuffling their components. If innovators emerge, they are neutralized in the administrative machine, if not ejected as foreign bodies. A new institution born from such parent organizations may be described as the child of administrative incest between in-bred minds. Hence the spectacle, in officialdom, of an apostolic succession of ideas masquerading as a system of social innovation while effectively embalming the *status quo*.

II

Early studies of groups, while they shed light on mental productivity in simple situations, were not, on the whole, particularly relevant to what most committees are actually called upon to do, nor were they alive to the part played in them by relationships between the members. A committee is not necessarily convened simply because its conclusions are likely to be more accurate than those that would be reached if each member were to meditate in isolation, or because it is more expeditious than individuals in finding the solution to a clear-cut problem. It may be set up, for example, to provide for an exchange of views between members. If so, the superior skill in problem-solving attributable to groups might not be an adequate measure of the committee's effectiveness.

A more recent approach has been to consider a human group as a system of communication. This view also has its shortcomings if it is restricted to the study of channels of communication, just as a visitor from Mars would have little idea of our social life if he only observed the networks of postal and telephone services without opening letters and tapping messages to find out the content and its meaning. At committee meetings, content and meaning are all-important. A member may utter a statement unwittingly conveying a different meaning from the one he consciously intended, and the message may be received by fellow-members in a corresponding ambivalence. If he pretends to mean what he says, instead of actually saying what he means, his utterance may be open to various interpretations. Furthermore, because of 'receiver bias', one and the same utterance may be received in different senses by several listeners.

Communication in groups need not be restricted to a verbal medium.[2] It may be merely vocal, in that meaning is conveyed by intonation, emphasis, rate of speech, or manner of articulation. In any event a form of words does not necessarily carry 'information'; the more conventional a statement the more various the possible interpretations we can give it. A casual remark about the weather cannot with confidence be taken either as a declaration of love or as a sentence of death.

Communication may be non-vocal as well as non-verbal. That is to say, silence may have one or more of several possible meanings, and by the judicious use of silence a member of a group may wish to convey one meaning to some and another meaning to others who are present. If he wishes to hide what he intended his silence to mean, he can retrospectively camouflage it when he subsequently speaks. A prolonged silence may be an ominous sign, unless it indicates compliance; to refrain from speaking in everyday life is a common expression of hostility; an individual does not trust himself to speak in case he 'bursts'. The frequency and distribution of silent intervals therefore is not to be overlooked.

Communication is also subject to perceptual distortion. A member of a group may ascribe characteristics to another member by seeing him not 'as he is', as judged by a general consensus of opinion among those who know him well, but as possessing features which in the perceiver's mind are associated with other people of significance for him, a phenomenon which is dramatically exemplified in psychotics.

III

How are we to judge the effectiveness of a committee or conference? Two kinds of criteria may be identified which we can call internal and external respectively. An internal criterion is one which simply requires that some activity should take place to the satisfaction of those engaged which they display by a mutual pat on the back. It would clearly be imprudent in some circumstances to rely on this alone. Otherwise, a captain of a ship, for example, would never know whether his vessel is advancing or merely moving round in circles. The activity of a social group might also be 'circular' if it is not assessed by the outside world.[3] Steering by reference to effects beyond the group constitutes an external criterion.

The use of external criteria presupposes that committees, conferences, and institutions may be evaluated in relation to the wider society of which they are part. Thus the effectiveness of a conference of management and workers might be assessed by looking for improvement in industrial relations. Duration of stay[4] of patients in hospital and their relapse rates may be regarded as external criteria of medical and nursing effectiveness, while the rate of recidivism could be an external test of the effectiveness of imprisonment. In general, if a social institution is to work effectively there must be a link between planner and executive and a feedback from the second to the first.

But external criteria can at best only maintain an *equilibrium* of ideas or action. If we seek inventiveness we shall need other methods, those which might provide a positive rather than a negative feedback. In the present context this means, first and foremost, eliminating of obstacles to receptivity. Novel ideas may be more likely to arise in a group if participants are optimally responsive to continuously changing patterns of the relationships between them. The mind (or brain, whichever we prefer) is essentially a social instrument, formed in close and intimate contact with other minds. If so, we should not expect new ideas to arise only when we are lost in lonely reflection. Conversation may kindle a 'thought spark' which will later burst into flame. Indeed, the capacity to integrate our perspectives with those of others, to achieve a mutual reciprocity, is perhaps a vital condition for intellectual productivity. It was this capacity which made possible the Platonic dialogues from which it is but a short step to the full dramatic mode in which Shakespeare formulated the innumerable aspects of his vision, to reveal the multifarious facets of reality;[5] and it was in this tradition that the mediaeval alchemist conceived of meditation as an inner dialogue. Plato defined thought as a dialogue of the soul with itself, a view revived among those contemporary biologists who describe thought and memory as communication of the self to the self.[6]

For such effects to take place it is essential to be able to *listen*, that is, to come as close as possible to a speaker's intended meaning, to enter his thoughts sympathetically before finding fault with them. There is a difference between merely *hearing* and *listening*, and the effectiveness of teaching and broadcasting, as well as of conferences and debates, depends on the latter rather than on the former. Training in the art of listening could enhance receptivity to new ideas by alerting people to their own tacit preconceptions, prejudices and stereotypes.

IV

We can find a clue to the formation of new ideas in groups by considering the intellectual characteristics of scientific workers, universally acknowledged as innovators.[7] What distinguishes the scientific world from the worlds of politics, administration and industry or from the judicial, military and religious worlds? First, there is the tendency to publish newly-won knowledge as soon and as widely as possible, thus scattering to fellow-workers a large and diverse number of 'signals'. Second, scientific issues are repeatedly and exhaustively debated in large numbers of formal and informal groups, and in specialist journals, exposing the scientist to a flood of comments and criticisms. Third, discussion is free. Anyone can talk to anyone, for the thing that matters is not who you are but what you have to say. Fourth, the scientist is constantly on the look out for situations where the usual way of doing or understanding things is inadequate. This quality contrasts particularly with that required of the military man as such. The scientist cultivates freedom of thought and expression, whilst the soldier learns to take and give orders, and if he makes a mistake, he is apt to conceal it from those whose confidence he enjoys. If a scientist makes a mistake, he must make the fullest and widest acknowledgment of his error. The virtue of the soldier, as Babbage[8] once said, is the vice of the scientist, who therefore challenges practices and assumptions whatever their history or prestige, however much they are hallowed or petrified by tradition, and when he thinks he has discovered a shortcoming in someone else's work he makes it a common experience, in the same way as a doctor reports to his colleagues a suspected case of infectious disease. All concerned can then be on their guard, and even if they are unwilling to accept the data or the interpretation or the inferences, their minds will have been prepared for receiving further observations of the same kind. The alternative to such a procedure is that nothing should be done until there is a crisis.

In Britain we are familiar with the fact that it is hard to introduce a change until a state of emergency compels us to; for example, a dangerous site frequently will not be made safe for traffic until an accident has actually occurred. Drastic alterations must thus be made when the crisis is actually upon us. It is harder to make a sensible decision at such a moment, if only because there is less time to consider alternative courses, apart from the fact that in an emergency we are apt to abandon foresight in favour of a superficially attractive solution.[9] The relative merits of the diverse courses of action should be judged, as far as possible, in advance of a crisis, for if things are left to the eleventh hour, when, so to speak, the house is on fire, a decision is forced on us by the situation.

V

Turn now to factors of a different kind, those which may hamper communication within a group. First of all there is the degree of homogeneity of the members relative to the purpose for which they are convened. Naturally they must share some minimal assumptions, otherwise they are in no position to discuss anything fruitfully; but if they are too homogeneous, they will tend to occupy themselves with minutae to which they will attach a disproportionate importance. In a homogeneous professional group, for example, tension from technical differences over trifles may spread to larger issues. By contrast, a relatively heterogeneous group is likely to ignore finer nuances and seek broad understanding of fundamentals. For this reason homogeneous groups in certain circumstances may be less stable than heterogeneous ones. Paradoxically, those who are intellectually remote from one another may reach understanding more readily than those who have much in common. A group of specialists can become passionately embroiled over some point which to the outsider seems of little significance; during World War II meetings of an official committee of specialist psychologists and psychiatrists were said to have been described by a Lord President of the Council as a 'bear-garden'. The same phenomenon is familiar in politics. British socialism is perhaps politically closer to communism than to conservatism. Yet the socialists are even more bitterly hostile to communists than to conversatives, and socialist leaders have been even less successful than the conservatives in their efforts to come to terms with communist regimes.

A second obstacle is the degree to which the participants resist new ideas, though this may in itself be a composite effect. Thus delegates sent to plead a special cause are given more or less definite instructions beforehand, and their minds are therefore closed to proposals not contemplated by the policy-makers behind them. In Britain there appears to be a tradition, at any rate in official institutions, to avoid creating precedents at all costs. This may be exemplified by the advice given by the leader of a British delegation to a Unesco General Conference. He

urged the Conference when it considered new proposals not to be afraid to say 'no' merely because no good reason could be urged against them.[10]

The British national commission for Unesco has retained this extraordinary talent for not doing anything that can be avoided.

A third influence is an unquestioned notion of the supposed role of members, as illustrated by the following example taken from the Report of the Royal Commission on the Dardanelles, an ill-fated British military adventure in World War I.

The question at the time was whether the Dardanelles could be forced by the use of sea power alone. It transpired later that a number of those principally concerned were strongly opposed to a naval attack unaided by land forces. But they never said so. And when one of them did express an opinion of this kind, it was at an inopportune moment. So these views never became known to the responsible Ministers. Why did the experts not reveal their misgivings? Duty, or at least what they believed was their duty. But no one ever discussed what 'Duty' was. They conceived their basic duty to be not to inquire into what was the meaning of 'Duty'. 'It was better not to talk about it and, if possible, not to think about it. They succeeded in not thinking about it.' The First Sea Lord stated that it was his duty to withhold his views until he could suppress them no longer and then resign. And just as the experts did not expect their subordinates to give advice unless they were asked for it, so they themselves did not offer advice until they themselves were invited to do so. 'We were the experts who were to open our mouths when told to', declared the First Sea Lord.[11]

A fourth factor is the tacit assumption that agreement between participants is a desirable end in itself. In other words, according to circumstances and individuals, attention is turned from points on which members diverge to matters on which they think alike. Members are thus led away from exploring differences, which may be by far the more fruitful enterprise, to discussing matters on which they concur. Such a state of affairs amounts to an inclination to conform to the group and to yield to its pressures, a *compulsion to agree*. When this is marked, the consciousness of the participants tends to exclude any item that deviates from the general trend of opinion, and free, uninhibited expression is discouraged. The nearer the group moves towards a decision, the more any divergence on the part of a member threatens its solidarity. Every committee member knows that a moment arrives when reticence is the better part of valour if he is not to incur the reprimand of his chairman or the hostility of his fellow-members. The compulsion to agree therefore grows in strength as the moment of decision approaches.[12, 13]

To the extent that preoccupation with agreement makes it difficult to listen to what others are saying, a lip service assent is likely to be given to what is not fully understood. Not that differences of view at committees fail to be made manifest but there commonly tends to be undue restraint; when a divergent opinion is ventured it is rarely sustained and it is the voluble or less dominant members who surrender. Under such conditions there is a weakening of the group's capacity to tolerate differences without distintegration. There can also be a compulsion to *disagree*, but this is more rare.[14] The crucial point is this: for group discussion to be more fruitful than private meditation, the minimal condition is that each member should feel as free to speak his mind in the presence of others as he would be in thinking his thoughts privately. Only when this condition is satisfied is there a possibility of fruitful interaction between members and a consequent intellectual enrichment of the outcome.

The idea that agreement in itself is a good thing is to rely on internal criteria of effectiveness. Judged by external criteria there is no merit in agreement as such, which may, indeed, merely be a device for preserving an illusory omiscience. 'I agree with you', when decoded could mean 'You must be right, because I share your view'. If agreement is a substitute for the exploration of differences it reduces the scope of interaction among members. The exchanges on which group thinking depends cannot take place when all participants are thinking alike. In point of fact, taking a longer view, individuals or groups may be co-operating more when they are in opposition than when they are content with superficial unanimity.

VI

Granted that differences must be explored, what, if anything, can be done to resolve conflicts due to genuine misunderstanding? Consider the situation in politics. We know that a political spokesman is, or is expected to be, familiar with the policy of his Party, and once he has begun to make a speech, we can sometimes guess how he will proceed. What we do not know is whether he has grasped the policy he is opposing. A court of justice offers a similar situation. There, too, we know full well that counsel for the prosecution can state his *own* case, just as counsel for the defence can state *his*, but we do not know whether each has a full and proper understanding of his opponent's case.

This state of affairs might be remedied if parliaments (and law courts) adopted a procedure that I have elsewhere called the technique

of role-reversal.[15] Let us assume, for purposes of illustration, that this technique has been established as parliamentary procedure and that a debate on Capital Punishment is about to commence. The opening speech for abolition is made by one who favours retention, and he is followed by an abolitionist stating the case for retention. Now when each speaker hears *his* view presented by his opponent, he will at least have the opportunity of seeing it in a new light. And, what is more, he may discover that he had himself been resisting ideas which he had not fully understood or had even misunderstood. If so, he would find it hard to insist on his objections so long as it is clear to others present that he has not apprehended the view which he rejects. Equally, he may be led to revalue his own ideas, and possibly begin to see some point in his opponents' criticisms.

Thus the procedure demands that no one should be allowed to criticize his opponents until he has satisfied them that he has grasped their point of view, and only then should he state his own case. Others present would also need to be assured of this. An arrangement of this sort might have the salutary effect of inducing disputants to make a true effort to understand the views which they reject, an effort which they have perhaps never found it necessary or even possible to make before. Their very struggle to understand might become the first step towards reconciliation.

Considered as a device for resolving political differences the proposed technique may appear naïve. In the first place, the critic could say that the procedure is already an established practice. Secondly, he would go on to argue, it is impracticable. Thirdly, even if practicable, it could never shake the rock-like beliefs of the professional politicians, even those conflicting convictions which are held by opposing parties with equal knowledge, intelligence and good will. 'Nothing that any of us can say can change his mind, which is that of a true believer', a well-known American commentator once said of the Soviet premier; and we may suppose that the Soviet premier formed the same opinion of the commentator. If an obdurate and refractory quality were characteristic of the political mind, can we escape the conclusion that political conferences and discussions are a waste of time?

The outlook would not be so bleak if we did not seek to 'change the minds' of other people. Hankering after agreement may be asking too much. The limited goal of *mutual understanding* is not only more realistic but could also, in very many instances, be adequate. The aim of role-reversal is not necessarily *to convince* the other party to the dispute. This is where it differs from similar procedures the objective

I

of which 'is to convince your opponent, to make him see things as you see them'.[16] In role-reversal this is not the goal; the disputant's primary aim is rather to try and see his opponent's view, not to impress his own view on his opponent.

VII

Role-reversal is a short-term device. What about the long term? Can something be done to cultivate the capacity for *understanding* others? This aspect of communication has been neglected, and it forms no part of information theory. Individual variations in the capacity for understanding may conceivably be due to ontogenetic factors. If parents do not understand their child, if teachers do not understand a pupil, they are unable effectively to communicate with him. So instead of providing for what he really needs they give him what they think he needs. If the child has been reared by control or manipulation, he has not had built into him the experience of 'being understood'. In adult years, therefore, he is, as a rule, only able to translate the passive control which he has experienced into an active manipulation of others. He cannot know what it is to understand another person if he himself has never had the feeling of being understood. There may be an optimal emotional stage of development, during pre-adolescence, for cultivating receptivity to the views of others. The tendency to substitute agreement for understanding may accordingly be regarded as a cultural phenomenon. It is not a law of nature.

I make no claim that role-reversal could lead to the reconciliation of divergent interests where there is *no* misunderstanding. If a man is hungry he must be fed, unless we can persuade him that hunger is good for his stomach. There is therefore no ground for the facile belief that manipulation of 'human relations' could 'do the trick'. But nor, on the other hand, should we assume, without more ado, that what *appear* to be irreconcilable interests are so *in fact*, and that all attempts to seek mutual understanding are futile.

Hence the importance of seeking an ensemble of perspectives in social and political life. 'Truth' from a single perspective is a provincialism, the expression of a person who thinks that only *his* point of view counts. Just as a photograph of a man can be taken from an infinite variety of angles, each photograph yielding only a single perspective, so each social opinion offers a single facet of 'social truth'. 'The very seeing of another vista', wrote Nietzsche, 'the very *wishing* to see another vista, is no little training and preparation of the intellect for its eternal "objectivity"—objectivity being understood not as

"contemplation without interest" (for that is inconceivable and non-sensical), but as the ability to have the pros and cons *in one's power* and to switch them on and off, so as to get to know how to utilize, for the advancement of knowledge, the *difference* in the perspective and in the emotional interpretations. . . . There is only a seeing from a perspective, only a "knowing" from a perspective, and the *more* emotions we express over a thing, the *more* eyes, different eyes, we train on the same thing, the more complete will be our "idea" of that thing, our "objectivity".[17]

Let us now return to our original question, which we can now see is less simple than it may have first appeared. We cannot dismiss *a priori* the possibility that, under suitable conditions, groups may become vehicles of innovation. Provided members feel free to utter their thoughts, and provided they listen, the group in which they participate offers opportunities of assimilating the ideas of others and of accommodating to them which are perhaps otherwise unattainable.

NOTES AND REFERENCES

1. SCHRÖDINGER, E., 1951, *Science and Humanism*, London: Cambridge University Press.
2. SULLIVAN, H. S., 1954, *The Psychiatric Interview*, New York: Norton.
3. LEWIN, K., 1947, 'Frontiers in Group Dynamics II', *Human Relations, 1*, 143.
4. COHEN, J., 1948, *Minority Report on the Recruitment and Training of Nurses*, London: H.M.S.O.
5. ARBER, A., 1954, *The Mind and the Eye*, London: Cambridge University Press.
6. HALDANE, J. B. S., 1955, 'Communication in Biology' in *Studies in Communication*, London: Secker and Warburg.
7. These characteristics were described by the late Geoffrey Pyke in an unpublished Memorandum.
8. BABBAGE, C., 1830, *Reflections on the Decline of Science*, London: Fellowes.
9. This behaviour in an emergency is analogous to the vacuum reaction discussed in section 7 of Chapter I.
10. 1949, *Report of the U.K. Delegation on the Third Unesco General Conference*, London: H.M.S.O. Cmd 7661.
11. See ref. 9. The analysis of the Report of the Royal Commission on the Dardanelles was also made by Geoffrey Pyke.
12. In this connection, Mr. Peter Cooper has pointed out, most compromises in committee tend to be forced, rather than willingly reached.
13. The phenomenon discussed in this paragraph also seems to characterize august bodies. 'The reluctance to oppose that which is disapproved', wrote Babbage, 'has been too extensively and too fatally prevalent for the interests of the Royal Society . . . some portion of it is due to that improper deference which was long paid to every dictum of the President and much of it to that natural indisposition to take trouble on any point in which a man's own interest is not immediately concerned.' In this connection it is of interest to

recall remarks made by Gilbert Murray about the manner in which ancient thinkers conceived of agreement as such. 'It has been well observed by Zeller', he writes, 'that the great weakness of all ancient thought, not excepting Socratic thought, was that instead of appealing to objective experiment it appealed to some subjective sense of fitness. There were exceptions, of course; Democritus, Eratosthenes, Hippocrates, and to a great extent Aristotle. But in general there was a strong tendency to follow Plato in supposing that people could really solve questions by an appeal to their inner consciousness. One result of this, no doubt, was a tendency to lay too much stress on mere agreement. It is obvious, when one thinks about it, that quite often a large number of people who know nothing about a subject will all agree and all be wrong. Yet we find the most radical of ancient philosophers unconsciously dominated by the argument *ex consensu gentium*. It is hard to find two more uncompromising thinkers than Zeno and Epicurus.' (MURRAY, G., 1935, *Five Stages of Greek Religion*, London: Watt, p. 128.)

14. It is worth remarking here that in the early stages of modern science violent polemics actually seem to have been the rule without retarding its development. For instance, the discovery of sympathin and the operation of complete sympathectomy were direct results of a polemic. In other spheres too, as exemplified by the celebrated Minority Report on the Poor Law, submitted by Beatrice and Sidney Webb, resistance to group conformity in the long run proved the more productive and effective course to take.

15. This technique was first described by the author in a report for UNESCO entitled *The Study of International Conferences* (1950), and was published in 1951, *Occup. Psychol.*, *25*, 64. For a consideration of its place in international debate see the author's 'Reflections on the Resolution of Conflict in International Affairs', *Proc. Internat. Cong. Appl. Psychol.*, 1962, Copenhagen: Munksgaard, *1*, 59: and in relation to parliamentary affairs see 'The 1959 House of Commons' (with Peter Cooper), *Occup. Psychol.*, 1961, *35*, 1.

16. RAPOPORT, A., *Fights, Games, Debates*, 1960, Ann Arbor: University of Michigan Press.

17. NIETZSCHE, F., 1910, *The Genealogy of Morals*, London: Foulis, 152.

APPENDIX *

The Natural History of Learned Societies

———

I

The body of the chapter is largely an attempt to examine (i) the influences which promote the intellectual productivity of groups and (ii) the obstacles to communication. In this Appendix I wish to illus-

* An abridged version of 'Natural History of Learned and Scientific Societies', by J. Cohen, C. E. M. Hansel and Edith F. May, *Nature*, 1954, *178*, 328.

trate contact between minds by reference to the growth of a certain type of social group, namely, the learned society. The aim in the investigation to be sketched was to seek a quantitative principle underlying the formation and growth of such societies, and the results to be given relate to about 220 national societies in Britain that still existed in 1952, though I shall be specially concerned with scientific societies.

In the descriptions of their origins given by the societies themselves, several patterns are discernible which reflect the modes of corporate life characteristic of the period in which the particular society came into being. The date when a learned society is founded is an arbitrary, if convenient, point in its history. Like the birth of a child, it marks a new phase but it is not a beginning. The society, like the infant, is first conceived and then passes through a phase of gestation before it formally sees the light of day.

The most common mode of generation, for society and child alike, is by the efforts of a single ardent individual. At least a third of the scientific societies examined were inspired in this way. About one-sixth owed their origin to a budding-off from an existing group. The remaining half seem to have been formed (i) to launch or support a journal; (ii) to preserve a library, a private laboratory, a collection of specimens left as a legacy, or to dispose of some fund; (iii) to enable the dying spirit of a moribund group to transmigrate into a new body; (iv) as a collective effort on the part of individuals already in informal contact; or (v) as an expression of professional defence against hostile interests.

Other influences, such as an important event or publication, or ease of transport and communication, were doubtless operative either directly or indirectly. Among such influences may be included the Scientific Societies' Act of 1843 and the Great Exhibition of 1851. Some of the earlier societies were necessarily limited to members living within reasonable distance of the place of meeting. The main body of the scientific societies in existence in 1952 came into being after the Napoleonic wars; in 1819 only four existed as compared with about 130 in 1952. But the rate of formation of new societies did not keep pace with the growth of membership of the combined societies. In a representative group of sciences, membership increased thirteen times whereas there was only a four- or five-fold increase in the number of societies. Between 1880 and 1952 forty-six new medical or biological societies were formed but not a single new mathematical or chemical society.

During the eighteenth and early nineteenth centuries, novel problems posed by local industry stimulated considerable scientific activity in British provincial centres. As a result many 'little clubs or coteries of scientific and literary men' flourished at Liverpool, Warrington, Bristol, Norwich, Manchester and Birmingham, and elsewhere in Britain! The number of learned societies established in each twenty-year period from 1800 to 1952 is shown in Table 1, and the membership by society is shown in Table 2.

TABLE I

FOUNDATION OF NEW SOCIETIES IN 20-YEAR PERIODS

	before 1799*	1800 to 1819	1820 to 1839	1840 to 1859	1860 to 1879	1880 to 1899	1900 to 1919	1920 to 1939	1940 to 1953
General Science	2	1							2
Astronomy			1			1		1	
Biology	1		2	3	3	9	8	7	2
Chemistry			1						
Physics				1	1		1	1	1
Mathematics				1	2				
Geology and Geography			1	1	2	1	1	2	1
Anthropology and Sociology				1	1	2	2	3	
Archaeological Studies				4	1	1	2		
Technology and Agriculture	1	1	2	2	1	1	9	4	4
Medicine†	3	2	1	1		3	4	8	5
Humanities (Law, Literature, History, Philosophy)	3	1	4	1	4	21	24	13	6
TOTAL	10	5	13	16	14	39	51	39	21

* Including the following five societies formed before 1780; the Royal Society (1660), Medical Society of London (1773), the Royal Medical Society of Edinburgh (1778), the Honourable Society of Cymmrodorion (1751), Society of Antiquaries of London (1707).

† Dates of foundation of three societies in this group are not available.

TABLE II

NUMBER OF SOCIETIES AND THEIR MEMBERSHIP

	Number of Societies	Membership*
GENERAL SCIENCE	5	7,900
NATURAL SCIENCES		
Astronomy	3	5,100
Biological Sciences	35	27,200
Chemistry	1	9,100
Physics	5	7,300
Mathematics	3	5,500
Geology and Geography	10	15,100
ANTHROPOLOGY AND SOCIOLOGY	9	13,200
ARCHAEOLOGICAL STUDIES	8	6,700
TECHNOLOGY AND AGRICULTURE	25	117,000
MEDICINE	30	24,100
HUMANITIES		
Law	7	6,000
Literature and Language	31	39,000
HISTORICAL STUDIES	33	25,600
Philosophy	6	4,400
TOTAL	211	313,200

* The figures are given to the nearest hundred.

II

In order to compare the rates of growth of the different groups of sciences, a sample was taken of those societies for which complete series of figures were available. From 1830 onwards rates of increase over decades, after correcting for changes in the population of Great Britain, are shown in Fig. 1. Fluctuations are more pronounced in the early parts of the curves because of the relatively small number of societies which were rapidly increasing in size. The rate of growth of membership must be due to a number of influences, the most obvious of which are increase in population and opportunities for higher education.

The curves in Fig. 1 may be studied in the light of developments in the different groups of sciences, on the one hand, and of economic and social influences, on the other. For example, the large peak in the curve

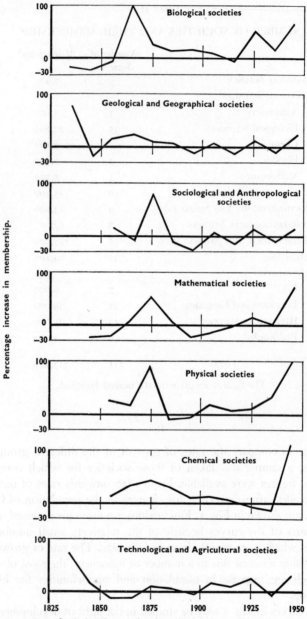

Rates of growth of scientific societies after allowing for population increases

FIG. 1.

of the biological societies between 1860 and 1870 may possibly be associated with the publication of Darwin's *The Origin of Species* in 1859. This peak is reflected to some extent in the curve for geology and geography. In the other groups of sciences a peak of growth occurs between 1870 and 1880. There is a marked difference in the effect of the First and Second World Wars respectively; a rapid increase in membership only appears after the second war.

III

Collection and analysis of the data was guided by the idea that the development of societies might show characteristics of growth similar to those displayed by cellular colonies or human populations. In particular the interesting analogies between mental and physical epidemiology, first drawn by Penrose,[2] leads us to expect that the growth in the size of the societies over a period of time could be susceptible to analysis in epidemiological terms. He considered crazes, panic reactions and religious enthusiasms in the light of these analogies. The societies in the present series may be regarded as extreme members of a class of much wider range. Intermediate members of this class might be represented by cults with pretensions to scientific status which grow fairly rapidly and decline with advance in knowledge as, for example, the 29 phrenological societies, which once enjoyed a transient existence in Great Britain. At the other extreme—the emotional end of the continuum—are the mass phenomena of the Middle Ages, such as the Flagellant Movement and the dancing manias.

Phases in the life of scientific societies may be expressed in epidemiological terms comparable to those identified by Penrose. (i) First there is a latent period in which the idea of a society is germinating in the minds of one or more individuals. (ii) The second phase is an increasingly rapid growth of members. (iii) This is followed by a third phase in which the rate of growth remains fairly constant or decreases; this may be due to exhaustion of potential membership, a factor analogous to saturation of the susceptible population in an epidemic.

(iv) The fourth phase is reached when there are counter influences such as competing societies and shifts of scientific interest which produce immunity to the societies' ideas in members and non-members alike. The development of immunity may be illustrated from the experience of a person who become a member of a society as a result of acute infection with its ideas. At the beginning he paid his subscription punctually without any prompting on the part of the society.

I*

After three or four years, a reminder was needed before the subscription was paid. At first the prompting yielded an immediate response. Subsequently, more than one reminder became necessary and the delay in payment become more prolonged. Eventually the threshold of response reached such a high level that the combined effect of several reminders was ineffective. In the end complete immunity was achieved.

(v) Finally, during the fifth phase, the rate of attraction of new members no longer offsets wastage from various causes. A society may then disappear or may recommence a new cycle of activity.

The development of learned societies seems, however, to be subject to many more influences than is the course of an epidemic, for socio-economic changes and technological discoveries have a profound impact on the spread of scientific ideas and on the possibility of forming and maintaining an association.

Gompertz curves fitted to the figures of membership of a number of societies (without allowing for increase in population) show a reasonably close fit to the data. In the case of the Chemical Society, the curve gives an excellent fit for the first eighty years of its existence. After 1920 the size of the society fell below the expected values and at 1950 it rose well above them. This curve may be used for representing stages in which a society is still growing as well as the size which it will reach if present conditions are maintained.

IV

Among the various independent estimates which may be made of development in the different fields of science in Great Britain we can consider the number of scientific journals, the number of patents sealed each year, and the number of students of science at the universities.

Briefly, there seem to be two or three journals per 1,000 members. So far as patents are concerned, there was a steady increase in the number sealed after 1850, comparable with the increase in membership of technological societies. During both World Wars, however, there was a distinct decline followed in each case by a recovery to the pre-war level.[3] The university output of graduates in science represent perhaps the main source of potential membership of scientific societies. In 1951–2 as compared with 1925–6, the number of honours science graduates showed an increase of more than 200 per cent, advanced science students 150 per cent, and membership of societies 100 per cent.

V

Studies of the kind described provide a comparative measure of the development and dissemination of ideas in different branches of learning at different periods. Secondly, they enable us to trace the growth of learned societies in relation to demographic, educational and technological changes. Thirdly, they offer a basis for comparing fields of interest which appear to be adequately represented by single societies with others which give rise to a diversity of groups. These studies may be extended to professional, voluntary and reform societies. A special case is the growth of societies in a limited population, such as a city, a factory or a university, where it is possible more readily to examine such phenomena as overlapping membership and intensity of participation. The studies lend themselves to elaboration on comparative lines at different levels, institutional, urban and national. Thus a comparison has in fact been made of student life at two universities;[4] and two cities might be compared with respect to the number and variety of societies they 'generate'.

NOTES AND REFERENCES

1. A similar growth in learned societies took place on the Continent particularly in Italy, where some 700 societies are said to have flourished during the sixteenth and seventeenth centuries, and later in France. There were, for example, academies at Ancona, Bologna, Brescia, Genoa, Mantua, Modena, Naples. Padua, Palermo, Perugia, Venice, and Verona. Rome had its *Umoristi* (1611) *Fantastici* (1625) and *Infecondi* (1653) amongst many others: Florence had an academy of Fine Arts as early as 1270. BROWN, HARCOURT, 1934, *Scientific Organizations in Seventeenth-Century France* (1620–80), Baltimore: Williams and Wilkins.

2. PENROSE, L. S., 1952, *On the Objective Study of Crowd Behaviour*, London: Lewis: see also COHEN, J., 1952, *Nature, 170*, 474.

3. See also ROSSMAN, J., 1931, 'War and Inventions', *Amer. J. Sociol., 36*, 625.

4. A Study of Student Societies in the University of Manchester, by Members of the Department of Psychology, University of Manchester, *Sociol. Rev., 1956, 4*, 243.

CHAPTER 16

THE ORGANIZATION OF MEMORY

BY IAN M. L. HUNTER

How are incoming data organized for storage and what forms of data retrieval and utilization does this storage permit under varying circumstances? Daily experience does not, at one extreme, pass and leave behind no trace whatever nor, at the other, leave a totally complete record. Between these two extremes, human activities reflect past experience in diverse ways which imply a complexity of memory organization that is far in excess of anything embodied in a lifeless repository wherein objects may be stored for later retrieval. The selective memory disorders which go by such names as amnesia, agnosia and apraxia[1] are conspicuously baffling: but no more so than the manifestations of memory organization which are commonplace in the human scene. Our present considerations will fall into three related parts. First, the salient features of a memory task which is carried through in two distinct ways. Secondly, the qualitative changes brought about in memory organization by pathological conditions and by the development of specialized accomplishments. Thirdly, the schematizing principle which underlies so much of the memory organization that sustains the development of high-level human accomplishment.

I

Mnemonic systems (sometimes called technical memories, mnemotechnics, or ingenious memorizing procedures) have a long popular history.[2] They enable their users to memorize lengthy sequences of unrelated items and, within their very limited realm of applicability, are dramatically successful. Why? The following experiment was conducted by the writer to yield some answer to this question. It should be borne in mind that the subjects are educated adults working under explicit instructions to learn, for later reproduction, material being presented under time pressure.

The following list is read out once to a group of students at a steady rate of one item every two seconds. ONE: SUGAR: TWO: DAFFODIL: THREE: BOAT: FOUR: TIGER: FIVE: NECK-LACE: SIX: TABLE: SEVEN: FEATHER: EIGHT: CUP: NINE: MOUNTAIN: TEN: BLACKBIRD. The students are told beforehand that there will be ten numbered and unrelated nouns; and that when the list has been read, they are to write down as many of the words as possible. Also beforehand, the students write down the numbers one to ten in their notebooks and are told that a recalled word will be scored correct only if written against its appropriate number. This task is given to two comparable groups: one group receives only the above instructions (Condition One) while the other is taught a mnemonic system (Condition Two).

The possible recall scores range from zero to ten, and the number of students making each score is shown in Table 1.

TABLE I

Showing the number of students with each recall score in conditions One and Two of the memory task described in the text.

Recall score	Under 5	5	6	7	8	9	10
Group One (N=32)	0	5	11	9	3	2	2
Group Two (N=32)	0	0	1	2	4	8	17

Some students do better than others but the task is too much for most because of the amount of words, their unrelatedness, and the time pressure imposed. When asked to describe how they went about the task, all students report dealing with incoming words in some individualistic but more or less systematic fashion. A few proceed by thematic chaining, that is, they cumulatively embed each word as a key item in a continuously elaborated story or theme which may be visual or verbal or both. A few count off the words on their fingers. The majority use cumulative rehearsal, that is, repeat the first word, then the first and second, then the first, second and third, and so on. But around the middle of the list, there is too little time for such rehearsal and students are uncertain how best to continue: some start a fresh chain of cumulative rehearsal; some keep repeating the chain they already have and ignore incoming words; some listen rather passively to the remaining words and 'hope they will stick'. In general, then, people proceed as best they can with a relatively unfamiliar type of task but, whatever their procedure, almost all report that there is too much to do in too short a time. The first four or five words give little trouble but, thereafter, students are trying to hold these, often by explicit rehearsal, while dealing with new incoming words and perhaps trying to devise more adequate procedures: they feel overloaded, hurried, confused.

This illustrates a pervasive memory characteristic which is more fully explored by experiments on short-term or immediate memory.[3, 4, 5, 6, 7] This characteristic is a limited capacity to do 'several things at once'. Thus, the average adult can receive, hold and recall a sequence of about seven digits: but he cannot do this with fourteen. Receiving the later digits interferes with holding the earlier ones, and recalling the earlier digits interferes with holding the later ones. In such short-term tasks, receiving, holding and recalling are all competing activities to be carried through by someone of limited capacity for activity within any specified time period. The main implication of these short-term memory studies is that any incoming item is rapidly lost unless the person is, in some sense, free to mull it over: if he is not free to do this, the item is lost in a matter of seconds. Otherwise expressed, people cannot take in and hold for later recall more than a brief sequence of incoming details. This fact contrasts with everyday observation that people seem able to recall quite lengthy episodes. The resolution of this apparent conflict will be taken up later.

When the word list has been read, students proceed to recall in ways that are consistent with what they have already done. Some start by producing the first few words of the list, but some begin at the end. Thus, one 'cumulative rehearser' reports, 'I quickly wrote down the last two words before I forgot them. Then I wrote the first four in correct order but found I'd forgotten the fifth. I remembered that one word was FEATHER but wasn't sure of its position. I put it against SIX but this turned out to be wrong.' Two further aspects of recall are noteworthy. First, if asked to produce the fifth word, most students must recall the list from the beginning, i.e. for the first four or five words at least, position is fixed by location in an inflexible, forward-order recall sequence. Secondly, omissions, position-errors (and even, in the case of 'thematic elaborators', intrusions) are typically concentrated in the late-middle part of the list.

Students in Condition Two are taught this system as follows. 'We start with a rhyme. One is a bun; two is a shoe; three is a tree; four is a door; five is a hive; six is sticks; seven is heaven; eight is a gate;

nine is wine; ten is a hen. I want you to learn this rhyme, but one thing is important. Think, for example, not of BUN ni general, but of a very particular bun. Vizualize the bun if you can. Is it large or small? Brown or yellow? Has it raisins? Has it icing? One is a bun? The experimenter continues through the rhyme encouraging students to think about each rhyming word as a vividly detailed, preferably visualized object. 'I want to tell you how to use this rhyme in learning the word list. When you hear the number, think of the rhyming object; and when you hear the word, relate this to the object as strikingly and vividly as you can. Suppose the first word is PETROL. See your bun covered in petrol, reeking petrol, swimming in a can of petrol, belching flames like a petrol-bun. The more outrageously odd the relation, the better. Do this sort of thing with each number-word pair you hear. The next point is that, once you have related each pair, forget it, dismiss it from mind, attend fully to the next pair. The rule is: compare only two things at a time and never attempt to go back and remember what a previous part of the list was.'

Table 1 shows that this group scores markedly higher than the first. The writer has done several variants of this experiment with more than eight hundred students in all, and the mnemonic system never fails to improve recall scores—often to the great surprise of students themselves. When we ask why the procedure should be effective, there are three main areas of activity to consider.

(a) The rhyming code is easy to learn and remember. The number sequence itself is already familiar, and the rest can readily be organized so that, when a word is given at one moment, it contains within itself specifications for the word required at the next moment. Thus, each pair comprises a number-word and an object-word: both words are embedded in a simple framework of shared phonetic attributes: and this enveloping framework is the same for all ten pairs. What is the code-word for FIVE? A familiar object-word almost phonetically identical with FIVE. Given FIVE, and given the superordinate framework, further activity is delimited; the required word is heavily signposted, readily produced as a correlate. The subsequent transition from rhyming-word to thought object is also easy, largely because it is part of the student's everyday repertoire of activity. In brief, each successive part of the rhyming code is so intimately specified that two or three repetitions amply secure mastery of the whole.

(b) Memorizing is decomposed into ten subtasks bound together by an overall procedural framework. This reduces moment-by-moment decision load as to what to do next since, given this framework, the hearing of each list item specifies the doing of whatever is appropriate. So the student is relatively free to treat each subtask in momentary isolation from the task as a whole. Each subtask is, itself, of limited scope and involves co-ordinating only two items into an ensemble, e.g. creating a BUN/SUGAR complex. Furthermore, in so far as each ensemble is created in isolation from every other, there is minimal risk of noting relations between inappropriate items (such as BUN and DAFFODIL). This co-ordination of, say, DAFFODIL and SHOE is a critical phase of the performance and illustrates a characteristic of memory organization. The noting of a relationship, or preferably of several relationships, between items has the effect of later facilitating the transition from one to the other. Thus, given some minimal level of linguistic competence, people can, in a few seconds, co-ordinate one object-word with another so as to be able, at least some minutes or hours later, to produce one word in response to the other. There seems no limit to the number of word pairs which people can so treat; and students can, in this fashion, learn hundreds of pairs without confusion or error.[8] Also, such co-ordinating seems most effective when carried out by each individual in his own preferred way.[9] It even happens that the noting of relations can substitute for deliberate memorizing. For example, if students are given an array of digits and asked to consider what they suggest (historical dates, telephone numbers, mathematical relations, etc.), they are later able to recall the digits as well as if they had been asked to memorize them: producing one part of the array leads, through noted relationships, to producing another part, and so on. There is something fundamental here and it is little wonder that psychologists, both in last century[10] and in this,[11] have been so persistently attracted to concepts of 'association' in one guise or another.

(c) Recalling involves carrying through independent subtasks within an overall framework. What is item SIX? STICKS—STICKS/TABLE—TABLE. What number is FEATHER? FEATHER/HEAVEN—HEAVEN—SEVEN. Each question signposts the production of a unique ensemble which embodies the answer as a component part. Students remark on the surprising ease of answering such questions, and many students are still able to produce correct answers several weeks later. In contrast to Condition One, it is noteworthy that the word list can be recalled as readily in reverse (or any other) order as in forward order.

The main features of the mnemonic system may be outlined as follows. It furnishes a schematically predetermined procedure for both memorizing and recalling activity: each phase of the procedure strongly specifies each succeeding phase, and no other: time is left for the phase of co-ordinating two items into an ensemble and, thereby, making one item specify the remaining item. The entire procedure emphasizes the general fact that memory organization is an interlocking system of constraints on activity sequences and that mnemonic systems, by and large, are merely contrived versions of an expedient noted by James Mill in 1829. Faced by a thing they want not to forget, people 'endeavour to form an association between the idea of the thing to be remembered, and some sensation, or some idea, which they know beforehand will occur at or near the time when they wish the remembrance to be in their minds'.

II

The above experiment emphasizes that consideration of the quality of activity is important if we are to understand the problem of 'what is learned', e.g. why, of two people who learn the 'same' lesson, one utilizes this learning flexibly and with 'understanding' while the other utilizes it only by inflexible replication. Now, what, in a general way, can be said about these qualitative features of memory organization? In answer, three descriptive assertions seem to be of fundamental importance, even if we continue to consider only deliberate memorizing. (a) The taking in of data is far from being passive registration. It is a successive complex of activity which co-ordinates the data to activity patterns that are already in the person's repertoire. Ease of memorizing depends notably on the readiness with which the person can co-ordinate the incoming data to activities that are, for him, familiar, self-consistent and adequately encompassing. The successful memorizing episode is, as it were, the running through of familiar activity in such a way as to lead into the new data: the novel becomes a follow-up or continuation of the accustomed; the new enters into a kind of lock-step with the old. Co-ordinating the new into an extension of the old is a modification of memory organization which seems to be a necessary condition for later recall. (b) Recalling is not a retrieval of the past from inert storage. It is a controlling of ongoing activities by constraints which, though operating in the present, derive from past co-ordinative modifications of memory organization. It is a problem task directed at constructing a facsimile of the original. (c) Both memorizing and recalling are shot through with individual differences. They depend on the predispositions and accomplishments which the person inevitably brings to the task, in short, on the details of the individual's unique memory organization.

Whether or not these three characteristics are common to *every* memory task, they certainly become more evident as the task becomes, in broad terms, more complex and less restricted. As material becomes more complex, its co-ordination demands more elaborate working out, more extensive involvement of diverse activities to effect a meeting of old and new. Likewise, replication becomes more conspicuously constructive, more obviously a matter of introducing diverse successions of constraints into the task activity and synthesizing therefrom an end-product which is judged adequately replicative. And as material becomes more complex, these memorizing and recalling activities become increasingly liable to vary from individual to individual.

Even with the same material, the person may have ample opportunity to proceed how he will, or be restricted by instructions and conditions of presentation. Such restrictions are familiar in the classical studies of Ebbinghaus.[12] He aimed to introduce into psychology the experimental rigour and quantification which had been so fruitful in physics. So he devised a form of memory task which minimized the learner's opportunity to 'work over' the material and emphasized dependence on repetition. He memorized and recalled nonsense syllable lists by the method of serial anticipation; schooled himself to treat syllables as inert, meaningless units; and the successive presentation of each unit was strictly controlled. In short, memory activity was already so severely restricted that co-ordinative memorizing, constructive recalling and individual variations were relatively, though not perhaps entirely, unimportant.

These three characteristics are especially evident in certain experimental memory tasks,[13, 14, 15, 16, 17] and also in people who, at one extreme, suffer from amnesia and, at the other, accomplish memory feats as a result of persistent specialized interests.

Marked inability to recall occurs in some pathological conditions, notably hysteria, brain injury and senility.[18] Hysterical amnesia dramatically exemplifies the selectivity of recall by resembling, sometimes closely, normal avoidance of thinking about certain unpleasant past experiences. But here, avoidance is extreme and not 'deliberate'. It might be said that the patient shows every appearance of trying hard to remember while, at the same time, he consistently breaks off at any point in the constructional activity which brings him close to recalling certain events. As regards memory organization, however, such amnesia probably reveals less than the organic conditions of concussion and brain degeneration. In concussion, loss of consciousness is followed by a distinctive pattern of recovery which may require minutes, hours, or weeks.[19] The patient does not 'come to' like a man awaking from sleep but passes through stages of progressively less disorganization. After return of simple reflex activity, restless movements, more purposeful movements, and even speech, he is still confused. He responds to environmental events, but misinterprets them: he behaves sensibly, but forgets current episodes almost as soon as they happen. He often cannot remember events which preceded the accident by some hours, weeks, or even years. Thus Russell[19] reports the case of a twenty-two-year-old man thrown from his motor cycle. A week after the accident, he was capable of sensible conversation but said he was a school-boy and, gave, as the date, a time which was eleven years before. He could recall nothing of five years spent in Australia or two years in Britain. Two weeks after injury, he remembered the Australian years and his return to Britain; but nothing further. Three weeks after injury, he went back to the village where he had worked for two years but saw it as for the first time. He then resumed work, but it was ten weeks after injury before the past two years were gradually remembered and he could recall a continuous personal past up to within a few minutes of the accident. It appears that the achievement of recalling a continuous personal past is possible only at a late, if not final, stage of recovery from concussion.

This case illustrates the additional finding that recall of recent experiences is more vulnerable to disruption by brain damage than is recall of remote experiences. As brain impairment lessens, the events which cannot be recalled contract toward the present. Conversely, in senility and other conditions of progressive brain impairment, the events which cannot be recalled extend toward the past. Initial failure of recall concerns very recent happenings but, as the condition worsens, the happenings involved become progressively more remote in time while the recall of yet more distant events seems unimpaired. Thus, 'an old lady speaking of the village where she had spent her childhood remarked, "I can remember it as clearly as if I had seen it yesterday"—she had'.[18]

The constructiveness of recalling is exaggeratedly shown in amnesic states. The patient who is recovering from concussion may spend hours deliberately trying to link up what he can recall so as to provoke further recall; and his efforts may be aided by encouragement, hints, and various happenings. This is but a laboured version of the normal piecing-together which is seen, for example, in trying to recall an elusive name. Also exaggerated is the filling-out of recall with likely details. The patient interpolates across the gaps in recall by producing fictitious, and often convincing, events which he accepts, at least for the moment, as genuine recall. In more severe cases, the patient may, if asked what he did this morning, describe how he went into town, met friends, did shopping, and so on. His account is detailed, untrue and, a short time later, is liable to change when some fortuitous event suggests a quite different theme for confabulation. But throughout, he seems completely convinced that he is engaged in genuine recall.

With eventual return to normality, the concussed person cannot recall much of what happened during the recovery period and, when any such event is recalled, it is unlocalized in the context of a continuous personal past. The implication is that, during his confused state, he did not react to current events in a way that made their subsequent recall possible, i.e. experiences were not stored so as to be retrievable. Also after recovery, he is typically and permanently unable to recall events which preceded head injury by a few seconds. Thus, the motorist recalls approaching the cross-roads, the workman losing his balance—and nothing further. The blow cannot have prevented his experiencing these further events, yet it prevents his subsequent recall of them. The inference (which accords with that drawn from studies on immediate memory) is that the blow, by disturbing normal brain activity, disrupted a storing process requiring some seconds for completion.

The above considerations lend new interest to the familiar fact that, in everyday life, many people can recall numerous events and data concerning issues which interest them. The general features of this accomplishment may best be expressed by quoting James.[10]

'Most men have a good memory for facts connected with their own pursuits. The college athlete who remains a dunce at his books will astonish you by his knowledge of men's "records" in various feats and games, and will be a walking dictionary of sporting statistics. The reason is that he is constantly going over these things in his mind, and comparing and making series of them. They form for him not so many odd facts, but a concept-system—so they stick. So the merchant remembers prices, the politician other politician's speeches and votes, with a copiousness which amazes outsiders, but which the amount of thinking they bestow on these subjects easily explains' (p. 662). Writing of Darwin's great memory for facts, James comments: 'Let a man early in life set himself the task of verifying such a theory as that of evolution, and facts will soon cluster and cling to him like grapes to their stem. Their relatedness to the theory will hold them fast: and the more of these the mind is able to discern, the greater the erudition will become' (p. 662). Again, regarding the ease developed by experienced actors in mastering their parts, James remarks on the effects of practice. 'What it has done for them is to improve their power of *studying* a part systematically. Their mind is now full of precedents in the way of intonation, emphasis, gesticulation: the new words awaken distinct suggestions and decisions; are caught up, in fact, into a pre-existing net-work, like the merchant's prices, or the athlete's store of "records", and are recollected easier, although the mere native tenacity is not a whit improved, and is usually, in fact, impaired by age. It is a case of better remembering by better *thinking*' (p. 664). Incidentally, the reference to impaired 'native tenacity' with age has been amply justified by experimental studies.[20]

Such observations point up a contrast between memory organization and any inanimate storehouse system. In a storehouse, the more objects already in stock, the less easily can further objects be accommodated; whereas in the memory system, the more a person has learned about some topic, the easier it becomes to encompass yet further data concerning this and related topics (except perhaps when the new data would violate the person's basic conceptualizations). Consonant with this is the fact that 'meaningful' learning is typically more rapid and lasting than learning which proceeds either by rote repetition or by meeting the material through 'superficial' mnemonic relationships.

III

The above observations also indicate a further principle of memory organization: incoming data are schematized (summarized, compressed, digested) into synoptic thought processes which, in recall, are de-schematized (expanded, reconstituted) to generate a facsimile of the original data. This principle is illustrated by shorthand transcription. Incoming dictation is segmented into units, each unit is recorded as a written symbol and, later, these symbols are decoded to give back what was dictated: and as the transcriber gains proficiency, he unifies larger segments of dictation into shorthand symbols which become more peculiar to himself. This general principle is also illustrated by that supreme coding device—the nervous system. This system comprises some ten thousand million interconnected nerve cells, is housed in a boney case, and has no direct contact with the outside world. Sensory data enter only in the form of neural events. Overt actions leave only in this neural form. All the happenings which mediate input and output are exclusively of this neural kind. Furthermore, this neural coding system contains, within itself, a complex variety of schematizing properties.[1] (The issues of neurological organization cannot be considered here but the interested student is referred to the classical, and still topical, work of Lashley.[21, 22] Suffice it to say that these issues remind us, if reminder is needed, that memory is no isolated function separable from the total, ongoing, many-sided flux which is the activity of a living being.)

Miller[23] was impressed by the memory feats of men working with digital computers that have small lights flashing to indicate which relays are closed. These men could grasp and remember a sequence of, say, twenty on-off signals. How was this achieved? They did not treat each light as an independent unit but dealt with successive groupings of three lights and translated each triplet into a code number. All three lights off is called 0, off-off-on is 1, off-on-off is 2, off-on-on is 3, etc. With this predetermined code for each of the eight possible triplets, an engineer groups a string of signals into successive triplets and labels each. So instead of remembering a sequence of eighteen lit and unlit lights, he remembers a sequence of six digits which he later decodes, according to the translation rules, to reconstruct the original. Almost anyone can use this coding device to extend his memory span for binary digits, that is, digits of two kinds only, e.g. 0 and 1. One trained subject[24] found that, without coding, his binary digit span was 12. When grouping and labelling pairs, his span was 24: grouping and labelling triplets brought his span to 36; and working in quartets gave a span of 40. Notice that the utility of this device is limited by the fact that the task of identifying and labelling groups becomes more demanding with increase in the number of elements in each group and also increase in the number of different groups which are possible.

Strict one-to-one coding of the above kind seems relatively rare in memory organization. But coding of a less strict kind (schematizing) is a pervasive characteristic which has been discussed, under various names, for at least three centuries. One of the earliest experimental psychologists to consider this point was Binet.[25] He referred to 'un curieux paradoxe de la mémoire: on allège le poids de sa charge en l'augmentant' (p. 264). A strange paradox indeed that memory load should be lightened by augmentation. Binet was, at the time, studying accomplished chess players who could recapitulate the myriad moves of many games they had played. They could also play several games concurrently, and even do so blindfolded.[26] He pointed out that, for the chess master, a game is not a piece-meal skirmish between wooden men but a large-scale contest between strategies. When playing or watching a game, he apprehends each move as but a component of a larger, unitary theme—analogous to a note in a melody. When recalling a game, he is not dealing with so many dozen independent moves but with a unique strategical struggle. Each move is recalled, not in isolation from every other, but as a necessary part of a purposeful, overall plan.

When a person learns chess, he progressively builds up organized systems of activity which are structured hierarchically. He learns the moves of individual pieces, then the move-complexes of groups of pieces. He learns to plan his probable moves farther ahead, anticipate the likely future moves of his opponent, and operate in strategies and counter-strategies. In short, he begins by mastering an assemblage of temporally circumscribed, small-scale activities which are relatively isolated from each other; and he proceeds by co-ordinating these into larger complexes. His individual moves become more and more embedded in superordinate plans. Novel performance characteristics emerge such as move-sequences, strategies, styles of play, and so-called position-sense. The carrying through of subordinate activities involves progressively less conscious awareness. He operates in large-scale units, recognizes these units in others, and talks about the game in terms of these units. As developmental syntheses proceed, there are, then, qualitative differences in playing and recalling any game—and the amount recalled is a function of the quality of skill in chess. His recapitulation of any game becomes a matter of reconstructing a particular variation on general themes with which he is already highly familiar.

What is true in chess is true in possibly all spheres of human accomplishment. Learning is not simply the repeating of activity until it becomes smoother, quicker, and more accurate: it is the progressive reorganization of activities into higher-order complexes of greater intricacy and compass. The development of competence involves profound qualitative changes which ramify through all aspects of performance, the building up of hierarchical systems of predispositions in which the action of each moment is augmented by being enmeshed in superordinate action. All this is true of telegraphy,[27, 28] typewriting,[29] simple sensory-motor skills[20, 30] and mental calculation.[31, 32] It is also true of verbal language. Contrast the literate and illiterate person in relation to a written line. In reading, the literate apprehends a significance in the black shapes which is lacking for the other to whom they make no sense. In copying, either in the presence or absence of the original, this significance of the whole guides and sustains the moment-by-moment scribing of the literate, while its absence leaves the illiterate with an unwieldy piece-meal chore comprising many unrelated parts.

The expert in any sphere has built up, through organized experience, a wide repertoire of what might be called large-scale themes or synopses or cognitive systems.[33] These augment and facilitate, among other things, his ability to memorize and recall material that lies within this sphere. They enable him more readily to note, in the data, relationships which are familiar and to apprehend a larger amount of data as a patterned unit falling under a single rubric—in brief, to incorporate the data into extensions of already established cognitive systems. In recall, these themes, now extended by a few variants, specify possible alternatives at each moment of construction and so enable him to regenerate the material in its required particulars.

The Schematizing Principle seems to resolve a paradox mentioned earlier in relation to the outcome of experiments in short-term memory. These studies show that immediate memory capacity is confined to a very few items and that many everyday performances are limited by this small capacity. On the other hand, there are performances in which people seem to be hampered little, if at all, by this basic limitation. How can these two observations be reconciled? The answer is suggested by the following example of the paradox. The university student cannot accurately remember a sequence of more than about six randomly presented monosyllabic words: yet he is expected to remember what is said in an hour's lecture. The difference between these two tasks is the size of 'unit' in terms of which performance operates. When a person listens to a lecture or a story, he does not hear each momentary sound complex as a unit, nor each phoneme, nor very often, each word or even sentence. He meets the incoming stimulation by progressively building up themes and sub-themes, climaxes, focal details and stylistic attributes. He extracts, as it were, the essence and retains each sound complex only long enough to up-date his précis. The lecture is translated into synoptic units or ideas and, as with the development of shorthand skill, the more familiar the topic the more summary each unit is. In recall, he elaborates this précis in accordance with translation rules which derive from general experience and present abilities and intentions. This results in word changes, shifts of emphases, dropping some details and importing others.[13, 34, 35, 36] The person may or may not be aware that he is giving the 'general idea' in his own words and, as always, there are stylistic differences between people in their procedures of schematizing and reconstituting.[37] Consonant with all this is the fact that, for most adults, memory for content persists longer than verbatim memory.[38] Also, in relation to a well-written article, people remember the salient points better when this article is presented in full rather than in an accurately prepared précis form:[39] in the one situation, the person is free to meet and schematize the material in his own preferred way while, in the other, he is denied some of this freedom by the circumstances of predigestion.

Clearly, schematizing may take many forms and involve transformation rules which vary greatly in their nature, complexity and self-consistency. But overall, schematizing is a powerful biological device which, among several economies, liberates the memory system from the confines of its limited capacity. There is, then, little wonder that it should be used deliberately for lightening the labour of memory. Through the centuries, men have devised procedures for translating whatever must be learned and remembered into compact, coherent schemes. In some respects the laws and models of science exemplify such schemes; so too do the parables and proverbs embodying codes [sic] of moral conduct. Furthermore, men have sought to present these schemes in ways which can most readily be met in terms of already established memory organization. And to this end, they have employed the analogies and metaphors which are so prevalent a feature of both social communication and private thinking.

REFERENCES

1. BRAIN, R., 1961, Speech Disorders; Aphasia, Apraxia and Agnosia, London: Butterworth.
2. HUNTER, I. M. L., 1957, Memory, Harmondsworth: Penguin.
3. KAY, H., and POULTON, E. C., 1951, 'Anticipation in memorizing', Brit. J. Psychol., 42, 34.
4. BROWN, J., 1954, 'The nature of set-to-learn and of intra-material interference in immediate memory', Quart. J. Exper. Psychol., 6, 141.
5. BROADBENT, D. E., 1958, Perception and Communication, London: Pergamon.
6. CONRAD, R., 1959, 'Errors of immediate memory', Brit. J. Psychol., 50, 349.
7. SPERLING, G., 1960, 'The information available in brief visual presentations', Psychol. Monog., 74, No. 498.
8. MILLER, G. A., GALANTER, E., and PRIBRAM, K. H., 1960, Plans and the Structure of Behavior, New York: Holt.

9. BRUNER, J. S., 1960, 'Individual and collective problems in the study of thinking', *Ann. New York Acad. Sci.*, *91*, 22.

10. JAMES, W., 1891, *Principles of Psychology*, Vol. I, London: Macmillan.

11. COFER, C. N. (ed.), 1961, *Verbal Learning and Verbal Behavior*, New York: McGraw-Hill.

12. EBBINGHAUS, H., 1885, *Über das Gedächtnis*, Leipzig: Duncker.

13. BARTLETT, F. C., 1932, *Remembering*, London: Cambridge University Press.

14. BOUSFIELD, W. A., 1953, 'The occurrence of clustering in the recall of randomly arranged associates', *J. gen. Psychol.*, *49*, 229.

15. KATONA, G., 1940, *Organizing and Memorizing*, New York: Columbia University Press.

16. ALLAN, M. D., 1961, 'Memorizing, recoding and perceptual organization', *Brit. J. Psychol.*, *52*, 25.

17. TULVING, E., 1962, 'The effect of alphabetical subjective organization on memorizing unrelated words', *Canad. J. Psychol.*, *16*, 185.

18. MAYER-GROSS, W., SLATER, E., and ROTH, M., 1960, *Clinical Psychiatry* (2nd edition), London: Cassell.

19. RUSSELL, W. R., 1959, *Brain, Memory, Learning*, London: Oxford University Press.

20. WELFORD, A. T., 1958, *Ageing and Human Skill*, London: Oxford University Press.

21. BEACH, F. A., HEBB, D. O., MORGAN, C. T., and NISSEN, H. W., 1960, *The Neuropsychology of Lashley*, London: McGraw-Hill.

22. ZANGWILL, O. L., 1961, 'Lashley's concept of cerebral mass action', in THORPE, W. H., and ZANGWILL, O. L. (ed.), *Current Problems in Animal Behaviour*, London: Cambridge University Press.

23. MILLER, G. A., 1956, 'Information and memory', *Scientific American*, *195*, 42.

24. MILLER, G. A., 1956, 'The magical number seven, plus or minus two', *Psychol. Rev.*, *63*, 81.

25. BINET, A., 1894, *Psychologie des Grands Calculateurs et Joueurs d'Echecs*, Paris: Hachette.

26. CLEVELAND, A. A., 1907, 'The psychology of chess and of learning to play it', *Amer. J. Psychol.*, *18*, 269.

27. BRYAN, W. L., and HARTER, N., 1897, 'Studies in the physiology and psychology of the telegraphic language', *Psychol. Rev.*, *4*, 27.

28. BRYAN, W. L., and HARTER, N., 1899, 'Studies on the telegraphic languages: the acquisition of a hierarchy of habits', *Psychol. Rev.*, *6*, 345.

29. BOOK, W. F., 1908, *The Psychology of Skill*, Missoula: University of Montana Press.

30. WELFORD, A. T., 1962, 'Research on skills', *Discovery*, *23*, 27.

31. BROWNELL, W. A., 1944, 'Rate, accuracy and process in learning', *J. educ. Psychol.*, *35*, 321.

32. HUNTER, I. M. L., 1962, 'An exceptional talent for calculative thinking', *Brit. J. Psychol.*, *53*, 243.

33. HUNTER, I. M. L., 1961, 'The development of problem-solving ability', *Discovery*, *22*, 344.

34. KAY, H., 1955, 'Learning and retaining verbal material', *Brit. J. Psychol.*, *46*, 81.

35. GOMULICKI, B. R., 1956, 'Recall as an abstractive process', *Acta Psychol.*, *12*, 77.

36. HAGGARD, E. A., BREKSTAD, A., and SKARD, A. G., 1960, 'On the reliability of the anamnestic interview', *J. Abn. Soc. Psychol.*, *61*, 311.

37. GOMULICKI, B. R., 1956, 'Individual differences in recall', *J. Person.*, *24*, 387.

38. ENGLISH, H. B., WELLBORN, E. L., and KILLIAN, C. D., 1934, 'Studies in substance memorization', *J. gen. Psychol.*, *11*, 233.

39. WASON, P. C., 1962, 'The retention of material presented through précis', *J. Communic.*, *12*, 36.

CHAPTER 17

THE PSYCHOLOGY OF
INTELLIGENCE AND G*

BY P. E. VERNON

In his *Introduction to Modern Psychology*,[1] Professor Zangwill states that intelligence testing is 'a technology whose theoretical foundations are distinctly insecure'. Professor Hearnshaw,[2] Dr Heim[3] and others have expressed similarly critical views in their recent writings. In this paper I hope to show that, by delving around, and making full use of the bricks and mortar that recent psychological and psychometric research have provided, we shall be able to integrate the apparently divergent and unrelated views of physiological, genetic and clinical psychologists, of mental testers and factor analysts, and to arrive at a more stable theory upon which the technological superstructure can be firmly based.

I

Merely for convenience, I am going to start, as it were, at the wrong end, and outline what seem to me to be the essential facts established by the psychometrist, which our theory has to explain. I am making no assumptions yet as to what it is that intelligence tests measure, and will refer to it as I.Q.†—Terman-Merrill I.Q., or Moray House or Wechsler Performance I.Q., and so on. Such I.Q.s are clearly quite different from physical measurements of stable attributes such as height. They are best regarded as standard scores corresponding to

* A Presidential address, delivered at Durham on April 16, 1955, at the Annual Conference of the British Psychological Society, published in *Bull. Brit. Psychol. Soc.*, 1955, No. 26, 1.

† Elsewhere,[4] I have supplemented Hebb's distinction between Intelligence A and Intelligence B by referring to test results or I.Q.s as 'Intelligence C'.

percentiles in a representative population. For example, I.Q. 130 is that score which cuts off the top $2\frac{1}{4}$ per cent of an age-group, provided we accept the arbitrary figure of 15 as our standard deviation. True, there are many tests which continue to calculate I.Q.s from Mental Age over Chronological Age in children, or over some constant divisor such as 15 in adults, notably the Terman-Merrill. But one is thankful to observe that they are gradually going out of fashion, since their standard deviations vary all over the place, and their I.Q.s have no consistent significance unless translated into percentiles. I.Q.s so calculated, moreover, are measures of rate of mental growth at that type of test—a concept which is far too obscure to be used in a logical manner. Thus teachers or clinical psychiatrists dealing with a child of 150 I.Q. certainly do not think of him as growing intellectually at one and a half times the average rate; but they *are* interested in his being the brightest child in a thousand of his age.

The standard score system assumes, of course, that whatever ability underlies I.Q.s is fundamentally normally distributed. I agree with those critics who say that this is an unprovable dogma. But it is a useful dogma, which seems to accord reasonably with common-sense observation of the relative rarity of very bright and very dull individuals. It obviously breaks down at the bottom end, and some alternative system of quantifying low-grade intelligence test performance is necessary. Maybe the Mental Age system is as good as any for this limited purpose. In other contexts where representative populations are not available, intelligence test scores are best expressed as percentiles relative to a specified group, for example Army recruits, or university students.

II

Now the I.Q. is a fairly stable measure over quite long periods—less stable than would be expected from some of the statements of psychometrists in the 1910's and '20's, but more stable than some recent writers deduce from Dearborn and Rothney's, Honzik's[5] and the Iowa School's results. The correlation between similar (not necessarily identical) tests over the 6 to 11-year period, or over 11 years to young adulthood, does not normally drop below 0·70; and with a standard deviation of 15, this means a median variation or probable error of 7 I.Q. points. Most individuals stay within the same band of I.Q., but some 17 per cent may rise or fall 15 or more points, and nearly 1 per cent may vary as much as 30 points either way. This refers to a single retest: with repeated retestings, fluctuations are about half as wide again.* Variability is increased also if the tests differ greatly in content, as when Terman-Merrill is compared with a group test; or a non-verbal with a verbal test. It is somewhat greater among high I.Q. than normal, or normal than low I.Q., groups; and it naturally rises when the standard deviation of I.Q.s exceeds 15 (as happens with Terman-Merrill at certain ages), or when the norms for either test are too lenient or too severe, or when one test has been coached or practised more than the other. Last but not least, the I.Q. is much more unstable if measured before the age of 5; indeed, developmental or other quotients from 0 to $2\frac{1}{2}$ have virtually no predictive value for later I.Q.

III

This stability is probably at least as great as that of any other mental measurement, say educational attainments, and it allows us to make useful predictions of all-round educability in the primary or the secondary school, and of probable vocational level. To quote but one illustration.[6] Terman's high I.Q. children, representing the top $\frac{1}{2}$ per cent of the Californian school population, were followed up twenty-five years later. It was found that they were five times as likely as average children to end up in the two highest professional and business occupational groups, and seven times as unlikely to become semi-skilled or unskilled workers. Note that this prediction is actuarial—a matter of probabilities. No psychometrist can say for certain that John Jones, age 11, I.Q. 150, will become a professional or a labourer. But precisely the same is true of any other type of prediction. As I have pointed out in my book on Personality Tests,[7] the clinical, educational or vocational psychologist who predicts from an all-round study of his subject's abilities, personality and circumstances is often no more successful, and sometimes less so, than the psychometrist with his objective aptitude, educational or other tests. Facts like these are generally ignored by those who criticize the mental tester for his inadequate theory or for his over-objective, quantitative approach to human beings. I.Q. tests alone may not carry us very far, especially in the vocational field. But the psychometrist is a scientist who discovers how valid they are, and supplements them by other types of predictive measure when required.

* The published investigations appear to confirm that the P.E. of variations at a single test is $0.6745\ \sigma\sqrt{1-r^2}$: while for repeated retests it is $1.349\ \sigma\sqrt{1-\bar{r}}$.

IV

Now returning to the undoubted variations that do occur in I.Q.s, these should not be attributed forthwith to environmentally produced alterations in the intelligence the tests are trying to measure. There are all sorts of chance factors at the time of testing, such as differences in motivation or attitudes, and inadequate sampling by the tests themselves, that account for most of the irregularities. However, some individuals do show consistent and prolonged upward or downward trends, and we have the evidence of Freeman's work on foster children and Newman and others on identical twins brought up apart that large environmental changes may bring about alterations of some 10, or at most 20, I.Q. points. The Iowa School and Schmidt have claimed considerably larger effects, but adequate confirmation from well-controlled experiments is not yet forthcoming. Extreme environmentalist statements are further contradicted by the appreciable correlation that exists between the I.Q.s of orphan children and the socio-economic status of true parents who have not brought them up.[8] Competent experts like Burks in America and Burt in England calculate from such figures as Freeman and Newman's that the hereditary contribution to I.Q. variance is three or more times as great as the environmental. Even this fairly small environmental component prohibits us from making genetic inferences, such as that national intelligence is declining or that one race is more intelligent than another. But a more important point which has been generally neglected is that the figures refer solely to environmental differences as they exist in the North American white or the British cultures. They do not cover the effects of environmental uniformities, and we shall see later that these play an extremely important part in intellectual development. And when cultures differ more widely, as say the British and the Australian aboriginal, any I.Q. comparisons become quite meaningless. Again, the calculations have mostly been based on I.Q.s of children of primary school age; environmental differences tend to become wider at the secondary stage and in early adulthood. After 11, the majority of the population receive rather poor quality education which they often resent; they leave school at 15 and enter jobs and indulge in leisure pursuits which provide little intellectual stimulus. But the more privileged receive a better education for a much longer period, tend to enter jobs which make more use of their brains, and are more likely to keep up cultural leisure activities. Such differences have been shown to have a considerable effect on

I.Q. Husén[9] finds that adults who obtain full secondary and university education have a 12-point advantage over others, of the same initial I.Q., who left school at 15. And I have demonstrated that the lower I.Q. strata, in less intellectual jobs, begin to decline in intelligence test performance earlier and do so more rapidly than do the higher strata.*

V

Turning now to the results of factorial research: how much can we accept as established psychological fact? Heim would say very little or nothing at all, and she illustrates her contention by the unresolved dispute between Slater and others regarding the age at which spatial ability emerges as a distinctive factor. Most British factorists would agree, I think, that factor analysis is an exploratory and suggestive rather than, by itself, a conclusive technique. But two features of Spearman's theory are thoroughly substantiated, and a third feature is definitely wrong. First there is the tendency towards positive correlation among all abilities. The child or adult who is superior in reasoning problems tends to be above average not only in memorizing and vocabulary, but also in arithmetic, mechanical comprehension, and even in handwriting, reaction time and sensory discrimination. Correlations may sink to zero or even slightly negative in highly selected groups, but in a representative sample the theory of an underlying g factor is perfectly tenable, whatever its psychological explanation may be. Secondly, the hierarchical organization of abilities is clearly indicated in the sense that the more complex intellectual functions generally show a greater involvement of this g factor than do the simpler rote cognitive functions and sensory-motor capacities. Note that although Thurstone and his followers favour a rather different picture of the mind's abilities from that of Burt and myself, their recognition of second-order factors implies agreement with my two statements.

The third point, where Spearman went wrong, was his belief in the determinacy of g—that any sampling of cognitive abilities would yield one and the same g. Sub-types of ability or group factors, or what Spearman called overlap of specifics, is far more pervasive than he envisaged; and the result is that all our samplings of abilities are more or less biased by group factors. For example, the g obtained from a battery of miscellaneous verbal group tests differs from that yielded

* Cf. also the fanning out of adult test norms in the Raven Matrices and Vocabulary tests.[10]

keep motivational factors reasonably constant, at least among normal children. Nevertheless, child guidance clinics often report cases whose intellectual development has been inhibited through emotional mal-adjustment, and who show spectacular rises in I.Q. after treatment, which do not seem to be attributable to mere lack of co-operation at the initial testing. In group testing we rely rather largely on the resemblance of the situation to that of school teaching and examining to induce the necessary rapport. Experimental studies of altered motivation (for example, offering monetary rewards) generally yield negative results. However, one investigation[11, 12] brought out some of the effects of testees' attitudes. When difficult, untimed power tests of ability were used, scores depended largely on the testees' per-sistence as well as their g; whereas when easy, speeded cognitive tests were given, the set towards speed on the one hand or accuracy on the other hand had a marked influence. Such attitudinal factors have generally escaped notice, because our group tests have compromised between the persistence and the speed types, and have managed to maintain a fairly uniform set throughout. They become more obvious when we try to extend American or British-made tests to other cultures whose work attitudes differ widely from our own. As Biesheuvel[13] and others have pointed out, the performances of primi-tive peoples are distorted not merely by their different educational backgrounds, but also by the fact that they don't seem to get the point of doing their individual best to answer silly questions, or to fit pictures and blocks together, as quickly as possible.

Despite our attempts to keep intellectual and emotional traits distinct, a certain amount of overlapping is widely reported. Neurotic patients in general do not score below average on intelligence tests, but delinquents and criminals usually do so. Terman's high I.Q. children were superior in character traits, and the w or character factor tends to correlate positively with g. Authoritarian and conservative $vs.$ radical attitudes seem to show little, if any, overlap with I.Q.; but patriotic attitudes yield more substantial coefficients of $-0\cdot3$ to $-0\cdot4$ in several American researches.

Further effects of emotion on intellectual functions are recognized in the clinical psychologist's methods of diagnostic testing. Though there is considerable doubt as to the consistency of Wechsler-Bellevue or other test score patterns in the various neurotic and psychotic syndromes, a beginning has been made in isolating group factors which are particularly susceptible to differential deterioration; for example, Furneaux's speed factor among psychotics, and Lovell's[14]

by Terman-Merrill type tests in having a stronger verbal compo
It also involves a group factor for doing multiple-choice as dist
from creative-response items; and the speeded conditions under wh
all the group tests are given introduce a different work-attitude fact
The reason why conventional intelligence tests used in selection
11+ seem to measure a rather narrow and artificial kind of ability—
or, as grammar school teachers complain, to select the 'spiv' type of
pupil—and the reason that clinical psychologists seem to get a better
indication of intelligence in everyday life from Terman-Merrill or
Wechsler, is the presence of these group factors. Such criticisms are
often much exaggerated, since the major factors in both types of test
are the same g and v. But they do contain sufficient truth to demolish
the psychometrist's contention that he can determine the essence of
intelligence purely through statistical analysis of test scores. Actually
we are back very much where we were in the early '20's, when no
two psychologists agreed in their definitions of intelligence. We must
recognize that there is no external criterion for deciding that this kind
of item is a better indication of intelligence than that; we can choose
whatever manifestations of complex cognitive processes that each of
us thinks most appropriate, and each will arrive at a somewhat different
intelligence. What factor analysis has really shown is that intelligence
must be regarded not as any single, identifiable type of ability, but as
a very fluid collection of overlapping abilities, comprising the whole
of mental life. It is perfectly legitimate, therefore, for Thurstone,
Guilford and other American factorists to classify abilities under a
dozen or fifty or more fairly distinctive categories and largely to
ignore the second-order or more general factors, whereas in this
country we mostly prefer to classify by progressive subdivision,
beginning with as inclusive a g as possible, then major verbal $vs.$
practical factors, and so on. But any classification is a matter of
convenience. We may eventually reach some agreed scheme, but it is
illusory to hope for any comprehensive and objective taxonomy at all
analogous to that of chemistry or botany.

VI

Another respect in which most of the psychometric work of the past
forty years or so has been somewhat misleading is that, inevitably, it
has treated intelligence as a purely cognitive variable, abstracted from
the social and emotional context in which intellectual functions normally operate. In individual testing it is possible for the skilled tester to

K

conceptualization, categorizing or flexibility factor.[12] A puzzling fact
to be explained by any theory of intelligence is that many types of
brain damage, including prefrontal leucotomy, seem to have no
consistent effects on I.Q. Nevertheless, deterioration attributable to
damage, or to age, is more readily observable in tests involving unfamiliar reasoning and performance test problems, in speeded tests,
and in tests involving flexibility and the formation of new concepts,
than in tests such as vocabulary which depend more on acquired
information and on habitual modes of problem-solving.

VII

So much for the facts. You can see that there are quite a lot of them,
although I have condensed as much as possible. Turning to theory:
there are said to be almost as many different definitions of intelligence
as there are psychologists. However, they can be classified into three
main groups, which I will designate as the operational, the biological
and the psychological. Operational writers consider that theorizing
about the nature of intelligence has proved fruitless; it is best regarded
as 'what the tests measure', and should be investigated by factor
analysis of the relations between different tests, and through empirical
research into what tests enable us to predict about people. While I am
sympathetic to such views, I have already pointed out that factors
are not determinate—that we must have a theoretical framework to
guide our choice. And the remarkable successes in prediction that we
have achieved so far have likewise depended on our having some
conception of what it is we are trying to measure.

The biological approach contrasts the relatively mechanical responses of lower animals, based on fixed tropisms, reflexes or instincts,
with the more versatile and adaptable behaviour of higher species,
including man. Thus many definitions stress capacity for profiting by
experience, adaptation to environment, plasticity or ability to learn
by trial and error, or, still more, by insight. There are many difficulties
here, particularly in view of the recent work of comparative psychologists such as Tinbergen.[15] It is only too obvious that our most
successful intelligence tests make very little attempt to measure
modifiability or learning capacity; also that many people whom we
would consider highly intelligent, who usually do quite well on our
tests, are not actually very well adapted to their social and physical
environment. But a more acceptable reformulation is possible, along
the lines suggested by Hebb and Piaget. In lower species, the

organism's behaviour is more directly and immediately determined by innate neural and biochemical patterns and by external stimulation (to which it becomes conditioned); whereas at higher levels, intervening processes occur to a greater extent in the central nervous system between stimulus and response, culminating in what we call thinking. By itself, of course, this does little to tell us how far any particular piece of behaviour is intelligent. But it has the great advantage of linking up, not only with psychological approaches, but also with factorial findings and current practice in intelligence testing. For the more complex intellectual problems which we use to differentiate between more and less intelligent humans, and which show the biggest g-saturations, are surely those which make most use of abstract concepts, and involve most internal thinking. The same theory takes us some way in describing perceptual generalization, transfer and problem-solving in such intelligent species as the rat and the ape.

Thirdly, psychological definitions: these have included a whole host of faculties—grasping relations, abstract thinking, reasoning, problem-solving, originality, foresight, judgment, all-round mental efficiency, etc. What strikes one is not so much that they disagree as that they all overlap, and that none of them provides any very precise guidance in devising intelligence tests. When tests are constructed in an attempt to sample two or more of them, they correlate very highly, though—as Guilford[16] has shown—moderately distinct group factors can often be established in highly selected populations. I would agree with Dr Heim that we should not expect to be able to specify any one clear-cut faculty, but should rather think of 'intelligent' as an adjective applicable to all types of response, perceptual as well as conceptual, practical as well as symbolic.

VIII

Now all earlier work on the nature of intelligence has been put in the shade by Piaget's recent books and by Hebb's *The Organization of Behavior*.[17] I cannot attempt to expound them fully or critically, but the following seem to me to be some of their most relevant points. They both show how the percepts and concepts, and the modes of perceiving and thinking, which adults accept almost as the natural order of things, are built up in childhood through contacts with the environment. In Hebb's view, the sensory-motor experience of the first year or two of life leads to the formation of groupings or 'assemblies' of neurones in the association areas of the brain. The fully developed perception of shapes, sizes or objects involves autonomous activities or cerebral discharges which he calls 'phase sequences'. I find some difficulties with his neurological speculations, and prefer the 'schema'—in Head's and Bartlett's sense—as the psychological element or unit of mental life, particularly since Piaget seems to employ schemata very similarly. The schema is an expectancy or anticipation which enables each experience entering consciousness to be charged with the integrated totality of previous relevant experience. Hebb provides considerable evidence of the dependence of such schemata on rich visual and kinaesthetic experience at an appropriate developmental age. Thus rats or dogs brought up as pets with a free run of a varied environment show greater learning and problem-solving capacity as adults than animals reared in the restricted environment of a cage. These early perceptual schemata are fundamental to the development of the higher-order ones which we call concepts or ideas, and which to a still greater extent operate as autonomous units in the association areas. They include not merely acquired information, but also modes of learning and thinking, and methods of tackling the sorts of problems we meet in daily life or in most intelligence tests. Like Harlow's monkeys, we learn how to learn.

Hebb's next point is his distinction between two uses of the word intelligence. Intelligence B is the intelligence that we recognize in daily life and which covers the intelligent thinking capacities that have been acquired during infancy and childhood, which also do not develop fully in the absence of suitable environmental stimulation. Intelligence A is an innate potentiality for forming, retaining and recombining schemata, which is presumably dependent on the genes. It is the innate capacity for acquiring what we ordinarily mean by intelligence. It is, of course, purely hypothetical; we can never directly observe its operation, nor measure it. But it is a legitimate hypothesis, since, as I have already mentioned, we can prove hereditary resemblance apart from environment. Another strong argument in its favour is the existence of large differences in Intelligence B between different children in the same family, or between orphans in the same orphanage, which could hardly be attributable to environmental differences.

Hebb believes that he can account for the smallness of the effects of brain damage on mental efficiency in everyday affairs and on the responses to Binet-type intelligence tests. Once phase sequences have become established, they are said to become independent of particular neurones or brain pathways. Thus Intelligence B can survive extensive brain injury, or operations; but the capacity for building up new schemata may be more greatly affected. I would suggest that we need to add to this the notion of rigidification, as brought out particularly in Welford's work on ageing[18] and in Allport's recent book on prejudice.[19] Each schema that we acquire not only provides a basis for further development but also tends in itself to become stereotyped or rigid, and thus to inhibit further development or reintegration. Thus all-round mental efficiency or Intelligence B depends not only on the total number and complexity of schemata, but also on the degree to which we are able to differentiate or break them down and keep them flexible. And it is this aspect which has repeatedly been shown to be impaired by certain types of brain injury as well as by ageing. This flexibility may depend rather largely on personality factors such as authoritarianism *vs.* tolerance, and is thus intimately bound up with early attitudes to the parents, and with the success or failure of upbringing and education in developing rationality and objectivity of outlook. But here clearly we must turn to Piaget.

IX

As Hearnshaw showed in his British Association for the Advancement of Science Presidential Address on thinking,[2] Piaget likewise emphasizes the historical aspects of our common modes of thought.[20] He insists also that intelligence is no one distinctive faculty, and cannot be reduced to, say, grasping relations or abstract thinking, but is present in all adaptations of the organism. Behaviour becomes progressively more intelligent the more complex the 'lines of interaction' between organism and environment, i.e. the greater the amount of autonomous cerebral activity. In the baby's early years, his behaviour consists predominantly of concrete and direct reactions to practical experience, and these sensory-motor adaptations tend to be one-way and inflexible. At the higher stages, culminating in abstract, logical reasoning, the individual's thinking is characterized by mobility—the capacity to generalize and transfer to new situations—and by reversibility—or ease of manipulation of ideas. After the first year, language plays an increasingly important part, not only in providing labels or symbols for conceptual schemata, but also in the classification and stabilization of perceptual ones. In between the sensory-motor and the logical stages comes an egocentric stage, when ideas are largely irrational, inconsistent, syncretistic and intuitive, bound up with the child's own needs and interests. Here I would differ from Piaget in regarding this, not so much as a stage of childhood around 5 to 7 years, but as a stage in the development of each class of ideas, which may occur at any age. In economic, political, social and religious matters, in the bringing up of children and the treatment of criminals, and in personal relations with other people, it persists even among most adults—as has been well brought out by Thouless in his books on straight and crooked thinking.[21] On the other hand, children much younger than 5 reach the rational stage in some of their practical activities, say in block-building or in manipulating furniture to reach a desired object.

This rationality aspect of intellectual development is largely ignored in intelligence testing, since test items are chosen as far as possible to avoid personal involvement or controversial content which might evoke egocentric thinking. At the same time, several investigations do suggest quite a close overlapping between conventional *g* tests, tests of flexibility, of concept formation in young children and older persons, and tests of rational, unprejudiced thinking in adults. But I feel that an adequate formulation of the role of drives and emotion is one of the main lacunae in intelligence theory. On the one hand, it is obvious that emotion disrupts the flow of cognitive schemata, and that maladjustment often inhibits intellectual growth; while on the other hand no intellectual development could occur in the absence of frustrations and need reduction, and motivation by interests. In most other respects there seems to me a very close fit between the theoretical framework suggested by Piaget's, Hebb's and Bartlett's writings, and the psychometric facts that I have outlined.

x

Both the psychological and the psychometric approaches agree in showing that intelligence in daily life, together with the approximation to Intelligence B which is measured by our standard tests of *g*, are largely acquired. The hereditary component, as shown by calculations based on foster children, twins, etc., appears to be predominant largely because of the vast amount of experience that all children within any one culture obtain in common, though it also, of course, does reflect genuine innate potentiality or Intelligence A. Environmental differences between families within a culture, or children within a family, certainly exist, and account for the 25 to 30 per cent environmental variance which Burt and others admit. But this component is comparatively small among young children, since such children are in the process of acquiring the comparatively simple perceptual and conceptual schemata, for which even quite poor homes provide sufficient environmental stimulation. Most children at this stage can see and manipulate similar shapes and objects, and come in contact with common pictorial and other symbols, and hear speech that is adequate to their mental level; moreover, from 5 to 11 they almost all undergo a highly standardized type of schooling. But in adolescence and early adulthood, when they are acquiring more complex concepts and modes of thought, the environmental differences attributable to different levels and lengths of schooling, and different vocational and leisure experiences, probably widen considerably. As I have shown elsewhere,[22] the correlation between g tests and educational attainments rises until, in an unselected population of recruits, it becomes virtually impossible to separate them into orthogonal factors.

I know that psychologists have usually postulated a clear distinction between intelligence or inborn ability and acquired information and education, but this seems to be breaking down, for example in contemporary American writings. I would say that a relative distinction may still be useful between the more general qualities of comprehending, judging, reasoning, and efficiency of thinking—on the one hand—which are largely acquired in the course of everyday living without much specific instruction, and—on the other hand—such skills and knowledge as are specifically taught, whose absorption and retention also depend to a greater extent on the person's interests in those fields and on his personality traits of industriousness and stability. That these two aspects of ability can be separated to some extent is shown by the existence of children with I.Q. much higher or lower than E.Q., though the correlation between them even in the primary school is of the order of 0·85. But I do not accept the formulation that intelligence (i.e. Intelligence B) causes or makes possible the acquisition of attainments. One might equally say that the attainments cause the intelligence.

However, we have still to consider the questions: why is Intelligence B, at least as measured by our best tests, as consistent as it is over quite long periods; and why does even the most thorough and sympathetic schooling seem to be incapable of raising the intelligence of really dull pupils or bringing their attainments up to anything like normal? To answer these we must, I admit, fall back to some extent on hypothetical individual differences in innate potentiality, Intelligence A. I would like, though, to couple this with the effects of deep-rooted emotional factors which favour or hinder intellectual and educational growth. For apparently irremediable backwardness is undoubtedly sometimes resolved by appropriate psychotherapy. But there is another important reason, namely the essentially cumulative nature of mental growth, and Hebb's demonstration that certain schemata are much more difficult to acquire if opportunity is denied at a particular age, or stage of development. A child who is brought up from o to 5 in an exceptionally unstimulating environment will be handicapped, however good the schooling from 5 onwards. Equally, of course, the intelligence tests that we apply at 11+ do, to a considerable extent, show potentiality for profiting from secondary education, although they certainly do not measure pure inborn ability. This potentiality is the product of initial genetic schema-forming capacity and of the cumulative effects of experience and emotional adjustment up to that age.

A corollary of these views is that it would be more logical to give up the term intelligence tests, particularly at the 11+ examination, where it causes continual misunderstandings and controversies with teachers and parents. If we substituted some such label as academic aptitude tests, it would leave us free to experiment with types of intelligence test items which could be proved empirically to add most to the prediction of future educational success, over and above what was predicted by conventional scholastic examinations and objective attainments tests and teachers' estimates. The items chosen for experimental trial should try to bring out the general level of concept development and symbolic thinking. But more specifically they should be based on a careful theoretical analysis of intellectual and educational growth in the 'teens, in the light of the writings of Piaget and other psychologists and of the great educational thinkers. Useful guidance might also be obtained from Guilford's[16] factorial explorations of the higher intellectual faculties.

XI

I will now attempt to reconcile the findings of factor analysis with psychological theory. How can we account for the tendency towards positive overlapping of all abilities? I would suggest that there are three reasons why such generality occurs. First there is Intelligence A —some innate quality of the nervous system which makes humans more capable than lower animals, and some humans more capable than others, of acquiring and recombining habits, percepts and concepts and schemata of all kinds. Secondly, the essentially cumulative

K*

nature of mental development implies that those who, in early life, acquire a richer stock of perceptual schemata and verbal labels, are better able to build up the more complex and more flexible schemata necessary for conceptual thinking. Thirdly, some individuals are reared in a more intellectually stimulating and emotionally adjusting environment than others; and this contributes during childhood, adolescence and early adulthood to the abilities they manifest in almost any kind of situation. Others are relatively starved, or emotionally frustrated, so that their schemata not only fail to reach as great complexity, but also become set and rigid, thus inhibiting the acquisition of new ones; and their overall intellectual efficiency begins to decline, perhaps before they have grown to full maturity.

On this view, we might also expect to find the hierarchical organization of abilities. Imagine that we could collect a broad sample, not merely of abilities commonly tapped by present-day tests, but of every conceivable kind of behaviour and thinking that was recognizably intelligent or adaptable or efficient. Then the highest common factor, or g, of this sampling would be identical with Intelligence B. And naturally the more complex and abstract items, those farthest evolved from the sensory-motor level, would turn out to be the most inclusive or g-saturated. Sir Godfrey Thomson's[23] theory of bonds seems helpful here, though I prefer the notion of schema to that of bond as being less apt to suggest the mechanical operation of associations. He criticizes any attempt to regard factors as unitary powers or organs of the mind, and thinks of the mind as consisting rather of an immense number of bonds. A mental test involves the operation of many such bonds, and two or more tests tend to correlate because they draw on the same pool. A certain structure or organization is imposed on the mind, partly perhaps through the influence of genetic factors (for example, in musical aptitude), partly through temperamental factors and interests, and largely through upbringing and education. Thus all the bonds or schemata concerned with number work, or with rote memorization, and so on, become rather closely linked. Hence, certain abilities or group factors do tend to emerge rather consistently and distinctly in the investigations of different factorists, despite their frequent disagreements. But g is almost impossible to pin down, as it were, because it represents a sampling of the totality of bonds; and whatever samples we draw are apt to be biased in the direction of the type of problems we choose, or by the type of presentation and the conditions of testing. Partly through Binet's and Terman's psychological genius, partly I daresay by luck, the g in Binet-Simon and

Stanford-Binet scales was a fairly good sampling of Intelligence B, that is of the totality of abilities which we recognize as intelligent in everyday life. No group test nor, I suspect, the Terman-Merrill, Wechsler-Bellevue or W.I.S.C. have been as successful from this point of view, in spite of their superior reliability and statistical sophistication. But I expect we could do better if we started again now and applied our psychometric expertise to tests which were based on a more clearly worked out psychology of mental development.

An important point to remember is that this totality of functioning will differ considerably in its nature and content at different stages of human growth. Our use of the term intelligence has made it appear that we are trying to measure one and the same thing in the 2-year-old, the 5-year-old, the 14-year-old and the 50-year-old, which is quite fallacious. In particular, this has landed us in difficulties over adult intelligence, and the age at which it is supposed to reach its maximum. If we are content to regard adult intelligence as capacity for dealing with abstract ideas, for manipulating verbal and other symbols, for grasping relations, and for new verbal learning, then our conventional tests sample it fairly effectively, as they do among children. In the average individual this g does go on increasing only so long as education and full exercise of the intellectual powers continues and, as I mentioned earlier, it usually starts to decline after leaving school or, at the latest, by about thirty years. But Intelligence B in adults should be something much broader. Full intellectual functioning is expressed in practical judgment, business acumen and artistic creativity, in success at skilled jobs and in social relations, and in all that goes to make up wisdom, judgment and experience. Obviously our tests constitute very poor samples of such an intelligence, and many of its aspects probably stay up or even go on improving until senescence.

Quite possibly—though here I have no strong views—we should make better progress if we gave up trying to measure the general factor for the time being, and instead concentrated on more specialized functions which could be shown by factor analysis to be fairly distinctive and to remain reasonably homogeneous in content over considerable age ranges. A profile of scores on tests which adequately sampled such functions would, of course, be much more valuable to the clinician or diagnostic tester than a vague, global I.Q. of indeterminate content. At the same time, such faculties would always show considerable overlapping, hence it would be legitimate to combine the scores from the various tests, weighting them in such a way as to yield any g in which we were interested. One weighting, for example, found by multiple regression analysis against educational criteria, would give us predictions of academic aptitude; another weighting would probably give a better indication of practical adaptability in daily life, yet another of schizophrenic deterioration, and so on. But I think that the effective realization of this step is a long way ahead. We need a great deal more fundamental analysis of the nature of mental development to guide us in choosing, and measuring, suitable faculties.

The crude sketch presented in this paper has many shortcomings; but I hope it shows that there is no inevitable conflict between the aims of the psychometrist and those of the comparative psychologist, the neurologist, the child or genetic psychologist and the educationist, and the clinical and medical psychologist. Rather the mental tester should welcome their collaboration in elucidating the nature of the abilities he is trying to measure.

REFERENCES

1. ZANGWILL, O. L., 1950, *An Introduction to Modern Psychology*, London: Methuen.
2. HEARNSHAW, L. S., 1954, 'Recent Studies in the Psychology of Thinking', *Advancement of Science, 42*, 220.
3. HEIM, A. W., 1954, *The Appraisal of Intelligence*, London: Methuen.
4. VERNON, P. E., 1955, 'The Assessment of Children', in VERNON, P. E. (ed.), *The Bearings of Recent Advances in Psychology on Educational Problems*, London: Evans.
5. HONZIK, M. P., *et al.*, 1948, 'The Stability of Mental Test Performances Between Two and Eighteen Years', *J. Exper. Educ., 17*, 309.
6. TERMAN, L. M., and ODEN, M. H., 1947, *The Gifted Child Grows Up*, Stanford, California: Stanford University Press.
7. VERNON, P. E., 1953, *Personality Tests and Assessments*, London: Methuen.
8. LAWRENCE, E. M., 1931, 'An Investigation into the Relationship Between Intelligence and Environment', *Brit. J. Monog. Suppl.*, No. 16.
9. HUSEN, T., 1951, 'The Influence of Schooling Upon I.Q.', *Theoria, 17*, 61.
10. FOULDS, G. A., and RAVEN, J. C., 1948, 'Normal Changes in the Mental Abilities of Adults As Age Advances', *J. Ment. Sci., 94*, 133.
11. MANGAN, G. L., 1954, 'A Factorial Study of Speed, Power and Related Variables', Ph.D. Thesis, University of London.
12. VERNON, P. E., 1954, 'The Factorial Study of Intellectual Capacities', *Bull. Brit. Psychol. Soc., 23*, Inset 9–10.
13. BIESHEUVEL, S., 1949, 'Psychological Tests and Their Application to Non-European Peoples', *Yearbook of Education*, London: Evans.
14. LOVELL, K., 1954, 'A Study of the Problem of Intellectual Deterioration in Adolescents and Young Adults', Ph.D. Thesis, University of London.
15. SCHNEIRLA, T. C., 1952, 'A Consideration of Some Conceptual Trends In Comparative Psychology', *Psychol. Bull., 49*, 559.

16. GUILFORD, J. P., *et al.*, 1950–54, *Reports from the Psychological Laboratory*, Nos. 1–11, Los Angeles: University of Southern California.

17. HEBB, D. O., 1949, *The Organization of Behaviour*, New York: Wiley.

18. WELFORD, A. T., 1951, *Skill and Age*, London: Oxford University Press.

19. ALLPORT, G. W., 1954, *The Nature of Prejudice*, Cambridge, Mass.: Addison-Wesley.

20. PIAGET, J., 1950, *The Psychology of Intelligence*, London: Routledge and Kegan Paul.

21. THOULESS, R. H., 1930, *Straight and Crooked Thinking*, London: Hodder and Stoughton.

22. VERNON, P. E., 1951, 'Recent Investigations of Intelligence and Its Measurement', *Eugen. Rev.*, *43*, 125.

23. THOMSON, G. H., 1939, *The Factorial Analysis of Human Ability*, London. University of London Press.

CHAPTER 18

THE SOURCES OF EMOTION*

BY PAUL FRAISSE

I

An analysis of the sources of emotion is only possible on the basis of an accepted standpoint as to the nature of emotion. Psychologists, however, are very far from being in agreement on this matter. The nineteenth century, dominated as it was by dualism, was disconcerted by the dual aspect of emotion as revealed to each of us in personal experience—the affective upheaval and the organic storm. The essential problem was to find out which was the effect and which the cause. Herbart and Wundt[1] were inclined to the view that bodily reactions are a mere consequence of mental perturbation, whereas William James[2] took an exactly opposite line, viz. that the knowledge we have of our organic reactions constitutes the psychic fact of our emotion. This futile dispute expired with the end of the era of introspection and of a psychology primarily concerned with the relationship between the organic and the psychic, between body and mind.

Dewey[3] was the first to view the problem in its proper perspective, that is, functionally. Emotion is born in a person when he experiences a resistance in his activity, that is when he encounters an obstacle to his adaptation. There is then a partial inhibition of activity, with organic consequences. This 'conflict theory' of emotion was the forerunner of the most advanced modern views. 'Emotion,' said Pierre Janet,[4] very truly, 'is a "behaviour" characterised by the disorganisation of adaptive acts, by a generalised disorder and its spread throughout the entire organism.'

There are, of course, physiologists and psychologists who, considering only one aspect of emotion, are periodically tempted to deny its

* Translated by Stephen Corrin.

specificity, in the teeth of all common sense. There are those, for example, who confuse emotion with affectivity and talk of 'aesthetic emotion'; or those who, in their preoccupation with physiological criteria, see no discontinuity in levels of activation and then proceed to wonder what characterizes emotion.[5] If it is to be properly understood, emotion must be regarded as a disturbance in adaptation; this was Dewey's view. It is not the intensity of the action which gives rise to emotion but perturbations and disorders of adaptation. Essentially these manifest themselves:

(*a*) by a functional degradation of activity. The subject is unable to cope: his gestures are less precise, his memory less certain and, generally speaking, one may say, with Janet, that there is a change from a higher activity to a lower one. This passing disorganization may take on forms akin to phenomena due to fatigue or age, but any confusion of these with emotion is prevented by the context.

(*b*) by organic manifestations dependent on the neuro-vegetative system.

These reactions, too, if considered separately, are to be found in other circumstances. Emotive reactions are specific only when integrated into behaviour patterns related to situations which have given rise to them.

These two aspects of the process of deterioration are not independent of each other, however. Other things being equal, one observes that the neuro-vegetative reactions are that much more frequent and intense when the adaptive reaction does not occur—either because it is not immediately possible or because it is blocked. It is then as though an unused energy were spreading through the neuro-vegetative system. As Wallon[6] points out, the relation between organism and environment may be disturbed and, as it were, interrupted by manifestations of a hyper- or hypo-tonicity of the neuro-vegetative system, and of posture, but it is true to say that these manifestations are more intense when the setting-up of relationships is, for various reasons, made more difficult.

Being disturbances in adaptation, emotions intervene in a dynamic process orientated by a motivation. Long before science, etymology had established the kinship between motivation and emotion, both of which derive from the Latin '*movere*'. Both motivation and emotion *move* the organism, but the 'e' (ex) in 'emotion' indicates an orientation of movement outside the self, and current usage accepts this interpretation. Between motivation and emotion there is continuity and break.

There must be sufficient motivation if adjustment to situations presented by the environment is to be achieved; but if there is over-motivation we are partly deprived of our ability to react and our adaptation to the real situation is less complete. Maladjustments then manifest themselves in the action, and emotive reactions sometimes entirely replace the adaptive reaction. If the problem is viewed from this angle, it may be said that there is an optimal motivation beyond which emotive patterns of behaviour will appear. In fact, psychologists of motivation are now agreed in acknowledging that a certain increase in motivation improves performance but that too intense a rise in motivation results in a deterioration. Freeman,[7] Hebb,[8] Malmo,[9] and Young[10] have attempted to represent this law hypothetically and (Fig. 1) are in agreement as to the course of this phenomenon, though their conceptions of motivation and its manifestations in action are divergent.

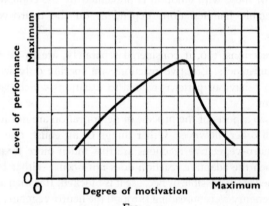

FIG. 1

Representation of the general relation between level of performance and degree of motivation

We may take as our starting-point a definition by Young[10]: 'Motivation is the process of arousing action, sustaining the activity in progress, and regulating the pattern of activity' (p. 24). Everything, therefore, which arouses animal or human activity constitutes motivation but these determinants may be of a very diverse nature. Broadly speaking we can detect two main sources. Motivation may have its origin in the organism proper, in which case one generally talks of needs. The list of needs seems to grow greater and greater as we become capable of using more refined psychological and physiological techniques. In recent years, for example, to the standard homeostatic needs have been added needs of excitation, activity, curiosity, etc., which appear to correspond to the necessity to maintain an adequate level of activation of the nervous system. The other source of motivation arises from stimuli in the world of environment. These stimuli may be of physical origin—a light, a noise may, at the very least, determine an orientation reaction. They may also be of psychological origin, that is to say, the situation as apprehended by the subject constitutes an incitement to action. This incitement to action is not independent of the past experience of the subject and the reinforcements associated therewith. In whatever way one envisages motivation, which is in reality a form

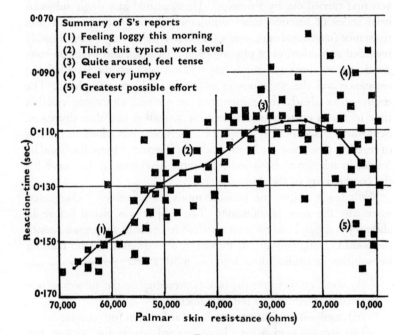

Summary of S's reports
(1) Feeling loggy this morning
(2) Think this typical work level
(3) Quite aroused, feel tense
(4) Feel very jumpy
(5) Greatest possible effort

FIG. 2

The relationship between palmar skin resistance and reaction-time per-formance in a single subject under various states of alertness (after Freeman[11])

of psychological activation, it becomes a quantifiable variable provided one confines oneself to a fundamental aspect of the situation envisaged. This explains why different writers have been able to schematize the process of motivation in different terms. It also explains why, later in this chapter, we shall have recourse to varied indices of motivation which may be the intensity of a noise, the duration of privation of the

organism, the use of instructions and a system of rewards and punishments more or less 'valorizing' the task under review.

Common experience supports the idea of the existence of an optimum motivation. We have only to think of those innumerable students
who are not half as successful on examination day in an exercise which
they so easily manage under normal school conditions. Officers are
well aware that their troops are far better at manoeuvres than in actual
combat. Experimentally it is not easy to prove the existence of this
optimum motivation for we cannot very well introduce a quantitative
variation. The most significant as well as the most complete experiment
was first carried out by Freeman.[11] He measured in a single subject a
brief series of reaction times simultaneously with the level of skin
resistance (psychogalvanic reflex). This last index may be legitimately
regarded as a criterion of physiological activation, and Freeman took
good care to check concretely the relation between the level of skin
resistance and the situations in which his subject was placed. The
results show clearly the existence of an optimal activation: reaction
time increases up to a certain level of activation and then decreases.
Schlosberg,[12] sceptical, repeated the experiment but added to the test
of reaction time a test for hand steadiness (degree of trembling) and he
found, in relation to both tests, the same maximum in the curve for
the conductivity of the skin.

With fewer values for variable motivation Stennett[13] discovered
essentially the same phenomenon. The subject was placed before an
auditory track and had to press a switch in order to suppress a sound,
the point O being periodically moved by a programmer. After training
his subjects he studied three levels of motivation:

(i) weak motivation: the task is presented to the subject as one
requiring adjustment of the instrument;

(ii) medium motivation: small rewards given for success;

(iii) strong motivation: large reward given for success but
electric shocks administered to the subject when the error was too
considerable.

He was able to confirm that the level of activation as measured by the
psychogalvanic reflex and tonic activity (PGR and EMG) increased
from situation *one* to situation *three*, but found that the best performances were obtained in situation *two*, with medium motivation.

Beyond optimum motivation performance deteriorates. This deterioration is specific if considered in relation to the task: a slowing-
down in tests where speed is required, awkwardness where precision

is called for, etc. Generally speaking, the deterioration shows up to the extent of the manifestation of neuro-vegetative reactions which disturb the organism and further reduce the chances of adjustment.

Optimum motivation varies, of course, with the job to be done. Yerkes and Dodson[14] carried out a basic experiment which was repeated with equal success on rats, chicks, cats and even men. It demonstrates that optimum motivation varies with the difficulty of the task. In the first experiment, the task was a choice based on discrimination between two brightnesses, one of the responses being arbitrarily false. The difficulty of this task varied as a function of the discriminability of the two stimuli. Elsewhere three levels of motivation were used as punishments for errors—namely, a slight, medium or strong electric shock. The general results are illustrated in Fig. 3.

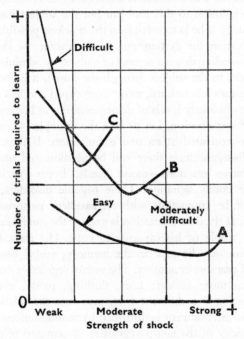

FIG. 3

Schematic diagram to illustrate the Yerkes–Dodson Principle

On the abscissae are shown the intensity of the shock, on the ordinates the number of attempts necessary to achieve the same criteria of success. The three curves correspond to the three levels of difficulty. In each case they show an optimum motivation for which learning is more rapid, and this optimum depends on the difficulty of the job. Yerkes and Dodson[14] deduced the following law: 'When the difficulty of the task increases, the intensity of the punishment which gives optimum speed in learning approaches liminal value.' More generally, one might say: 'the greater the level of difficulty, the lower the optimum motivation'. In other words, in any useless activity, over-motivation might not produce disturbances in behaviour patterns, though this danger may be present in higher grade tasks. Let us take as an example an experiment carried out on a human being. Patrick[15] bolts the subject in a cabinet with four doors, from which he has to try to get out as quickly as possible. In each situation one of the doors is not bolted and after each attempt this door is changed, though it is never the same door which is unbolted twice in succession. There is no single solution to this problem but the subject has to adopt a rational strategy if he is to solve it in the quickest possible time. Now if the motivation for getting out of the cabinet is increased (for example, by sending down a shower of nails or by administering slight electric shocks to the subject through the floor), it is found that the strategy becomes less rational, more stereotyped and less efficient.

There are obviously levels of disorganization in behaviour as there are levels of organization. Let us take the example of a student who arrives over-motivated at an oral examination. If there is a slight degree of disorganization there will be needless and unaccustomed, neuro-vegetative reactions—moist hands, hyper-tonicity, difficult digestion or bodily agitation. These organic disorders, if not too violent, may be compatible with an excellent performance in the examination. If the disorganization is greater the candidate may lose a part or the whole of his capacity to cope. His mental activity is affected: there may be gaps in the memory, verbal blockages, and confusion of one sort or another. The neuro-vegetative manifestations become even more violent: tears, flushing, pallor, even fainting. Wallon,[6] putting it a different way, says that the relation between organism and environment is disturbed by manifestations of a hyper- or hypo-tonicity of the neuro-vegetative system and of postures. In other words, over-motivation involves disorders which are first specific, then become more and more generalized, so that they can only be discerned if considered together with the task and neuro-vegetative reactions.

If the emotion arises from an over-motivation related to the difficulty of the task, we shall have to demonstrate emotion:

(*a*) *When the task becomes very difficult.* Where motivation is constant, the more difficult the task the greater the chance of observing emotive reactions. In fact, optimal motivation is reduced as the task becomes more difficult. Generally speaking, a task is difficult or simple only in relation to the capacities of the subject. Difficulty arises from the relationship between the demands of the environment and the subject's innate or acquired potentialities. The adolescent is worried by a mathematical problem which to his teacher is merely play. We shall illustrate this source of emotions by analysing in particular those tasks which are almost *absolutely* difficult because adaptation is difficult whatever the potentialities of the subject.

(*b*) *When motivation is greatly increased.* The difficulty of the task remaining constant, the more motivation is increased the greater the chance of going beyond optimal motivation. We have already pointed out that this increase in motivation could have very different origins. We shall consider in particular those cases in which increase in motivation is very systematic, regardless of the subject's usual tastes or interests.

(*c*) *When the subject is very emotional.* The difficulty of the task and the objective circumstances remaining the same, certain subjects feel a stronger motivation. They are described as emotional because they move beyond optimal motivation more easily than others.

It would therefore appear that the determinants of emotion are never simple. Emotion is a consequence of the mode of relationship established between a subject and his environment, with due allowance made for his past experience and present state.

II

I have already pointed out that the difficulty of the task is always relative to the capabilities of the subject and that optimal motivation shifts correspondingly. Even a simple task could be a source of emotional reaction in an incompetent subject. It is not possible therefore to draw up a list of difficult tasks.

There are, however, categories of tasks which are *absolutely* difficult. They are those in which the very circumstances of the stimulation make impossible the working out of a completely adequate response. Generally speaking this would be the case with a person caught unawares. His uncertainty and incapacity are then translated into emotional reactions through the direct effect of an incitement to react which has no actual outcome in the chain of relationships. We can describe under three heads, the variety of situations in which a man is caught unawares—the new, the unaccustomed and the sudden, fully aware that in numerous situations these categories may well overlap.

(*a*) A situation is really new when nothing has prepared us to react to it. We have in mind, of course, situations which elicit a response on our part. Here, emotion could hardly be said to impair a reaction which is merely rudimentary or inchoate. The excitement produced can only be discharged in emotive reactions of the neuro-vegetative type. The expert swimmer, summoned by someone drowning, feels little if any emotion; he simply dives in. But, in the same situation, the non-swimmer watching from the bank, remains powerless but intensely excited. This rule explains in part why the younger the child the greater the emotion he feels. It is characteristic of the child that it is constantly confronted by situations for which it does not yet command an adequate system of responses. A baby immersed in a warm bath will scream, an adult will let in the cold water. The same rule also explains why the repetition of a situation blunts the emotions and even cuts them out because the individual gradually develops adaptive reaction patterns. Take the simple example of an evasive response to a painful stimulus. Suppose an animal is fixed in a harness with an electrode on one leg. The shock which produces the painful reaction is preceded by a noise or a flash of light. Initially, when the animal spots the signal, it displays great anxiety: the situation is new and it has not yet learned the correct response. But gradually it is seen to adjust. It calmly raises its leg as soon as the signal appears so as to avoid the electric shock. This simple process of conditioning enables us, by analogy, to understand the behaviour of children. When they are very young everything is new to them and their emotive manifestations are numerous and diverse. Training certainly helps them to exert a better self-control but its main effect is to equip them with reaction patterns adapted to the most frequently recurring life situations.

On the other hand, the same principle explains why most animals display less emotion than human beings: they are in fact equipped with instinctive patterns of reaction corresponding to nearly all the stimuli to which they are sensitive. Thus, generally speaking, the greater the part learning plays in these necessary adaptations, the greater the risk of being confronted by situations which give rise to emotive reactions.

It is not in the least surprising, therefore, that Hebb[16] was able to show the emotive influence of novelty in monkeys. To thirty chimpanzees he showed different fixed or mobile objects representing animals, detached bits of the bodies of chimpanzees and even human heads. Before these inert and dismembered portions the chimpanzees took fright. Hebb interprets this fear as being caused by a new stimulus to which the upper centres of the brain are not adapted—which, in other words, is the explanation we have just suggested. Wallon[17] notes that a child may be terrified if it sees its mother, contrary to her custom, wearing gloves or a hat. The child's habits have been turned topsy-turvy, it is not prepared for situations in which the known is mixed with the unknown. They can even cause greater disturbance than completely new stimuli, which may arouse only curiosity.

(b) There are situations which always remain new even when repeated because there is no 'correct' response. Thus a violent noise will produce an emotive reaction in a person of any age. This reaction will, of course, be stronger in a child which, since it is untrained, will possess no inhibitory schemata. The reaction will be particularly intense in the newborn babe because a violent noise unleashes a tonic reaction of a primitive type 'the cause of which, at an age when the acoustic fibres are not yet medullated, is attributable to the close association of the auditory apparatus with the labyrinthine apparatus rather than to the sense of hearing proper'.[18]

Of the same type is the reaction to loss of support which Watson classified under the primary or even reflex emotions. This reaction evolves as a person grows older and its emotive character is consistent. 'Every postural insecurity involves a fear reaction', adds Wallon, with reference to this point.

To these unaccustomed situations may be added those which remain potentially charged with uncertainty whatever happens. This is the case with darkness and, to a lesser degree, with loneliness (dreaded, too, by chimpanzees), and also with fantasies of the imagination.

(c) But 'the great cause of emotion is surprise', P. Janet has justly remarked.[19] Emotion caused through surprise is one of the most familiar kind and it is also the one which has been most fully investigated in the laboratory. In order to grasp its specific quality, we must distinguish it from the effects of new and unaccustomed stimuli the suddenness of which often reinforces their emotive character. Let us borrow an example from pathology, given by P. Janet,[9] which puts the problem clearly. A young woman is expecting the arrival of an article of furniture which she has previously ordered and which she is very keen on having. It is delivered sooner than she has expected and instead of feeling pleased she is seriously upset. In her own words: 'If I had been notified, if I had seen the van through the window, I wouldn't have become ill.' There has been a time-lag between the rhythm of the activity and that of the request. In cases like these the possibilities of adjustment do exist, but the suddenness of the stimuli prevents their being assimilated. We all know how important it is to prepare our friends for bad news—and sometimes even for very joyous tidings—if we are to avoid upsetting them.

These reactions to the new, the unaccustomed and the sudden are akin. Their most usual form corresponds to a generalized excitement. Gastaut[20] showed that the reaction of surprise is the primary emotive reaction, corresponding to the simple activation of the reticular formation. Excitement is to some extent the nascent form of every emotion. 'Excitement and emotion supplement our routine modes of response which at the moment appear inadequate', says Stratton;[21] he showed how excitement differentiates subsequently, following the two poles of depression and elation.

The cases which we have just looked at are model examples in which the emotive reactions are all the stronger because there is no possible way of reacting. We have seen that the first effect of emotion is to lower the level of performance and where this is not possible it would seem that all the available energy manifests itself in neuro-vegetative reactions.

III

Where the difficulty of the task remains constant, anything which causes strong motivation may involve over-motivation, which, in turn, is a cause of emotive response. Here again there is no specific situation but we shall review a few classic instances involving an intensification of motivation in order to prove that, very frequently, they are in fact accompanied by emotive reactions.[22]

(a) To transform individual behaviour into social behaviour means to submit it to the judgment of others, sometimes to give it the character of a competition. As soon as behaviour becomes social there is an increase in our motivation and this over-motivation often results in a certain disruption. It is, moreover, generally agreed that an act which is easy to accomplish when one is alone becomes difficult as soon as it is subjected to the gaze of others. Consequently, optimal motivation is more often exceeded in the case of social behaviour than in that of solitary behaviour. Social situations of the type that we meet in schools are a daily illustration of this principle. The child who knows his lesson well is disturbed and starts stammering when the teacher questions him in class. Few people can write without irritation when someone is looking over their shoulder and even intellectuals admit to a dislike of writing in the presence of others.

(b) Frustration occurs whenever a physical, social or imaginary obstacle impedes or blocks movement directed towards a goal. Frustration often engenders emotive reactions for two complementary reasons. The first and most important is that frustration generates a supplementary motivation for protection orientated towards the obstacle in its path. The risk of over-motivation and going beyond the optimum then becomes very great. But the risk does not necessarily exist if the initial motivation is not too strong and the task not too difficult; the additional motivation due to the frustration may then prove useful in helping to work out a new and efficient solution.[23] However, more often than not, frustration involves an excess of motivation. Secondly, frustration is very often the source of emotive reactions for, by definition, its effect is to suspend or to render more difficult reactions adapted to the situation. This blockage makes available a great amount of energy which is discharged as emotion.

It is usually agreed that the standard reactions to frustration correspond to different types of emotive reactions:

(i) Aggressiveness: the most common reaction to frustration is the development of a generalized aggressiveness, usually orientated to the cause of the frustration. The reaction adapted to the obstacle is designed to suppress it quietly where possible; to get round it; or, if we are quite powerless, the reaction would be to give way. But frustration often leads to aggressive, violent or unsuitable reactions which readily change to anger. This aggressiveness represents the first beginnings of the tendency to eliminate the obstacle, but what marks it is precisely the fact that it does not do so but only gives indications of disorder in behaviour.

When Watson describes constriction of the body as a primitive form of emotion he is merely picking out one of the forms of frustration to which the child becomes sensitive very early in life, namely, the deprivation of its freedom of movement. That irritation, aggressiveness and even anger are most often engendered by frustrations is attested in the study made by Gates.[24] He asked forty-five women students to note down their experiences of irritation or anger for the period of a week. Most of these experiences correspond to frustrations: accusations, injustices, sarcastic remarks, reprimands, waiting, being jostled, having one's place taken, being met with a refusal, having a pen or telephone which does not operate. In 115 cases out of 145 the cause of the frustration is another person rather than another thing and, in 113 cases, these frustrations give rise to aggressiveness: verbal rejoinders, insults, physical attacks on the person (pinching, hitting, pushing) or on the object (breaking or maltreating it).

(ii) Regression: regression occurs when, for the same situation, the subject chooses an easier solution than he is capable of. This classic consequence of frustration, spotlighted by Barker, Dembo and Lewin,[25] illustrates exactly what we have just said on the nature of emotion. It entails a disorganization of activity simultaneously with disordered organic manifestations. Barker, Dembo and Lewin have justly established that when one forces children to play with toys or games less interesting than those they have been accustomed to, not only are their efforts on a lower level but they also become agitated and aggressive.

(iii) Retreat or escape. In the case of a quasi-permanent frustration and one which appears to have no solution, it is not rare for the subject to react by attempting to escape from the frustration itself. In a social situation, a person can take refuge in silence or even leave the room. These manifestations may appear relatively adapted but they are generally accompanied by an intra-punitive or extra-punitive aggressiveness which is then manifested only implicitly, or by an inner language. Generally speaking, we observe disturbances of posture characteristic of fixations. Thus, in a Lashley jumping-apparatus, a rat unable to find the solution remains convulsed on the departure platform from which nothing can dislodge it. A child frustrated will shut itself up in its room, prostrate, incapable of any useful activity, deaf to all requests from its surroundings.

(c) It is commonly agreed that conflict occurs when an individual finds himself confronted by two simultaneous and incompatible promptings to action. Conflicts, like frustration, increase motivation, for each incitement to act has a frustrating effect on the other. It is not surprising, therefore, that conflicts are one of the main sources of emotion. We have seen that Dewey regarded them as the characteristic source of emotions. Claparède was saying the same thing when he wrote[26] 'Emotions occur precisely when adaptation is impeded for whatever reason.'

Not every conflict engenders emotive reactions. There are both minor and major ones, which can be resolved. But they are particularly a source of emotion when the subject finds himself in a real dilemma. Applying Lewin's useful classification[27] and adopted by Miller[28] and Brown[29] we can distinguish three different kinds of conflict—approach-approach, approach-avoidance and avoidance-avoidance. The first kind is never dramatic even if a difficult choice is preceded by a period of hesitation. Approach-avoidance conflicts are more delicate, particularly if the two motivations have comparable weightings. Thus in a Skinner box,[30] if a rat, accustomed to press a pedal in order to obtain food, receives, after a warning sound, an electric shock through the selfsame pedal, it will be in an approach-avoidance conflict relative to the pedal. As this situation is repeated, the rat is seen to manifest more and more anxiety and to hesitate in pressing the pedal if not to cease activity entirely. What Pavlov termed experimental neurosis corresponds to a type of situation of the same kind. In Pavlov's main experiment, a dog is trained to respond positively to a circle and negatively to an ellipse. But if the shape of the ellipse is gradually modified to render it more like a circle, there comes a stage when differentiation is no longer possible. The animal then manifests violent motor excitation: it strives to break its harness and to bite the apparatus.

Avoidance-avoidance conflicts are even more dramatic for there are never any satisfactory solutions. The individual is between Scylla and Charybdis. The educator often places the child in such a situation by threatening it with punishment for failure to carry out an act which is distasteful to it (eating of food, doing homework, etc.). All these conflicts develop the same type of reactions as frustration: aggressiveness, physical or mental evasion, regression and inhibition—all of which are emotive disorganizations of behaviour with, in addition, agitation, anxiety and neuro-vegetative disturbances.

(*d*) Occasionally over-motivation arises simply as a result of the setting up of a motivation which does not correspond (or no longer corresponds) to an immediately possible activity. These cases can sometimes be interpreted as being relevant to a conflict situation—though there is no general rule about this. Let us take a few examples:

(i) excess of motivation before action: the 'funk'. When a man is strongly motivated toward a difficult action which he cannot carry out right away, he experiences 'funk', that is, anxiety manifesting itself in agitation or painful neuro-vegetative reactions. It is as though the still unused energy were canalized in emotive discharges. Usually the 'funk' ceases as soon as the subject begins to act, for at that moment there is an adequacy of motivation with action.

(ii) excess of motivation after action. P. Janet[31] reports the story of a mountaineer who had slipped into a névé (granular ice); having successfully checked his fall and got out of the névé he climbs on to a rock where he is no longer in danger. He is then seized by a violent trembling: 'My heart pounded,' he said, 'my body was covered with a cold sweat and only then did I have a feeling of fear, of extreme terror.' In this instance there was a surplus of motivation arising from the fact that the subject now realizes, on the cognitive level, the danger from which he has just escaped. This actualization of the danger gives rise to a motivation which now has no object. Akin to this is the behaviour of students when their results are announced: some clap, others embrace and some scream with joy—these are the successful ones. Others turn pale and even weep—these are the failures. The nature of the emotion depends on the result but the cause is the same. Expectation has developed an anxious motivation without a goal and so it flows into emotive reactions whose nature depends on the whole situation. People who lived through the armistice of November 11, 1918, recall the crowds, noisy and excited, invading the streets of the towns and villages. Now that the tension was over nobody could keep still. Wallon[32] has made the following fine analysis: 'There are subjects whose work instead of satisfying their need for activity increases their irritability. Their temperament no doubt requires that movement should arouse more tonus than it is capable of discharging and that the act should not, when it is being executed, exhaust the attitudes which it has called forth . . . These are the impatient types who obtain a kind of advance on what they have to do, anxious types who never abandon themselves to an action without an excess of preparation . . . inept types who, because they do not command, in the motor or intellectual sphere, the necessary powers for the realization of their inner desires, translate their impotence into irritation and anger.' There is an analogy here with those emotive behaviour patterns that occur in mourning. After the death of a loved one, social obligations and the many other duties involved, use up an intense motivation, but as soon as this activity ceases, in the hours and days that follow, when the bereavement is still an open wound, it does not require much— sometimes simply a tender reference—for the pent-up grief to burst out into tears.

The child, like the man, can utilize these goal-less motivations which, when their intensity is weak, give rise to pleasurable emotive discharges. Such is the principle of play when children pretend to be afraid in order the better to laugh at their fears. This is also the principle of suspense in the theatre or cinema. When Bergson remarks that laughter arises from the incongruity between what is and what it would be normal to expect, we can fit it into our schema: something unusual which is not frightening and which does not call for action is translated into laughter. Freud is no doubt saying the same thing when he presents laughter as a defence mechanism. When the subject is in a state of excitement he liberates himself by laughter before the tension becomes painful.

We ought not to be surprised that tension may just as easily produce laughter as tears. Laughter and tears are discharges of energy which have the same origin; whether it should be the one reaction or the other will be determined by the context. In children the passage from one to the other will be very rapid when there is an abrupt change in their interpretation of the situation.

(e) Finally, it need not be any particular situation that may predispose us to an emotion but someone around us in the throes of an emotion. Fear is as infectious as joy. This no doubt accounts for the strong correlation (0.67), which Hagman[33] found between the number of fears mentioned by mothers and those related by their children. This contagion can even spread through a whole group, and panic exists in the animal as well as in man. In trying to analyse this phenomenon, two cases must be distinguished. In the former, the same situation engenders first in one, then in several persons, the same reaction of fear, anger or joy. We come back to the preceding analyses, except that the existence of a group involves, as always, an increase of motivation through the very fact of emotive reactions.

The second case is more specific. Sometimes an emotion takes hold of us without the situation concerning us directly. If we see two men quarrelling violently, we may remain indifferent or simply curious but we ourselves may also become angry. In this case, as has been remarked by Young,[34] we identify ourselves with one of the protagonists, his motivation becoming, as it were, ours. Anger, as well as laughter and tears, can be infectious, but only if identification is possible. Thus everything that facilitates identification increases emotive contagion. On the one hand, it will be the more frequent and intense if the emotive manifestations are more exteriorized; on the other hand, everything that decreases the social distance between two beings facilitates contagion. This is the case with love as with physical proximity. Wallon[35] rightly considers that the distinction between self and others is only acquired progressively. Emotion takes us back to earlier stages of communion. 'It is amid great concourses of people, when the notion of individuality is at its lowest, that emotions explode with the greatest ease and intensity.' Societies which recognize the value of these collective manifestations attach great importance to ceremonies, games and rites which strengthen their cohesion in the unity of the same emotive reactions.

(f) There are passing sources of emotion; there are also chronic ones. If a situation which habitually produces emotive reactions repeats itself without our having the possibility of developing adaptive reactions, anxious or neurotic conditions may develop. Liddell[36] has carried out some excellent experiments on sheep. After a warning signal he gave them electric shocks of average intensity which they could not avoid. After repeating the situation several times daily and for several days in succession, a veritable neurotic condition developed characterized by a diffuse agitation, generalized movements, irregular breathing and an accelerated pulse. This condition is not confined to the duration of the session in the laboratory. The animal becomes hyper-vigilant by day and by night. Anthropomorphically, we may say that it is the repetition of a certain rhythm of anxiety states which is at the root of these disturbances. This experiment may help us to a better understanding of human attitudes. In many lives there are more or less permanent causes of over-motivation. The source is frequently social in origin: a wife who fears rightly or wrongly that she is being deceived, a workman living in a state of insecurity through fear of being given the sack, a soldier living in fear of death. This state can also arise from an unresolved inner conflict and, for example, from the repression of the sexual impulse. These fears, when repeated, maintain a more or less accentuated anxiety state. Selye[37, 38] deserves credit for drawing the attention of psychologists to these states of stress which determine what he calls a general syndrome of adaptation. If the stress is not too intense, it will simply involve an alarm reaction and a state of resistance, but if it is too intense, or if it lasts too long, there will develop what he terms a state of exhaustion. These periodic tensions engender states of anxiety more or less general and sometimes even neurotic conditions. The consequences are found to be not only on the usual plane of emotion; since these are physiological components, they may also give rise to organic lesions through sympathetic irritation. They can come into the purview of psychosomatic medicine.

IV

Other things being equal, certain people are known to have stronger emotive reactions than the average. All typologies consider emotivity to be a fundamental personality trait. Hippocrates had already singled out the choleric temperament as one of the four basic ones. Pavlov[39] has a very similar viewpoint; at the basis of the temperament he distinguishes two antagonistic nervous processes—excitation and inhibition. According to the strength of the process of excitation, he classifies the strong and the weak. Among the strong, and according to the relation between excitation and inhibition, he distinguishes the balanced and the unbalanced. There is therefore a very excitable and unbalanced type through lack of control of excitation by inhibition— a type which Pavlov puts alongside Hippocrates' choleric. Heymans and Wiersma[40, 41] have distinguished three constituent factors in personality: emotivity, activity and persistence. Their definition of emotivity is given in question 9 of their questionnaire: 'Is he emotive (takes things to heart more easily than others, becomes happy or tearful for slight reasons) or non-emotive (less sensitive than others, cold in character)'? Burt[42] whose early work on this problem goes back to 1915, through his method of factorial analysis applied to the results of interviews and observations in standardized situations, discovered a general factor of emotivity which accounts for 40 to 50 per cent of the total variance and which is more important in children than in adults. R. B. Cattell[43] in cross-checking multiple factorial analyses of personality, found that they had in common a factor which he called C. This C factor he finds in analysis based on estimates of behaviour in real situations. There is a bipolar trait opposing an affectively stable character to a general neurotic emotivity. The main signs of opposing behaviour are the following:

C +	C —
Affectively stable.	Dissatisfied, emotive.
Showing no neurotic symptoms.	Showing various neurotic symptoms.
Showing no hypochondriac components.	Hypochrondriac, complains readily.
Stable, self-controlled.	Fickle.
Calm, patient, etc.	Excitable, impatient, etc.

This C factor also appears in the analysis of responses to questionnaires and seems to show a general emotivity in opposition to stability and affective maturity. Here, for example, are two questions which seem selective in relation to this factor:

'Do infringements of good manners and morals in others annoy you to an extent out of all proportion to their importance?'
'Do you often feel worried and tense for trivial reasons?'

The older classifications, therefore, like the more reliable analyses, are at one in agreeing that certain individuals are more emotive than others. The description given by Heymans and Wiersma, as well as the characteristic traits singled out by Cattell, confirm our preceding examination. Emotive types are characterized by a disproportion between the situation and the reaction to it. This disproportion is accounted for by the existence of an overestimation of motivation. In these people optimal motivation is lower compared with those who are unemotive, or emotive only to a slight degree.

Is this emotivity constitutional or acquired? The answer to this question is not a simple one and it is probable that both factors play a part. Hall,[44, 45] in the following experiments, demonstrated this dual origin. Using an emotivity test he was able to select rats and to show that from generation to generation the difference in the two groups kept increasing. Conversely, he also demonstrated that rats subjected to a traumatic stimulus during the first week of their lives later became more motive than rats in a control group who had not undergone this experience. We may recall also the experiments carried out by Liddell[46] who succeeded in creating in a sheep a lasting emotivity by a series of conditionings to hurtful stimuli which the animal could not avoid.

Comparable experiments are not possible with human beings and we have to be content with more debatable indications. Lacey[47] found high correlations between the neuro-vegetative responses of mother and children. These correlations can of course be attributed to the influence of the mother, but they are more likely to be linked with hereditary structures. Stratton[48] found, on the other hand, in studying the medical histories of students, that those who had had illnesses when young were also those who, in a questionnaire, admitted to having more frequent fears or outbursts of temper.

That emotivity is acquired is demonstrated by experiments on conditioned emotive reactions. The experiments carried out by Watson and Rayner[49] on an eleven-month-old infant clearly revealed this tendency. At the beginning of the experiments the child had no fear of a white rat. Later, whenever the child touched the rat, a violent noise was produced which caused the child to tremble and weep. On the succeeding days the mere sight of the rat caused the child to scream and to attempt to escape. Fear of the rat had been conditioned, and, following the laws of conditioning, this fear became applied to other furry animals or to anything that had the same feel, though these stimuli, before the experiment, had been found to have a neutral value. Jones[50] obtained the same results and showed that these reactions could be 'stifled' by fairly complex processes (showing the dreaded object together with another which is desired, or making use of social imitation).

Neuro-vegetative responses, as well as motor and verbal reactions, are subject to conditioning. Thus vaso-constriction can be conditioned to the sound of a bell, a movement, a light, the pronunciation of a syllable.[51] Bykov[52] showed that these neuro-vegetative reactions could also be conditioned by interoceptive stimuli, a fact which considerably extends the field of possible conditioning. Such conditioning no doubt explains many emotive reactions, often diffuse, which we can observe in ourselves without being able to detect their precise antecedents. It is understandable that the frequency and variety of these reactions explain the emotivity of certain individuals.

Emotivity which is mainly acquired may have a very general character or may be quite specific. Wallon[53] reports the case of a person who had been informed of the accidental death of her daughter while she (the person) was seated at the table. She was then seized by an attack of vomiting and from then onwards whenever she was confronted by the same dishes she wanted to vomit. Conditioned reactions of fear can also be quite specific. Phobias are nothing other than elective fears (claustrophobia, nosophobia, etc.) and are often the sequelae of emotional shocks. A complex, in the Jungian sense, corresponds to a mode of feelings and attitudes, not integrated in the personality, originating in conflict and manifesting itself by violent and often ambivalent reactions to certain situations. Adler's inferiority complex is a classic illustration of this. At a more generalized level, the feeling of imminent and indeterminate danger, together with a feeling of impotence, is a source of very numerous emotive reactions. Anxious people, whatever the origin of their anxiety, are emotive types: Malmo[9] showed that if placed in a painful situation (thermal stimulation of the forehead), these individuals are subject to more trembling, more head movement, more tension in the neck muscles, and less regular respiration, than subjects of a control group placed in the same situation. In a word, inemotive subjects—emotive by tem-

L

perament or as a result of painful experience—there is increased sensitivity to certain situations which frequently give rise to emotive reactions where, in less emotive individuals, only adaptive reactions may be observed.

V

Emotion is not a specific behaviour having its own stimuli. It is a consequence of failure in adaptation. Emotion is all the more likely to occur when circumstances render adaptation more difficult. This difficulty always arises from a relationship between the demands of the situation and task and the subject's potentialities. The difficulty of the task may depend on many factors but the novelty or suddenness of the situation are intrinsic factors which explain numerous emotions. The possibilities of action on the part of the subject obviously depend on the variety of schemata of reaction which he has at his command; from this point of view, the adult is better equipped than the child. Mobilization of these possibilities, however, depends on the intensity of the motivation. Without motivation nothing is possible, but the moment motivation becomes extreme, we lose control of our activity which then becomes disorganized simultaneously with the manifestation of neuro-vegetative reactions. These are the more intense as we find ourselves in situations where action is somehow paralyzed by external circumstances or inner inhibitions.

But the man incapable of facing all the exigencies of a situation often falls back on emotion, which is a misfire of adaptation in social activity. Tears may arouse pity or may be an appeal for help; outbursts of temper can frighten and also fortify efforts to surmount an obstacle. Emotive expressions in general socialize our emotions and enable action to be carried out on others. This last observation confirms our analysis and demonstrates that emotion, even when it is not a simple disorder of behaviour or of the organism, is an inferior form of adaptation.

NOTES AND REFERENCES

1. WUNDT, W., 1886, *Eléments de psychologie physiologique*, Trad. franç. de Rouvier, I., Paris: Alcan.
2. JAMES, W., 1884, 'What is emotion?', *Mind*, 9, 188; 1902, *La théorie de l'emotion*, Trad. franç. et introduction de Dumas, G., Paris: Alcan.
3. DEWEY, J., 1894, 'The theory of emotion, I. Emotional attitudes', *Psychol. Rev.*, 1, 553; 1895, 'The theory of emotion, II. The significance of emotions', *Psychol. Rev.*, 2, 13.

4. JANET, P., 1928, *De l'angoisse à l'extase*, Paris: Alcan.

5. LINDSLEY, D. B., 1950, 'Emotions and the electroencephalogram', in REYMERT, M. L. (ed.), *Feelings and emotions*, New York: McGraw-Hill.

6. WALLON, H., 1949, *Les origines du caractère chez l'enfant*, Paris: Bouvin.

7. FREEMAN, G. L., 1948, *The Energetics of Human Behaviour*, London: Oxford University Press.

8. HEBB, D. O., 1946, 'On the nature of fear', *Psychol. Rev.*, *53*, 259.

9. MALMO, R. B., 1950, 'Experimental studies of mental patients under stress', in REYMERT, M. L. (ed.), *Feelings and emotions*, New York: McGraw-Hill.

10. YOUNG, P. T., 1961, *Motivation and emotion*, New York: Wiley.

11. FREEMAN, G. L., 1940, 'The relationship between performance level and bodily activity level', *J. Exper. Psychol.*, *26*, 602.

12. SCHLOSBERG, H., 1954, 'Three dimensions of emotion', *Psychol. Rev.*, *61*, 81.

13. STENNET, R. G., 1957, 'The relationship of performance level to level of arousal', *J. Exper. Psychol.*, *54*, 54.

14. YERKES, R. M., and DODSON, J. D., 1908, 'The relation of strength of stimulus to rapidity of habit formation', *J. Comp. Neurol. Psychol.*, *18*, 458.

15. PATRICK, J. R., 1934, 'Studies in rational behaviour and emotional excitement; the effect of emotional excitement on rational behaviour of human subjects', *J. Compar. Psychol.*, *18*, 153.

16. HEBB, D. O., 1946, 'Emotion in man and animal. An analysis of the intuitive process of recognition', *Psychol. Rev.*, *53*, 88.

17. See ref. 6, p. 102.

18. See ref. 6, p. 100.

19. See ref. 4, p. 491.

20. GASTAUT, H., 1957, 'Données actuelles sur les mécanismes physiologiques centraux de l'émotion', *Bull. de Psychol.*, *11*, 119.

21. STRATTON, G. M., 1928, 'The function of emotion as shown particularly in excitement', *Psychol. Rev.*, *35*, 351.

22. We shall deliberately confine ourselves to psychological analysis. But we could also mention experiments which show that the threshold of emotion is lowered when a subject is under the effect of a stimulant acting on the nervous system which renders him sensitive to the demands of the environment. (SCHACTER, S., and WHEELER, L., 1962, 'Epinephrine, chlorpromazine and amusement', *J. Abn. Soc. Psychol.*, *65*, 121.)

23. BROWN, J. S., and FARBER, I. E. ('Emotions conceptualized as intervening variables with suggestions toward a theory of frustration', *Psychol. Bull.*, *1951*, *48*, 465), have emphasized the fact that frustration creates a mainspring, and MARX, M. H. ('Some relations between frustration and drive', in *Nebraska Symposium on Motivation*, Lincoln: University of Nebraska Press, 1956) has demonstrated experimentally that frustration produced an upsurge in the strength of motivation.

24. GATES, G. S., 1926, 'An observational study of anger', *J. Exper. Psychol.*, *9*, 325.

25. BARKER, R. G., DEMBO, T., and LEWIN, K., 1941, 'Studies in topological and vector psychology; II. Frustration and regression', *University Iowa Stud. Child Welfare*, *18*, No. 1.

26. CLAPAR'DE, E., 1928, 'Feelings and emotions', in REYMERT, M. L. (ed.), *Feelings and Emotions*, New York: McGraw-Hill.

27. LEWIN, K., 1931, 'Environmental forces in child behaviour and development', in MURCHISON, C., *A Handbook of Child Psychology*, Worcester, Mass.: Clark University Press.

28. MILLER, N. E., 1944, 'Experimental Studies of Conflict', in HUNT, J. MCV. (ed.), *Personality and the Behaviour Disorders, Vol. I*, New York: Ronald Press.

29. BROWN, J. S., 1948, 'Gradients of approach and avoidance responses and their relation to level of motivation', *J. Comp. Physiol. Psychol.*, *41*, 450.

30. ESTES, W. K., and SKINNER, B. F., 1941, 'Some quantitative properties of anxiety', *J. Exper. Psychol.*, *29*, 390.

31. See ref. 4, p. 147.

32. See ref. 6, p. 98.

33. HAGMAN, R. R., 1932, 'A study of fears of children of pre-school age', *J. Exper. Educ.*, *1*, 110.

34. YOUNG, P. T., 1943, *Emotion in Man and Animal*, p. 332, New York: Wiley.

35. See ref. 6, p. 76.

36. LIDDELL, H. S., 1950, 'Animal origins of anxiety', in REYMERT, M. L. (ed.), *Feelings and emotions*, New York: McGraw-Hill.

37. SELYE, H., 1946; 'The general adaptation syndrome and the diseases of adaptation', *J. Clin. Endocrinol.*, *6*, 117.

38. SELYE, H., 1956, *The Stress of Life*, New York: McGraw-Hill.

39. PAVLOV, I. P., 1955, *Typologie et pathologie de l'activité nerveuse supérieure*, Paris: Presses Universitaires de France.

40. HEYMANS, G., and WIERSMA, E., 1908, 'Über einige psychische Korrelationen', *Zeit. für angewandte Psychol. und psychol. Sammelforschung*, *1*, 313.

41. HEYMANS, G., and WIERSMA, E., 1909, 'Beiträge zur speziellen Psychologie auf Grund einer Massenuntersuchung', *Zeit. für Psychol und Physiol. der Sinnersorgane*, *51*, 1.

42. BURT, C., 1950, 'The factorial study of emotions', in REYMERT, M. L. (ed.), *Feelings and emotions*, New York: McGraw-Hill.

43. CATTELL, R. B., 1956, *La personnalité*, Paris: Presses Universitaires de France.

44. HALL, C. S., 1941, 'Temperament: a survey of animal studies', *Psychol. Bull.*, *38*, 909.

45. HALL, C. S., and WHITEMAN, P. H., 1951, 'Effects of infantile stimulation upon later emotional stability in the mouse', *J. Comp. Physiol. Psychol.*, *44*, 61.

46. LIDDELL, H. S., 1956, *Emotional Hazards in Animals and Man*, Springfield, Illinois: Thomas.

47. LACEY, J. I., 1956, 'The evaluation of autonomic responses. Toward a general solution', *Ann. New York Acad. Sci.*, *67*, 123.

48. STRATTON, G. M., 1929, 'Emotion and the incidence of disease', *Psychol. Rev.*, *36*, 242.

49. WATSON, J. B., and RAYNER, R., 1920, 'Conditioned emotional reactions', *J. Exper. Psychol.*, *3*, 1.

50. JONES, M. C., 1924, 'A laboratory study of fear: The case of Peter', *Ped. Sem.*, *31*, 308.

51. MENZIES, R., 1937, 'Conditioned vasomotor responses in human subjects', *J. Psychol.*, *4*, 75.

52. BYKOV, C., 1956, *L'écorce cérébrale et les organes internes*, Moscou: Editions en langues étrangères.

53. See WALLON, H., ref. 6, p. 70.

CHAPTER 19

RESPONSE TO STRESS IN MILITARY AND OTHER SITUATIONS*

BY D. E. BROADBENT

I

It is a source of some pride to soldiers, sailors and airmen that they are prepared to expose themselves to conditions far outside the usual range which civilians will tolerate. They are inclined, therefore, to be somewhat contemptuous, and even resentful, of biologists who start enquiring into the effects of these abnormal conditions upon efficiency. Matters are not improved by the apparently abstract and impractical techniques of investigation which are used in studying human beings. A story is told by Sir Henry Dale, for instance, of the very early investigations of anoxia amongst British military pilots forty-five years ago. Considerable indignation was aroused by a proposal to take samples of blood from men who had been flying high; because obviously their difficulty was in breathing, and the pilots did not feel that this had anything to do with their blood.

While it is still fortunately true that unpleasant conditions do not make men unwilling to fly, to man submarines, to drive tanks, or to go out into space, it is not true that they can afford to be inefficient while they do these things. As a result research has had to go a lot farther than taking a little blood, and studies have been made of human beings in all sorts of ways and under all sorts of peculiar circumstances. It would be impossible to consider them all, and no such attempt will be made here. All discussion of physiological measurements will be left out, and even among studies of behaviour many important researches will be omitted.

* Originally presented to a conference organized by NATO in 1961.

We shall start by considering cases in which human efficiency is bound to be low for purely physical or mechanical reasons, but the main thesis is that under stress there are high level changes in the organization of behaviour, and we will work up gradually to these phenomena of the central nervous system.

II

To start then with the case of gravity, it is clear that a man who is being launched in a rocket or who is changing direction in a fast aircraft may be unable to carry out his work simply because his arms and legs are difficult to move, their apparent weight being increased; and of course the blood may be driven down from his head towards his feet and so may cause his vision to fail. The first signs of this will appear when the man's weight has been increased to three or four times its normal value, and he is liable to lose vision altogether at five or six times his normal weight (that is, 5–6G). The lower of these levels of acceleration is reached by conventional aircraft in quite normal manoeuvres such as loops, and complete blackout can be produced without too much difficulty. In rocket launching one would like to use even higher accelerations and the men recently sent into space have been exposed to about twice the blackout value. Even if one does not go so far as to consider space flight, the success of the interception of one aircraft by another may depend upon the extent to which the interceptor can make sharp turns. The ordinary G-suit, which applies pressure to the body so as to keep the blood in the head, will allow an extra G or thereabouts, which is useful: but a very striking recent finding reported by the U.S. Navy is that a man immersed in water can stand up to 16G without noticeable effects on his vision.[1] This is a big advance, but of course it might be thought rather extravagant to send a man into space accompanied by his own swimming pool, and therefore there is also much interest in the possibility of increasing tolerance by changing the man's seating position. If he lies on his back instead of sitting normally, he can stand 12 or 14G, and the limit becomes one of breathing.[1] A couch in which the feet are slightly lower than the head seems to be ideal, and the U.S.A.F. investigators report that as much as 20G can be sustained under these conditions. The controls used by the man under these conditions need, of course, to be very small levers built into the rests on which his arms lie—it would call for great strength to move ordinary aircraft controls or anything of that sort. The American astronauts in their recent flights into space controlled their own re-entry under 11G, which speaks well for the technique employed.

The simple mechanical effect of acceleration is not the whole story, however. When gravity is increased or decreased, the messages from the sense organs in the semicircular canals cease to bear their usual relationships to the messages from the eye. Consequently visual perception may be disordered; the apparent vertical may be out of true[2] and visual after-images may appear to rise or fall compared with their normal position, the direction of their movement depending upon whether gravity is increased or decreased. Even more interesting, an increase in apparent weight may produce a loss of concentration in tasks that are not dependent on a good blood supply to the eyes or easy movement of the hands. It has been shown that under a mere 3G men are unduly slow at a task of counting backwards by threes from 100 to zero.[3] The same study also showed that the perception of time was distorted, a long time seeming under high G to be relatively longer, when compared with a shorter time. These sorts of effects appear before the dramatic mechanical ones, and they certainly seem likely to be purely central and due to the discomfort and generally stressful nature of the situation.

High and prolonged acceleration is perhaps only likely to affect airmen and spacemen. But quite high accelerations can occur for short periods on the ground, except that their direction is rapidly and repeatedly reversed. In other words, vibration is a factor which will appear in tanks and ships as well as in aeroplanes. The visual acuity of a man sitting on an ordinary tank seat will deteriorate if the seat is vibrated between 5 and 28 c.p.s., with an amplitude sufficient to give accelerations of $\frac{1}{4}$G.[4] In this case, incidentally, a reclining seat is worse than a conventional one, probably because it transmits the vibration to the man's head more perfectly. The amount of the vibration is not untypical of a tank; at 28 c.p.s. it is only a few thousandths of an inch, or well under a tenth of a millimetre. In aircraft also, short sharp accelerations are frequent even when straight and level flight is being maintained. Measurements made at high altitudes have shown gusts of over $\frac{1}{2}$G up and down: and at low altitudes below 300 feet bumps of up to nearly 3G have been measured. It is not surprising that vibration is becoming of very general interest. Most of the investigators have concentrated upon visual acuity, which is the function most dramatically affected, probably because it is hard to see when the image of the retina is blurred by vibration. The effect is usually reported to be greatest at frequencies of about 4–5 c.p.s., at which the shoulder girdle resonates and the head therefore shakes most. Recently, however, one investigator has found that vision still suffers even when the object being examined is vibrated in time with the man.[5] This looks as if there may be a central effect like the one already mentioned for high G—although the matter is still not quite certain, because the vibration of the head might not be quite identical to that of the object being examined. There is, however, at least the possibility that a man who is being vibrated suffers from a generalized inefficiency distinct from the particular difficulties he has in seeing and manipulating the outside world.

III

Such a generalized inefficiency might be expected to appear most clearly when one considers the problem of men who are short of oxygen: since in this case the functioning of the brain itself is presumably being affected. Indeed anoxia does impair efficiency in tasks which involve peripheral factors as little as possible: in one case inferior performance has been reported at only 13,000 ft (say, 4,000 metres) on a test of conceptual reasoning.[6] In the test used the subject is faced by an assortment of wooden blocks each possessing a number of different features, and he has to find out by trial and error which of these features are relevant to a division of the blocks into two categories. This is clearly an intellectual job, without the senses and the muscles being very much involved. There are also many anecdotes of over-confidence, temporary changes in personality, and similar disturbances amongst men living at high altitudes. But perhaps the most widely reported feature of anoxia is the intermittent nature of the impairment which it produces. In most studies of this topic, a deficiency of oxygen did not simply increase by a constant amount the time taken for each reaction. On the contrary, the effect was that the man had moments of very acute inefficiency, giving enormous response times; but between these incidents he seemed to perform as well as ever. This 'blocking', as it has been called, is quite a common symptom in stressful situations, and, as we shall see later, it does seem that tasks which merely measure the average efficiency of a man over a prolonged period are not very sensitive to changes in his efficiency. They do not detect these momentary lapses.

IV

Almost everybody recognizes the dangers to efficiency which may come from acceleration and from anoxia: but the effects of high temperatures have not always been so widely realized. It was for many years expected that warships should operate in the tropics without special equipment for cooling their men. In the Persian Gulf in the summer the temperature on a ship's deck is normally over 90°F— perhaps one should say 35°C for the benefit of the more civilized reader. Below decks, in the engine room for example, the temperature has been recorded as higher by 10° or even 20°F; this was in a ship ten years ago, when some air-conditioning had been installed. A report written at that time remarked of the men in the engine room 'some of them have even forgotten what it is to feel well'. Of the men in the galley, where the ship's bread was baked, it said 'with working environments such as this it can only be a question of time before there is a serious accident or fatality'. That was, of course, a purely clinical assessment, but there is a very great deal of evidence that working efficiency does get less as the effective temperature rises above 80–85°F (say 30°C). A deterioration at this same approximate level has been found in British and American soldiers and sailors and in British miners.[7, 8, 9, 10] Perhaps most remarkably, it has also been found in a study in a Johannesburg gold-mine on the work output of African labourers filling trucks with rock.[11] There is little doubt, therefore, that if one requires men to work in temperatures above this level, one must watch out for inefficiency. At the same time there is also much evidence that some functions will survive unimpaired even under heat conditions: in one experiment a tracking task in which the control lever had to be moved through quite a large distance was impaired by heat, but a similar task in which the control was moved much smaller distances against a spring loading was only impaired by cold.[7] Another investigator failed to find effects of heat on a task only slightly modified from one which had previously shown such effects.[12] This should be mentioned because one must emphasize that these various stresses do not simply produce a deterioration on any score one chooses to measure. Their effects show up only on certain kinds of measurement: in anoxia one should, for the greatest sensitivity, use a task on which 'blocking' shows up, and in heat also there are measures which show no effect.

Two points about heat should be added: first, we have mentioned the effective temperature scale, which has long been used to provide

L*

a combined measure of the temperature, the humidity, and the air movement. Some experiments, however, have shown that for the same effective temperature, performance was worse at high humidities. A new scale for combining these variables has in fact been devised and published under the name of the Equatorial Comfort Index.[13] This index gives a greater weight to humidity and seems more in agreement with the experimental results.

The second point is that, in the rather borderline temperature ranges where effects on efficiency first appear, there seems to be little correlation between the physiological and the psychological effects. Men who are showing bodily reactions to heat do not necessarily work less well, while those whose work deteriorates may show little physiological effect. As with the other stresses, heat has some sort of effect on the nervous system as well as on simple functions.

V

When one starts to introduce air-conditioning and other means of combating heat, one usually finds that the noise level rises. In warships it is not uncommon to find that fans bringing cool air into a compartment may produce over 80 db S.P.L. and make it necessary to raise one's voice in order to talk. This interference with speech is a real hazard, and must be borne in mind when the nature of the work makes communication essential. In the past it has not been unknown for a tank to be equipped with a loudspeaker system for the crew to talk to each other and for the mechanism of the gun-turret to make so much noise that the loudspeaker was inaudible. However, if the man's work does not involve his ears, there is no evidence that 80 db or so of noise will have any effect on his efficiency. If one must choose between having fan-noise and being hot, it is probably better to have the noise. Even with louder noises, such as those in ships' engine-rooms, in tanks, or near aero-engines, there is little doubt that many jobs can be performed just as efficiently in noise as in quiet. Not quite all, however. In continuous loud noise of 100 db or more (so loud that speech is quite impossible) there seems to be a tendency for mistakes to be made in continuous work, although the speed of work remains unchanged.[14, 15, 16, 17] There also seems to be some sign of an effect on the alertness with which a man watches for occasional signals, provided that he has several places to watch rather than only one. So there are some, rather specialized, effects of continuous noise. One can also consider the case of a sudden sharp noise, such as a rocket being launched intruding into a continuous task such as the making of a series of decisions from a complex display. In this case it has been found that a temporary inefficiency will appear shortly after the burst of noise.[18] This inefficiency is only momentary, and thus if the task is one in which the man can compensate for a brief lapse, no effect will be found. If for instance the job is one of checking equipment against a written list, so that a second's delay at one point can be caught up at another, the presence of noise probably does not matter. If, on the other hand, a series of targets is being allocated at a high speed, and a target which is once missed will pass out of the field of fire before it can be dealt with, then a burst of noise may be harmful. In this case, as in the case of continuous noise, the intensity of the sound needs to be around 100 db or more.[15, 18] Such levels may sound extreme, but inside a tank on an ordinary road the noise is quite often 115 db, and a recent report on a British tank towing vehicle gave figures of 103–108 db.[19] The engine room or the flight deck of an aircraft carrier provides similar levels. Protection against these levels is desirable in any case because of the risk of deafness, but in addition there is this slight but undoubtedly real effect on working efficiency.

VI

One of the inconveniences which even modest noises can produce is interference with sleep. Even if noise is absent, however, it may be necessary in battle for normal sleeping habits to go by the board. The effects of loss of sleep, like those of noise, are much harder to demonstrate than most people would imagine. Until recently, the most sensitive way of finding out if a man had been too long without sleep was to notice whether he was disorientated and hallucinating. In our own laboratory, for instance, we have noticed a sailor, who had missed a couple of nights' sleep, step off a path to make way for a lady. This spoke well for his manners, but as the lady was invisible to everybody else it was a little alarming. Incidentally, the next sailor along the path stepped off as well—this type of behaviour affects a group of people very easily. But even at this stage many tests will show no change in the man's performance. Fortunately, we need not rely purely on this appearance of almost psychotic symptoms: some types of tasks have been shown to be affected quite seriously by loss of sleep. Once again the sensitive tasks are those which are continuous, having no instants in which it is safe for the subject to relax his attention. These may take the form of a continuous serial reaction task, in which each response is followed immediately by another signal; or of a vigilance task in which the man watches continuously for some signal which will arrive at an uncertain time. Given this type of task, even one night's loss of sleep can be detected quite sensitively.[20, 21, 22] With these tasks we are in fact beginning to be able to measure the rather subtle deteriorations of which most of us are conscious in everyday life, but which have resisted measurement so far.

VII

This, then, is the point at which we shall stop discussing individual stresses, and begin to consider the overall pattern. As we have seen, there are quite specific peripheral effects from some particular stresses —G and vibration interfere with vision and with manipulation, noise interferes with speech—but there are also central effects. The tests which reveal these share certain similarities, so that one would not now start to investigate some new problem using the techniques which seemed obvious thirty years ago. The ordinary psychometric test of intelligence, or of arithmetic, does not seem to be sensitive. Simple isolated functions also such as reaction time, the ability to judge distances, sensory thresholds, digit span, and so on, have repeatedly failed to show effects of grossly extreme stresses.

Be this as it may, the most sensitive tests we have for the various stresses are rather similar. Does this mean that the effects of the stresses are the same? Looking over the literature as a whole, one gets the impression that they are not. On the whole, for instance, if a task has scores for both speed and accuracy, it is accuracy which is affected by noise, while loss of sleep affects speed. Perhaps it would be more accurate to say that in noise people do things which they should not, while when sleeping they do not do things which they should: because the most sensitive measure of sleep loss is blocking, as already mentioned, rather than errors. The absence of effects of loss of sleep upon commissive errors is particularly strongly urged by one group of investigators;[20] and the absence of effects of noise upon speed is so striking that some investigators have dismissed as unimportant their own findings about accuracy.

However, the exact nature of a test clearly makes a big difference— error in one task may not be psychologically equivalent to errors in another. Different populations of subjects may conceivably react differently too: to take a far-fetched but not impossible point, a very cautious man might well slow down rather than make mistakes while a man who is prepared to gamble on long odds will keep up his speed and risk a few errors. There are data in the literature which suggest that in experimental situations soldiers are more prepared to gamble on long odds than students are. Therefore, it might be that one laboratory studying soldiers might get an effect on errors when another laboratory studying students would have got an effect on speed from the same stress. One can, however, rule out this possibility in the case of certain stresses, since our own laboratory has used the same tests on similar groups of subjects under various environmental conditions. The scores which show deterioration are not the same in every case: there is no identical pattern of breakdown under stress. We are now beginning to approach the nature of the central effects which stresses have in addition to their sensory and muscular ones: and it seems that these effects are different for different stresses.

Let us take as an example the task on which most work has been done. This is a serial reaction test of the kind already mentioned. There are five lights on a panel in front of the subject, and five contacts. When a lamp comes on, he must touch the corresponding contact. As soon as he does so, another light comes on, and when he makes a response to that another light comes on, and so on. This task is performed for half an hour, and one can, of course, score errors, speed, and the frequency of blocking. Speed and blocks are affected by loss of sleep: errors are not.[21, 23] Noise and heat increase errors but leave speed unaffected.[14, 15, 23] Whereas noise and loss of sleep affect the end of the work-period more than the beginning, heat affects the beginning as much or even more than the end.[14, 23] There are, therefore, three distinct types of deterioration. In heat you do the wrong thing as soon as you start the job: in noise you do the wrong thing only after working for a while. After loss of sleep you don't do the wrong thing, but you don't do the right thing either.

This kind of difference strongly suggests either that quite different mechanisms are involved, or that the same mechanism is being disturbed in different directions. The first of these possibilities is straightforward and requires no explanation: as an example of the second, there might for intance be a general mechanism of arousal, which could increase and decrease the overall activity of the nervous system. If one supposed that the efficiency of work decreases, when arousal is too low *or* when it is too high, one could imagine that some conditions might disturb efficiency by reducing arousal and others by making it too high. Now one can distinguish these possibilities by applying two stresses simultaneously: since if the mechanisms are quite separate the effects will simply be additive, while if the same mechanism is involved the effects will modify each other. In the case where the two stresses act in opposite ways, they might even cancel each other out.

One experiment on the combined effects of heat and loss of sleep has been carried out.[23] It showed no statistically significant interaction between the two stresses; each produced its own effect without modifying the other. This suggests that the two conditions affect different mechanisms. It is worth noticing another difference between them: the effect of loss of sleep can be reduced by applying incentives, such as knowledge of results or an offer that the experiment will be stopped when a certain score is reached.[24] When these incentives are present, men who have slept normally do no better than men who lost a night's sleep. The effect of heat, however, seems to be just as big whatever incentives are applied: the incentives improve performance, but they do so equally at high and low temperatures.[8, 9] This again looks as if the effects of sleep loss and of heat are quite separate. Unfortunately, the only substantial experiment on the combined effects of heat and noise is one in a different laboratory, which only used 90 db noise.[25] Such a level is scarcely enough to give much of an effect: but for what it is worth, no interaction appeared between noise and heat. The existing evidence, therefore, suggests that heat affects mechanisms which are at least partially independent of those of loss of sleep, and of noise. It is only fair to add that one or two measures do show statistically insignificant interactions between loss of sleep and heat, and also that heat in this context means one particular temperature—105°F dry-bulb and 95°F wet-bulb. There may, therefore, be some partial overlap of the effects, yet to be verified, and it may also be that a different degree of heat might reinforce the effects of loss of sleep: intuitively, a moderate but not extreme warmth makes sleep rather easy.

Two experiments have been carried out on the combined effects of loss of sleep and noise.[26, 27] They both found that the presence of loud continuous noise reduced the effect of loss of sleep, which suggests that the two variables affect the same mechanism in opposite directions. In that case, since incentives reduce the effect of sleeplessness, one immediately wonders what happens to the effect of *noise* when incentives are applied: this experiment has been carried out, and showed that the effect of noise is greater when incentives are present.[27] This fits so neatly into the view that the effects of noise are exactly opposite to those of loss of sleep, that it is almost too good to be true.

On the other hand, it also fits in with a fact which has been somewhat of an embarrassment: in a study in an industrial situation, the effects of noise appeared to be very much larger than those measured in the laboratory.[28] At the time this was found, there was no obvious reason why the effects should be greater, but in industry the worker's pay depended upon the amount he produced. In the light of the more recent work, this makes it very reasonable that the effects of noise were greater than in the more detached conditions of the laboratory.

At all events, the present results are consistent with the idea that loss of sleep is opposite in its effects to noise, and that heat is distinct from both. The effects of heat might possibly be connected with a disorganization of response due to changes in proprioceptive sensitivity: this view has at least been suggested by some investigators.[7, 23] As already mentioned, of two tracking tasks, the one in which the subject's control was through pressure rather than movement was not affected by heat.[7] This suggests that the organization of response is somehow concerned in the effects of heat.

Perhaps most interesting, however, is the nature of the mechanism affected by noise and loss of sleep. It could, for instance, be a general level of arousal, as suggested earlier: if a man is normally at peak efficiency, noise over-arouses him while loss of sleep reduces his level below the optimum. Incentives would raise the level, and so increase the effect of noise but reduce that of loss of sleep. There are some difficulties in this view, such as the snag that noise and loss of sleep both have their effects at the end of the work-period, whereas one would expect the effects of over-arousal to be greatest when the task was novel.

VIII

We have now reached the point of saying that, apart from their peripheral effects on, say, vision, the stresses have an effect on the general control of behaviour, and that this effect is not the same for all abnormal environments. Specifically, noise and loss of sleep seem to oppose one another, one producing too much activity and the other too little. Incentives come in here by raising the general level of activity. This immediately raises the questions which many people regard as the main subjects covered by the term 'stress'. What happens to behaviour in situations where the motives in play are extremely strong? Specifically, in the highly dangerous situation of a battle, is a man more or less efficient than he would be in a laboratory? Are some personalities better at resisting the forces at play in such extremities?

One way of attacking such questions is to apply psychological tests to men in real frightening situations. This was done in a very well known study of troops in the Korean War[29] and also in at least one study of parachute jumping. In neither case did psychological tests show anything very much.

This might be due to bad luck in the choice of tests, or to the time interval which is bound to elapse in a real situation between the test and the source of the fear. Another line of attack is to use milder stresses, such as electric shock, various forms of social pressure, or the challenge of the various abnormal environments, which we have discussed, and look at the resulting behaviour in the laboratory. The argument here is that if one can obtain a few points on a graph relating behaviour to degree of motivation, one may perhaps have a basis for extrapolating to higher degrees. While this is obviously not a completely safe thing to do, it is nevertheless a good idea. If one could obtain an understanding of the changes which varying motives produce in the laboratory this would at least guide the choice of tests for later use in real situations; and so offer some hope of avoiding wasted time in circumstances where such time is very valuable. One cannot afford much random experimentation on troops coming out of battle.

What does happen then when one raises the strength of the motives acting on a man in the laboratory? Suppose one uses simple tasks, such as making well-practised reactions, acquiring elementary conditioned reflexes, or learning to associate words which have an obvious connection even before the experiment. At such simple tasks the man whose motives are strong usually does better than the man whose motives are weak. Experiments showing this come from many laboratories. To take a single example, if one is teaching a man to respond with the word 'serene' when he sees the word 'tranquil', he will learn better if every minute or so he gets an electric shock. This improvement applies to cases where the right response is a natural and obvious one.[30]

When, however, the correct response is under strong competition from other incorrect responses, it may not be true that a rise in the threatening or rewarding features of the situation will improve performance. In the same experiment, one can alter the task slightly so that the man is trying to learn to say the word 'rugged' when he sees the word 'tranquil', rather than the more obvious association 'tranquil-serene'. When this was done, people who received an electric shock occasionally did worse at learning than people who had no shock. Once they had learned a little, however, and began to do better than chance, the shock seemed to help them to gain rapidly and reach a high level of performance. One can formulate this result by saying that the electric shock increases the strength of whatever response is strongest: if the most natural response is the correct one, shock is a help, while if the most natural response is incorrect, shock makes it harder to eliminate this error and achieve the correct responses.[30]

These results are typical of a number of others, and particularly of results found by comparing people who show a number of signs of chronic anxiety with those who do not: or at any rate, people who score highly on certain questionnaire scales of anxiety. The anxious people are reported to acquire conditioned eye-blinks more rapidly, and to do well in easy rote learning tasks, but to do badly when there are strongly competing alternative responses in a learning task; when, in fact, there are other things they might do instead of the correct action. This might be taken, and has been taken by some authors, as meaning that a high level of any motive will have a generalized effect, strengthening strong responses at the expense of weak ones. But certain results do suggest that different motives do not necessarily interact. For instance, it has been shown that smokers kept without tobacco, and so in a state of need, do not give better conditioned eye-blinks than people not so deprived.[31] On the other hand it has also been found that anxious people do not show conditioned salivation particularly well.[32] Even before conditioning takes place, those individuals who have a high blink rate are not necessarily those who salivate a great deal, since both blinking and dryness of the mouth may be in some way connected with anxiety. These results make me think that a rise in the hazardous or unpleasant features of a situation will affect primarily those responses which are associated with anxiety. If a man's behaviour is in any case largely based upon fear, an external reason for that fear will have widespread effects upon his efficiency: those effects being good or bad according to the circumstances.

This may underlie an experimental finding which is now very widely accepted: namely, that there is an interaction between the score of an individual person on a questionnaire of anxiety, and the size of the effects which unpleasant conditions such as electric shock have upon his behaviour. A variety of experiments have found this.[33, 34, 35, 36] The interaction is sometimes in the direction of good performance and sometimes of bad, but whichever way it is, the unpleasant conditions have their greatest effect upon the anxious man.

In practical terms, one may perhaps expect the highly arousing circumstances of a battle to improve the performance of simple and

routine jobs, but to impair the flexibility with which new and unfamiliar problems are tackled. These effects will be greatest in the
anxious individual. One immediately wonders how this view is to be
related to the findings on arousal, noise, and loss of sleep mentioned
earlier. One ought perhaps to distinguish different kinds of arousal
depending upon the type of motive in play: and one should perhaps
relate the bad effects of over-arousal to the presence of competing
responses. This might help to explain some of the difficulties indicated
previously; noise, for instance, may be regarded as helping performance so long as the correct response is dominant but it increases the
tendency to error when through prolonged work that tendency begins
occasionally to exceed the tendency to make correct responses.

There are, therefore, many promising lines for future research. It
is already clear, however, that stress has general effects on efficiency,
that an important part of these effects is the raising and lowering of
levels of arousal or motivation, and that these changes in level affect
the flexibility of action. The implications of this view need to be
followed out in specific fields, and no doubt this will be done in the
years to come.

REFERENCES

1. KAEHLER, R. C., MEEHAN, J. P., and FREEDMAN, T., 1959, 'Designing for human
   capabilities under acceleration in satellite operations', Paper 59-AV-34,
   American Society of Mechanical Engineers.
2. GRAYBIEL, A., 1952, 'The oculogravic illusion', *Arch. Ophthal.*, *38*, 605.
3. FRANKENHAUSER, M., 1958, 'Effects of prolonged gravitational stress on
   performance', *Acta Psychol.*, *14*, 92.
4. FORBES, A. R., 1959, 'A survey of the effects of buffetting and wholebody
   vibration on human behaviour', *Flying Personnel Research Committee
   Memorandum*, No. 105.
5. DRAZIN, D. H., 1959, 'Effects of low frequency high amplitude whole body
   vibration on visual acuity', *Flying Personnel Research Committee Memorandum*, No. 128.
6. MAAG, C. H., 1957, 'Characteristics of mental impairment in hypoxia', *Amer.
   J. Psychol.*, *70*, 243.
7. RUSSELL, R. W., 1957, 'Effects of variations in ambient temperature on certain
   measures of tracking skill and sensory sensitivity', Report No. 300, U.S.
   Army Medical Research Lab., Fort Knox.
8. MACKWORTH, N. H., 1950, 'Researches in the measurement of human performance', *M.R.C. Special Report Series*, No. 268.
9. PEPLER, R. D., 1958, 'Warmth and performance: an investigation in the tropics',
   Ergonomics, 2, 63.
10. FRASER, D. C. (1956 ? original undated), in *Reaction of Mines Rescue Person-
    nel to work in hot environments*, National Coal Board Medical Service.

11. WYNDHAM, C. H., *et al.*, 1959, 'Studies on the effect of heat on performance of work in mines. Part 3', Report No. 3/59 Applied Physiology Laboratory, Transvaal and Orange Free State Chamber of Mines.

12. CHILES, W. D., 1958, 'Effects of elevated temperatures on performance of a complex mental task', *Ergonomics*, 2, 89.

13. WEBB, C. G., 1959, 'An analysis of some observations of thermal comfort in an equatorial climate', *Brit. J. industr. Med.*, *16*, 297.

14. BROADBENT, D. E., 1953, 'Noise, paced performance and vigilance tasks', *Brit. J. Psychol.*, *44*, 295.

15. BROADBENT, D. E., 1957, 'Effects of noises of high and low frequency on behaviour', *Ergonomics*, *1*, 21.

16. GRIMALDI, J. V., 1958, 'Sensori-motor performance under varying noise conditions', *Ergonomics*, 2, 34.

17. JERISON, H. J., 1959, 'Effects of noise on human performance', *J. Appl. Psychol.*, *43*, 96.

18. WOODHEAD, M. M., 1959, 'Effect of brief loud noise on decision-making', *J. Accoust. Soc. Amer.*, *31*, 1329.

19. DENNIS, J. P., SIDDALL, G. J., and COLBOURNE, P. J., 1956, 'Noise levels recorded in "Antar" and some observations on their possible effect', *Ministry of Supply C.S.E. Report*, No. 66.

20. WILLIAMS, H. L., LUBIN, A., and GOODNOW, J. J., 1959, 'Impaired performance with acute sleep loss', *Psychol. Monog.*, *73*, 1.

21. WILKINSON, R. T., 1959, 'Rest pauses in a task affected by lack of sleep', *Ergonomics*, 2, 373.

22. WILKINSON, R. T., 1960, 'The effect of lack of sleep on visual watch-keeping', *Quart. J. Exper. Psychol.*, *12*, 36.

23. PEPLER, R. D., 1959, 'Warmth and lack of sleep: accuracy or activity reduced', *J. Compar. physiol. Psychol.*, *52*, 446.

24. WILKINSON, R. T., 1961, 'Interaction of lack of sleep with knowledge of results', *J. Exper. Psychol.*, *62*, 263.

25. VITELES, M. S., and SMITH, K. R., 1946, 'An experimental investigation of the effect of change in atmospheric conditions and noise upon performance', *Trans. Amer. Soc. Heat Vent. Eng.*, *52*, 167.

26. CORCORAN, D. W. J., 1962, 'Noise and loss of sleep', *Quart. J. Exper. Psychol.*, *14*, 178.

27. WILKINSON, R. T., 1963, 'The interaction of noise with sleep deprivation and knowledge of results', *J. Exper. Psychol.* (in press).

28. BROADBENT, D. E., and LITTLE, E. A. J., 1960, 'Effects of noise reduction in a work situation', *Occup. Psychol.*, *34*, 133.

29. DAVIS, S. W., 1956, 'Stress in combat', *Scientific American*, *194*, 31.

30. CHILES, W. D., 1958, 'Effects of shock-induced stress on verbal performance', *Wright Air Development Centre Tech.*, Report 58-117, *ASTIA Document* AD 151083.

31. FRANKS, C. M., 1957, 'Effect of food, drink, and tobacco deprivation on the conditioning of the eye-blink response', *J. Exper. Psychol.*, *53*, 117.

32. BINDRA, D., PATTERSON, A. L., and STRZELECKI, J., 1955, 'On the relationship between anxiety and conditioning', *Canad. J. Psychol.*, *9*, 1.

33. SPENCE, K. W., FARBER, I. E., and TAYLOR, E., 1954, 'The relation of electric shock and anxiety to level of performance in eye-lid conditioning', *J. Exper. Psychol.*, *48*, 404.

34. DAVIDSON, W. Z., ANDREWS, T. G., and ROSS, S., 1956, 'Effects of stress and anxiety on continuous high speed colour naming', *J. Exper. Psychol.*, *52*, 13.

35. DEESE, J., LAZARUS, R. S., and KEENAN, J., 1953, 'Anxiety, anxiety reduction and stress in learning', *J. Exper. Psychol.*, *46*, 55.

36. SARASON, I. G., 1958, 'Effects on verbal learning of anxiety, reassurance and meaningfulness of material', *J. Exper. Psychol.*, *56*, 472.

CHAPTER 20

TEMPORAL INTEGRATION AND BEHAVIOUR*

BY L. S. HEARNSHAW

I

It is just over a hundred years since the idea of psychology as a science
as distinct from a philosophy of mind became firmly established. In
this country J. S. Mill[1] proposed that there is, or may be, a science of
human nature, and adopted the then unfashionable term 'Psychology'
to denote it. But alongside the abstract, general science of psychology
Mill set a more concrete science, closely in touch with the realities of
human life, which he termed 'Ethology'. The tension latent in Mill's
distinction—the tension, in fact, between the demands of scientific
method and the appreciation of the richness of human individuality—
has been endemic throughout the development of psychology and has
been a major source of the division of psychology into rival schools of
thought. One thinks of Dilthey's protests against the aridity of the
Wundtian experimentalism of his day; of the recent rise of the psychology of personality as a reaction from the reduction of behaviour to
linked muscle twitches; and, to give contemporary instances, the
protest of Ketchum[2] to the Canadian Psychological Association against
the assumptions of learning theory, and Cantril's[3] eloquent plea for a
humanistic psychology.

There always has been, and there still is, a danger of psychologists
splitting into two insulated groups, one dedicated to scientific methodology in all its rigour and purity, the other to understanding living
human beings, their achievements and their problems. Such a split
would, I think, be unfortunate for psychology. The record of human-

* An abridged version of the Presidential address delivered at Manchester,
on April 7, 1956, at the Annual Conference of the British Psychological Society,
published in *Bull. Brit. Psychol. Soc.*, 1956, No. 30, 1.

istic psychologies is not encouraging. Their claims are enticing; their performance distinctly dusty. By now it should be clear that psychology cannot afford to compromise on the matter of methodology and techniques, nor hope to find short cuts to its goal.

But this is not the whole story. It is easy to oversimplify the methodology of science; to lay too much stress on formal precision and to ignore components which in the actual advance of science are of at least equal importance. To be brief, and perhaps dogmatic, the great scientists have always had an eye for significance. They have seen just where to apply their scientific method and tools. And this eye for significance has derived primarily from two things: from the fact, firstly, that they have been reflective thinkers, often indeed dreamers; and, secondly, from their deep and intimate first-hand acquaintance with their subject-matter. It is just these vital components which our scientific purists in psychology are in danger of excluding, and which the humanistic and clinical psychologists help to contribute. It is for this reason that the interaction of psychologists of different persuasions, whatever the tensions between them, is so important, and why the boundary which Mill drew between an abstract psychology and a concrete ethology must not, if we can help it, lead to divorce.

But let me come to my point, which is to justify my choice of subject. I can see only one way of narrowing the gap between the scientific and the humanistic psychologies, and that is through a gradual encroachment of scientific techniques upon territory already roughly mapped by humanistic insight. This means in effect a constant search for concepts which, while capable of scientific definition and employment, nevertheless possess humanistic implications in the sense that they throw light upon the peculiar or, as they are sometimes termed, the higher attributes of men. The concept of temporal integration, which I have taken as my theme, is, I suggest, such a concept.

II

Instead of beginning with a definition or an abstract discussion of the meaning of temporal integration I will begin with some illustrations, and first of all with a very ancient one, a subtle introspective description of temporal integration by St Augustine:[4]

"I am about to repeat a psalm that I know. Before I begin, my expectation alone reaches itself over the whole; but so soon as I shall have once begun, how much so ever of it I shall take off into the past, over so much my memory also reaches; thus the life of this action of mine is extended both ways; into my memory so far as it concerns that part which I have repeated already, and into my expectation too, in respect of what I am about to repeat now; but all this while is my marking faculty (*attentio*) present at hand, through which, that which was future, is conveyed over, that it may become past; till the whole expectation be at length vanished quite away, when namely that whole action being ended, shall be absolutely passed into memory. What is now done in this psalm, this holds too throughout the whole course of man's life."

We have here in these words of St Augustine a clear account of the integration of expectation, present action, and immediate memory into a temporally extended whole, which serves to guide the course of the recitation.

My second illustration, if you will forgive the incongruity of the sudden leap from a father of the Church to myself, is a simple experiment of my own.

A series of approximately 2,500 letters on a continuously moving tape is passed through an aperture at the rate of 100 letters a minute, the aperture being large enough to expose five letters at a time. Fig. 1 shows the first 120 letters of the series: it cannot, of course, reproduce

P X F F R U Q Z S T N F F R I E K F F R

D M H F F R I D M F F R J C B F F R G L

A F F R Q N S T V Y F F R Y Q O P W S F

F R H E M F F R M B A F F R W Z N V Y Q

F F R W Q N T Y Z F F R A B H F F R S Y

N V T P F F R T Z W O Q N F F R N Q Z O

FIG. 1

The FFR series—the first 120 letters in the series, which is shown on a moving tape in a single continuous line.

the serial nature of the exposure, which is an essential feature of the experiment; but it does serve to bring out certain characteristics of the series. Double F is repeated at intervals: it is invariably followed by R. The intervals between F F R are either long or short. At the beginning of the series the long intervals contain six letters, and the short intervals three; the length of the intervals gradually increases until at the end of the series they consist of eight and five letters respectively. This long-term trend cannot, of course, be shown on the slide. The long intervals are always filled with letters from the second half of the alphabet (N–Z, excluding R) arranged at random, no letter being repeated within any one interval. The short intervals are always filled with letters from the first half of the alphabet (A–M, excluding F) also arranged at random, with the one exception that A is always followed by B and *vice versa*, unless A or B immediately precede F. Long and short intervals are randomly arranged. The series, therefore, in more ways than one is only partially predictable. The subjects are simply asked to comment at once on any feature which strikes them as significant, and given no further instructions as to what to look for.

I do not intend to give a full report of this experiment here, but merely note that all my subjects (the majority of them first-year psychology students) without exception very rapidly structured the series. F F R were always separated out. All the subjects at some stage or other counted the letters between the F F R groups, and the counting never included the F F R groups themselves. There was therefore objective evidence that the F F R groups were differently regarded from the rest of the series, and the series structured round them.

Now grasping the pattern of the series in this way is more than, though it may be based on, an associative probabalistic process. All but one of my sixteen subjects learned to associate A and B (in seventy-three out of ninety appearances of either letter A and B are conjoined in the series). But this did not lead to any structuring of the series round A and B. A and B remain part of the series and are counted when counting takes place. F F R stand apart as a result of a reorganization of the series as a whole. This patterning cannot be a perceptual patterning because the number of letters perceived at any one moment is limited to five. It is a temporal patterning, extending from the past to the future, the discovery of a repetitive rhythm which though not perfectly regular does follow certain ascertainable rules. The process which enables a series of successive events to be patterned in this way may be appropriately termed temporal integration.

My third and most familiar example of temporal integration is the production and comprehension of speech. Speech consists of sequences of words; and if it is to be intelligible these words must be grouped in recognizable syntactical patterns as well as in patterns of meaning. To grasp these patterns requires an integrative process which, because of the sequential nature of speech, is necessarily a form of temporal integration, involving, as in the case of St Augustine's recitation, both memory and expectation. Attempts have been made to explain the coherence of normal speech by the statistical interdependencies among successive items in a verbal statement and the weaker influence of more remote associations. Such statistical structure does exist, and explains a variety of phenomena, such as speed of recognition and level of difficulty. But explanations wholly in terms of statistical frequency of association fail to account for the logical coherence of rational discourse, and Lashley,[5] who has reviewed some of the literature on this topic, has argued that 'any theory of grammatical form which ascribes it to direct associative linkage of the words of the sentence overlooks the essential structure of speech'.

Whatever the theory, however, it can be shown by George Miller's method of approximation that temporal span is necessary to account for the sequences of normal speech. What Miller[6] calls a zero-order approximation to normal English picks words at random from the dictionary. A first-order approximation takes account of the relative frequencies of occurrence of individual words; a second-order approximation of relative frequencies of pairs of words, the word 'of', for instance, frequently being followed by 'the' but very rarely by 'pullulation'. Higher approximations get closer and closer to normal English. A fifth-order approximation, which can be produced by getting different persons to choose each next word in the context of the preceding four, is still nonsense, but not necessarily ungrammatical nonsense. Here is a short example of a fifth-order approximation obtained by Miller's method:

The town is situated on a conspicuous building ornamented with pillars shaped like those of my professor.

To produce and to understand rational speech involves a much longer span of temporal integration than the artificially restricted span which in effect is the outcome of Miller's method.

There is, of course, a great deal of material relevant to the problem of temporal integration in the literature on speech disorders. In particular it is the capacity for temporal integration which seems to be impaired in the type of aphasia termed by Head[7] 'semantic'. It is described by him as 'due essentially to want of power to combine mentally into a single act a series of relevant details . . . want of ability to appreciate and retain the ultimate significance of intention of words and phrases combined in normal sequence'. And it is linked to disturbances not only of speech but of other activities involving temporal integration; for instance, an inability to assemble articles requiring an ordered series of moves, to play games like chess and cards, or to reproduce the plan of a building which cannot be viewed at once and comprehensively.

In the light of these illustrations perhaps temporal integration may be provisionally defined as the formation of contemporaneous patterns of action and meaning when the units from which these patterns are constituted are serially ordered and in temporal succession. In the very brief space available to me I want to do three things: firstly, consider the historical roots of the concept and the obstacles which have for long prevented its development; secondly, illustrate its experimental potentialities; and thirdly, discuss its wider psychological implications.

III

First, then, some history. At the risk of distortion, I must work with broad and rapid brush strokes.

Modern psychology began when Hobbes brought motion into the mind, and mind became no longer a collection of faculties but a train of thoughts, a succession or sort of discourse. Two problems followed: how is this train or succession guided? How is continuity maintained? To the first question Hobbes gave a clear answer. The second he largely evaded.

With Hume[8] there were no evasions. He found 'nothing but a bundle or collection of different perceptions which succeed each other with an inconceivable rapidity, and are in perpetual flux and movement'. It is 'the successive perceptions only that constitute the mind', and 'our notions of personal identity proceed entirely from the smooth and uninterrupted progress of the thought along a train of connected ideas'.

From the time of Hume onwards the primary nature of temporal succession was commonly recognized. For Kant it was the special mark of the 'inner sense', and hence of all experience. For Bain, Spencer and J. S. Mill successiveness was the basic character of psychical life, and at the end of the century William James vividly described the stream of consciousness. Kant was the first to see that, given succession as a primary datum, an indispensable condition of experience was synthesis or integration; for the purpose he postulated complex transcendental machinery, which is perhaps not really so much more outrageous than the hypothetical constructs of some psychologists!

For two generations after Kant British Associationists, as T. H. Green[9] complained in his weighty introductions to Hume, failed to come to terms with the issue. J. S. Mill,[10] indeed, looked and retreated. He saw the need for 'a permanent something contrasted with the perpetual flux of sensations and other feelings or mental states which we refer to it', but had nothing better to suggest than 'a permanent possibility of these states'. 'The paradox that something which *ex hypothesi* is but a series of feelings can be aware of itself as a series' he regarded as the final inexplicability.

After 1870 the problem could no longer be ignored. Ward, Stout and James all grappled with it in their various ways. For Ward[11] there was a persisting subject and a memory continuum resulting from the continuity of attention. For Stout[12] noetic synthesis implied the determination of a train of thought by the central idea of the whole topic. Two factors, in particular, were involved, conative continuity and primary retentiveness, which he held to be the foundation of meaning, and which was indeed apart from the lack of expectancy a direct anticipation of the concept of temporal integration.

"The last note of a melody (remarked Stout[13]) may be and often is the only note of which we are aware at the moment it strikes the ear. Yet in it the entire melody is in a sense present. It comes before consciousness as part of a quite specific whole, and derives a specific character from its place in that whole. . . . This cumulative effect of the preceding phases of a conative process on the succeeding may be called primary retentiveness, in order to distinguish it from the retentiveness which is involved in reproduction and association."

James[14] was more radical, and proposed that passing thoughts in some mysterious way both inherited the title of all past thoughts and also contained 'vast premonitory glimpses' of what was to come.

The weakness of all these proposals, as well as of the German theories of apperception, was their abstract nature and lack of experimental support. Before the end of the century, however, experimental evidence was forthcoming. G. E. Müller and Schumann[15] in a famous series of experiments demonstrated the fact of serial grouping in the learning of nonsense syllables, and showed that grouping could override contiguity. The Würzburg psychologists established the existence of persisting determining tendencies directing and integrating associative successions, and on the basis of clinical evidence Head[16] proposed his theory of the schema.

Nevertheless in the two great contemporary movements of Gestalt psychology and behaviourism the concept of temporal integration never quite emerged. Though the concept has affinities with Gestalt theory, though Humphrey[17] and Katona[18] came close to formulating it, and though we find references to action patterns and the organization of simple rhythms in their writings, the Gestalt psychologists, largely owing to the extraordinary dominance of spatial concepts in their thinking, failed to develop their theories in this area. Behaviourism, on the other hand, in the form of learning theories has shown an increasing proclivity towards temporal concepts, such as antedating reactions, expectancies and pure stimulus acts, and in one study at any rate, O. H. Mowrer's 'Time and Integrative Learning',[19] we have a direct attack at the rat level on the problem 'of integrating the future and the present, of learning how to surmount the natural limitations imposed by the naturally given gradients of reinforcement'. It is doubtful, however, whether, owing to the limited temporal capacities of animals, including even the primates, animal experiments can contribute more than foundations—valuable and indeed indispensable as these are—to our understanding of temporal integration. Lloyd Morgan in his pioneering work on comparative psychology[20] pregnantly observed that the emergence of higher levels of mentality was closely linked with the grasping of the time plan of events, with retrospective memory and reflective anticipation, and Piaget's studies of the child mind have amply confirmed Lloyd Morgan's observations. For Piaget[21] characterizes the first and essential difference between sensori-motor and conceptual intelligence thus:

"Acts of sensori-motor intelligence, which consist solely in coordinating successive perceptions and (also successive) overt movements, can themselves only be reduced to a succession of states, linked by brief anticipations and reconstructions but never arriving at an all-embracing representation; the latter can only be established if thought makes these states simultaneous, and thus releases them from the temporal sequence characteristic of action."

It is at this latter level that temporal integration proper emerges with what Piaget calls 'an all-embracing representation', and it is this level that animal studies by their very nature cannot elucidate.

With the recent writings of Hebb,[22] Lashley[5] and Fessard[23] the concept of temporal integration has emerged into clearer daylight.

But it is strange, in spite of what Lashley terms 'the ubiquity of the problem', and in spite of its being a required corollary of the Hobbesian train of ideas, that for so long 'it has (again in Lashley's words) been largely ignored; it is not even mentioned in recent textbooks, nor is there any significant body of experimental studies bearing on the problem'. We can only speculate on the reasons for this. Perhaps faculty psychology was a main culprit—and who can doubt on inspecting the chapter headings of our textbooks that the influence of faculty psychology is far from dead? Temporal integration cuts across faculty boundaries. It implies perception of the present, memory of the past, and expectation of the future—stimulus patterns, traces, and symbolic processes—integrated into a common organization. But there is, I think, another reason. In their approach to the more complex forms of learning, memory and thinking psychologists have been unduly influenced by the set exercises of the school classroom, where problems are frozen on to blackboards and exercise books, and lessons can be conned repeatedly until learned by heart. World War II ended the exclusiveness of this preoccupation. Psychologists were confronted with situations that would not stand still, indeed which often moved with dramatic speed. There is no need, and I have no time, to review the reorientation of psychology that became inevitable. Sir Frederic Bartlett[24] has recently done so authoritatively. Let it suffice to note that the investigation of skills, mechanical devices for prediction and control, theories of communication and the renewed study of language, studies of decision making, and finally progress in the understanding of the neurological basis of memory and integration have all contributed to the recent emergence of the concept of temporal integration. But as we look back over the history of our science, and this is why I have ventured to include this historical section in my chapter, we can see that the concept was implicit from the beginning and potentially of central importance throughout modern psychology.

IV

I should like to conclude by briefly alluding to the wider psychological implications of the concept of temporal integration, since it seems to me that here its special value lies.

Temporal integration essentially involves the formation, from temporally disparate units, of configurations in which the present moment and immediate stimuli lose the dominance they possess at the perceptual level. The capacity to form and to scan such temporal configurations frees the organism from control by the present situation, and is the foundation of most of man's characteristic attributes. For the behaviour of the normal human adult takes place in an extended temporal framework. A promise made years ago, and nowhere objectively recorded, may influence a man's actions for the remainder of his days; long-term goals and aspirations may be major regulators of his day-to-day conduct. The whole aspect of the world can be changed by a future event known to be immanent—the certain knowledge, for example, that one has not long to live. About the hardest thing for the adult to do is to immerse himself wholly in the present; even in his relaxations he tends to be goal-directed and time-conscious, to be imbued with some sense both of history and of futurity.

By contrast animals, even the primates, live mainly in the present. They are sense-bound; learned reactions are tied to present stimuli, or subject to but short delay; anticipations are brief. Köhler's[25] observation is classic: 'A great many years spent with chimpanzees leads me to venture the opinion that besides in the lack of speech it is in the extremely narrow limits (in time) that the chief difference is to be found between anthropoids and even the most primitive human beings'. In confirmation of this observation we find the temporal maze is a peculiarly difficult task for animals; and that the capacity for delayed response is far less than with quite young children.

Hebb[26] recently put the matter thus:

"The problem of consciousness is not only a problem of integration, that is, the finding of an area or a system in which diverse things may be brought together, but also a problem of temporal order. As far as integration as such is concerned, you can find it in the flat worm or in the spinal dog, but we cannot assume that this is consciousness. If we make a separation between an organism such as man, in which we are sure of consciousness, and lower forms in which consciousness is doubtful or negligible, we find that the greatest difference in behaviour is the complex temporal integration in the higher animal—implying a series of events going on in the cranium which are to some extent independent of the environment."

If Hebb is right the concept of temporal integration is likely to illuminate many aspects of human psychology—language, for instance, conceptual cognition, planning and foresight. It reopens, moreover, neglected approaches to the study of emotion. You will recollect that Shand[27] named an important group of human emotions, e.g. hope and disappointment, 'prospective emotions of desire', and that to these McDougall[28] added a group of retrospective emotions, e.g. regret and remorse. Few psychologists except Stern, who included a chapter on 'The Temporal Reference of Feeling' in his *General Psychology*,[29] have paid much attention to the Shand-McDougall scheme. Yet explanations in terms of physiological concomitants and expressive movements have not taken us far in the understanding of the more complex human emotions. Temporal reference may, after all, hold the key to a more fruitful interpretation.

But more than this temporal integration may not impossibly throw light on some of the primary problems of personality development and breakdown. Bowlby[30] recently noted that the young child's personality develops hand in hand with a sense of continuity in time. The deprived child never acquires this sense, and remains at the mercy of momentary impulses. An important factor in the development of a sense of continuity is the constantly recurring presence of the mother, who thus acts as what Bowlby terms 'a psychic organizer' to the child. A year before Bowlby published his report Lauretta Bender[31] had noted essentially the same thing. 'Defect in time concepts is one of the most significant problems', she writes, in children isolated from the mother. 'This may be related to lack of identification as a continuous temporal process . . . it appears that we develop our time concept from passage of time in our earliest love relationships, in the going and coming of the mother. These children do not remember the past; they cannot benefit from past mistakes; consequently they have no future goals and cannot be motivated to control their behaviour for future gains.'

In breakdowns of personality, both mild and severe, temporal disorganization is a common feature. Schizophrenic patients tend to lose the sense of temporal sequence, 'the ability to enmesh the flux of activity within a temporal schema', as Heinz Werner[32] puts it. After frontal lobe operations and brain damage there seem also to be temporal disturbances which generally go with an inability to plan and anticipate. And is not the difference in the capacity for temporal integration the common feature of Goldstein's distinctions between concrete and abstract behaviour?

Even in milder forms of personality disturbance temporal constriction is commonly reported. Professor Hamson,[33] of Cambridge, who was himself a prisoner of war, states that the mark of transition from the mental daze that follows captivity was that 'the prisoner no longer lived from day to day passively largely or with exclusively immediate object, but began to plan so far as he might and to dispose of himself and his circumstance over some span of time and with some variety'. Or consider *les clochards*, the Parisian down-and-outs recently described by Schneider,[34] whose horizon is the moment, who have no history, nor aspirations, but have surrendered unconditionally to the passage of events.

Finally, observe how temporal integration within the individual mind is supplemented and supported by society; by official time measurement and by calendars; by records of the past and by blueprints of the future; by the whole ordered scheme of regular and timed communal activity, about which Norbert Wiener has proposed some interesting speculations in his recent Fawley lecture.[35]

According to Mowrer[36] 'the essence of integrated behaviour is the capacity to bring the future into the psychological present'. Perhaps we might extend Mowrer's analysis and say that integrated behaviour involves at the human level at least three things: it involves the assimilation of the past, both personal past experience and, as man cannot function except as a social being, the accumulated traditions of his community; it involves, secondly, prudence and foresight; and, thirdly, it involves the sense of self-identity and continuity. If we are to explain behaviour in its most characteristically human forms without having recourse to animism it is to the concept of temporal integration that we must turn. It is because it seems to me among the most promising immediate lines of advance in psychological theory that I have ventured, with a full awareness of my inadequacies, to write about temporal integration and behaviour.

REFERENCES

1. MILL, J. S., 1843, *A System of Logic*, London: Parker.
2. KETCHUM, J. D., 1955, 'Psychology Versus Man', *Canad. J. Psychol.*, IX, 91.
3. CANTRIL, H., 1955, 'Toward a Humanistic Psychology', ETC: *A Review of General Semantics, XII*, 278.
4. AUGUSTINE, ST, 397, *Confessions*, Book XI, 28 (Loeb edition).
5. LASHLEY, K. S., 1951, 'The Problem of Serial Order in Behaviour', in LLOYD A. JEFFRESS (ed.), *Cerebral Mechanisms in Behaviour*, New York: Wiley.
6. MILLER, G. A., 1951, *Language and Communication*, New York: McGraw-Hill.
7. HEAD, H., 1926, *Aphasia and Kindred Disorders of Speech*, London: Cambridge University Press.
8. HUME, D., 1740, *A Treatise of Human Nature* (ed. GREEN, T. H., and GROSE, T. H.), London: Longmans, Green.
9. GREEN, T. H., 1874, see ref. 8, Introduction.

10. MILL, J. S., 1865, *An Examination of Sir Wm. Hamilton's Philosophy*, London: Longmans, Green.

11. WARD, J., 1886, 'Psychology', *Encycl. Brit.* (IXth edition).

12. STOUT, G. F., 1896, *Analytic Psychology*, London: Sonnenschein.

13. STOUT, G. F., 1899, *A Manual of Psychology*, London: Clive.

14. JAMES, W., 1890, *The Principles of Psychology*, New York: Holt.

15 M LLER, G. E., and SCHUMANN, F., 1894, 'Expt. Beiträge zur Untersuchung des Gedächtnisses', *Z. Psychol., VI*, 81.

16. HEAD, H., *et al.*, 1920, *Studies in Neurology*, London: Frowde.

17. HUMPHREY, G., 1933, *The Nature of Learning*, London: Kegan Paul.

18. KATONA, G., 1940, *Organising and Memorizing*, New York: Columbia University Press.

19. MOWRER, O. H., 1945, 'Time and Integrative Learning', *Psychol. Rev., LII*, 61.

20 MORGAN, C. LLOYD, 1930, *The Animal Mind*, London: Arnold.

21. PIAGET, J., 1947, *The Psychology of Intelligence* (English trans. 1950), London: Routledge and Kegan Paul.

22. HEBB, D. O., 1949, *The Organization of Behaviour*, New York: Wiley.

23. FESSARD, A. E., 1954, 'Mechanisms of Nervous Integration and Conscious Experience', in DELAFRESNAYE, J. F. (ed.), *Brain Mechanisms and Consciousness*, Oxford: Blackwell.

24. BARTLETT, F. C., 1955, 'Fifty Years of Psychology', *Occup. Psychol., XXIX*, 203.

25. KÖHLER, W., 1925, *The Mentality of Apes*, New York: Harcourt, Brace.

26. HEBB, D. O., 1954, in DELAFRESNAYE, J. F. (ed.), *Brain Mechanisms and Consciousness*, Oxford: Blackwell.

27. SHAND, A. F., 1914, *The Foundations of Character*, London: Macmillan.

28. MCDOUGALL, W., 1919, *An Introduction to Social Psychology*, Supplementary chapter to XIVth edition, London: Methuen.

29. STERN, W., 1938, *General Psychology from the Personalistic Standpoint* (English trans.), New York: Macmillan.

30. BOWLBY, J., 1951, *Maternal Love and Mental Health*, W.H.O. Report.

31. BENDER, LAURETTA, 1950, 'Anxiety in Disturbed Children', in HOCH, P. H., and ZUBIN, J. (ed.), *Anxiety*, New York: Grune and Stratton.

32. WERNER, H., 1948, *Comparative Psychology of Mental Development*, Chicago: Follet Publ. Co.

33. HAMSON, C. J., 1955, 'Reflections on Captivity', *Listener, LIII*, 368.

34. SCHNEIDER, P., 1955, 'The Minimum Man', *Listener, LIV*, 397.

35. WIENER, N., 1955, *Time and Organization*, Fawley Lecture, No. 2, University of Southampton.

36. MOWRER, O. H., 1950, *Learning Theory and Personality Dynamics*, New York: Ronald.

M

RESEARCH TECHNIQUES IN PSYCHO-ANALYSIS AND IN GENERAL PSYCHOLOGY: AN ESSAY IN CONTRASTS

BY EDWARD GLOVER

Just over ten years ago I published a review of research methods in psycho-analysis[1] the primary aim of which was frankly political, namely, to promote the development of an international organization devoted to research in psycho-analysis. This project, I maintained, would involve a preparatory phase during which the working concepts of psycho-analysis would be re-examined and re-defined in order to establish standard units of comparison.

I

Briefly the argument ran as follows: owing partly to the conditions under which psycho-analysis is conducted and partly to the use of interpretative techniques of investigation it is not possible to employ fully or fully to depend on the forms of scientific control customary in most other sciences. Not only so, there is some evidence that psycho-analysts tend to abstain from applying such reliable controls as are available, with the result that views gain currency and sanction on hearsay evidence. The *ipse dixit* acquires the validity of an attested conclusion, largely by a process of repetition. This process is naturally accelerated when the proponent of the views in question happens to be a training analyst. In such instances the factors of transference and counter-transference operate. Added to which the influence of fashion in psycho-analytical thinking results in the development of 'slogans' which obstruct free development. Psycho-analytical candidates are trained to practise therapy rather than the techniques of research. There is in fact little discrimination in the psycho-analytical field between controlled research and individual opinion, which cannot always be distinguished from unchecked speculation.

Reviewing the problem of controlled research in psycho-analysis, it was maintained that the data of observation are rarely defined in a manner suitable for purposes of control and that in particular there is so far no reliable control of the process of interpretation. Moreover, psycho-analysis has not yet provided quantitative measures, e.g. measures of the intensity of psychic stimulation determining the persistence or absence of any given mental state. The severity of symptom-formation (the customary psycho-analytical measure of intensity) measures only the *margin* of mental instability. Not only so, there are no agreed definitions of basic concepts, such as those of mental structures or mechanisms. In other words, there is a lack of suitable psychic 'entities' which would permit the application of a mathematical 'operator' system by which mental properties can be examined, and the conclusions subsequently tested by the techniques of prediction. Lack of control of interpretative techniques is the Achilles heel of psycho-analytical research. Therapeutic criteria (e.g. whether a given interpretation brings about symptomatic improvement) are illusory partly because the influence of 'suggestion' cannot be excluded and partly because we have no reliable statistics of therapeutic results. Granted that intuition is the most precious of all instruments of research, we must nevertheless take what steps we can to prevent its debasement to a form of authoritarianism.

Standardization of terms and concepts is an essential preliminary to controlled research; and this in turn involves the organization of an agreed clinical system of psycho-analysis. In particular the various character disorders have yet to be accurately rated and correlated with symptom-formations. So far no two observers follow the same diagnostic and differential systems. Unsatisfactory as the questionnaire method is in many respects, its employment might bring us nearer to the facts than the accumulation of an increasingly extensive, but unorganized, literature. Training analysis is no guarantee of research capacity; there is still considerable confusion between the aims of research and those of therapy. The problem becomes more and more pressing every year. What is urgently needed is the compilation of a complete survey of psycho-analytical concepts, as it were a Domesday Book of the science. We must settle down to the arduous task of defining terms, verifying criteria and developing reliable statistics.

II

At this point it is desirable to remind the reader of the circumstances under which the paper summarized above was written and the specific aim of the survey. Otherwise those who do not subscribe to the tenets of psycho-analysis may jump to the conclusion that the criticisms advanced constituted a damaging attack on the validity of psycho-analytic technique. And if they should happen to be students of general descriptive or laboratory psychology, where the processes of controlled observation and experiment are comparatively easy to follow, they may even be ready to congratulate themselves on the scientific advantages that they obtain in their own particular field.

This was not at all the intention of the paper, which was concerned primarily with the need to sharpen the methods of scientific investigation employed by psycho-analysts. It did not imply that non-analytical methods of investigation, however much they exploit the 'control' systems favoured in natural science, are therefore more free from error. In a recent research note[2] I have endeavoured to set out the fundamental weakness of the systems applied in general and educational psychology, in social psychology and in sociology, taking as paradigmatic the methods of 'controlled' observation practised in the field of criminology. The argument is therefore complementary to that already set out. It runs as follows: research on delinquency (and in other psychological fields) is retarded by the absence of comparative surveys of *methodology*. The 'controlled' observation is one of the most valuable of scientific procedures and psycho-analytic findings are frequently criticized because of lack of such controls. Nevertheless, owing to the existence of unconscious mental structures and functions, the so-called 'controlled' experiment in mental science is subject also to gross error. In any case the final estimation of mental factors depends not just on statistical investigations but on the *interpretation* of the statistical results. And this in spite of the fact that the interpretative process is itself liable to gross subjective error. Whilst admitting the possibilities of error the psycho-analyst maintains that the data which constitute the groundwork of 'controlled' investigations in general psychology are merely *end results* which seldom give any direct indication of the mental processes leading to them: hence the interpretation of unconscious factors, however subject to error, is indispensable.

Study of the 'family history', one of the most elementary forms of 'control', indicates that in spite of the apparent similarity of familial conditions many of the siblings in the delinquent's family are non-delinquent. And *mutatis mutandis* this generalization is also true of the neurotic and psychotic. The familial control is not in any scientific sense a control: it is a problem in psycho-dynamics. What then are we to think of those standard investigations in which a system of *extrafamilial* 'matched controls' is adopted? What the descriptive psychologist describes as the total personality is an end product which in ordinary circumstances does not give any clear indication of its origin and development, its strength and its weakness. The dynamic, structural and economic factors which determine the personality vary from person to person. Although, therefore, in any two cases the end result may appear to be identical (as in some forms of theft) the antecedent processes may be entirely different. In the ordinary processes of control we are really checking one unknown with another. If, for example, we limit our investigations to behaviouristic data we have no means of distinguishing a 'latent' delinquent who is apparently law-abiding from a true or stable non-delinquent. This applies with particular force to the study of psychopathy, for we have no means of checking the number of potential psychopaths in the 'normal' population from which control cases are usually recruited. Indeed, if we want effective controls of anti-social individuals we might well choose them from amongst the homosexual population where ethical standards are often of a high level! In short, to make the control system effective we must submit each control case to as rigorous an investigation of his unconscious and conscious reactions as we do in the psycho-analytical diagnosis of pathological types.

From all this there follows the somewhat disconcerting conclusion that under present systems of control we have no sound justification for abandoning a causal theory simply because the application of statistical controls appears to show that it is non-specific. When allegedly scientific procedures appear to point conclusively in one direction, the investigator of deep and unconscious factors should not be too perturbed if these conclusions run counter to his own interpretations. Although apparently wrong by the standards of natural science he may yet be right by the standards of depth psychology. Freud was able to establish some of the most important laws regarding human behaviour on the strength of isolated observations of unconscious function. Depth rather than numerical extension of observations has been and still is the consistent policy of the dynamic psychologist. In short since we understand 'normality' much less than we do 'abnormality', the 'control' case is more of a puzzle than the pathological type he is intended to control.

III

Although the two points of view summarized above may appear to end in a number of logical contradictions, there is in fact a simple explanation of these. Mental phenomena can be ordered in distinct layers ranging from (pre)-conscious to the deepest unconscious. General psychology is concerned with the behaviouristic aspects of the (pre)-conscious system: psycho-analysis with the interaction of the dynamic unconscious and the (pre)-conscious system. Up to the present the disciplines suitable for investigating the (pre)-conscious have proved inadequate for exploring the dynamic unconscious. The immediate problem can therefore be stated clearly enough: how can our (pre)-conscious investigations be made to dovetail with explorations of the unconscious. So far the most fruitful technique would appear to depend on a fuller exploration of questionnaire methods, provided always the questions take cognizance of unconscious function and endeavour to tap the roots of unconscious motivation. This means however that the psycho-analyst must play a leading role in framing the questionnaires. Some work along these lines has recently been published and promises fairly well.[3]

Such methods however, do not solve the problem of standardizing theoretical concepts for purposes of control. A certain amount of progress in this direction can however be recorded during the past ten years. The literature is too extensive to be summarized in a brief review, but it may be said that the work falls into two distinct groups, viz. contributions in which existing analytical concepts are re-examined *per se* and contributions in which existing concepts are modified or substituted by fresh concepts and theories. Of these groups the former is the more reliable: but the time has not yet come when a sufficiency of definitions can be formulated for purposes of statisticial control. With the best will in the world many of them are still of too general and imprecise a nature. As for the clinical data of psycho-analysis progress in precise definition is still extremely slow: indeed the data cannot be reduced to order in the absence of systematic investigation by an international board of psycho-analytical clinicians. And incidentally, until this is done, statistics of therapeutic results must be treated with a considerable degree of reserve.

Finally, regarding the vexed but nevertheless vital problem of criteria of interpretation, it can only be said that so far only a beginning has been made with attempts to control the process in a satisfactory way. Interestingly enough, whilst some of these have been made by psycho-analysts, others have been contributed by psycho-analytically oriented general psychologists.[4] Suggestive as these are we cannot expect too much of them for some time to. come; and this because of two main difficulties; first, because of gaps that still exist in our knowledge of early (deep) unconscious processes; and, second, because many unconscious functions are exceedingly hard to measure (cf. the processes of unconscious suggestion and transference). The attempt to weigh imponderables may in course of time gain momentum; in the meantime we must fall back on the summation of probabilities arrived at by processes of interpretation, however fallible or subject to error these may be.

REFERENCES

1. GLOVER, E., 1952, 'Research Methods in Psycho-analysis', *Internat. J. Psycho-anal.*, *33*, 4 (reprinted in GLOVER, E., 1956, *On the Early Development of Mind*, London: Allen and Unwin).
2. GLOVER, E., 1962, 'Psycho-analysis and "controlled" research in Delinquency', *Brit. J. Criminol.*, *3*, 63.
3. See for example:
   (i) BONNARD, A., 1955, 'Clinical Standards of Prognosis in Delinquency', *Proc. 3rd Cong. Internat. Crim. Assoc.*;
   (ii) CARR-SAUNDERS, A. M., MANNHEIM, H., and RHODES, E. C., 1942, *Young Offenders*, London: Cambridge University Press;
   (iii) GLUECK, S., and GLUECK, E. T., 1957, *Unravelling Juvenile Delinquency*' New York Commonwealth Fund, Cambridge: Harvard University Press;
   (iv) GRYGIER, T. G., 1955, 'Infantile Complexes, their Measurement and Significance for Social Psychology', *Bull. Brit. Psychol. Soc.*, *26*, 56; 1957, 'The Dynamic Personality Inventory. A Preliminary Notice', *Bull. Nat. Found. Educ. Research*, *9*, 39: 1958, 'Statistical and psychoanalytical criteria in the development of the Dynamic Personality Inventory', *The Rorschach Newsletter*, *3*, 5.
   (v) HOLT, R. R., 1958, 'Clinical and statistical prediction; a reformulation and some new data', *J. Abn. Soc. Psychol.*, *56*, 1; 1960, 'Recent developments in psycho-analytic ego psychology and their implications for diagnostic testing', *J. Project. Tech.*, *4*, 254;
   (vi) KROUT, M. H., and KROUT-TABIN, J., 1954, 'Measuring personality in developmental terms: the personal preference scale', *Genet. Psychol. Monog.*, *50*, 289;
   (vii) LOEVINGER, J., 1957, 'Objective tests as instruments of psychological theory', *Psychol. Rep.*, *3*, 635;
   (viii) MANNHEIM, H., and WILKINS, L. T., 1955, *Prediction Methods in Relation to Borstal Training*, London: H.M.S.O.
4. See *inter alios;*
   (i) BELLAK, L., and SMITH, M. BREWSTER, 1956, 'An experimental exploration of the psycho-analytic process', *Psycho-anal. Quart.*, *25*, 385;

(ii) BELLAK, L., 1958, 'Studying the psycho-analytic process by the method of short-range prediction and judgment', *Brit. J. med. Psychol.*, *31*, 249;

(iii) BELLAK, L., 1961, 'Research in psychoanalysis', *Psychoanal. Quart.*, *30*, 519:

(iv) KUBIE, L. S., 1952, 'Problems and technique of psycho-analytic validation and progress', in PUMPIAN-MINDLIN, E. (ed.), *Psycho-analysis as science*, Stanford, California: Stanford University Press;

(v) KUBIE, L. S., 1956, 'Some unsolved problems of psycho-analytic psycho-therapy', in FROMM-REICHMANN, F., and MORENO, J. (ed.), *Progress in Psychotherapy*, New York: Grune and Stratton;

(vi) KNAPP, P. W., 'Short term psycho-analytic and psychosomatic predictions' (to be published);

(vii) RUBINSTEIN, E. A., and PARLOFF, M. B. (ed.), 1959, *Research in Psychotherapy*, Washington, D.C.: American Psycho-analytic Association;

(viii) STRUPP, H. H., 1960, *Psychotherapists in Action*, New York: Grune and Stratton;

(ix) STRUPP, H. H., 1962, 'Psychotherapy', *Ann. Rev. Psychol.*, *13*, 445.

CHAPTER 22

THE EFFECTIVE USE OF MANPOWER*

BY ALEC RODGER

I

The aim of this chapter is to draw attention to some of the ways in which occupational psychologists may be expected to contribute to the delineation and solution of recurrent manpower problems.

Occupational psychology, as I shall present it, is both a science and a technology: it encompasses not only the discovery of knowledge but also its well-contrived use. The occupational psychologist gathers and applies knowledge about the behaviour of people as workers of every kind and every level. As a scientist he seeks better understanding of internal determinants of their behaviour; and as a technologist he helps, through that understanding, to improve their effectiveness at work. When he does all this in an industrial setting, the occupational psychologist is called an industrial psychologist; and when he does it in a military setting he is called a military psychologist.

It is of course as a technologist, an applier of scientific knowledge, that the occupational psychologist is best known. In this role he can usefully describe his fields of interests in terms of the main problems he helps others to solve. These are, basically, the problem of *fitting the man to the job* (through the improvement of methods of vocational guidance, personnel selection and occupational training) and the complementary problem of *fitting the job to the man* (through the improvement of methods and organization of work, equipment design, and working conditions of diverse kinds, including rewards).[1]

They are problems he 'helps' others to solve, because his techno-logical function is essentially advisory, not executive. Even as an

---

* A revised and shortened version of the 1955 presidential address to Section J of the British Association for the Advancement of Science.

M*

adviser he may be, and often should be, one of several. He does not set himself up as *the* expert in any of the fields in which he operates. His particular brief is to look at all of them with his mind on those internal determinants of human behaviour which I shall call, broadly, capacities and inclinations. That is, he is concerned everywhere, and all the time, with personal characteristics which govern what people, as workers, *can* do, and what they may be *inclined* to do. The whole point of his training as a psychologist has been to make him a specialist in this sphere; to make him more precise than others in his knowledge of the nature, development, pathology, assessment and use of individual human capacities and inclinations.

He will commonly think of these characteristics as rooted in 'traits' of various degrees of generality and persistence,[2] but for some of his purposes he may set trait theories aside in favour of, for example, field theory or information theory.

In short, no matter what sort of problem it is he is helping others to solve—whether it is concerned with fitting the man to the job or with fitting the job to the man—the occupational psychologist's practical task is to bring to bear on it, in a skilful fashion, our knowledge of human capacities and inclinations. If he cannot do that better than the next man, there is no justification for his existence.

To this series of bald pronouncements, let me add a qualification. For some may well ask, 'What is the place, in all this, of other related sciences—physiology, for example, on the one hand; and sociology on the other?' It is clear that the physiologist, as well as the psychologist, is concerned with human capacities and inclinations; and that the sociologist, even though he is not concerned with such personal characteristics directly, is at least concerned with some of the circumstances that mould them and are moulded by them. It is not my intention to examine here the links between psychology, physiology and sociology; but let me suggest in passing that the connection between psychology and physiology deserves more rigorous treatment than it receives in those textbooks of psychology which make unconvincing distinctions between muscles, glands and nerves, to be found at one level, and something called 'the individual as a whole' to be found at another—higher—level.

It is sometimes both convenient and salutary for the psychologist modestly to regard his science as what I have called elsewhere[3] 'residual'; to look upon it, indeed, as a biological science dealing with 'left-overs', whose function is to take up the explanation of human behaviour at the point at which the physiologist has to say, 'I'm sorry, but I can't do any more—not yet, anyway'. This is the point at which human capacities and inclinations become so hard to think about and detect in the physiologist's way, that other explanatory concepts and other methods of investigation are needed. It is the point at which we cease to talk of a man's muscles, glands and nerves, and talk instead about his abilities and his interests, or about his skills and his attitudes, or even—if we are so minded—about his ego and his id. The task of the psychologist, on this view, is primarily one of clearing up after the physiologist. I hope I shall not be accused of minimizing the scope and importance of psychology in expressing it. Certainly, at the present time, what is left over when the physiologists have done all the explaining they can manage is varied, complex and extensive enough to justify confidence that psychologists need have no fear of working themselves out of a job. But there is, too, the fact that the psychologist, in playing his part in the explanation of human behaviour, may help the physiologist to play his. In recent years there have been numerous demonstrations[4, 5] of ways in which techniques used by psychologists can illuminate the problems of physiologists.

Such, then, is the base for which I approach my theme, the effective use of manpower. In discussing it, I shall assume that it is desirable that manpower should be used effectively; that what we call our 'work' should make good use of our capacities and be in accord with our inclinations. Of course, we may experience great difficulty in using all our capacities in our work, and we may have inclinations that are in conflict with one another. In the event, we may have to compromise: some of the components in an individual's psychological armoury may have to be modified, and others may have to find expression outside his work. My assumption about the desirability of the effective use of manpower is one that I ask you to accept, at least temporarily. There are, of course, various grounds on which you might do so, from the 'national economy' plea to the 'enlightened self-interest' argument. Some may give it, as I do myself, a religious basis.

II

I shall marshal my reflections under six headings. The first three— *vocational guidance, personnel selection, occupational training*—belong to the group of problems I have labelled 'fitting the man to the job'. The other three—*methods and organization of work, equipment design, working conditions and rewards*—are problems of 'fitting the job to the man'.

But let me introduce here a general point I shall emphasize later. These six fields of interest of the occupational psychologist are continuous and not easily separated. What seems to be a personnel selection problem may turn out to be largely a training problem. Many organizations have hankered after better personnel selection procedures to improve the quality of their operatives, of their apprentices, of their clerks, of their salesmen, of their supervisors, when what they have needed in the first instance has been a better training method to enable them to make more effective use of the people they already have available.[6] Similarly, a methods of work problem may be revealed as —at least primarily—a working conditions problem. However substantially a new method may be capable of increasing productivity, it may in fact prove highly disappointing, if those who are asked to use it pursue restrictive practices, either of the well-recognized kind derived from group pressures or of the neglected but important variety which arises quite simply from private quarrels between fellow-workers.

A major cause of the comparatively slow development of occupational psychology as a whole has been a continuing disregard of the unity of our problems.[7] It springs to some extent from the unfortunate fact that those who are interested in fitting the man to the job tend to lack enthusiasm for fitting the job to the man, and vice versa. This we must recognize as a serious matter, because it often leads to the dissipation of research funds on projects too narrowly conceived. An investigator whose concern is mainly with fitting the job to the man may be reluctant even to explore the possible influence, on work performance, of persisting individual differences in capacities—for instance, in what some still call general intelligence—which are often found to be important by those whose concern is mainly with fitting the man to the job. He may indeed be inclined to assume that for his purpose all men may be regarded as equal in their capacities, or nearly so; that there is 'a standard man'. If he makes this assumption, it is natural that he should not worry greatly about the nature or size of his population samples.[8]

III

Now let me tackle the first of my six specific topics, vocational guidance. There is, surely, a case for supposing that arrangements for the giving of some occupational advice to individuals would be generally regarded as the firmest foundation for any plan for the effective use of manpower. We have learned to be cautious about making the assumption that satisfaction with work will be closely associated with satis-factoriness in it;[9, 10] but it seems probable that people who are not suited to their work by both capacity and inclination are unlikely to become highly productive.[11] Yet this, and the consequent need for advice, is not commonly recognized. It is occasionally suggested that vocational guidance is unimportant, because people—especially young people—are very adaptable; or that it is useless, because even in days of full employment most people have to take what they can get locally; or that it is undesirable, either because it is good for people—again, especially young people—to make a few mistakes or because we should not interfere with people's lives. Of course, there is something worth discussing in all these views, and in several others commonly expressed: so there is in the attitude of many employers, who are not unnaturally anxious lest potential employees providentially living on their door-steps should be steered elsewhere. Nevertheless, it seems unquestion-able that here, in the vocational guidance field, we have a serious gap in our defences against waste.

From the occupational psychologist's standpoint, the chief and most pressing need of a vocational guidance service is for systematic, long-term 'follow-up' studies designed to reveal, by the independent application of appropriate criteria, strong and weak features of currently-used concepts and methods. Inevitably, in a period of labour scarcity, this idea causes apprehension among employers, who fear that such studies would have an undesirably unsettling effect on the samples of young workers from whom, and about whom, enquiries would be made. In a period of job scarcity, proposals of the kind cause workers to become worried, lest the outcome should be their replace-ment by others considered more suitable. On the availability of rele-vant, accurate, comprehensive follow-up information depends the solution of all our major problems in this field, including the most fundamental of all, that of deciding how to group and grade occupa-tions for vocational guidance purposes. What is required here is a substantial series of integrated studies of the main things which, by a method of contrasts, can be shown to differentiate those who succeed in an occupation from those who prove less successful in it or who fail.[12, 13, 2]

Of the other vocational guidance problems awaiting our attention, I must mention one in particular, because, if we are justified in assuming that a person is unlikely to be maximally productive unless he is satisfied with his work, it is important. It is created by the setting-up in large organizations, public and private, of what are designated 'general' classes of employees. The situation is typically one in which a number of previously fairly specialized small occupational groups—engaged, for example, on this and that kind of clerical work—are absorbed into one big group—for example, a general clerical class—with the intention of providing both more flexibility within the organization and more adequate opportunities for promotion. The 'generalist' system tends of course to involve a person in more changes of work than the 'specialist' system. Not infrequently he finds that, when he wants to move onward and upward, he is expected to 'broaden his experience' by taking assignments of little direct interest to him. Here we have a source of waste that unquestionably needs investigation. The authorities would be wise to take appropriate chances of comparing the satisfaction and satisfactoriness of specialists and generalists engaged on the same type of work in different organizations; and of specialists in an organization before and after their absorption into a general class in the same organization. It may be that some of the more obvious advantages of the general class notion are cancelled out by its tendency to produce a higher proportion of people who have no enthusiasm at all for some of the jobs they have to do. And it may therefore be that, if general classes are to be worth having, those who arrange their work and allocate their members will have to take more account of what should be essentially a vocational guidance approach to their problems. I do not suggest that organizations which have general classes have not considered this matter at all; but I strongly suspect that thorough, open-minded study of it would prove to be rewarding, not least in the British Civil Service, one of whose 'desk' classes, the executive, now deals with work which ranges all the way from public relations to computer programming.

IV

After vocational guidance comes personnel selection. Here we are thinking of the man or woman, the boy or girl, who—we may suppose —has been given advice on the choice of an occupation and is now a candidate for a particular appointment or training course. It is often said in times of full employment, 'Our selection procedure just doesn't work nowadays: we have to take anybody we can get'. When applicants are plentiful, there is a tendency for employers to say, 'We don't need selection procedures, because we can easily replace anyone who turns out to be unsatisfactory'. The comments suggest that many have been misled by a name. For a personnel selection procedure is primarily a procedure for the assessment of capacities and inclinations; and if it is appropriately planned it is usable not only for selecting and rejecting but for other purposes too. There is a considerable need for careful stage-by-stage assessment procedures designed to enable employers and training institutions to make the most effective use of their recruits, by providing a suitable service midway between guidance and selection, and spread over a period. It is true that the notion operates already to some extent, for example, in the 'executive trainee' schemes of some big firms; but in industry there is not much sign of the systematic and continuous study of the capacities and inclinations of people below the management level. However, the mere fact that it is appearing high up is presumably a sign that the boardroom thinks it may be on to something good, so perhaps we may be cautiously optimistic. We must, of course, be wise in our formulation of assessment procedures. A rashly contrived scheme is very likely to defeat its own ends by frightening potential recruits away and antagonizing those who remain.

In advocating what would be essentially a running audit of the capacities and inclinations of a whole organization, I am not pleading for a nightmare of psychological testing. The corner-stone of the personnel audit, like the corner-stone of ordinary vocational guidance, should be well-designed and conveniently-operated reporting procedures, which aim at the quick and painless extraction of thoroughly relevant facts and opinions from knowledgeable people. On this method of preparing to make effective use of human capacities and inclinations, industry has much to learn from the British Civil Service[14] and from the Defence Services. For reporting on people below management level there is a great potential value in the type of workshop report form used in IRUs, on which a supervisor is asked to rate his workers on a short series of five-point scales, composed of items defined at the extremes of the scales by opposed descriptive statements expressed in ordinary workshop language.[15]

On management selection specifically I shall venture only one comment. It is time some responsible organization embarked on the delicate but fundamental task of studying management 'requirements' by the method of contrasts I have mentioned in my remarks on vocational guidance. Its aim would be to distinguish between the capacities and inclinations of managers who by agreed criteria are held to be successful and managers who by the same criteria are held to be less successful.[16, 2] It might, of course, be found that the word 'management' covered duties so many and various that useful generalization would prove very hard indeed. It might be revealed also that accepted standards of performance in them differed so much, from place to place and time to time, that they served merely to drive home the fact that what we call the requirements of any occupation are always dependent on the state of its labour market. But even negative findings of these kinds would be valuable if they helped to protect us from the unverified—and often unverifiable—statements about management selection and training which flow rather freely in some business circles.

v̂

Now I turn to my third heading, occupational training. Clearly, a good programme for the effective use of manpower must ensure that sound guidance and sound selection or allocation are followed by sound training: all are important phases in the process of fitting the man to the job. There are three parts of this field which should increasingly engage the attention of the occupational psychologist in industry— those concerned with the training of managers, apprentices, and operatives.

In the management field there is a particular need to explore ways in which men whose education has been mainly in the humanities can be turned into production managers. Wartime experience in the selection and training of potential engineer officers suggests that we have no right to assume that a young man who has followed such course to the age of eighteen, or even later, cannot hope to become competent in an occupation which demands quick appreciation of things technical. Nor need the discovery of these occupational hermaphrodites be a laborious and hazardous affair of trial and error. There is probably no problem the occupational psychologist has tackled more successfully than that of helping an organization, civil or military, quickly to detect technical potentialities in apparently unlikely people.

When we look at apprentice training in Britain, we should be greatly disturbed by what we see. A prominent educational administrator has recently described the apprentice system as 'archaic'. It is more than that: in its commonest forms, it is wasteful too. Fortunately, we are gradually realizing the fact, helped rather than hindered by some of the system's most determined supporters, who refuse to consider clearly desirable changes in age of entry and length of apprenticeship. Many boys remain at school considerably beyond the upper age limit for acceptance for most apprenticeships, and are therefore precluded from entering them. These tend on the whole to be the abler boys. They are lost to trades which need them. In the meantime, some employers' associations and trade unions who have seen the red light are stealing a march on the reactionaries. Changes are being made in the rules about starting-ages and length of training in certain occupations. Certainly, it would seem expedient to allow apprentices some credit for having continued their ordinary education, provided they have reached suitable standards in it.

But this would provide only a partial solution of the problem. We need a thorough examination of the system and all the good and bad restrictive practices associated with it. Many apprentices are not being trained in a profitable way; they often waste their time on jobs no one would dare to mention in a printed syllabus; they are often kept on particular jobs far too long, because production is given priority over training; and they often stand no chance of gaining the breadth of experience the potential journeyman should have. It is true that in some industries all these problems are receiving attention. Requirements are being modified; training is becoming more systematic; and exceptions to rules are being made. But we must not imagine that progressive-looking agreements reached on these matters at the national level are always acted on at the local level: they are not.

The problem is important, because the coming of automation and other technological changes are forcing us to review all our ideas about training, all our ideas of who should be trained for what and how. Now, clearly, is the time for fresh thinking on the training of young people, especially for the skilled trades; and for reflection on relevant evidence of the sort already assembled in military and civil establishments which have managed to produce skilled adult workers for various trades in far less time than is commonly admitted to be practicable. The medical profession have long since dropped their apprenticeship approach to training, but—particularly in recent years, through their further development of the system of junior hospital appointments and trainee assistantships—have conserved its most valuable feature, by ultimate attachment of the newly qualified doctor to a 'master' who provides experience in the practical use of technologies of medicine and surgery.[17] Why should not this be done more widely in the skilled trades?

The training of people to operate machines of one kind and another in industry and the Defence Services has presented the occupational psychologist with some knotty problems, and research in this field is gradually eliciting new facts, especially about the so-called 'perceptual' element in operating skills, which may prove important.[18] I say 'may', because much of this work is conducted in a laboratory setting, on a restricted range of operations, and with small groups of subjects who lack the ordinary industrial trainee's inducements to learn and are often of much higher intellectual calibre. Generalization from facts revealed in such circumstances must be hazardous. Moreover, it may turn out that some of these inquiries are appreciably less relevant to industrial than to military operations. For example, studies of some of the stresses which corrode skills may continue to be of practical importance to the Defence Services when the development of automation in industry has reduced their value elsewhere. But certainly the need for other investigations in this group—for instance, on the effects of stresses associated with increasing age—must be regarded as pressing. The time is not far off when one-fifth of the population of this country will be of pensionable age, by present standards; and presumably another fifth will have to be regarded as 'getting on'. One useful finding of research on ageing[19] has been that what is often needed for the older worker is not 'light' work but less strenuously paced work. And if we put together the main conclusions emerging, we should probably decide that a substantial contribution to the effective use of manpower could perhaps be made by the re-training of many machine operators in their forties, for work of other kinds, while they are still trainable.[20]

VI

From my first trio of topics (*guidance, selection, training*), grouped together as problems of fitting the man to the job, I now pass to the second trio (*methods and organization of work, equipment design, working conditions and rewards*) grouped together as problems of fitting the job to the man.

The investigation of methods and organization of work in industry, known under various titles of the 'motion study' and 'methods study' sort, has of course been hampered by fears of rate-cutting, overwork and redundancy, as well as by sheer dislike of inquiry and change. The fears have not been without foundation, and for this reason such problems as these cannot in practice be divorced from problems of pay, security and status, which belong to the last of my six topics, working conditions and rewards. But let us for a moment try to consider them in isolation, to identify the nature of the occupational psychologist's concern with them. Is he merely another efficiency-monger to be entered on the list as a straight competitor of the industrial consultant, the work-study practitioner, the time and motion study engineer, the production engineer, the methods engineer, the costs and works accountant, the organization and methods man, and all the rest? From my early general remarks about his function it will be clear once more that my answer to these questions is, 'No, he is—or should be—a collaborator with a special assignment'. In day-to-day studies of methods of work, his particular business is to help to ensure that new procedures are suited to the capacities and inclinations of those who will be expected to use them. If he is competent, he will be able to perform this task with greater precision, speed and economy than others.

But he has important research interests in this field. Let me mention three of them. In the first place, though extensive use is made in methods study of certain principles of motion economy enunciated by Gilbreth[21] and others,[22] we know very little indeed about the circumstances in which they do and do not hold good. Secondly, the time studies which are widely used as a means of comparing the relative values of different methods, as well as—more extensively—for rate-setting, usually have no scientific leg to stand on because of the nature and extent of the arbitrary judgments they involve.[23] What is going on in a time-study man's mind when he 'rates' a job as, say, a 60, an 80? How exactly does he make his subsequent 'allowances' for what is called 'compensating rest'? How does he, especially when he is in a hurry, decide which workers he is going to study? We know hardly anything about the answers to these questions; and until we have them in reasonably satisfactory form we shall be entitled to wonder whether a good deal of current practice in time study is not perhaps a piece of mumbo-jumbo, developed—by agreement between managements and workers—to provide an apparently rational basis for the payment of wages whose amount has already been settled by quite other means. It was the research director of the Textile Workers' Union of America[24] who said: 'Time study . . . is a procedure for careful personal evaluation of a job and human application in terms of vague, ill-defined personal norms held by the analyst.' A third problem deserving of attention here is that of discovering more about the actual functions, status and qualifications of practitioners in this whole field, now generally known as the field of work study; and about the ways in which they are related—informally as well as formally—to other technical men in their organizations, to management at various levels, and to workers and their representatives.

VII

My fifth heading is equipment design. The occupational psychologist's concern with this is well indicated by a statement on a notice-board in the Pentagon at Washington. It ran: 'No research or development project or production item is satisfactory until it is successfully in use by the user. This means in use by the personnel who are there, not by the personnel we would like to have there. The material must be designed for that user.' Considerable progress has been made in this field, much of it through the work of the Medical Research Council's Applied Psychology Unit at Cambridge, which has supplemented in a valuable way the investigations of physiological and other scientists and technologists. But Sir Frederic Bartlett,[25] the first director of the unit, has had to deplore the fact that even in weapon development the physiological and psychological tolerances of the human operator are still frequently ignored. He has rightly warned those who put their faith in human adaptability that this adaptability has limits; and that stresses of various kinds likely to be created in operators should all be taken properly into account at the design stage.

But it is not enough that the capacities and inclinations of operators of equipment, military or industrial, should be considered. Attention must be paid to the maintainers too. The importance of this was well brought out[26] at a meeting of the British Institution of Radio Engineers, held to discuss the maintainability of equipment in the Defence Services. As I listened, my thoughts went back to the war period, when I was in charge of the Admiralty psychological department, and particularly to a minute I once wrote on ways of coping with a dearth of suitable candidates for training for the radio mechanic branch of the Navy. For here were the same points being made again—on the urgent need for the simplification and standardization of equipment, for the devising of clearer fault-finding procedures, for the provision of fast and slow courses of instruction, and for the removal of unnecessary theory from the syllabus. The object of the minute was, of course, to argue that the radio mechanic branch could 'make do' with a smaller proportion of really able men, if co-ordinated steps were taken to fit the men to the job and fit the job to the men. It cut no ice then. However, the desirability of approaches of this kind to the manpower distribution problem—approaches which take account of quality as well as quantity—is now widely accepted, at least in the Defence Departments.

However, we cannot afford to be complacent about the matter. Automation is upon us; and though we may suspect that its effects on the working population of our own country will continue to be softened by our arrangements for full or nearly full employment, and by slow development resulting from the fact that our industry is rather conservative and made up largely of small firms with little capital, we must begin to think seriously about the manpower problems it will produce the world over. No one seems to have had much to say about certain serious implications of the change that automation tends to produce in the proportion of skilled to unskilled workers. Even in the early days, it was reported[27] that the Moscow factory which made pistons for the whole of the Russian light car industry was worked by a staff of nine men on each shift: one controller at the electronic nerve-centre, one labourer, two machine-minders (who appeared to be at least semi-skilled), and five skilled maintenance men. That is, two-thirds of the team were of the skilled trades level. If this is the shape of things to come, how are we going to manage? It is perhaps a bit fanciful to suggest that we may create a situation in which the abler half of the working population have to work themselves silly to earn enough to pay enough taxes to keep the other half sitting around doing nothing; but reflection along these lines would probably do us no harm. It might at least help our designers and their employers to recognize that transfer machines, automatic assembly equipments and such like must be matched to the capacities—and to the inclinations—of those who are actually available to operate and maintain them.

VIII

Now I come to the sixth and last of my special topics, working conditions and rewards. The occupational psychologist devotes less attention than formerly to the effects of working conditions of the physical environmental kind (heating, lighting, ventilation, and so on) and more to the effects of those which—perhaps because they influence the workers inclinations rather than his capacities—tend nowadays to be gathered up under the rather flabby title 'human relations'. Here he is, in fact, touching on some of the stark and explosive realities of management organization, payment systems and restrictive practices.

In the study of physical environmental conditions he has accomplished a great deal, particularly, in this country, through the Industrial Health Research Board and other Medical Research Council groups. But his progress in the rest of the field has been slow. A remark made long ago about social psychology seems applicable here: 'Research has been spotty, scattered, unco-ordinated.'[28] Why?

I have three explanations to offer, to supplement others occasionally put forward which range all the way from the conservatism of industrialists to the youth and inexperience of the psychologists they meet.

In this brief additional list I seek to blame no one but ourselves. In the first place, the occupational psychologist has too often been unclear about his own specific role, and has been inclined to dabble in other people's areas to the neglect of his own. This tendency has increased with the popularity of the multi-disciplinary approach, whereby mixed teams of investigators tackle a human relations problem. The idea is, of course, admirable; but the organizers of such teams appear some-times to overlook the fact that a team should be composed of experts, each with his own particular function to perform. We should not expect much of a football team composed of people of the 'can play in any position' variety. Nor can we expect much of a research team so composed. Secondly, the occupational psychologist has frequently sought after wide generalizations when he should have been satisfied with something narrower. If more often he asked himself, *In what circumstances* is X true? instead of simply, *Is* X true? he would more rapidly build up a useful body of knowledge. The formulation of his problems in this way would compel him to be more comprehensive and thorough in his initial survey of the conditions likely to affect his findings. Moreover, it might incidentally make him less disdainful of the use of certain statistical techniques—for example, of factor analysis —which might improve his sorting-out of the variables he decided to take into account. Thirdly, he has been too content to do his job as an outsider, as a visitor. It is unquestionable that some of the best in-quiries in the human relations field have been conducted by people who have 'belonged' to the organizations whose problems they have studied. No doubt there is a place for the peripatetic research worker who has his base in a university department or an independent research body, and who comes to his task with a fresh eye and experience of comparable problems elsewhere; but it may be a smaller place than we detached outsiders like to suppose.

Until we attend to these things—that is, until we clarify our roles, limit our objectives, and work more from the inside—we are not likely to make rapid advance, because few will feel that we are likely to prove competent in tackling crucial problems. We shall be left on the periphery, having little direct contact with the people who make far-reaching decisions and little knowledge of their real worries.

Let us consider, very briefly, an illustration. The coming of the 'welfare state' notion has thrown up several big problems in this field of working conditions, including problems created by the narrowing of wage-differentials. For instance, in the British building industry we find that, after a period of four hundred years in which unskilled men received two-thirds of the pay of skilled men, they now receive nine-tenths.[29] Why should it be left to sociologists[30] and economists[31, 32] to reflect on the psychological issues this wage problem raises? We may be glad they have tried their hand at it, for they have been both provocative and entertaining. But should not the occupational psychologist be concerned with the matter himself? Hugh Gaitskell once said that his political party wanted to see wage-differentials based more securely on occupational differences in skill, responsibility, effort, danger and dirt. Surely, in the study of all these criteria—and others that might be added—the psychologist has a very substantial part to play? Are they not all matters of human capacity and inclination?

But is he likely to have a chance to play this part, if he does not make his function clear, if he does not formulate his questions well, or if he stays on industry's touchline? Does it not seem obvious that, if he is to be concerned with crucial issues, he must more often be *in* industry? I should like to see more psychologists within industrial and commercial organizations, spending part of their time on useful bread-and-butter work, paying their way in, for example, the fields of selection, training and work study; and part of it in cautious development and research in their other fields of interest. This is, in fact, a pattern of psychological activity already showing itself in public services and private enterprise. In my view, we should seek to extend it, for it may offer us our best approach to some of the tricky problems we should be helping our users to solve. It goes without saying that the acquisition of competence and confidence in following this pattern is more likely to be achieved quickly by psychologists with appropriate systematic, comprehensive postgraduate training than by graduates who have not had opportunities for further study of the occupational psychologist's territory.

SUMMARY

My first object has been to map out the occupational psychologist's fields of interest; and to suggest that it is convenient to group these under two complementary headings—fitting the man to the job, and fitting the job to the man. My second object has been to specify and illustrate his concerns within each field. My third object has been to press the point that in all his fields, and all the time, the occupational psychologist concentrates his attention on the study of what I have called human capacities and inclinations: for this is his peculiar contribution to the solution of scientific and technological problems. That, in short, is what I have tried to do. What I have tried not to do is to make out that the occupational psychologist is *the* expert in tackling any of them. Without others—the physiologist, the economist, the sociologist, especially—he is not likely to go far. But in his collaboration he must constantly remind himself of the nature of his specific function. No science, no technology, can hope to thrive unless those who follow it are clear about their own particular duties and responsibilities.

ADDENDUM TO SECTION III

In writing of the inadequacies of arrangements in Britain, I do not overlook the work of the Youth Employment Service. If we take account of the conditions under which it has to operate,[32] we must agree that this Service manages very well. However, if we look at it in the light of the far-sighted report made by the Ince Committee in 1945, we can readily see that, despite advances in recent years in such matters as the training of its staff, it is not yet doing all it should. It offers occupational information; it gives advice; and, after placement, it conducts what are called reviews of progress. But, mainly because of the unfavourable attitudes I have mentioned, it does all these things with a very delicate touch indeed.

In another part of the vocational guidance field—that covered by the Ministry of Labour's Industrial Rehabilitation Service—the outlook is brighter, mainly because this Service has been able to get on with its duties unobtrusively and in its own way. It has built up for itself a good international reputation; and it has developed to some extent a research outlook. There can be little doubt that, in this area of industrial rehabilitation, the Ministry of Labour could provide the occupational psychologist with an opportunity of proving his worth comparable with the opportunity given to him by the Service Departments during the war. That does not mean that he has no exasperating frustrations: what it does mean is that he has a good chance to advance in relevant knowledge and skill; and to show that he can do a practical job of work that satisfies three criteria put forward on another occasion.[33] It is of the utmost importance that psychologists in public services should exert themselves to make their work technically sound, administratively convenient, and politically defensible.

Perhaps the Ministry of Labour will soon be able to regard their industrial rehabilitation units (IRUs) not merely as places intended to take people for courses lasting several weeks, but also as centres which will, on the basis of only two or three days' attendance, provide help for the Ministry's employment exchanges in the tackling of more ordinary vocational guidance problems. A precedent exists in an arrangement whereby some units give assistance to youth employment officers in difficult cases. Eventually, perhaps, we shall see vocational guidance bureaux for adults, basing their activities on the experience gained in IRUs and elsewhere, attached to all major employment exchanges of the Ministry. This is desirable, for there could be no more convenient way of ensuring that well-considered advice is available to the community as a whole. From their very nature, the Youth Employment Service and the Industrial Rehabilitation Service are concerned with special groups; and in times of change that involve many mature and healthy people in substantial job changes, we cannot possibly rest content with our existing facilities.

REFERENCES

1. RODGER, A., 1961, *Occupational Versatility and Planned Procrastination*, London: Birkbeck College.
2. RODGER, A., and CAVANAGH, P., 1962, 'Personnel Selection and Vocational Guidance', in WELFORD, A. T., *et al.* (ed.), *Society: Problems and Methods of Study*, London: Routledge and Kegan Paul.
3. RODGER, A., 1949, 'What is Industrial Psychology?', *Occup. Psychol.*, *23*, 170.
4. MALMO, R. B., 1954, 'Eccles' Neurophysiological Model of the Conditioned Reflex', *Canad. J. Psychol.*, *8*, 125.
5. BROADBENT, D. E., 1961, *Behaviour*, London: Eyre and Spottiswoode.
6. MCMAHON, D., 1962, 'The Identification and Use of Talent', *Advancement of Science*, *19*, 322.
7. HEARNSHAW, L. S., 1942, 'The Unity of Industrial Psychology', *Occup. Psychol.*, *16*, 43.
8. RODGER, A., 1959, 'Ten Years of Ergonomics', *Nature*, *184*, 20.
9. KRISTY, N. F., 1952, *Criteria of Occupational Success among Post Office Counter Clerks*, unpublished Ph.D. thesis, University of London Library.
10. CONNOLLY, T. G., 1955, *A Contribution to the Measurement of Occupational Interests*, unpublished Ph.D. thesis, University of London Library.
11. HERON, A., 1954, 'Satisfaction and Satisfactoriness; Complementary Aspects of Occupational Adjustment', *Occup. Psychol*', *28*, 140.
12. RODGER, A., 1939, 'The Work of the Vocational Adviser', in *The Study of Society*, BARTLETT, F. C., *et. al.* (ed.), London: Kegan Paul.
13. RODGER, A., 1945, 'On the Selection of Business Executives', *Labour Management*, *27*, 30.
14. MENZIES, I. E. P., and ANSTEY, E., 1951, *Staff Reporting*, London: Royal Institute of Public Administration.
15. CAVANAGH, P., 1950, 'The Work of an Industrial Rehabilitation Unit', *Quart. Bull. Brit. Psych. Soc.*, *1*, 250.

16. RODGER, A., 1951, 'Group Selection Techniques: Do They Yield Better Results than Individual Interviews Alone?', *Brit. Man. Rev., 10,* 45.

17. WHITE, FRANKLIN A., 1955, 'The Apprentice in Medicine', *Brit. med. J., 1,* 966.

18. SEYMOUR, W. D., 1962, 'Experiments on the Acquisition of Industrial Skills (Part 5, Stages in the Acquisition of Skills)', *Occup. Psychol., 36,* 15.

19. WELFORD, A. T., 1951, *Skill and Age,* London: Oxford University Press.

20. HERON, A., and CUNNINGHAM, C. M., 1962, 'The Experience of Younger and Older Men in a Works Reorganisation', *Occup. Psychol., 36,* 10.

21. GILBRETH, F. B., and GILBRETH, L. M., 1923, 'A Fourth Dimension for Measuring Skill for Obtaining the One Best Way to Do Work', *Soc. Indust. Eng. Bull., 5.*

22. BARNES, R. M., 1963, *Motion and Time Study,* 5th edition, New York: Wiley.

23. RODGERS, W., and HAMMERSLEY, J. M., 1954, 'The Consistency of Stop-Watch Time Study Practitioners', *Occup. Psychol., 28,* 61.

24. BARKIN, S., 1954, 'An American Trade Union Leader's View of Wage Incentives', (Australian) *Personnel Practice Bulletin, 10,* 23.

25. BARTLETT, F. C., 1955, Two Special University Lectures arranged by the Board of Military Studies of the University of London, unpublished.

26. DUMMER, G. W. A., BRENCHLEY, R. B., GODFREY, G. C., NAISH, A. J. B., et. al., 1955, 'Maintainability of Services Equipment', *Journ. Brit. Inst. Radio Engrs., 15,* 283.

27. LILLEY, S., 1955, 'Automatic Factories', *Discovery, 16,* 147.

28. MURPHY, G., MURPHY, L. B., and NEWCOMB, T. M., 1931, *Experimental Social Psychology,* 1st edition, New York: Harper.

29. ROBERTS, B. C., 1955, in 'Topic for Tonight', BBC Light Programme, April 22nd.

30. CAPLOW, T., 1954, *The Sociology of Work,* Minneapolis: University of Minnesota Press, London: Geoffrey Cumberlege.

31. WOOTTON, B., 1955, *The Social Foundations of Wage Policy,* London: Allen and Unwin.

32. RODGER, A., 1962, 'Arranging Jobs for the Young', *New Society,* December 6th.

33. RODGER, A., 'Peacetime Government Psychology', Paper to the 12th International Congress of Psychology, Abstracted in *Proceedings,* published 1950, Edinburgh: Oliver and Boyd.

CHAPTER 23

SOME CONCEPTS OF ETHOLOGY*

BY W. H. THORPE

—————

I

Ethology is a convenient word to denote behaviour study in the widest sense, and if used in this way ecology, ethology, bionomics and taxonomy can be regarded as the four divisions which together comprise the study of the whole living animal as distinct from anatomy, physiology, embryology and genetics (with all their included subdivisions such as histology, cytology, biochemistry, etc.), which constitute the study of its parts and of its development. The term ethology has recently come into much more general use than before as a result of new theories primarily concerning instinct, which are due in the first place to the work and writing of Konrad Lorenz;[1, 2, 3] but it would be a great mistake to confine its use solely to the work of those who are known to base their studies on any particular theoretical scheme, whether of Lorenz or another. The word is potentially much too useful to be restricted in this way. Nevertheless, wide as the real meaning of the term is, there is little doubt that the present popularity of behaviour study is in fact largely due to the stimulating and clarifying effect of Lorenz's theories; and it is interesting to consider how some of the essential concepts in this field have fared during the fifteen years or so since[1, 2, 3] his scheme was first put forward in its definitive form.

The essential elements of Lorenz's formulation are as follows:

(1) The division of behaviour into a flexible appetitive behaviour and the relatively rigid consummatory act.

(2) The assumption that the fixed action pattern of the latter is

* An adaptation of 'Some Concepts of Ethology', *Nature*, 1954, *174*, 101.

generating some specific action potential (a term which now includes the essentials of the original action specific energy concept of Lorenz and in effect supersedes it). This brings back in a new form the concept of internal drive, so resuscitating the essential idea of instinct.

(3) The concept of the 'innate releasing mechanism' which assumes there to be within the central nervous system a series of mechanisms of a particular type which effectively inhibit or block all discharge of activity unless the animal encounters the right environmental situation or stimulus to remove or release the block.

These and other considerations led almost inevitably to the hierarchy scheme of Tinbergen,[4] according to which there are a number of tiers or levels within the total organization which makes up an 'instinct', and incorporated in each level are one or more innate releasing mechanisms. On the receptor side these are in some way attuned to the biologically right stimuli or situations in the environment—as, for example, the appearance of the sexual partner or the specific prey—and are, as it were, unlocked by the appropriate environmental releasers and only by them, thus allowing behaviour to proceed to the levels below, only in the biologically right situation. These lower levels in their turn incorporate blocks which, while they remain unmoved, prevent action of these lower centres proceeding. So long as such lower centres remain blocked the action potential will therefore be diverted into the type of action known as appetitive behaviour, which is 'directive' in that it tends to bring the animal into the kind of environment where the appropriate releaser is likely to be encountered.

Finally, to make clear that this scheme is not one of innate or inborn behaviour only, it should be mentioned that although Lorenz regarded the learning abilities of animals as mainly operative in the sphere of appetitive behaviour, his theory is by no means an anti-learning one; indeed, besides accepting the categories of learning already usually assumed, he found it necessary to propose a new one—imprinting—to effect, in certain special cases only, the required rapid adjustment between the simplified or skeleton organization which constitutes the releaser and its correlate, innate releasing mechanism, and the more elaborate or detailed pattern to which the individual animal has to respond.

The immediate attractiveness of this scheme lay first in its apparent avoidance of the vitalistic approach—for the objective of the animal is no longer the attainment of the final biological goal or result (which it is, of course, inconceivable in most cases that it could know about) but rather the performance of the rigid consummatory acts themselves. Besides thus providing a physiologically reasonable system in place of an obviously untenable vitalistic one, this system at once showed some other tremendous advantages. In particular, it stressed the fact that evolutionary relationships are often expressed even more clearly by similarities and differences in behaviour than they are by structures and morphological characteristics, and so the theory provides an excellent approach to the taxonomic analysis of behaviour. Moreover, the very fact that these behaviour patterns are so constant as to be taxonomically valuable makes it inconceivable, at least in so far as the invertebrates and the majority of the non-mammalian vertebrate groups are concerned, that learning can be playing a significant part in their production. It seems apparent that within the insects, for example, countless thousands of instances of specific behaviour (such as acts related to pupation which are performed only once in the life of the individual) cannot possibly be the sole expression of anything that can by any conceivable definition be called learning. Nor, to take another example, is there evidence that the olfactory selection of hosts by hymenopterous parasites or other insects is primarily learned. On the contrary, in *Nemeritis* Thorpe and Jones[5] (misquoted by Lehrman[6] to give the exact opposite of the true meaning) found the choice to be preponderatingly inborn and only to a relatively minor degree modified by learning.

Finally Lorenz's idea of internal drive held back by the block or inhibitory action of the innate releasing mechanism system until the right releaser is encountered at once attracts the field naturalist and especially the field ornithologist, for it supplies a ready explanation for a vast amount of puzzling behaviour—displacement and vacuum activity—which it seems otherwise extremely difficult, if not impossible, to interpret.

It appears that the most fundamental concepts at the base of these theories of animal behaviour are centred around the idea of internal drive; but before discussing this central problem it will perhaps be as well to consider one or two of the criticisms which have recently been directed against these current theories of instinct.

First, it has been objected that there is an unwarranted dualism in instinct theory. Thus Kennedy[7] in effect says that all behaviour is, in fact, reflex and that all evidence for any internal drive is spurious. He argues that the current objection to the universal employment of the term reflex among behaviour students is due to the fact that they have an out-of-date picture of reflex which is 'a wooden caricature of reality'. But he himself clings to its use because he regards it as the sole behaviour concept which embodies the principle of determinism—which, if it means anything, is tantamount to saying that it is rigid. The whole matter is, in fact, a quibble. If the term reflex is regarded as implying relative or absolute rigidity, then it is still useful to behaviour students (as it is to physiologists) in certain restricted contexts. If, on the other hand, it simply means 'response'—then it is better to say so and to drop the term reflex. It is significant that Pavlov,[8] who did in fact widen the use of the term so that it became practically meaningless, nevertheless handicapped his followers by his retention of it and by his contention that instincts are 'nothing but' reflexes. He urged (as Kennedy says) that the investigation of instincts is the 'next important task', but none of his followers heeded this. The reason is not far to seek: the idea of the reflex did not alone provide them with the concepts necessary for the work, and it was, as I think all critics admit, the coming of Lorenz's formulation which was the signal for the great modern development of analytical work on instinct. This was not so much because the ideas contained in it were new—actually none of them was entirely new—but it was rather because here was a new system which facilitated and invited experiment and, by the way in which it is articulated, directed attention to those points in the vast and varied phenomena of instinct where experimental analysis was both profitable and immediately practicable. It has also been argued[6] that present-day instinct theory often blinds those who use it to the evidences of adjustment by learning which their animals display. It may indeed be possible to point out occasional relevant instances of animal learning which some modern workers on instinct have missed because of their concentration on the latter field; though it would also be possible to point to examples where such theories have actually inspired research on learning. But it would be far easier to name scores of workers who have missed the whole field of instinctive behaviour because of their obsession with the learning process. It is largely because of this that the work of those modern schools of comparative psychology which are based exclusively on the theory and investigation of learning is only too often virtually useless to the zoologist, and it is the failure of such schools which has thrown into relief the immediate relevance for the naturalist of so much of modern instinct theory. To say either 'all behaviour is learned' (as Hebb[9] or Lehrman[6] appear in effect to do) or 'all behaviour is reflex' is at the present time as stultifying for research as it would be to say that all behaviour is innate. It may, of course, be possible so to extend the definition of the terms 'reflex', 'learned' and 'innate' in such a manner that such statements are virtually true; but when this is done the terms themselves thereupon become practically useless, for such statements give a spurious simplicity and uniformity to what is, in fact, highly complex.

Kennedy argues that it is for social reasons that the dualistic approach which he finds so reprehensible has lingered in biology, psychology and philosophy long after it was abandoned in physics and chemistry. To me it appears to be rather for epistemological reasons: and may it not be that dualism is still necessary in biology simply because living organisms are different from non-living ones? Directiveness or purposiveness, whatever anyone may say, is characteristic of living systems; and Sommerhoff[10] has recently made a brilliant and courageous, although I consider ultimately unsuccessful, attempt to express the essential directiveness of organisms in purely physical terms. Until this has been done convincingly and without any room for doubt, there is no justification for denying the place of dualism in biology.

Lehrman[6] takes exception to a number of ideas which he claims workers upon instinct hold, but some at least of these objections appear to be due to misunderstanding. He himself apparently starts out with the idea that all behaviour must be learned—a conclusion surely only possible to one who has confined his studies to certain very special cases among mammals, and difficult to maintain even then. Moreover, he finds difficulty in accepting the abundant evidence that complex behaviour patterns are inherited because he is unwarrantably thinking of such inheritance as involving some sort of preformationist doctrine of the instinct being itself within the germ plasm. This would indeed be an unjustifiable reification; but I am not aware of any ethologist ever having implied any such thing. What modern instinct theorists mean when they speak of a motor pattern or an innate releasing mechanism being inherited or inborn is that it is genetically 'coded' and so determined in the sense that the behaviour is constant, even though the environment may be relatively inconstant and may contain no stimulus adequate for the determination itself. They do not mean, and never have meant, any such absurdity as the statement that 'the organism is independent of its environment'. On the other hand, Lehrman seems to oppose reification where it is not only useful but even necessary. Crude isomorphism is rightly suspect: we need not, for example, suppose that the engram of a cube is itself cubic. But his objections would seem to lead to the rejection—as unjustifiable reification and isomorphic preconception—of the basic assumption of neurophysiology that there is to be expected within the central nervous system a system of organization sufficiently similar in certain essential relations to the observed behaviour to be able to serve as a code; and this is all that instinct theory need imply. It is exactly in this sense and in this sense only that the behaviour of embryonic tissues and their constituents (such as blastomeres, histoblasts and the cells of imaginal buds), where the problem of organization is presented most vividly, may be said to be inherited. Lehrman thus appears essentially antiphysiological, although uttering appeals for more physiology. The term innate, however, is admittedly liable to cause confusion in that it incorporates three different strands of meaning: (1) internally co-ordinated, (2) inborn, and (3) driven from within. The first applies to practically all behaviour; (2) may apply equally to instinct and reflex, while (3) appears to be especially characteristic of instinct.

II

This brings us to the problem of drive and consummatory act, which must be considered more fully since it is in many ways central to the whole subject. Tolerably objective definitions of these two terms have been given as a result of an international conference[11] at which a number of behaviour students representing the most varied aspects and methods of approach to behaviour study were present; but critics are apt rather conveniently to overlook this admittedly provisional attempt of ethologists to be as objective as possible. We may therefore give three of these definitions here:

Drive—the complex of internal and external states and stimuli leading to a given behaviour.

Appetitive behaviour—the variable introductory phase of an instinctive behaviour pattern or sequence.

Consummatory act—an act which constitutes the termination of a given instinctive behaviour pattern or sequence.

The term 'drive' in its earliest usage in behaviour literature probably meant little, if anything, more than a state of internal activity or disequilibrium of the central nervous system or of internal organs in their turn stimulating the nervous system. So long as the meaning was itself restricted it was unobjectionable enough even to the avowed opponent of 'instinct'. So early as 1911, however, Ladd and Woodworth[12] were using the term to cover the mechanism by which activity was internally governed and directed along certain channels, and so no sooner had the term 'instinct' been abandoned by psychologists and behaviourists than we find 'drive' taking its place and standing for just those ideas which had led to the rejection of the former term. Later Woodworth[13] pointed out that habit mechanisms, in any event in human beings, may become drives and implied that since, in his view and that of many earlier writers, habit and instinct had much in common, the co-ordinating mechanism of the behaviour pattern itself might be generating the drive.

In the late 'thirties, Lashley[14] and Lorenz[1, 2, 3] realized independently that the aspect of instinct which would be most profitable for study was not specifically the drive itself, central though that idea is to the whole field, but rather the internal system of co-ordination of special behaviour patterns on the one hand and the special receptive sensory mechanisms on the other. In fact they concentrated their attention on the whole specific sensori-motor organization of the behaviour patterns, considering the complex and stereotyped action system to be more fundamental to the subject than any immediate question of drive; and both these workers proposed that a study of these mechanisms themselves might throw light on the problems of drive and motivation. Lashley in effect suggests that all cases of motivation might well turn out to be the result of the activities of specific co-ordination mechanisms and that general drive is really nothing more nor less than the partial excitation of a very specific sensori-motor mechanism irradiating to affect other systems of reaction. We thus arrive at something very like the concept of specific action potential which, in the form of action specific energy was to play such an important part in Lorenz's system. Lashley's ideas, penetrating though they were, perhaps aimed at little more than supplying some general directions for future experiments and theorizing, whereas Lorenz's contribution was to produce a thoroughgoing theoretical system of behaviour more comprehensive than any which had preceded it.

The idea of a relatively rigid consummatory act is thus a theoretically fundamental one, and it brings with it the methodologically invaluable distinction, which had in fact been made years before by Sherrington,[15] between appetitive behaviour and consummatory act (pre-current and consummatory responses, as Sherrington called them). While this separation into two categories probably continues to be as useful as it has ever been, it has now become abundantly clear that the distinction is not a hard and fast one. Much appetitive behaviour contains consummatory acts of what might be termed the minor grade, and the work of Hinde[16] (to whom I am indebted for

N

much useful discussion of such problems) on the behaviour of the great tit (*Parus major*) and that of Hinde, Thorpe and Vince[17] on the following responses of young moorhens (*Gallinula chloropus*) show quite conclusively that in these cases appetitive behaviour and consummatory act vary in degree of rigidity and flexibility; no absolute distinction can be made between them. Both are to some extent spontaneous in that they show evidence of internal activation, both are stereotyped to some degree and show some rigidity, and both are to some extent flexible. Thus the classic examples of appetitive behaviour and consummatory act can be regarded as the two ends of a series, ranging from extreme variability and plasticity on the one hand to almost complete fixity on the other. Moreover, much appetitive behaviour consists in a process of searching which can be described as locomotion with a particular orientation. Since it may often happen that the conclusion of the appetitive behaviour is the finding of a particular object or attainment of a particular situation (that is, a particular perceptual set) and not necessarily the performance of a particular act, so similarly it is sometimes a perceptual set or locomotion with a particular orientation thereto which turns out to be consummatory. So we can be fairly clear that not all drive arises from the co-ordination mechanism of a specific consummatory act. Moreover, since many consummatory situations or perceptual sets are extremely general, some drive at least must also be generalized, suggesting as in the system of Tinbergen[4] an effect coming from higher centres; these higher centres being, according to much evidence, the ones most closely and directly linked in activity with levels of hormone production; and so once more we seem to be approaching the concept of some entity flowing down pre-formed channels. Although, of course, for the sake of simplicity the organization of the appetitive behaviour is entirely omitted from Tinbergen's scheme, so that the hypothetical channels are only shown as leading from the appetitive behaviour to the consummatory act, there is no doubt that appetitive behaviour is no less complex than the latter, and that if such pathways are present in the one they must also be present in the other. Consummatory situations are clearly demonstrated if we analyse carefully the process of, say, the building of a complex domed nest by a bird such as the long-tailed tit (*Aegithalos caudatus*). Here we cannot escape the conclusion that in addition to an elaborate series of releasers (probably most of them visual patterns) which determine the way in which the various individually rather simple building actions are employed to construct the nest, there are other situations which are themselves consummatory. They may well be thought of as specific 'inhibitors' activating what might be called 'innate inhibiting mechanisms', in that they bring to an end a particular series of actions which result in a particular part of the nest construction, but do not necessarily themselves initiate the next stage in behaviour. So here, too, we see that the goal of such sections of behaviour is not the consummatory act by itself, but at least as much the experience of having constructed a particular object, or having achieved a particular situation. Bastock, Morris and Moynihan[18] have also pointed this out with reference to both birds and fish.

In view, then, of these conclusions, what can we think about the origin of the drive in such situations? Since it is not related to a particular act or act sequence, it cannot properly be regarded as arising from the co-ordination mechanism of that act. Again, if we look at the recent literature on behaviour we are continually being confronted with the terms aggressive drive, fighting drive, fleeing drive, etc. Here again in many cases we cannot find a specific consummatory act which is sufficient by itself to complete the behaviour sequence. In aggression, the pattern of attack or of fighting may, it is true, be a consummatory act in a sense, but it is often a pattern which can be used in a number of different situations, and it only becomes consummatory for a certain piece of behaviour when it takes place in a certain situation. So here again it is a situation which is consummatory at least as much as the act. When we consider the fleeing drive the position is even more clear, as was seen by Wallace Craig[19] in his discussion of aversions; it is very doubtful in many cases whether there is a specific consummatory act terminating a fleeing drive. In such situations, as, for example, in bird behaviour, the act of recognizing a rival fellow member of the species, of expressing antagonism or dominance to it or of fleeing from it, must all in part be consummatory, although they do not by any means in all cases lead to a particular act, and it becomes difficult to describe the actual situation except in terms involving the self and another member of the species recognized in relation to the self. The outcome of these considerations is that in order for there to be any flexible working towards a goal situation of whatever kind, there must be some schema of the act and the releasing situation together, as, for example,[20] the learning of song by a chaffinch (*Fringilla coelebs*), where the 'goal' seems to be a descending series of notes of 2·5 sec. duration of a certain degree but quite unspecified kind of complexity. This schema, inborn or learned, but usually a combination of both, appears to be generating 'potential'.

Hayes, Russell *et al.*[21, 22] see this clearly and they suggest, purely for purposes of illustration, that if we were able to introspect an innate releasing mechanism while its output was still below the release level, we should be aware of a goal. For a specific drive ('act-available-message-set' in the information theory terminology of these authors) the schema must be relatively precise, while for a superordinated drive ('animal-available-message-set') coming from a 'higher' region of the hierarchy system it must be far more general.

III

But whether the climax of the behaviour is a specific or a general situation, the concept of appetitive behaviour is crucial for the problem of drive. Where it is relatively stereotyped and consists of random or unoriented locomotion, as in klinokinesis, it raises few difficulties. But where it is more variable and has to be precisely directed or oriented, some important problems arise. In order to account for the flexible directiveness which is the most characteristic feature of appetitive behaviour—that is, in order to account for the appearance of purpose displayed—there are two possible alternatives. One can assume a very great variety and complexity of pre-formed pathways, each of which is, as a result of evolutionary selection, directive in the sense that all well-designed machines are directive, and which serve as possible alternatives. Certain of these would then come to be preferred by a trial-and-error process as a result of reinforcement by the attainment of a releasing situation and the ensuing consummatory act. Besides this, one can suppose a 'directiveness' of a more subtle kind in the sense that progressive approximations to the 'ideal' releasers are perceived and so reinforced, with the result that the animal, by means of a real but extremely short-term purposiveness and anticipation, succeeds in steadily sharpening the configuration of the innate releasing mechanism. Thus by gradually building up its own releasers, the appetitive behaviour as a whole becomes, in effect, welded into a directional unit which gives an overall impression of purpose much greater than the apparent sum-total of the minute gleams of purposiveness which are supposed to have played their part in its development in the individual.

It is evident that the first alternative must be very widely operative in animal behaviour. The question is how far is the second concept necessary. It seems that to account adequately for all varieties of appetitive behaviour it is necessary to assume that not only are the fixed action pattern and the inhibitory mechanism by a feedback device together generating some motivation for the next phase, but that also some short-term purpose in the super-ordinated drive itself must be postulated. The concept of appetitive drive as nothing more than a completely non-directive 'force' rigidly confined within a previously co-ordinated system of conduits together with the specific action potential of a consummatory act seems inadequate to cover the great variety of behaviour observable. Many biologists will no doubt object to the introduction of such a concept as purpose into their subject and, of course, there are great fields of biology in which, however directive the organization and activities may appear, the concept of purpose is either definitely redundant or, to say the least, is of doubtful utility. Sommerhoff tries to solve the problem by separating 'purpose' (as subjective adaptation) from 'purposiveness' (as objective adaptation) and claims that his system of directive correlation is all that is necessary for the objective description of purposiveness in living organisms. But here he seems to fail; for, as Scriven[23] shows, on Sommerhoff's analysis some machines would be classed as living beings and some living organisms (including some human beings) would be classified as nothing more than machines. So we still lack a satisfactory set of terms and concepts which will serve for the description of all examples of directively correlated animal behaviour and thus we still require the concept of purpose. In using such a term we, as biologists, need not, of course, come to any conclusion as to the relation between mechanism and mental events. If we decide, as the result of experiment, that the behaviour of an animal gives reasonable evidence of purpose as distinct from directiveness, we mean that its behaviour cannot be fully or reasonably explained by mechanisms at present known to be operating within the body of the animal— although if we can point to a sufficient mechanism, that does not necessarily mean that true purpose is absent. As Agar[24] says, it is the task of biologists to investigate such mechanisms down to the most minute detail; but while the assumption and investigation of mechanisms is an essential method of biology, it is hard to conceive as a really fundamental explanatory principle in a biological philosophy. On the other hand, as Woodger[25] has indicated, it is doubtful whether the causal efficacy of purpose can be proved in the sense that all other explanations are excluded. 'It is always possible to defend microscopic mechanisms in principle . . . by making your mechanism complicated enough and by postulating enough sub-mechanisms to meet all contingencies. It cannot then be refuted, but neither can it be verified.'

IV

But, purpose apart, Kennedy has objected to the ethologists' use of many other much more orthodox terms which he regards as subjective. He ignores the definitions above referred to, and appears to argue that the use of many of these terms is inadmissible in that in employing them ethologists have abandoned all pretence of being objective and are back in the jungles of subjectivistic animal psychology. Tinbergen does indeed claim that the particular value of his system is that it is objective, and in this he is undoubtedly right. When compared with much of the naturalistic comparative psychology which was not infrequently met with prior to the publication of Lorenz's main papers, its objectivity is plain and is certainly an inestimable advantage. But there is a danger lest objectivity come to be thought of as the sole requirement of a system of behaviour study. Of course, although all concepts are ultimately subjective in origin, it is usually possible to restate them in more or less objective terms and thus to clothe them with whatever degree of respectability may be required by the climate of scientific opinion at the moment. Actually, to me, the great merit of the behaviour theory of Lorenz—for much of the development of which Tinbergen is responsible—is that, in fact, as the writings of both these authors show, it combines both objectivity and subjectivity and (in the first place by distinguishing flexible and inflexible behaviour) helps one to specify where each has its rightful place and each its dangers. Sommerhoff's failure in his main task shows in, I think, a particularly dramatic fashion that both subjectivity and objectivity are necessary in the scientific study of life and that a biology which succeeds in being purely objective (however successful it may be in parts of its field) must fail to provide a full biological philosophy— just as surely as a purely subjective biology must, of course, fail. In other words, subjective concepts derived from introspection are among the essential tools for the study of life, and the only hope for a complete biology is to combine subjective and objective in the right proportions, using each approach with due circumspection and adequate safeguards, as it is required. All our concepts, in whatever field, are of course in the last resort subjective in that they are the conscious expressions of our own experiences. Although, as stated above, there are wide fields of biology where it is possible, and indeed essential, to achieve a very high degree of objectivity, there are many sections of ethology concerned with the modifiable behaviour of the higher animals where we sometimes simply cannot progress without concepts of a high degree of subjectivity. Polanyi[26] has said that science does not require that, in the study of man and society, we attempt always to remain detached observers: 'On the contrary, the part played by personal knowledge in science suggests that the science of man should rely on greatly extended use of personal knowing.' I would add that the same applies to certain fields of biology other than those which deal exclusively with man. But we have above all to beware of falling into the trap—which has so frequently caused the downfall of past students of living matter—of supposing ourselves objective when, in fact, we are being subjective. First and all the time we must know precisely where and to what extent we are using and relying upon subjective concepts. It is essential to avoid confusion here if biology is to deal adequately with the vast theoretical problems that confront it.

Appendix

Since the above chapter was written in 1954 there have been considerable developments in a number of the fields dealt with. In this appendix I have tried to cover these developments by quoting some extracts from my paper 'Progress and Prospects in Ethology'.[27]

V

Another way of deciding what the term 'instinct' should include is to consider how we recognize an instinctive action when we see one—to give, that is, a purely practical definition. The best method of approach is to consider the origin of behavioural complexity. Where does the complexity of the behaviour come from? If we can see the necessary complexity in the input from the environment which is being, or has previously been, experienced, then we are justified in assuming provisionally that it has been learned. If, however, there is complexity in the behaviour pattern which is not seen in the immediate, or indeed the whole, previous experience of the individual animal, then we have to assume that this complexity comes from somewhere else; and that it can have come only from the inborn organization of the animal. To take an obvious example: if a whitethroat or a garden warbler hand-reared from the egg in a soundproof room and maintained under a constant and simple regime of physiological stimulation comes in due course to produce the perfectly characteristic and exceedingly elaborate song of its own species, then we can say quite definitely that there is no system of stimulation in the environment to which it has been exposed which can 'account for' the complexity of this behaviour pattern of singing. Therefore we conclude that the behaviour pattern is innate in the sense that it must be in some way coded genetically and in the central nervous system, and that it is not even dependent on auditory feedback—as has been shown by operatively deafened birds. This, I think, is the most useful method of deciding whether we are dealing with something which has been learned or something which is instinctive, and it gives us many clues as to what the nature of instinct really is.

VI

Only a few years ago it could still be argued with some degree of plausibility that there were serious neurophysiological difficulties in accepting the view that instinctive behaviour patterns could be truly endogenous in the sense of arising within the central nervous system independently of peripheral stimulation. The modern development of techniques for recording the output of single neurons and groups of neurons has provided new evidence of fundamental importance as to the origin of patterned nervous discharge. Indeed Bullock[28] has expressed his conviction that such neural discharges are probably normally patterned—that is to say, temporally and spatially distributed —in a meaningful, non-random way. He says 'One way of stating the function of the nervous system, or of any significant part of it, is that it formulates appropriately patterned messages in code'. Indeed such a variety of examples of nervous organizations for controlling behaviour are now neurophysiologically established, mainly in the invertebrates, that we have ample factual evidence for the existence of neuronal devices which, singly and in co-operation, can account for all postu-lated types of organization of behaviour: from behaviour of the highest degree of complexity on the one hand, to extreme flexibility on the other, and from systems exhibiting complete peripheral initia-tion and control to those where this is exclusively central. Thus to account for the temporal patterning of nervous discharge we can, according to Bullock, have (a) systems which take their timing clues solely from peripheral causes, as in the reflex eye-blink to an approach-ing object, (b) sensory feedback from proprioceptors, such that a feedback loop may (c) exist with a central pacemaker so that the feed-back may start the next cycle of events before the central pacemaker comes into operation. A system of this kind is well suited to give a spontaneous rhythm modulated in frequency by feedback, i.e. a central physiological milieu for the development of sexual behaviour patterns through experience.

The original concept of 'the innate releasive mechanism', implying some central structural organization keyed to respond to the perception of the releasing stimulus itself, owed its attractiveness primarily to the way in which it seemed to bring order out of a whole chaos of observations relating to the complex situations to which animals were seen to be reacting in the normal course of their lives in the wild. But experimental study soon threw up difficulties. So the original clear-cut picture of the releasing mechanism as a lock exactly fitted to receive the key of the stimulus situation has come to be doubted. Obviously, if most or all of the usual constituents of the releaser can be varied and improved upon in experimental situations, there is little left of the original concept of the innate releasing mechanism, and so further experimental analysis has become particularly urgent. This urgency is increased by the fact that studies of recent years have brought about a fuller realization of the extent to which our understanding of sensory physiology is bound to influence our idea of releasers; for it is now clear that, as von Uexküll emphasized many years ago, each species is living in a world of its own, a world determined in the first place by the nature of its sense organs. When we thought of a releaser as something very precisely and definitely peculiar to the species, it was difficult then to imagine that such precise perceptions, involving form, colour, temporal cycles and so forth, could possibly be coded in the sense organ itself, and therefore it was natural to suppose that the coding must be in the central nervous system. Of course the characteristics of the eye of the animal, considered as an instrument for distinguishing between different groups of wavelengths, will help to determine what kind of visual stimulus gives the strongest response. Again, certain types of movement can be effective as releasers only if the eye has a flicker-fusion frequency such as to allow the animal to see them, and obviously a sound-pattern consisting of notes of high frequency very rapidly succeeding one another cannot influence the animal unless its ear has an adequate range of frequency response and a short enough 'time perception smear'. All these characteristics of the sense organs will, therefore, play their part in determining the degree to which different kinds of sign stimuli will appear strong or weak to the animal. Thus now we realize that all the component sign stimuli which go to make up a releaser may be acting separately, but that their effects can summate and that they themselves are often very simple relational key stimuli, it at once becomes probable that much more than we formerly imagined of the selectivity of the animal for its environment must be due to its receptors. Instinctive visual responses to those visual stimuli which solely or primarily comprise colour and movement may well be very largely dependent on the structure of the receptor. If, on the other hand, they are indeed concerned with form as distinct from movement, a distinction often very difficult to make in practice (e.g. the response of an inexperienced bird to the visual perception of the owl pattern, or to the auditory pattern of specific songs and call notes), we tend to be forced back on the theory of central control. In this connection the work of Lettvin, et al.[38] is of particular interest. These workers find that over a large part of the frog's retina it is not the light intensity itself, but rather the pattern of local variation of intensity that is the factor exciting the fibres of the optic nerve. There are, in fact, four distinct parallel distribution channels—sustained contrast detectors, net convexity detectors, moving edge detectors and net dimming detectors—which are capable of passing on to the brain specific information about the visual image. If similar mechanisms exist in the higher vertebrates, many of the views of ethologists about releasing mechanisms may before long be in need of reformulation.

The idea that the complex stimulus relationships which make up the external releaser as we can see it are—before they cause the animal to respond—subject to a series of physiological filtering mechanisms, has recently been developed by Marler,[39] and as a result we have a much better basis for the analysis and understanding of releasing mechanisms than was available before. Marler discusses three types of filtering: (a) that imposed primarily by the receptors, (b) by the receptors' afferent pathways and central nervous system as they function together in normal perception, and (c) by a central filtering mechanism more or less equivalent to the original concept of the innate releasing mechanism. This subject as a whole, then, is one of particular promise and interest at present, and is not only related to the study of instinctive behaviour but also arises, of course, in connection with learning. In instinctive behaviour we are thinking of a filtering mechanism which is built-in or self-differentiated; in learned behaviour we are considering filtering which arises from the individual experience of the animal. It should, however, be pointed out that while learning may be playing a hitherto unsuspected part in the perception of what may often have been regarded as instinctively coded releasers, there are nevertheless innumerable cases in which built-in sensory processes may in fact be playing a far more important role in learning than had previously been thought—even, as Marler shows, in creatures like mammals, where instinctive processes have been thought to make only a minor contribution to behaviour. Broadbent[40] has recently pointed out the profound importance of studies of animal perceptual learning for the understanding of human perception. As he says, human perception is selective, just as is that of animals; we attend to some things and ignore others. Attention wanders, so that a monotonous series of signals will rapidly produce inefficiency. But on the whole we learn only what we have 'perceived'. The mammalian nervous system is of too small a capacity to transmit all the information reaching the sense organs, and therefore the incoming information must be filtered before any coding mechanism—which allocates a particular output to each input—comes into play. Probably the information passing this filter depends both on the properties of the stimulus and on those of the organism; in particular it decreases with recent passage of information on the same channel and with low physical intensity of the stimulus. Moreover, different classes of stimuli differ in their probability of passing the filter. Thus, in man, pain stimuli have a higher probability than touch, and high-frequency noises than low-frequency ones. Thus, just as in animals, so in man, there are complex and important filtering mechanisms between the periphery and the centre. Striking evidence of this is supplied, in mammals, by Hernández-Peón's work, which showed a change in the type of recording obtained from the cochlear nuclei of the cat when it sees a mouse; the response to the click-like auditory stimulus being suppressed while the visual representation of the mouse takes over in the central nervous system. Barlow[41] has reconsidered what is essentially the same fundamental problem from the point of view of the physiologist, exploiting the idea that removing redundancy by compressing the sensory message into the smallest possible channel might be the first step in learning to discriminate sensory stimuli, a task which would be easier if the sensory information was presented in this compressed form. And so the message compression which takes place between the sensory stimulation provided in the releasing situation and the innate releasing mechanism may be very much the same as that which takes place between sensory experience and discrimination memory in man. This is an instance where the formulations of information theory yield much of promise, and Barlow suggests that the factors and necessities which lead to message compression—which, in other words, leads to the production of a code in the central nervous system—may be the same as those which lead to the ordering of memories and so may be part of the more elaborate psychological functions underlying what we speak of in human beings as 'intelligence'. To follow these ideas out further would be beyond the scope of this article. They are appropriate for conclusion in that they show that not only can neurophysiology and ethology be regarded as two parts of what is in effect a single discipline, but also that the study of human and animal behaviour are, at many levels, inseparable.

REFERENCES

1. LORENZ, K., 1937, 'Über den Begriff der Instinkthandlung', *Folia Biotheor.*, 2, 17.

2. LORENZ, K., 1937, 'Über die Bildung des Instinktbegriffes', *Naturwiss.*, 25, 289, 307, 324.

3. LORENZ, K., 1939, 'Vergleichende Verhaltensforschung', *Zool. Anz. (Supp. Band)*, 12, 69.

4. TINBERGEN, N., 1951, *The Study of Instinct*, Oxford: Clarendon.

5. THORPE, W. H., and JONES, F. G. W., 1937, 'Olfactory conditioning in a parasitic insect and its relation to the problems of host selection', *Proc. Roy Soc. B, 124*, 56.

6. LEHRMAN, D. S., 1953, 'A critique of Konrad Lorenz's theory of instinctive behaviour', *Quart Rev. Biol.*, 28, 337.

7. KENNEDY, J. S., 1954, 'Modern Ethology Objective?', *Brit. J. Animal Behaviour*, 9, 1.

8. PAVLOV, I. P., 1928, *Lectures on Conditioned Reflexes*, New York: Internat. Publishers.

9. HEBB, D. O., 1953, 'Heredity and environment in mammalian behaviour', *Brit. J. Animal Behaviour*, 1, 43.

10. SOMMERHOFF, G., 1950, *Analytical Biology*, London: Oxford University Press.

11. THORPE, W. H., 1951, 'The definition of some terms used in animal behaviour studies', *Bull. Animal Behaviour*, 9, 1.

12. LADD, G. T., and WOODWORTH, R. S., 1911, *Elements of Physiological Psychology*, New York: Scribner.

13. WOODWORTH, R. S., 1918, *Dynamic Psychology*, New York: Columbia University Press.

14. LASHLEY, K. S., 1938, 'Experimental analysis of instinctive behaviour', *Psychol. Rev.*, 45, 445.

15. SHERRINGTON, C. S., 1906, *The Integrative Action of the Nervous System*, New York: Scribner.

16. HINDE, R. A., 1953, 'Appetitive behaviour, consummatory acts, and the hierarchical organization of behaviour—with special reference to the great tit', *Behaviour*, 5, 189.

17. HINDE, R. A., THORPE, W. H., and VINCE, M. A., 1954 (unpublished).

18. BASTOCK, M., MORRIS, D., and MOYNIHAN, M., 1953, 'Some comments on conflict and thwarting in animals', *Behaviour*, 6, 66.

19. CRAIG, WALLACE, 1918, 'Appetites and Aversions as Constituents of Instincts', *Biol. Bull.*, *34*, 91.

20. THORPE, W. H., 1954, 'The Process of Song-Learning in the Chaffinch as studied by Means of the Sound Spectrograph', *Nature*, *173*, 465.

21. HAYES, J. S., RUSSELL, W. M. S., HAYES, C., and KOHNSEN, A., 1953, 'The mechanism of an instinctive control system; a hypothesis', *Behaviour*, *6*, 85.

22. RUSSELL, W. M. S., MEAD, A. P., and HAYES, J. S., 1954, 'A basis for the quantitative study of the structure of behaviour', *Behaviour*, *6*, 153.

23. SCRIVEN, M., 1952, Review of 'Analytical Biology' by SOMMERHOFF, G., *Mind*, *61*, 416.

24. AGAR, W. E., 1943, *The Theory of the Living Organism*, Melbourne: Melbourne University Press.

25. WOODGER, J. H., 1929, *Biological Principles*, London: Kegan Paul, Trench, Trubner.

26. POLANYI, M., 1953, 'On the Introduction of Science into Moral Subjects', *Cambridge J.*, *7*, 3.

27. THORPE, W. H., 1961, 'Progress and Prospects in Ethology', in RAMSAY, J. A., and WIGGLESWORTH, V. B. (ed.), *The Cell and the Organism*, London: Cambridge University Press.

28. BULLOCK, T. H., 1961, 'The Origins of Patterned Nervous Discharges', *Behaviour*, *17*, 48.

29. THORPE, W. H., 1961, *Bird Song: The Biology of Vocal Communication and Expression in Birds*, London: Cambridge University Press.

30. ASCHOFF, J., 1958, 'Tierische Periodik unter dem Einfluss von Zeitgebirn', *Z. Tierpsychol.*, *15*, 1.

31. PITTENDRIGH, C. S., and BRUCE, V. G., 1959, 'Daily rhythms as coupled oscillator systems and their relation to thermo-periodism and photo-periodism', in WITHROW, R. B. (ed.), *Photoperiodism and Related Phenomena in Plants and Animals*, Washington, D.C.: American Association for the Advancement of Science.

32. HARKER, J. E., 1958, 'Experimental production of mid-gut tumours in *Periplaneta americana*', *J. Exper. Biol.*, *35*, 251.

33. THORPE, W. H., 1956, *Learning and Instinct in Animals*, London: Methuen.

34. HINDE, R. A., 1961, 'The establishment of the parent-offspring relation in birds, with some mammalian analogies', in THORPE, W. H., and ZANGWILL, O. L. (see ref. 35).

35. THORPE, W. H., and ZANGWILL, O. L. (ed.), 1961, *Current Problems in Animal Behaviour*, London: Cambridge University Press.

36. THORPE, W. H., 'Some Characteristics of the Early Learning Period in Birds', in DELAFRESNAYE, J. F. (ed.), 1961, *Brain Mechanisms and Learning*, C.I.O.M.S. Symposium, Oxford: Blackwell.

37. ROSENBLATT, J., and ARONSON, L. R., 1958, 'The decline of sexual behaviour in male cats after castration, with special reference to the role of prior sexual experience', *Behaviour*, *12*, 284. 1958, 'The influence of experience on the behavioural effects of androgen in pre-puberally castrated cats', *Animal Behaviour*, *6*, 171.

38. LETTVIN, J. Y., MATURANA, H. R., MCCULLOCH, W. S., and PITTS, W. H., 1959, 'What the frog's eye tells the frog's brain', *Proc. Inst. Radio Engrs.*, *47*, 1941.

39. MARLER, P., 1961, 'The filtering of external stimuli during instinctive behaviour', in THORPE, W. H., and ZANGWILL, O. L. (see ref. 35).

40. BROADBENT, D. E., 1961, 'Human perception and animal learning', in THORPE, W. H., and ZANGWILL, O. L. (see ref. 35).

41. BARLOW, H. B., 1961, 'The coding of sensory messages', in THORPE, W. H., and ZANGWILL, O. L. (see ref. 35).

ANNEXE

A WORKING SCHEME OF PSYCHOLOGICAL DOCUMENTATION

BY G. PATRICK MEREDITH

The classification adopted at the Department of Psychology, University of Leeds, grew out of a simpler scheme devised some years ago to give students a synoptic view of the general structure of psychology and the interrelations of its branches. (The advantage of an over-all view first struck me in the '20's through daily exposure to a chart called 'the Psychological Tree' which Spearman displayed in the Psychology Department at University College, London. But the Leeds chart bears no other relation to the London one. The 'tree' has become a whole forest.)

The central concept is that psychological literature springs up when individuals or groups (X) are studied or treated by psychologists or psychiatrists (Y) in various environmental situations (Z).

The literature is broadly divided into 'pure' and 'applied', or contributions to theoretical learning (L) and contributions to professional practice (P). Each of these can relate to the training of psychologists and psychiatrists, or to the study of individuals and groups or to the adjustments to environments.

Thus the scheme falls into three main divisions, each of these being in three parts, but the first two are further subdivided, making fifteen sections in all as shown in Chart I.

The advantage of a well-defined classification chart is that all supporting library activities can be organized so as to contribute to definite categories in the scheme. (One feature of the scheme which is of growing importance is the use of an Information Box for each of the ninety categories.) Since the Library itself is only a sample of a vast range of literature in neighbouring Libraries, in national Libraries and in the bookshops, the books themselves in any category should be supplemented by book-lists, with indications, where possible, as to where they may be obtained outside. The compilation of these book-lists is a service to which all users can contribute.

The classification, storage and retrieval of reports, pamphlets, and offprints, together with the procedure for dealing with current journals and back numbers are complex problems which, though not yet satisfactorily solved, are receiving close attention.

Each section of this classification contains up to a dozen categories, and more can be added as need arises. At present there are about ninety categories. Every book in the Departmental Library is classified under one of these categories, with subsidiary cross-classification to allow for the inevitable over-laps.

The main body of the psychological curriculum is represented by books in the 2nd and 3rd divisions (X, LM, LY, PM, PY, Z, LB and PR). The first division is a token representation of the range of theoretical and practical studies which contribute to the conceptual and professional background of psychology.

A departmental Library cannot meet all the documentary needs of students preparing for a variety of special, combined and higher degrees, or for the requirements of teaching and research. It is to be regarded as a representative sample of the literature of psychology and associated studies, with special care being devoted to *categoreal* representation (however unequal the *numerical* samples may be) so that every user of the Library becomes aware of the full scope of the subject and can see his special interests in relation to the rest.

The Library is the primary instrument of study and must play a central role in the organization of the curriculum. It is not a static instrument but one which grows. Its growth is one not only of accretion but also of continual internal refinement of service. What is perhaps unusual in the concept of departmental documentation with which we are experimenting is that every user of the Library is invited to contribute to the improvement of its services. In this sense the whole department constitutes the Library staff.

These contributions may range from merely making suggestions, or drawing attention to defects or confusions, up to the undertaking of specific documentary tasks such as making a national survey of Child Guidance Clinics or an outline of contemporary trends in French psychology. More particularly we are concerned with obtaining a realistic assessment of actual student practice with regard to the use of the Library. Books and reading provide many problems of space, time and number for which economical solutions must be found. Current developments include a project in Co-ordinate Indexing.

PSYCHOLOGICAL DOCUMENTATION OUTLINE

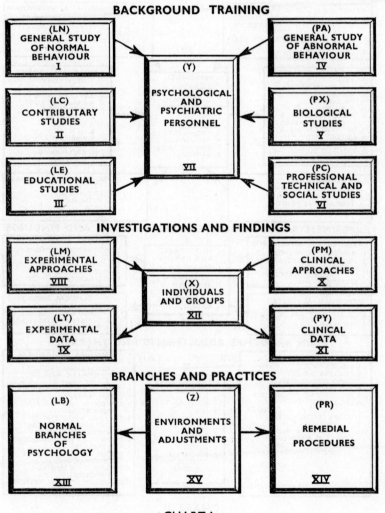

CHART I

PSYCHOLOGICAL DOCUMENTATION
A SYNOPTIC VIEW Library classification

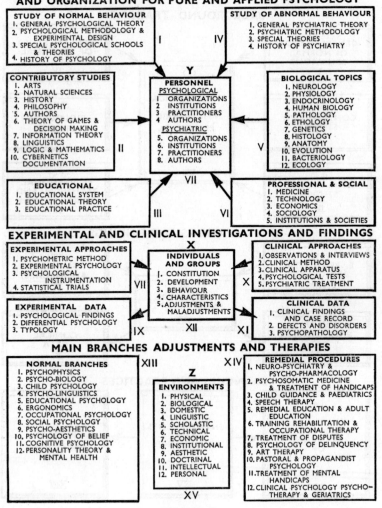

THEORETICAL AND PROFESSIONAL BACKGROUND OF TRAINING AND ORGANIZATION FOR PURE AND APPLIED PSYCHOLOGY

STUDY OF NORMAL BEHAVIOUR
1. GENERAL PSYCHOLOGICAL THEORY
2. PSYCHOLOGICAL METHODOLOGY & EXPERIMENTAL DESIGN
3. SPECIAL PSYCHOLOGICAL SCHOOLS & THEORIES
4. HISTORY OF PSYCHOLOGY

I

IV

STUDY OF ABNORMAL BEHAVIOUR
1. GENERAL PSYCHIATRIC THEORY
2. PSYCHIATRIC METHODOLOGY
3. SPECIAL THEORIES
4. HISTORY OF PSYCHIATRY

Y

CONTRIBUTORY STUDIES
1. ARTS
2. NATURAL SCIENCES
3. HISTORY
4. PHILOSOPHY
5. AUTHORS
6. THEORY OF GAMES & DECISION MAKING
7. INFORMATION THEORY
8. LINGUISTICS
9. LOGIC & MATHEMATICS
10. CYBERNETICS DOCUMENTATION

II

PERSONNEL
PSYCHOLOGICAL
1. ORGANIZATIONS
2. INSTITUTIONS
3. PRACTITIONERS
4. AUTHORS
PSYCHIATRIC
5. ORGANIZATIONS
6. INSTITUTIONS
7. PRACTITIONERS
8. AUTHORS

BIOLOGICAL TOPICS
1. NEUROLOGY
2. PHYSIOLOGY
3. ENDOCRINOLOGY
4. HUMAN BIOLOGY
5. PATHOLOGY
6. ETHOLOGY
7. GENETICS
8. HISTOLOGY
9. ANATOMY
10. EVOLUTION
11. BACTERIOLOGY
12. ECOLOGY

V

VII

EDUCATIONAL
1. EDUCATIONAL SYSTEM
2. EDUCATIONAL THEORY
3. EDUCATIONAL PRACTICE

III

VI

PROFESSIONAL & SOCIAL
1. MEDICINE
2. TECHNOLOGY
3. ECONOMICS
4. SOCIOLOGY
5. INSTITUTIONS & SOCIETIES

EXPERIMENTAL AND CLINICAL INVESTIGATIONS AND FINDINGS

X

EXPERIMENTAL APPROACHES
1. PSYCHOMETRIC METHOD
2. EXPERIMENTAL PSYCHOLOGY
3. PSYCHOLOGICAL INSTRUMENTATION
4. STATISTICAL TRIALS

VII

INDIVIDUALS AND GROUPS
1. CONSTITUTION
2. DEVELOPMENT
3. BEHAVIOUR
4. CHARACTERISTICS
5. ADJUSTMENTS & MALADJUSTMENTS

X

CLINICAL APPROACHES
1. OBSERVATIONS & INTERVIEWS
2. CLINICAL METHOD
3. CLINICAL APPARATUS
4. PSYCHOLOGICAL TESTS
5. PSYCHIATRIC TREATMENT

EXPERIMENTAL DATA
1. PSYCHOLOGICAL FINDINGS
2. DIFFERENTIAL PSYCHOLOGY
3. TYPOLOGY

IX

XII

XI

CLINICAL DATA
1. CLINICAL FINDINGS AND CASE RECORD
2. DEFECTS AND DISORDERS
3. PSYCHOPATHOLOGY

MAIN BRANCHES ADJUSTMENTS AND THERAPIES

NORMAL BRANCHES
1. PSYCHOPHYSICS
2. PSYCHO-BIOLOGY
3. CHILD PSYCHOLOGY
4. PSYCHO-LINGUISTICS
5. EDUCATIONAL PSYCHOLOGY
6. ERGONOMICS
7. OCCUPATIONAL PSYCHOLOGY
8. SOCIAL PSYCHOLOGY
9. PSYCHO-AESTHETICS
10. PSYCHOLOGY OF BELIEF
11. COGNITIVE PSYCHOLOGY
12. PERSONALITY THEORY & MENTAL HEALTH

XIII

XIV

Z

ENVIRONMENTS
1. PHYSICAL
2. BIOLOGICAL
3. DOMESTIC
4. LINGUISTIC
5. SCHOLASTIC
6. TECHNICAL
7. ECONOMIC
8. INSTITUTIONAL
9. AESTHETIC
10. DOCTRINAL
11. INTELLECTUAL
12. PERSONAL

XV

REMEDIAL PROCEDURES
1. NEURO-PSYCHIATRY & PSYCHO-PHARMACOLOGY
2. PSYCHOSOMATIC MEDICINE & TREATMENT OF HANDICAPS
3. CHILD GUIDANCE & PAEDIATRICS
4. SPEECH THERAPY
5. REMEDIAL EDUCATION & ADULT EDUCATION
6. TRAINING REHABILITATION & OCCUPATIONAL THERAPY
7. TREATMENT OF DISPUTES
8. PSYCHOLOGY OF DELINQUENCY
9. ART THERAPY
10. PASTORAL & PROPAGANDIST PSYCHOLOGY
11. TREATMENT OF MENTAL HANDICAPS
12. CLINICAL PSYCHOLOGY PSYCHO-THERAPY & GERIATRICS

CHART II

UNIVERSITY OF LEEDS — DEPARTMENT OF PSYCHOLOGY
DEPARTMENTAL LIBRARY
Resources & Working

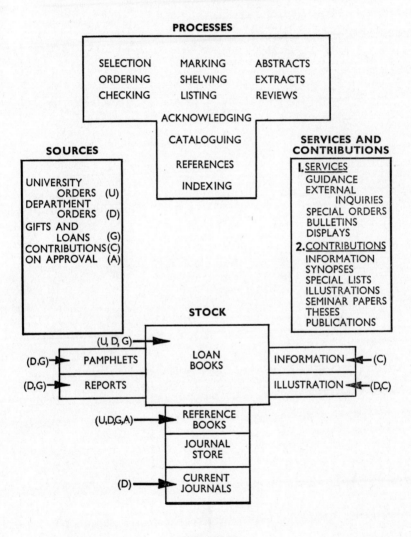

PROCESSES

SELECTION	MARKING	ABSTRACTS
ORDERING	SHELVING	EXTRACTS
CHECKING	LISTING	REVIEWS

ACKNOWLEDGING

CATALOGUING

REFERENCES

INDEXING

SOURCES

UNIVERSITY
    ORDERS   (U)
DEPARTMENT
    ORDERS   (D)
GIFTS AND
    LOANS   (G)
CONTRIBUTIONS (C)
ON APPROVAL (A)

SERVICES AND CONTRIBUTIONS

1. SERVICES
    GUIDANCE
    EXTERNAL
        INQUIRIES
    SPECIAL ORDERS
    BULLETINS
    DISPLAYS
2. CONTRIBUTIONS
    INFORMATION
    SYNOPSES
    SPECIAL LISTS
    ILLUSTRATIONS
    SEMINAR PAPERS
    THESES
    PUBLICATIONS

STOCK

(U, D, G) →

(D,G) → PAMPHLETS

(D,G) → REPORTS

LOAN BOOKS

INFORMATION ← (C)

ILLUSTRATION ← (D,C)

(U,D,G,A) → REFERENCE BOOKS

JOURNAL STORE

(D) → CURRENT JOURNALS

CHART III

UNIVERSITY OF LEEDS — DEPARTMENT OF PSYCHOLOGY
DEPARTMENTAL LIBRARY

PROCESSES

CHART III

INDEX

GEORGE ALLEN & UNWIN LTD

London: 40 Museum Street, WC1

Auckland: 24 Wyndham Street
Bombay: 15 Graham Road, Ballard Estate, Bombay 1
Bridgetown: P.O. Box 222
Buenos Aires: Escritorio 454–459, Florida 165
Calcutta: 17 Chittaranjan Avenue, Calcutta 13
Cape Town: 109 Long Street
Hong Kong: 44, Mody Road, Kowloon
Ibadan: P.O. Box 62
Karachi: Karachi Chambers, McLeod Road
Madras: Mohan Mansions, 38c Mount Road, Madras 6
Mexico: Villalongin 32–10, Piso, Mexico 5, D.F.
Nairobi: P.O. Box 4536
New Delhi: 13–14 Asaf Ali Road, New Delhi 1
São Paulo: Avenida 9 De Julho 1138-Ap. 51
Singapore: 36c Prinsep Street, Singapore 7
Sydney, N.S.W.: Bradbury House, 55 York Street
Tokyo: 10 Kanda-Ogawamachi, 3-Chome, Chiyoda-Ku
Toronto: 91 Wellington Street West, Toronto 1